SLOW TR...

Isle Wight

Local, characterful guides to Britain's special places

Mark Rowe

EDITION 1

Bradt Guides Ltd, UK
The Globe Pequot Press Inc, USA

First edition published March 2022
Bradt Guides Ltd
31a High Street, Chesham, Buckinghamshire, HP5 1BW, England
www.bradtguides.com
Print edition published in the USA by The Globe Pequot Press Inc,
PO Box 480, Guilford, Connecticut 06437-0480

Text copyright © 2022 Mark Rowe
Maps copyright © 2022 Bradt Guides Ltd; includes map data © OpenStreetMap contributors
Photographs copyright © 2022 Individual photographers (see below)
Project Managers: Laura Pidgley and Anna Moores
Cover research: Ian Spick, Bradt Guides Ltd

ISBN: 9781784777968

British Library Cataloguing in Publication Data
A catalogue record for this book is available from the British Library

Photographs © individual photographers credited beside images & also those picture libraries credited as follows: Alamy.com (A); Dreamstime.com (DT); Shutterstock.com (S); Superstock.com (SS)

Front cover Freshwater (Alessandro Saffro/4Corners)
Back cover The Eastern Yar (MikeIOW/S)
Title page View towards Bembridge (visitisleofwight.co.uk)

Maps David McCutcheon FBCart.S
Typeset by Ian Spick, Bradt Guides Ltd
Production managed by Zenith Media; printed in the UK
Digital conversion by dataworks.co.in

AUTHOR

Mark Rowe is an environmental journalist and author who writes for a wide range of national newspapers and magazines, including BBC *Countryfile Magazine*, *Geographical*, *The Independent* and *National Geographic Traveller*. He considers this new book on the sheltered climes of an island off the south coast of England a reward for good behaviour and the many winters endured researching his guides to the Outer Hebrides and Orkney for Bradt.

AUTHOR'S STORY

If you're new to the Isle of Wight or have not been since childhood, it's fair to say you're likely to have your preconceptions thoroughly dismantled on arrival. I speak from personal experience: having not visited for 20 years, I returned 15 years ago with young children in tow, seeking a beach holiday. While we certainly found that, we were utterly blown away by the island's sheer variety of landscapes – from high cliffs and sweeping downs to picturesque, easily explored woodlands, open countryside, tiny creeks and nature reserves. Birdsong was common in a way it simply wasn't in my home city of Bristol. The food, too, was a surprise, though of course with hindsight I realise this shouldn't have been the case. Having expected to plod around a dreary supermarket for the holiday shop we instead found family-run stores heavily stocked with local meat, vegetables and drink.

Since that return in 2005, I am still finding beaches, coves and footpaths to explore and I am slowly – but determinedly – working my way through a lengthy list of inviting pubs.

Researching this guide has been a sheer delight, providing me with an excuse for outdoor exploration during one of the strangest and most difficult times most of us will ever know. At a point in our history where the great outdoors and the need to seek support and comfort from nature have never been more important, the Isle of Wight is the perfect place to turn to. If the UK – and perhaps the world – is learning that a low-key, less intensive – indeed, Slow – approach to life is key to rebuilding in the wake of the Covid-19 pandemic, then the Isle of Wight offers a pretty strong template for doing so.

ACKNOWLEDEGMENTS

Over the years, people who run pubs, cafés or accommodation have become trusted friends on the Isle of Wight and have gone out of their way to ferry me around the Island, confirm or dispel a quirky fact I've run past them, and generally shared their love for their Island home. Those who deserve particular thanks include Sue Emmerson, Abi Fox and Simon Clark at Visit Isle of Wight, Tracy Mikich at the Seaview Hotel, David Howarth of the Island Ramblers group, Paul Armfield of the Medina bookshop, Ian Boyd of Arc Consulting, Megan Jacobs of Wight Coast Fossils and Martin Munt, curator of Dinosaur Isle. I should also mention Josie Morris and Emma Theunissen at Nettlecombe Farm and Paul Mocroft at The Bay Boutique B&B. The team at WightLink, from head office to the guys on the bridge, have also been generous with their time. The same goes to the crews of the hovercraft. I'd also like to thank my editors Laura Pidgley and Emma Gibbs who have inadvertently found themselves vicariously shadowing me around the UK's offshore islands, as well as Bradt's Anna Moores and Claire Strange for their kind support, cartographer David McCutcheon for patiently turning my squiggles into maps that are both practical and attractive, and Adrian Phillips, who kept a steady hand on the rudder as this publisher navigated the choppy waters of recent years.

DEDICATION
To Hannah

CONTENTS

GOING SLOW ON THE ISLE OF WIGHT 8

The Island **11**, Island food **12**, Isle of Wighty **17**, Festivals & events **18**, Getting there **20**, Car-free travel **20**, Low-impact car travel **22**, Activities **23**, The Island landscape – a brief natural history **30**, Further information **34**, How this book is arranged **36**, Accessible Isle of Wight **38**

1 YARMOUTH & THE NORTHWEST 41

Getting there & around **42**, Yarmouth **43**, West of the River Yar **54**, East of the River Yar **57**, The hinterland **67**

2 COWES, RYDE & THE NORTHEAST 75

Getting there & around **76**, Cowes & East Cowes **76**, Osborne House to Whippingham **86**, Southeast to Binstead **95**, Ryde & the northeast coast **103**

3 TENNYSON DOWN & THE SOUTHWEST 121

Getting there & around **122**, From Tennyson Down to Freshwater Bay **124**, Freshwater Bay & around **135**, Back o' the Wight **152**

4 THE SOUTH 169

Getting there & around **170**, Along the Undercliff to Niton & on to St Laurence **171**, Ventnor & around **188**, The southern hinterland **207**

5 NEWPORT & AROUND 217

Getting there & around **218**, Newport & Carisbrooke **218**, North of Newport **234**, The Arreton Valley **238**

6 SANDOWN, SHANKLIN & THE EAST 255

Getting there & around **256**, Bembridge, Brading & around **257**, Culver Down, Yaverland & around **273**, Sandown, Shanklin & Luccombe **282**, The east coast hinterland **296**

ACCOMMODATION 303
INDEX 307
INDEX OF ADVERTISERS 311

SUGGESTED PLACES TO BASE YOURSELF

These bases make ideal starting points for exploring localities the Slow way.

YARMOUTH page 43

For many visitors, Yarmouth is their first Island landfall and its Norman cobbled streets, fine walking opportunities and delicious food do not disappoint.

Hampshire

Parkhurst Forest

Newtown

YARMOUTH

Shalfleet

A3054

A305

A3054

Western Yar

CHAPTER 1
page 40

Calbourne

Totland

Freshwater

B3399

Brighstone Forest

Tennyson Down

Freshwater Bay

A3055

CHAPTER 3
page 120

The Needles

Brook

Shorwe

Brook Bay

Brighstone

A3055

FRESHWATER page 143

The gateway to The Needles and magnificent Tennyson Down, Freshwater is surrounded by woods, river and downland.

BACK O' THE WIGHT page 152

Rural even by the standards of the Island, villages such as Brighstone and Shorwell offer good food, superb walking and views from coast and hills.

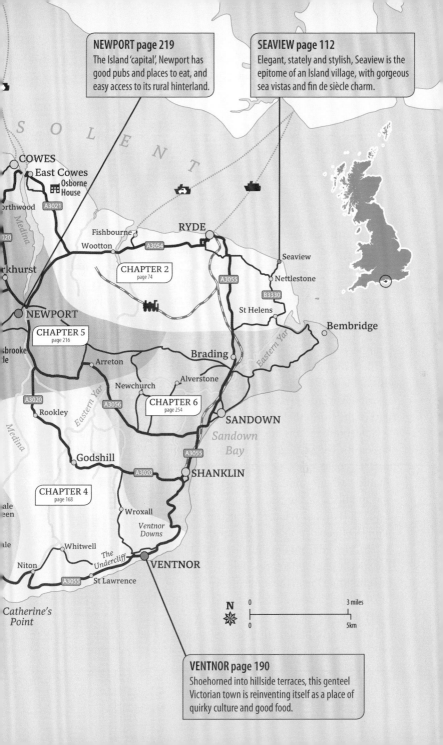

NEWPORT page 219
The Island 'capital', Newport has good pubs and places to eat, and easy access to its rural hinterland.

SEAVIEW page 112
Elegant, stately and stylish, Seaview is the epitome of an Island village, with gorgeous sea vistas and fin de siècle charm.

S O L E N T

COWES
East Cowes
Osborne House
orthwood
A3021
020
rkhurst

Fishbourne
Wootton
A3054
RYDE
Seaview
Nettlestone
A3055
B3330
St Helens
Bembridge

CHAPTER 2
page 74

NEWPORT

CHAPTER 5
page 216

sbrooke
le

Arreton
Brading
Alverstone
Eastern Yar

A3020
A3056
Newchurch
CHAPTER 6
page 254

Rookley
Eastern Yar
SANDOWN
Sandown Bay

Medina

Godshill
A3020
SHANKLIN
A3055

CHAPTER 4
page 168

ale
een

Wroxall
Ventnor Downs

ale
Whitwell
The Undercliff
VENTNOR
Niton
A3055
St Lawrence

Catherine's Point

N

0 ——— 3 miles
0 ——— 5km

VENTNOR page 190
Shoehorned into hillside terraces, this genteel Victorian town is reinventing itself as a place of quirky culture and good food.

GOING SLOW ON
THE ISLE OF WIGHT

At the narrowest point of the Solent, between Hurst Castle in Hampshire and Fort Albert on the Island's northwest edge, the Isle of Wight floats barely a mile off the coast of the British mainland. Yet with no commercial airport or tunnel you must take to the sea to reach it: that requirement alone demands that, in a literal sense, you must slow down and begin to shed the hurried pace of everyday life before you have even arrived. Then, when on dry land, you will find little reason to quicken your pace.

The Island is large enough to lose yourself on, but small enough for this not to matter: just keep walking and that creek you amble along will eventually wind its way to a village pub or, failing that, another slice of a part of the world that is easy on the eye.

Guidebook authors are invariably asked to single out a favourite place, but on the Isle of Wight I find that impossible. Where would I possibly start? I could point to the haunting coastline around Newtown and Shalfleet where woodland edges dip their roots in the ebbing shallows and mudflats, or the Norman town of Yarmouth with its fine cafés and delis. The red squirrels pretty much anywhere you look, the extraordinary jumble of geology that makes up the Undercliff or dawn flooding the Solent, viewed from the shingle spit that keeps Seaview dry. Then there's the spectacle of a peregrine falcon darting along the guillotined edges of Tennyson Down, the mournful call of a nightjar in Brighstone Forest, or stumbling across dinosaur fossils. Each one has a strong claim on the heart strings of visitors.

The cheek by jowl nature of seaside paraphernalia and natural drama on the Island often borders on the surreal. Just a few minutes' cycle

View from Niton towards St Catherine's Point. ▶

THE SLOW MINDSET

Hilary Bradt, Founder, Bradt Travel Guides

> We shall not cease from exploration
> And the end of all our exploring
> Will be to arrive where we started
> And know the place for the first time.
>
> T S Eliot, 'Little Gidding', *Four Quartets*

This series evolved, slowly, from a Bradt editorial meeting when we started to explore ideas for guides to our favourite part of the world – Great Britain. We wanted to get away from the usual 'top sights' formula and encourage our authors to bring out the nuances and local differences that make up a sense of place – such things as food, building styles, nature, geology or local people and what makes them tick. Our aim was to create a series that celebrates the present, focusing on sustainable tourism, rather than taking a nostalgic wallow in the past.

So without our realising it at the time, we had defined 'Slow Travel', or at least our concept of it. For the beauty of the Slow Movement is that there is no fixed definition; we adapt the philosophy to fit our individual needs and aspirations. Thus Carl Honoré, author of *In Praise of Slow*, writes: 'The Slow Movement is a cultural revolution against the notion that faster is always better. It's not about doing everything at a snail's pace, it's about seeking to do everything at the right speed. Savouring the hours and minutes rather than just counting them. Doing everything as well as possible, instead of as fast as possible. It's about quality over quantity in everything from work to food to parenting.' And travel.

So take time to explore. Don't rush it, get to know an area – and the people who live there – and you'll be as delighted as the authors by what you find.

from the archetypical resort of Sandown you can lean your bike against a hedge and watch an egret hunting for fish in a serene mire; you might catch a red squirrel out of the corner of your eye, furiously clambering upside down along an overhanging branch. Elsewhere, you might heave yourself up the vertiginous slopes of Ventnor Downs, taking in a sweeping coastline that pulls away to the middle distance. But while one moment you may get carried away with the 'being at one with nature' ethos, the next you may encounter a Victorian seaside amusement park. Some visitors can find such a combination intrusive; others have certainly been known to sneer. To me – and for most Islanders – they seem to rub along perfectly well. Far from being mutually exclusive, they are all part of the Island DNA.

These two elements have co-existed for the best part of 180 years: sweet shops and bustle characterise Shanklin yet Darwin found the town, which sits in the shadow of magnificent Jurassic cliffs, sufficiently peaceful and scenic that he chose it as the place to write up his paper *On the Origin of Species*. Nor did poets, from Alfred, Lord Tennyson to Lewis Carroll and John Keats, find their reveries interrupted by the Island's appeal to the wider public.

I once chatted to Simon Davis, founder of Wight Salt (see box, page 198) on Ventnor Pier. As he patiently peeled off his wellies after a morning wading in the shallow seas harvesting saltwater, he laughed when I said my journey across the Island to Ventnor had taken much longer than I'd expected. 'The Island forces you to go slowly,' he said, 'there are no trunk roads where you can drive at 70mph and I think that has a trickle-down effect on Island culture.' Simon was spot on: you don't have a choice, you have to slow down on this Island and that helps you get the most out of a visit.

THE ISLAND

Take a map of the Isle of Wight, step back from it and you may – at a push – perceive the Island to resemble a large vertebra in shape. This would be apt, for 125 million years ago the Island once hovered where North Africa is today and the humid climate of the time led to it being an ideal habitat for several species of dinosaurs. A little more recently – for the past 6,000 to 10,000 years or so – the Solent has kept the Island separate and discrete from the mainland, not just physically but culturally and environmentally. Romans, royalty and the great and good of the literary world have all lain their helmets, crowns, wide-brimmed hats and quills here.

Island life has been sustained by sunny climes congenial to growing crops and grazing livestock. Everything has been to hand: building materials from the beach and quarries in the form of stone; reeds from the marshes; timber from the forests; lime from chalk pits; and abundant cowpats that could be used to make bricks or for waterproof insulation. The northerly forests were once full of wild boar and deer, while the Solent's creeks still harbour fish, oysters and crabs along with plump (but now off limits) migrant geese. The coastal and southern chalk downlands are still generally given over to sheep, while the foothills of these downs feed streams that water lower-lying fields where beef and dairy herds graze.

The Island extends 13 miles north–south and is around 26 miles broad in the beam, its west and east fringes joined by a chalk backbone that wobbles from one coast to the other. Along the way that chalk ridge buckles into superb rolling downlands, the folds of which were created 300 million years ago. On the north coast these undulations calm down and fragment into haunting wetlands and creeks. To the south they come to an abrupt full stop in the form of high cliffs.

This chalky geology is sometimes thought to be the origin of the Island name. Probably the only certainty is that the colour 'white' has nothing to with the provenance of the island name. An Anglo-Saxon explanation comes from Wihtwara, a kingdom of Jutish origin that was founded on the Island, which mean 'men of Whit' (Whit is a possibly fictitious 6th-century king of this land). This version is challenged vigorously by some historians. The Romans Latinised the Island, referring to it as both *Vectis* and *Vecta*. By the time of the Domesday Book this had become 'Wit'. The word and its earlier and subsequent corruptions may mean 'place of the division', a reference to its location halfway along the Solent, or to possibly the mouth of the River Medina at present-day Cowes, which to the arriving sailor does look like a significant dividing point. No explanation is universally accepted: if it exists at all, the definitive answer remains elusive.

ISLAND FOOD

When it comes to the Slow approach, it seems those early Romans – who built no towns but did establish at least seven farmsteads on the Island – were ahead of their time. While the boar and deer are gone, other resources they latched on to remain in abundance and explain why the Island supports an extraordinary range of local, independent food producers. You'll find everything from fresh fish to cheese, tomatoes, cherries, flour, sweetcorn, pumpkins, broccoli, sprouts, bread, jams, dressings, vinegars and ice cream here.

At the last count, there were more than 50 local food producers on the Island, all either independent or family owned. There are two

---

1 The Tomato Stall. **2** Adgestone Vineyard. **3** The Garlic Farm. **4** Local jams for sale. ▶

ISLE OF WIGHT TOMATOES

ADGESTONE VINEYARD

VISITISLEOFWIGHT.CO.UK

THE GARLIC FARM, NEWCHURCH, ISLE OF WIGHT

vineyards (pages 97 and 271) and three breweries: Goddards Brewery (⌀ goddardsbrewery.com); Island Brewery (⌀ islandbrewery.co.uk); and Yates (⌀ yates-brewery.co.uk). The Island has also caught on to the UK gin obsession with the emergence of Mermaid Gin (see box, page 116). 'There are no big companies or businesses here to take up lots of space,' says Will Steward, who runs Living Larder (⌀ livinglarder.co.uk;

A FORAGE THROUGH THE ISLAND

The Island is abundant not only in food producers drawing from the land but also in edibles you can gather yourself. 'I used to be a rubbish cook, I was never that interested in food,' laughs Alex Richards of Island Wild Food (⌀ islandwildfood.co.uk), who leads foraging walks on the Island. 'Foraging is not just about what you find, it's about the nature, the views and where you explore. The Isle of Wight just feels so accessible, you can go somewhere and be by yourself and there is park, coast and woods all close to each other.'

On a typical half day with Alex you'll walk in stop-start fashion for around three hours, gathering up to 15 seasonal food items. 'I may show guests a flower and then send them to look for it,' she says. The walk ends up with a picnic, either using the foods that you've come across, or eating something Alex has prepared from foraging in advance. The joy is that every trip is different. 'One year I might go to a spot in March and it's overrun with wild garlic but the next year when you go back at the same time it's not out.'

The seasons dictate what Alex comes across. Spring brings nettles, wild garlic and elderflowers while autumnal offerings range from cobnuts (hazelnuts) which are great in butter to rosehips (for tea) and Alexander seeds (similar to black pepper in taste). The flavours can be surprisingly intense and bring a whiff of Asia to this southerly British island. For example, the roots of wood avens (a flower that looks a little like a bunch of miniature strawberries) exude the smell of cloves and go well with sloe gin or elderflower cordial. The seeds from the heads of common hogweed, when crushed up, taste like a combination of cardamom and orange and are wonderful when grated on to a crumble – perhaps one made from windfall apples. Sorrel is a good companion to hummus, while deep-fried dulse seaweed tastes rather like healthy crisps.

Alex offers a gentle reminder that you can forage for the four 'Fs' – fungi, flowers, fruit and foliage. You must not uproot a plant (but you can collect roots that have worked loose from soil); you can forage on public land (including footpaths) but not on SSSIs or National Trust land. Seaweed can only be gathered if it is floating loose on the water; it must not be plucked, nor gathered if washed up on the shore. Forage sustainably and avoid trampling over other flowers to reach your target. Remember that some mushrooms can be poisonous, even deadly, and that some flowers can be too. Do your homework. Even better, tag along with Alex.

page 301), which delivers boxes of fresh fruit and vegetables around the island. 'That creates opportunities for local and smaller operators. If you're from the Island or have lived here for a long time then you feel an obligation to make it a better place. I think that is why there are so many local food producers.'

A good example of this is the meat reared by the **Isle of Wight Meat Co** (Cheverton Farm, Shorwell PO30 3JE ✆ 01983 741234 ⊘ isleofwightmeat.co.uk). The emphasis here is on quality rather than quality – their meat is hung on the bone in a salt chamber for up to eight weeks – and visitors to the website will be struck by the statement, especially from a butcher depending on meat sales for their livelihood, that 'we don't have to eat meat every day'. The change in emphasis came in 2019 when farmer-owner Andrew Hobson decided to move away from supplying restaurants and supermarket chains and instead supply the local market with Island-produced pork, beef and lamb. For his efforts, Andrew was awarded Beef Innovator of the Year at the 2020 British Farming awards. Note that the company does not have a farm shop as such but does operate a click and collect system for online orders, with options ranging from peppered pork and shish kebabs to boxes of different cuts of meat. The company recently merged with Greef's Biltong (formerly based in Seaview). This specialist product is produced by Zimbabwe-born Nick Greef, who learnt his trade as a child on his father's cattle farm. The dry-cured meat is lean and high in protein – for meat eaters, it's a good alternative to Kendal mint cake if you're out on the downs all day – and free of nitrates and emulsifiers.

Like the Isle of Wight Meat Co, many of the Island producers aren't geared up to sell from their production sites (which are often their homes or farm steadings) so instead you will find them available in shops across the Island. Probably the best known is Minghella Ice Cream (⊘ minghella.co.uk), founded by Edward and Gloria Minghella, and which produces high-end Italian-style ice creams and sorbets. (Their son, Anthony, achieved worldwide fame as a film director and playwright.) Others include The Fruit Bowl (⊘ thefruitbowliw. co.uk) run by Alistair and Barbara Jupe in Newchurch. The couple produce jams and preserves – plum, loganberry and cherry, rhubarb, ginger and apple, among more than a dozen varieties, and are aiming to become the UK's first 'green' jam producer. Their three-acre smallholding accounts for 90% of the fruit they use. Another local producer, Godshill Orchards (godshillorchards.co.uk), grows cherries, apricots, greengages and plums. Meanwhile, Wight Crystal (wightcrystal.org.uk) collects, treats and bottles water from a spring at Knighton and uses their profits to fund the training and employment of people with disabilities on the Island. I've included many other producers throughout the guide.

PALMERSTON'S FOLLIES

While the Isle of Wight has proved attractive to invaders over the centuries, the real aim for aggressors has always been access to the mainland via the Solent, the corridor of water that separates the Island from the UK. Fortification of the Island is not new – Henry VIII commissioned a series of defences around it, such as Cowes Castle (page 81) – but the increasing importance of the naval yards at Portsmouth and the docks at Southampton meant that the Island and its waters were seen as pivotal to a wider defence of the nation during the 19th century, from France in particular. The impetus for a series of forts and batteries was driven in the 1860s by Lord Palmerston (Prime Minister 1859–65); though forts were constructed around much of the southeast and east coasts of England, few places saw as much activity as the Isle of Wight. In all, 23 redoubts of one kind or another were built, including at The Needles (page 129) and off St Helens (page 118) often in the shape of a redan (an arrow-shaped embankment) though not all during Palmerston's tenure or even his lifetime.

Ultimately, the endeavours proved obsolete as the French threat never really materialised and France became distracted by a war with Prussia. What's more, even as the forts were being completed, technological advances rendered their brick walls and muzzle-loading guns useless against larger ships that now sailed with more powerful artillery. The term 'Palmerston's Follies' was doing the rounds long before the last breeze blocks and bricks were put in place. The practicalities of the forts' design left a lot to be desired too: by definition they were in or by the sea and heavy ammunition was left on the ground floor by necessity, where it often became damp and useless. Although the forts proved to be utterly useless for their original intended purposes, some did ultimately play military roles during World War II, providing anti-aircraft defences, serving as troop barracks and as locations to trail searchlights.

You'll see plenty of surviving forts around the Island, some of which wear their history better than others. All the accessible ones offer fine vantage points while a handful have been converted into residential and self-catering accommodation, such as Fort Albert and Golden Hill Fort. It's even possible – if your pockets are deep enough – to stay at a couple of offshore forts, including No-Man's Fort (northeast of Seaview) where a night can set you back a mere £990.

ISLE OF WIGHTY

A question you might ask of an Islander is whether they are a *caulkhead* (born on the Island) or an *overner* (migrated from the mainland). To qualify as a caulkhead your family must have lived on the Island for at least three generations. The name comes from 'caulk', a resin used to keep boats watertight. You may hear the added wry observation that 'you tend to need to be good at that [keeping boats watertight] if you live on an Island.'

These names are the most common examples of the local dialect, known as Isle of Wighty, that you will hear on the Island. Other colloquialisms include *gallybagger* (scarecrow) and *nammet* (originally bread and cheese with a drink of beer consumed by people working in the field, now broadened to apply to sandwiches).

The definitive glossary on the subject was drawn up by William Henry Long in 1886 and he found enough examples to fill 97 pages, many of which he catalogued, in a reflection of the times, as 'provincialisms'. Words and phrases which arguably deserve reintroduction into today's lexicon include *atterclaps* (something disagreeable happening in a matter which is considered settled); *scrannel* (to eat greedily); a *dabster* (an adept or proficient person); *queer as Dick's hatband* (to be in a morose or sullen temper); *dumbledore* (a bumblebee); and *joltehead* (defined by Long as 'a heavy, dull or stupid fellow').

> *"While the accent is dominated by standard southern English, it does carry more melodic hints of rural Dorset or Hampshire."*

It's fair to say not all of the words have survived into the 21st century but they can still sometimes be found lurking in the local accent. While this is nowadays dominated by standard southern English, it does carry more melodic hints of rural Dorset or Hampshire. For example, when an Islander says 'I might have been', you could phonetically transcribe their words as something Long would have recognised: 'I med a ben'. You may also encounter a distinctive feature of speech where pronouns are not inflected, such as '*He never opened his mouth to we* [us] *about it.*' Long's guide can be found online in various forms nowadays, including at ⊘ archive.org/details/dictionaryofisle00longrich/page.

The language reflects a distinct sense of identity that can surprise visitors who think what separates the Isle of Wight from the mainland is merely a short geographical hop across the Solent. You'll notice this in particular in the common usage of 'Island' (with a capital 'I') to refer to both the physical landscape and pretty much anything you find on it. Caulkheads get quite uppity should you forget that capital letter and so, for the sake of a quiet life, 'Island' is used throughout this book.

FESTIVALS & EVENTS

An island that gave a platform to Jimi Hendrix (see box, page 138) knows how to put on a show and the Isle of Wight is a gregarious place with events held throughout the year. Sailing, for obvious reasons, features heavily but walking, the arts and of course music are also hugely popular. Covid-19 has had an impact on local festivals and events, so check ⟨⟩ visitisleofwight.co.uk/whats-on/events and event websites for up-to-date information.

MAY

Isle of Wight Walking Festival ⟨⟩ isleofwightwalkingfestival.co.uk. The UK's largest walking festival and typically features around 100 walks over a fortnight, all led by local knowledgeable guides with specialist themes including wildlife, shipwrecks and military history. Culminates in Walk the Wight, an epic 26½-mile traverse of the Island from Bembridge to Alum Bay (see box, page 24). In 2022, organisers were planning a second festival in October. If demand is high, they plan to run two festivals a year in subsequent years.

Hullabaloo ⟨⟩ hullabalooiw.com. In Sandown, this event offers a long weekend of performance and workshops, with a quirky combination of arts and science. Expect to take in a lecture on dinosaur poo while listening to samba from a nearby stage.

Festival of Running ⟨⟩ isleofwightfestivalofrunning.co.uk. A week-long mixture of tough hill climbs, breezy jogs across downland and along the Coastal Path and fun runs that collectively make for one of the most spectacular cross country settings in the UK. The super-fit can tackle the Needles half marathon with a slog up Tennyson Down thrown in for fun.

JUNE

Isle of Wight Festival ⟨⟩ isleofwightfestival.com. The original UK music festival, dating back more than 50 years and still one of the summer's major rock festivals, featuring headline acts year after year.

Shorwell Midsummer Fair ⟨⟩ shorwellmidsummerfair.org. Arguably the most traditional of the Island's village fairs, with falconry displays, great homemade food and music.

Round the Island Race ⟡ roundtheisland.org.uk. A wide range of crafts circumnavigate the Island.

JULY

Open Studio ⟡ isleofwightarts.com. Held in Newport over two weekends. Painters, potters and designers open their studios to all-comers. A good chance to chat and buy.

AUGUST

Cowes Week ⟡ cowesweek.co.uk. The world's oldest and largest regatta (page 80) and the most iconic festival on the Island. Expert yachtsmen and women take to the sea in various races.

Seaview Regatta ⟡ seaviewvillageregatta.co.uk. Arguably more scenic and certainly more local in terms of competition than its larger rival.

Isle of Wight Garlic Festival ⟡ garlicfestival.co.uk. Does exactly what it says on the tin but with great flair and imagination. Pungent bulb-based activities including cookery classes and celebrity chef presentations along with (presumably, garlic-free) music.

OCTOBER

Harp on Wight ⟡ harponwight.co.uk. Classical and innovative performances in Ryde – such as flamenco and Breton harp music – by harpists from both the UK and overseas.

Isle of Wight Literary Festival ⟡ isleofwightliteraryfestival.com. Held at Northwood House in Cowes every year, this literary festival runs for four days and features around 60 authors. Talks cover novels, history, children's literature and, as you might expect, there's a strong element of maritime writing.

DECEMBER

The Isle of Wight embraces the **Christmas** spirit with gusto and several markets are worth visiting. There is usually a large outdoor market in Cowes, another in Ventnor and a third at the Donkey Sanctuary at Wroxall, plus pop-up markets in Newport, Yarmouth and Ryde as well as Briddlesford Farm near Wootton Bridge. Robin Hill also usually runs a strong Christmas theme with goods and food on sale. For the latest on times and dates, visit ⟡ visitisleofwight.co.uk.

If you can't make it in December, then the Jingle Bells Christmas Shop (107 High St, Shanklin PO37 6NS ⬛) is open all year round. Another perennial (or at least, from Mar–Dec) outlet is the Christmas Imaginarium (7 Cross St, Ryde PO33 2AD ⟡ christmasimaginarium.com), the home of Russell Ince, an Island-born author and illustrator. Russell achieved worldwide success with *Santa Claus: The Book of Secrets* and has built on the interest the book has generated to establish a shop selling decorations, advent calendars, seasonal foods and great deal more.

GETTING THERE

In the absence of a tunnel and a commercial airport, the only way to reach the Isle of Wight is by sea. Despite the frequency of services (some run around the clock), you should always book ahead, especially for Friday and Sunday travel – and as far in advance as you can for school holidays.

Wightlink (⊘ wightlink.co.uk) runs ferry services between Lymington in the New Forest and Yarmouth (journey time 30 minutes) and between Portsmouth and Fishbourne (45 minutes).

Red Funnel (⊘ redfunnel.co.uk) operates the service between Southampton and East Cowes, with a journey time of around one hour. The company also runs the Red Jet high-speed foot passenger service from Southampton to Cowes (on the west bank of the River Medina), which takes just 25 minutes.

Ryde enjoys two services. The FastCat (foot-passengers only) is operated by Wightlink and takes 22 minutes to nip across from Portsmouth Harbour. Adjacent to this service is the hovercraft, operated by **Hovertravel** (⊘ hovertravel.co.uk) which takes ten minutes to traverse the Solent from Southsea (see box, page 108).

CAR-FREE TRAVEL

The Isle of Wight has an excellent range of bus services, as well as an extraordinarily dense network of public footpaths and rights of way. The beauty of this cat's cradle of paths is that many places of interest can be visited on foot, either from a bus stop or by walking between one attraction and the next. You can easily spend a week on the Island without need for a car, and just about every sight featured in this book can be visited through a combination of bus and short- or medium-distance walks. Cycling options cater for all levels of fitness and vary from flat-as-pancake scoots through the heart of the Island to more rigorous steep climbs that will expose any twinges in your calf muscles.

For nostalgists there is even a train line that deploys rolling stock deemed surplus to requirements by the London Underground network (though visitors' enthusiasm for this service is not necessarily shared by Islanders who point to its exasperating unreliability).

Just as importantly, the ferry ports on the mainland that serve the Isle of Wight – Lymington, Southampton and Portsmouth – are all well

VILLAGE SIGNS

Not only does the Island as a whole exude a strong sense of identity, community pride is palpable from the point at which you enter many of its villages. The road signs, as expected, bear the name of the village concerned but they often feature beautifully drawn images that in some way represent the community. The borders of Niton are marked by a road sign accompanied by a drawing of St Catherine's lighthouse; at Fishbourne, which overlooks the Solent, the sign features a yacht; at Wootton Bridge it's a heron; St Helens sports a goose, while at Gurnard it's the eponymous fish. This also applies to towns: Ryde's entry signs feature a silhouette of a hovercraft and Brading sports a montage of a sailing ship, a Tudor-framed building and its church. Quite how or when this tradition evolved remains unclear. The most likely explanation is that it began when one parish council had a bright idea of clamping its identity to its entry points and others followed.

connected by rail with the rest of the UK, making a car-free holiday to the Island entirely plausible and practical, from start to finish.

BUS

Almost all corners of the Island are well served by bus routes, and with a frequency that is no longer the case in much of the rest of the UK. The vast majority of services are run by Southern Vectis (⊘ islandbuses.info). The centre, north, south and east of the Island are particularly well served throughout the day by buses; the west less so after 17.00. Most services tend to radiate out of Newport, the Island's capital which sits more or less in the middle of the Island; Ryde is the other bus hub.

The #2, #3 and #9 move between Newport and Ryde: #9 via Wootton Bridge; #2 takes in Godshill, Sandown and Brading; and #3 takes a longer route, travelling via Ventnor on the south coast. Another useful route from Newport is the #6, which heads for Ventnor but this time via Chale, Blackgang Chine, Niton and Whitwell. Meanwhile, the #4 travels from Ryde to East Cowes and is the bus you need for Osborne House. In the west of the Island, routes #7 and #12 connect Newport to Alum Bay (the #7 travelling via Yarmouth and also passing Parkhurst Forest) while the FYT (Freshwater–Yarmouth–Totland) bus links Yarmouth to destinations to the southwest coast, such as The Needles (Alum Bay) and Freshwater. The #1 heads out of Newport to Cowes but the #5, which joins Newport to East Cowes, is more scenic as it takes in Osborne House (and you can take the chain ferry across the River Medina from East Cowes to Cowes).

If you are planning on using the bus a lot, consider either a one- or two-day rover card or a weekly freedom card, which offer savings compared with the standard single fares.

TRAIN

The Island Line (⌖ southwesternrailway.com/destinations-and-offers/island-line) operates in the east of the Island, between Ryde and Shanklin, stopping along the way at Smallbrook Junction, Brading, Sandown and Lake. The total length is 8½ miles and journey time from north to south is around 30 minutes. For most visitors, a brief trip on the train can be fun as you'll get good views of Brading Marshes and occasional glimpses of the sea.

The service is also genuinely useful. The northerly terminus is at Ryde Pier Head, adjacent to the bus terminal and hovercraft landing stage and the line enables you to explore much of the east and northeast coasts without a car and provides access to Sandown beaches and attractions such as Dinosaur Isle and Brading Roman Villa. In addition, the line connects with the Isle of Wight Steam Railway (page 97) at Smallbrook Junction.

The line now uses retro-fitted shells of 1978 former London District Line stock that have been updated, refitted and feature wheelchair access, Wi-Fi and USB charging points. The reason for using London Underground trains of a certain vintage is that their dimensions enable them to squeeze within height restrictions in a tunnel at Ryde (the track was lifted here to address flooding problems but reduced the headroom) and at a bridge near Smallbrook Junction.

LOW-IMPACT CAR TRAVEL

Even with the excellent Island bus network and port links to the rest of the country, the reality is most visitors to the Isle of Wight drive. One option you could consider is using a car hired through the community-interest company Co-Wheels (⌖ co-wheels.org.uk), which has vehicles available at Cowes and Ryde as well as at many UK locations. This is a social enterprise network that works on the principles of a car club but the emphasis is on hybrid and electric vehicles (this is apt, for the Isle of Wight is where Britain's first electric car was introduced, the battery-powered Electric Enfield 8000 designed by John Avery in 1973). For a small membership fee you can hire a car at low rates and you only pay mileage, not fuel.

Wightlink now offers EV charging points at Portsmouth car ferry terminal, Lymington, Fishbourne and Ryde. In addition, the Island council has installed charging points in five car parks: Chapel Street Car Park, Newport; Quay Road Car Park, Ryde; Cross Street Car Park, Cowes; St John's Road Car Park, Sandown; and Moa Place Car Park, Freshwater. The number of charging points is expected to increase within the lifetime of this book and you can get up to date by checking ⵔ zap-map.com.

ACTIVITIES

There's no shortage of outdoor fun to be had on the Island. Whether you're a walker, cyclist or want to embrace the sea in some fashion, you'll be spoilt for choice.

WALKING

Simply put, the Isle of Wight offers some of the most magnificent walking in the entire UK, with more than 500 miles of rights of way, permissive paths and bridleways squeezed into its modest dimensions. This is as dense a network as you will find anywhere in the country. From sweeping downland to high cliffs, sleepy bays, woodlands, forests and sunken valleys, the variety of routes, and where they thread through, is astonishing. The England Coast Path runs for 88 miles around almost all the Island's edges, allowing a circumnavigation of the Island on foot. Most walkers can complete the path in a week at a leisurely pace; clockwise, beginning at Yarmouth, is popular, as for much of the second half of the route Tennyson Down will hover in and out of view.

You can walk across these landscapes unencumbered by roads, your route perhaps broken only by a winding country lane. Sometimes these paths will cross narrow, steep lanes, known locally as shutes: these make their way through pint-sized valleys or ravines, and often have deeply ancient origins in allowing the earliest inhabitants of the Island access to the sea by the most direct route. One moment you might be in

CROSSING THE ISLAND ON FOOT

The granddaddy of Island walks is the 26½-mile Walk the Wight, sometimes called the Cross Island Trek or, more dauntingly, the Cross Wight Traverse. Running from Bembridge Point on the east coast to Alum Bay in the west, this is a classic coast-to-coast walk taking in just about all the features of the Island, from downlands to shutes, rivers and woodlands. The recommended route is from east to west because, while it does mean you will tend to be walking into the prevailing westerlies, the hike culminates in the stupendous cliffs of Alum Bay and Tennyson Down, which represent as superb and eye-popping a climax as any walk in Britain. You can, of course, do the walk by yourself at any time but it also features in the annual Isle of Wight Walking Festival (page 18), where it becomes a fundraising event for an Island hospice, with around 6,000 people typically taking part.

The walk should take about 12 hours for someone of average fitness to complete. The route (⏁ mountbatten.org.uk/main-walk) follows the Bembridge Trail from Bembridge via Brading and Arreton to Newport and then heads via Carisbrooke Castle along Mottistone Down to Compton Down, Freshwater Bay and onwards to the sea. Given the plethora of footpaths on the Island, there is probably an infinite number of variations on this route to take you across the Island; you could tailor the walk to take in anywhere that catches your eye, beginning for example in Sandown and taking the Red Squirrel Trail to Newport.

woodland, listening to the earliest spring migrants, the next you emerge on to magnificent downland with views of sweeping cliffs, or springing yourself on to a little-visited bay. Always, there is the sea.

You are also extremely unlikely to get lost. Every footpath on the Island has an official ID, which is displayed on its signpost. These IDs refer to the parish through which the footpath runs, or originates. For example, a path near Ventnor will start with 'V', followed by the number of the footpath; elsewhere you will see 'BB' for Bembridge (eg: BB21), 'CS' for Cowes… you get the idea.

The Island Ramblers group is highly active, and welcomes new members and visitors. Their website, ⏁ iowramblers.com, is an excellent source of information and they also have a good booklet of walks, *12 Rambles by Bus*, which is available through their website and outlets such as ferry ports and bookshops.

Finally, if you are big fan of walking, consider visiting in early May when the Isle of Wight Walking Festival (page 18) usually takes place (though check the website as it switched to autumn in 2021). This week-long celebration involves guided hikes by experts in everything from wildlife to geology and military history and culminates in the Walk the Wight, a cross-island traverse.

CYCLING

The Isle of Wight is one of the best places for cycling in the UK and three main routes, which are generally waymarked and signposted, cover a good deal of the Island. Other smaller inter-linked cycle paths fill in the remaining gaps.

The **Taste Round the Island** route (visitisleofwight.co.uk/dbimgs/RTICycleMapNew.pdf, visitisleofwight.co.uk/things-to-do/cycling/

EASY RIDER: CYCLING ON THE ISLAND

It's not just visitors who benefit from the cycling opportunities that the Island provides. Those living here do too, both for work and pleasure. Brian McElhinney, who works at the Seaview Hotel (page 115) in Seaview on the northeast coast, is a keen cyclist and always keeps his two wheels to hand.

Brian's 'commute' to work along the sea wall from his home in Ryde is the envy of millions. 'My cycle home is to me a joy as – no matter how my day has gone – the peace and quiet is fantastic. During summer I see all the little beach parties and young people out having fun, and in the winter coming along the sea wall and avoiding the big waves can be fun! I also get to stop on a good night and chat with the fishermen angling from the beach.'

On his days off Brian explores further and strongly encourages others to do the same. 'For me, the appeal of cycling on the Island is the many different routes that can be taken depending on the level of a workout you want,' he says. 'With many dedicated cycle tracks and little cafés along the way there are also lots of lovely places to stop and take in the sights, and usually you have it to yourself.'

A route favoured by Brian is one that many visitors could reasonably tackle. 'I leave my house in Ryde and follow the coast around through Seaview and St Helens and through the nature reserve at Brading,' he says. Continuing to Shanklin, he picks up the Red Squirrel Trail west to Newport and then returns to Ryde via Wootton Bridge where he can get back on an off-road trail which runs past the front door of Quarr Abbey (page 99). This route takes Brian about three hours with a few stops to rest – but a visitor can make a delightful day out of it.'

Brian also openly admits to being a convert to electric bikes. 'In the beginning I thought it was cheating,' he laughs, 'but now after a few years of renting them to guests and advising on cycle routes I've come round to them. I also use them now and again if it's been a really busy day or if there's a strong easterly wind at home time!'

bicycle-island/taste-round-the-island-route) does just what it says and circles the Island for a total of 66 miles, almost entirely on roads and signposted all the way. This is a good route to follow to pick up most of the coastal sites of interest. It was originally intended as a way to direct gourmands to places that promoted local food (farm shops, cafés) as they sojourned around the Island, but over time it has become more of a useful route for exploration. It is handy for exploring little-visited hinterlands, such as the area northeast of Yarmouth, from Shalfleet to Cowes, as well as embracing a pleasingly scenic crescent behind Sandown, from Brading to Wroxall. With a couple of unavoidable exceptions (along the Military Road around Blackgang and between Niton and Freshwater), it sticks to quieter roads.

If a cycle trail can be a poster child for two wheelers, then it would be the **Red Squirrel Trail** (⏀ visitisleofwight.co.uk/things-to-do/cycling/bicycle-island/red-squirrel-trail). This lasso-shaped route explores the east of the Island and is popular with families. The basic loop runs for 13 miles from Newport to Sandown and Shanklin, with the 'noose' of the lasso representing the extension up through Newport towards West Cowes and into Parkhurst Forest. About 95% of the route is off-road, ranging from flat, former train lines to mud and puddles, and is suitable for trail bikes and mountain bikes, and bicycles with chunkier tyres. The route is really excellent for all age groups, so younger families can easily manage it with a trailer. If you're looking for a day's family cycling then, from personal experience, hiring bikes to go from Newport to Dinosaur Isle and the Wildheart Animal Sanctuary on the edge of Sandown is one of those experiences that can leave you feeling like a good parent.

Just as the Island can get patronised by those unable to peer beyond the bucket-and-spade stereotype, so hardcore cyclists might sniff and fix their gaze determinedly towards hiller landscapes on the mainland. In which case, you might suggest that they try out the **Island Chalk Ridge Extreme Trail** (⏀ visitisleofwight.co.uk/things-to-do/cycling/bicycle-island/chalk-ridge-extreme): the route is aimed at cyclists with a slightly higher level of fitness as it follows the chalk ridge along the 'back' (in this case, this means the ridges set back from the coast) of the Island. Across the entire 53 miles you will climb a total of 4,934ft:

---

1 Paddleboarding. **2** Isle of Wight Festival. **3** Cycling options cater for all levels of fitness.
4 Fossil hunting, Atherfield Bay, looking west. ▶

proper mountain-bike territory. Easier sections include those around Arreton and the Garlic Farm, where you can enjoy far-reaching views in a truly bucolic setting. The gradients kick in among the extended downland element of the trail, running from Chale Green, up above Brighstone and up and down Brook Down, Afton Down and Compton Down, where truly superb views are bookended by St Catherine's Down to the east and Tennyson Down to the west and open sea to the south. Be mindful that both this trail and the Red Squirrel Trail are shared with walkers.

If you find some of the potential climbs rather daunting you can always hire an **electric bike**. 'Many people want a leisurely experience,' says Tracy Mikich of the Seaview Hotel (⊘ seaviewhotel.co.uk) in Seaview, which hires out electric bikes. 'Electric bikes allow you to enjoy what you are seeing around you rather than pumping your calf muscles all the time. Not all cycling has to be about gung-ho lycra.' It's a point well made and one you might agree with when cycling from the sea-level promenade of Sandown up to Bonchurch.

If you're planning to cycle, pick up a copy of **Bicycle Island**, the Island cycle map, from any ferry port or tourist centre, and you can knit together routes that don't leave much of the Island out of touch. The Island is small enough that you can hop from one route to another.

CYCLE HIRE

The availability of electric bikes is improving all the time, so always ask at rental shops; some hotels and B&Bs also hire them.

Routefifty7 Bike Park Dean Resorts, Lower Hyde, off Landguard Manor Rd, Shanklin PO37 7LL ⊘ 07491 000057 ⊘ routefifty7.com. Offers bikes for hire across the Island and will drop them off for free (dependent on a minimum hire charge). They also hire cycles for promenading up and down the bay from Shanklin to Sandown and back, a distance of 5½ miles.
TAV Cycles 140–140a High St, Ryde PO33 2RE ⊘ 01983 812989 ⊘ tavcycles.co.uk. A wide range of adults' and kids' bikes with half-day, daily and weekly rates available.
Two Elements 10 Bath Rd, Cowes PO31 7QN ⊘ 07947 912886 ⊘ twoelements.co.uk ☺ Mar–Sep. Offers a good range of mountain bikes, ideal for tackling the Island's chalk ridges. They also hire paddleboards.
Wight Cycle Hire Yarmouth Station, Station Rd, Yarmouth PO41 0QT ⊘ 01983 761800 ⊘ wightcyclehire.co.uk. Conveniently located right on the Yarmouth to Freshwater cycleway (page 52).

SAILING

The Island that gave us Cowes Week is far from an exclusive haunt of salt-soaked sailors. If you plan to sail to or around the Island, the best initial contact is the Cowes Harbour Commission ($\mathscr{O}$ cowesharbourcommission. co.uk), which is a helpful source of information about berthing and slipways for small and medium-sized vessels.

Beginners' courses are available if you want to get stuck in but don't know your tack (sailing upwind) from your jib (sailing downwind). The United Kingdom Sailing Academy ($\mathscr{O}$ uksa.org) is based by the waterfront in Cowes and offers courses to satisfy both the confirmed landlubber and those dreaming of circumnavigating not only the Island but perhaps the globe. They also run a dinghy mini-course for children and extend their training to kayaking, windsurfing and kitesurfing. Another organisation, Girls for Sail (**f**) does what it says and is designed to appeal specifically to women of all sailing abilities.

KAYAKING

With sheltered coves in places such as St Helens and Newtown Creek, the Island is ideal for taking a canoe or kayak out on to the water. The more adventurous may look to paddle further afield around the coasts of Freshwater and along Sandown Bay. If you do, seriously consider using a qualified instructor to guide you or provide advice. There is a handful of operators offering these services as well as coasteering. Tackt-isle ($\mathscr{O}$ 01983 875542 $\mathscr{O}$ tackt-isle.co.uk) is based at St Helens on the west coast while Adventure Activities ($\mathscr{O}$ adventureisleofwight.com) is based at Freshwater Bay on the south coast.

HORSERIDING

The Island's downlands, beaches and quiet lanes make it a fine place for horseriding. Experienced riders as well as beginners can ride horses from the Island Riding Centre (Staplers Rd, Newport PO30 2NB $\mathscr{O}$ 01983 214000 $\mathscr{O}$ islandriding.com). The centre can also accommodate any horses you wish to bring with you.

FOSSIL HUNTING

The Isle of Wight is one of the best places in the world to find fossils, with important discoveries regularly exposed along the coast, including everything from dinosaurs to ancient turtles (see box, page 32). A guided walk is the best introduction for visitors and is really worthwhile: being told in a highly engaging manner what you are looking at can be like having a curtain drawn back to reveal something extremely special.

Guided walks are available from Dinosaur Isle at Yaverland (page 280) and with Wight Coast Fossils ($\diamond$ wightcoastfossils.co.uk), both of which offer walking tours to the curious, whether they be experts or novices.

THE ISLAND LANDSCAPE – A BRIEF NATURAL HISTORY

The landmass that we today call the Isle of Wight became an island around 6,000 to 10,000 years ago when the Solent broke through the lowland valleys between the present-day island and the New Forest, creating valleys and estuaries. Before that time, the Solent had been no more than an eastward flowing river and you could have walked from what is the present-day Isle of Wight across Doggerland (now under the North Sea) to continental Europe without getting your feet wet.

Wading back even further into the deep past, some 125 million years ago, the Island was located where North Africa is today, attached to parts of what we now call France, Germany and Spain. A hot, sultry place, it offered exposed, sweaty plains for animals to die on, and swampy water and flash floods aplenty to quickly envelop them and begin the process of fossilisation. Over time, this turned the Island into one of the world's top spots for dinosaur hunting (page 32).

All the Island rocks are sedimentary, that is, muds, clays, limestones and sandstones laid down by water in the forms of rivers, lakes, ponds and seas. This has led over time to a landscape that has similarities to the chalk downs of the South Downs and, on the north coast, the sylvan, estuarine coastline of the New Forest. In fact, the Isle of Wight could geologically be shunted into Hampshire, Dorset and Sussex: putting the Solent aside, the Island is essentially a continuation of the landmass of the island of Britain. While the Island has no mountains, those chalk downs are part of the same geological events that created the Swiss Alps.

Much of the Island has been categorised as an Area of Outstanding Natural Beauty (AONB) but with a difference, in that it is the only one of the 46 AONBs in England, Wales and Northern Ireland to comprise five areas of unconnected land: two areas along the north coast; the central and east downs; the south coast and downs; and the southwest coast and downs. 'The landscape is phenomenal,' says Joel Bateman of the Island's Area of Outstanding Natural Beauty (⌀ wightaonb.org.uk). 'We have a little bit of everything that southern Britain has to offer, from Kent to Somerset. You have downland across the centre of the Island and again further south at Bonchurch and Ventnor. Because most of our population is found in discrete areas, our rural areas are very rural indeed.'

Wherever you go, however, you are likely to be sidetracked by nature. 'The Island is so rich in character for such a small place,' says Carol Flux, project manager for Gift to Nature, which manages 29 wildlife sites across the Island. When it comes to animal magnetism, the red squirrel (page 236) is the Island's headline act but the diversity of fauna and flora – from white-tailed eagles (page 276) to butterflies such as the Glanville fritillary and flowers including the rare early gentian and explosions of bluebells in spring – is remarkable. Woodland covers around 11% of the Island, which is a similar proportion to the wider UK. The Solent is both an abundant year-round habitat for birds and an important stopover for wading birds and terns on the Eastern Atlantic Flyway, a migratory route that links the west coast of Africa with western Europe and the Arctic Circle. You are likely to see flocks of hundreds of Brent geese, graceful Mediterranean gulls (with their distinctive white eye-liner appearance) along with ducks such as teal, which are notable for a colour scheme that resembles bits of a jigsaw fitted together. The Island is the only place in Britain where the wood calamint, a pink funnel-shaped flower, can be found – on just one sun-exposed bank in a chalk valley to the south of Carisbrooke Castle (older readers may dimly recall the flower used to be printed on the side of Woolworths' carrier bags). In 2014, exotic-looking bee-eaters, a rare visitor to the UK, bred in the Wydcombe Estate, north of Niton.

A high percentage of land is covered, protected or managed and free to access. In fact, 75% of the Island is designated as protected – both land and sea – for its wildlife and ecology, while 70% of its farmland is managed to some level of environmental stewardship.

The Island is uniquely tranquil and, says Joel, 'represents a mixture of sympathetic tenants and landowners, informed wildlife management and a lot of goodwill.'

One of the joys of the Island is how local wildlife sites are detailed in an extremely thoughtful and knowledgeable way. Two good resources

THE FLOWER MAN

William Bromfield sits comfortably within the *oeuvre* of great brains from the Victorian age, with which the Island is well endowed. He may have been born in the New Forest but it was on the southern side of the Solent that he rose to fame. Although he graduated in medicine, botany was his first love and he spent a great deal of his life on the Isle of Wight, cataloguing as many of its known (and unknown) species of flora as the hours of every day permitted.

Bromfield came from a family of considerable wealth and he deployed his means to travel to Europe and the USA in pursuit of his love of nature, always returning to his home in Ryde. In his garden he nurtured plantings and seeds he accumulated on his travels, and he compiled *Flora Vectensis*, a systematic description of the plants and ferns of the Island. He reckoned that, collectively, he devoted 14 years to the tome, which includes a listing for *Calamintha sylvatica*, or wood calamint, which he identified as a new species in 1843. His wanderlust burned strong, however, and ultimately it was to get the better of him. On a venture to the Middle East he contracted typhus in Damascus and died. The book can still be bought from specialist bookshops or online; he bequeathed his herbarium of preserved plants and a library of about 600 specialist books to the Royal Botanic Gardens at Kew. Unfortunately there is nothing left to see of his garden in Ryde.

to browse through are Island Rivers (⊘ islandrivers.org.uk) which, as it suggests, covers the Island's watercourses large and small and includes several fine walks, and the website of Arc (⊘ arc-consulting.co.uk), which is run by a small team of experts who seek to integrate the Island's ecology, landscapes and communities in a low-impact way.

DEAD INTERESTING

Not all the Island wildlife of interest to visitors is living. There's a strong case for arguing that the Isle of Wight is in the canon of top global dinosaur hotspots and Martin Munt, curator of Dinosaur Isle (page 280), puts it on the top ten localities in the world. So far, 35 (and counting) types of dinosaur have been found here. The Jurassic Coast of Dorset has long been more heralded but dinosaur finds are significantly scarcer there than they are on the Island.

Running down the east side of the Island, where Yaverland Beach and Dinosaur Isle are located, is a Cretaceous coastline (dating from 125 million to 90 million years ago). In contrast, the north coast features more swamplands, which is why places such as Bouldnor have yielded fossils of creatures harking from the early Oligocene (30 million years ago) that favoured such habitats, such as crocodiles and turtles.

Three species found on the Island, the Yaverlandia and two contemporary carnivores, the Neovenator and Eotyrannuare, are possibly endemic (that is, they are yet to be found anywhere else on the planet) while others include two species of Iguanodon, a small bipedal herbivore Hypsilophodon, the armoured Polacanthus and a large, unnamed brachiosaurid.

It's thought the dinosaurs would have migrated along a long river valley all the way from what is modern-day Devon. As they died, either from natural causes or picked off by predators, the unimaginably slow process of fossilisation began amid the river muds and sands. Over time these sunk into hollows created by tectonic shifts and upheavals that eventually led to the exposure of the fossils along the Island's coast.

Coprolite – dinosaur poo – has also been found here: the passing of time has solidified such offerings into rock, which makes it hard for the lay visitor to identify. Should you feel the need to study some in detail you'll find examples at Dinosaur Isle.

One of the striking things about fossils on the Island is that they turn up all over the place. The main centres of interest are Yaverland (page 277) and Hanover Point/Brook Bay (page 147), locations that tend to be the focus of most tours. But other areas include the shoreline around Bouldnor and Newtown on the north coast and St Catherine's Point on the south coast. Along the western edges of the south coast are found some of the oldest rocks of all, dating back 127 million years.

'The rocks on the old landslips around St Catherine's Point are rich in fossils,' says Megan Jacobs, one of three guides – the others are Theo Vickers and Jack Wonfor – who formed Wight Coast Fossils (⌂ wightcoastfossils.co.uk), 'but you have to know what you are looking for – there is no point in just turning up with a hammer and chisel on your own. There are big boulders there that have filled up over thousands of years with phosphate nodules which are covered with sharks' teeth and ammonites – these are completely different from the rocks of Yaverland but you need to know your geology to find them.' What is striking is that all three were born on the Island and caught the palaeontology bug while growing up here. They have all worked at Dinosaur Isle and are keen to take visitors to less-explored corners of the Island and offer both general and private walks.

The trio of young fossil hunters also take visitors to the Atherfield Ledge (between Chale Bay and Brighstone Bay) where you may find fossilised lobsters dating 100 to 110 million years in age. The lagoon-like and marshy landscape of Bouldnor also offers rich pickings. 'If you don't come back from Bouldnor with a big bucket of crocodile teeth and turtle shells then you haven't been looking properly,' Megan says.

Around Newtown Harbour you are likely to come across palaeosols, which you can think of as a cracked proto-soil, a survivor from the clay landscape of millions of years ago. These clays have been desiccated over eons and dried out but retain the deeply ancient outlines of roots of plants and trees. The clays are a haunting red as a result of oxidisation which has rusted the iron pigments in the soils. 'What is amazing is that the soils we have today are the same as the soils that were around millions of years ago,' says Megan. That allows us to pinpoint what weather conditions were like at different times millions of years ago – whether the weather was seasonal, wet or dry.

'The preservation is brilliant. What is amazing about the Isle of Wight is we have fossils from so many different environments and that allows us to track the history of the Island from 130 million to 30 million years ago – from the end of the dinosaurs to sea levels rising and the appearance of marine creatures and then the sea retreating and the evolution of mammals.'

Go on a fossil hunt on the Island and your imagination can run away with you: the possibilities are endless. 'The wonder of the Island is that there is so much out there, under our feet,' says Megan. 'With every high tide, something gets washed up or washed off the cliffs. The Island has so many amateur fossil hunters who work really closely with us. We're also sure that they pick stuff up and wait to collect the whole skeleton before presenting it to us.'

FURTHER INFORMATION
BOOKS
For an insight into what makes the Isle of Wight tick, look no further than any of the many books written by the prolific Jan Toms, whose methodical eye has documented everything from shipwrecks to quirky tales that lay bare the soul of the Island. Choice compendiums include *Rogues, Rascals and Reprobates* and *The Little Book of the Isle of Wight*. A fine account of

the Island's extremely long list of famous and esoteric visitors is *The Isle of Wight's Missing Chapter* by James Rayner. If you feel that the Victorian influence on the Island, particularly West Wight, can be a little dreary or serious, I'd recommend *Tennyson's Gift* by Lynne Truss as an excellent antidote, for this is a novel whose central theme of farce has shades of both P G Wodehouse and Oscar Wilde. The unlikely love affair between the doomed Russian royal family and the Isle of Wight is documented in *Isle and Empires* by Stephen Roman; it's an engrossing and, in the context of the fate that awaited the royal household back home at the hands of the Russian Revolution, a rather sad read.

Those seeking an insight into the foodie culture on the Island, and the ethos of localism behind those who produce it, should consider *Nammet: A Celebration of Isle of Wight Food and Drink* by Caroline Gurney-Champion. Should you get bitten by the fossil bug then get hold of the *Isle of Wight: Geologists' Association Guide No. 60* by Andy Gale, which provides an excellent introduction to the Island's cliffs and geology and where to find different fossils.

ONLINE

For somewhere so rural and where it is possible to leave the cares of everyday behind, the Isle of Wight is extremely well connected online. Every organisation that has a presence in the Island's great outdoors seems to have a comprehensive website, as does just about every accommodation, food outlet and visitor attraction.

ONLINE RESOURCES

Gift to Nature ⌀ gifttonature.org.uk
Hampshire and Isle of Wight Wildlife Trust ⌀ hiwwt.org.uk
Isle of Wight Area of Outstanding Natural Beauty ⌀ wightaonb.org.uk
Isle of Wight Biosphere ⌀ en.unesco.org/biosphere/eu-na/isle-of-wight, ⌀ iwbiosphere. org. For more on the Island's biosphere designation, see box, page 133.
Matt & Catt ⌀ mattandcat.co.uk. An excellent, punchily written online foodie guide to the Island.
On the Wight ⌀ onthewight.com. Good for up-to-date news and travel.
Slow Travel Isle of Wight ⌀ bradtguides.com/isleofwight
Slow Travel Isle of Wight accommodation ⌀ bradtguides.com/iowsleeps
Taste of the Wight ⌀ tasteofthewight.co.uk
Visit Isle of Wight ⌀ visitisleofwight.co.uk

Visit IOW Green Star scheme ✍ visitisleofwight.co.uk/travel/sustainable-travel/green-star. A comprehensive list of accommodation that meets the tourist board's Green Star standards, though in a handful of cases the bar for inclusion seems quite low.

HOW THIS BOOK IS ARRANGED

I've chosen to divide the Island into six geographical areas: northwest; north and northeast; southwest; south; east; and, in the middle, the main town of Newport and its immediate surroundings. The boundaries of these areas can – and do – overlap but the rationale for these divisions is that visitors can explore a chosen region in detail, without rushing backwards and forwards or covering large distances. The geographical nature of these chapters also, I hope, sits well with the way in which points of interest are connected by bus routes and by short- and medium-distance paths and cycle routes. Here's an example: on the north coast, Cowes and East Cowes may be nearer to Newport but I've generally found that the logical route of exploration from them is eastwards, towards Ryde and Seaview; hence these are all gathered together (in *Chapter 2* in this instance). Similarly, Parkhurst Forest (the epicentre of the Island's red squirrel community) may be close to Cowes but I find I tend to visit it from Newport, which offers slightly easier access by bike or bus.

PRACTICAL INFORMATION

Telephone numbers are given where possible and are marked with the symbol ✍ (for both landline and mobile numbers), while websites are marked ♂. Opening periods (and, if necessary, times) are indicated by the symbol ⊙. Generally speaking, most places open 09.00–17.00 (or a little later) Monday to Saturday. Where the times are significantly different (for example, a shop or museum is closed on a weekday) this is stated. Opening details can of course change, particularly in the context of the Covid-19 pandemic, so it's always worth checking ahead if you can – online is the best way as almost every Island business seems to have an active website. A number of attractions, such as stately homes, are closed in the depths of winter but cafés, hotels and many B&Bs stay open year-round. Postcodes are included to help locate destinations.

Most walks on the Island are easy to follow, thanks to the common practice of signing and numbering every footpath (page 24), but where a location or route direction may be ambiguous, I've included grid references (indicated by the symbol ♀) and included possible bus – and, just occasionally, train – links.

ACCOMMODATION, EATING & DRINKING

The accommodation in this guide has been chosen for its value for money, scenic location, historical interest and unique features, but most of all because it fits in with the Slow approach and because their owners also buy into a wider ethos of being greener where possible and are supportive of keeping carbon footprints low. These are people who care about the landscapes and environment of the Island and who often form part of local, mutually independent communities. The variety and choice of accommodation is remarkable, from modern or traditional B&Bs to lighthouse cottages. Camping also covers the entire spectrum from simple field set-ups to yurts and lotus bell tents. Hotels and B&Bs are indicated by 🏠, self-catering options by 🏠 and camping by 🛆; all are listed under the heading for the area in which they are located. For further accommodation reviews and additional listings, go to ⌀ bradtguides.com/iowsleeps.

Places to eat have been chosen for the excellent food they serve, the surroundings in which they are set and their character – sometimes for all three. Above all, they have been included because they support the Island's vibrant food-growing industry. You can buy a sandwich made at a factory in Sussex or Norfolk on the Island but you won't find it recommended in this book.

MAPS

You'll find a map of the Isle of Wight with suggested places to base yourself on page 6, while heading each chapter is a numbered map of the area that corresponds to the numbered place headings in the text. On the area maps you'll also find a ♀ symbol showing the location of the walks outlined in the chapter. While some of the walks in this book come with a sketch map, it's worth investing in the Ordnance Survey OL29 *Isle of Wight* map, which is double sided and covers the entirety of the Island. You may also come across the AA *Isle of Wight Walkers Map* but it's hard to discern much of a difference between this and the OS version. Cycling maps and local walk maps can be picked up in village shops and ferry ports. This must be one of the most comprehensively mapped parts of the UK.

ACCESSIBLE ISLE OF WIGHT

For a comprehensive list of accessible places and activities on the Island, visit the accessible travel pages of the Visit Isle of Wight website (⊘ visitisleofwight.co.uk/travel/accessible-isle-of-wight). This website also gives details of how ferries and hovercraft can accommodate visitors with mobility issues. It also has click-through links to Isle Access (⊘ isleaccess.co.uk), an Island-based charity promoting accessibility and which lists accessible places to visit, stay and eat and drink in. **Euan's Guide** (⊘ euansguide.com), the disabled-access review site, covers the Island comprehensively too, with reviews by disabled visitors, their families, friends and carers.

Major attractions, such as Osborne House, Blackgang Chine and the Isle of Wight Zoo are disabled-friendly. However, uneven pavements (and indeed pavements that suddenly disappear, leaving you faced with a step down to a road or just confronting oncoming traffic) are a feature of a number of villages around the Island. More positively, there are several excellent disabled-access and wheelchair-friendly scenic paths. These include most of the promenade of Sandown Bay, the stretch of coast between Seaview and Ryde, and the network of paths on the east side of the River Eastern Yar at Yarmouth.

As you walk around the Island you will become increasingly aware of the number of gates that have replaced stiles. This is the result of the Ramblers' Donate-a-Gate scheme, where a walker can donate (ie: fund rather than build) a gate that remembers a loved one. The idea is a rather nice touch, making progress easier for walkers who struggle with stiles. More than 200 such gates are now in place, with more added every year.

FEEDBACK REQUEST

At Bradt Guides we're aware that guidebooks start to go out of date on the day they're published – and that you, our readers, are out there in the field doing research of your own. You'll find out before us when a fine new family-run hotel opens or a favourite restaurant changes hands and goes downhill. So why not tell us about your experiences? Contact us on ☏ 01753 893444 or ✉ info@bradtguides.com. We will forward emails to the author who may post updates on the Bradt website at ⊘ bradtguides.com/updates. Alternatively, you can add a review of the book to Amazon, or share your adventures with us on social media: 🅕 BradtGuides 🅣 BradtGuides & @wanderingrowe 🅘 BradtGuides

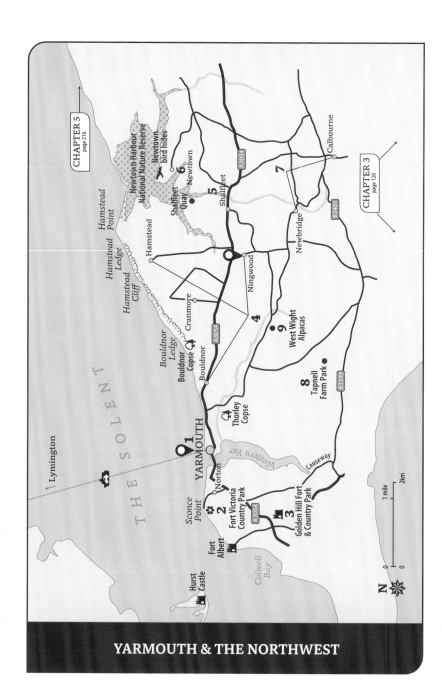

YARMOUTH & THE NORTHWEST

1
YARMOUTH & THE NORTHWEST

The northwest of the Isle of Wight is something of a paradox. While it most definitely sees its fair slice of the tourist pie, it retains at the same time a keen sense of being somewhere for those 'in the know'. You'll find the shortest ferry crossing (in terms of distance) from the mainland here, to the port of Yarmouth – and it is perhaps the fact that arrivals will have first traversed the New Forest, an area of similar bucolic charm, that makes this feel a rather sleepy, sparsely populated part of the Island.

While the landscapes are reminiscent of the New Forest, with woodlands and small villages to stumble upon, the topography is unique and unlike anywhere else in the UK. This is where you realise just what an extraordinary shape the Isle of Wight is. Looming up to the south of Yarmouth, the western tailcoats of the Island downs make for a spectacular rolling backdrop as they begin their journey east. Their solid lumps, in the form of Afton and Compton downs and the more distant upward curve of Tennyson Down, contrast with the spirit-level flat marshes around the River Yar. It's a top-heavy landscape and you sometimes wonder if the northwest of the Island isn't about to tip, like an ill-balanced iceberg, headfirst into the Solent.

Yarmouth is an attractive town and merits more time than its Lilliputian size might at first glance suggest. The town will also introduce you to the high-quality local produce for which the Island is deservedly renowned. The coast either side of the port is worth exploring, too: to the west lies **Fort Victoria**, a 19th-century defence post surrounded by woodlands that offer your first chance of spotting red squirrels, as well as the easily accessible sands of **Colwell Bay**. To the east of Yarmouth is what might be termed the Isle of Wight's 'Empty Quarter'; around the small and scattered villages of **Hamstead** and **Bouldnor** are woodlands full of birdsong, which open up unexpectedly into slivers of heathland and, in turn, tumble down to little-visited shores offering the chance of fossil

TOURIST INFORMATION

There is no tourist office as such in Yarmouth, but staff at the Wightlink Office at the ferry terminal are helpful – you can also pick up leaflets, flyers and more comprehensive brochures from here.

hunting. Further east, the historic villages of **Shalfleet** and **Newtown** straddle a seemingly infinite number of creeks and mudflats along the Hamstead Heritage Coast, which forms the northerly outlier of the island's AONB. This environmentally special stretch is home to hundreds of wading birds, including lapwing and dunlin, migrating Brent geese and ducks such as wigeon, as well as the rather larger white-tailed eagles.

GETTING THERE & AROUND

WALKING & CYCLING

Almost all of the northwest can be walked or cycled. The **Coastal Path** runs east and west from Yarmouth (including with a few deviations away from the coast where access is tricky), while both banks of the River Yar are accessible on foot (see box, page 52, for a circular route), with the east side particularly good for bikes. Cyclists can expect easy, generally flat routes and beautiful views of the Yar Estuary, with the option of pausing at Colwell Bay for a picnic. A circumnavigation on two wheels of the area covered in this chapter would make for a very easy and rewarding day. You could start at Yarmouth, follow the cycle path along the east bank of the Yar to the Causeway, then follow signs into Freshwater village and the coast. If you're feeling energetic you could cycle up Afton Down for views west up Tennyson Down and east, on a clear day, all the way to St Catherine's Down, some 15 miles away. You could then wind your way back to Yarmouth along the west coast lanes and roads via The Needles Landmark Attraction, parking the bike to explore Headon Warren, Colwell Bay and the coast and woods behind Fort Victoria. You will also find some excellent route suggestions from the team at Wight Cycle Hire (see below).

 CYCLE HIRE

Wight Cycle Hire Yarmouth Station, Station Rd, Yarmouth PO41 0QT ✆ 01983 761800
⌂ wightcyclehire.co.uk ☉ Mar–Oct. Bike hire and repair service. Handy location five

minutes' walk from the ferry and right next to the Off the Rails café. The team are generous with their knowledge and suggestions for several cycling routes can be downloaded from their website.

PUBLIC TRANSPORT

The bus station by Yarmouth's pier provides connections with most destinations in this chapter, and those that are not on a bus route (such as Tapnell Farm) are easily reached on foot from a nearby stop. The proximity of many places also means you can take the bus to one location, walk from there to another, and then pick up a bus to return to your starting point. The key **bus** route is the #7, which runs from Newport to Yarmouth (some services via Calbourne, others via Shalfleet on the north coast) before continuing south to Freshwater and Alum Bay. Route A of the ultra-local FYT Bus (Freshwater–Yarmouth–Totland ⏚ fytbus.org.uk) connects Yarmouth to Bouldnor, with services running in both directions until lunchtime on weekdays. The Needles Breezer (page 124) runs around the western chunk of the island, taking in Yarmouth along the way.

1 YARMOUTH

🏠 **Jireh House** (page 303) ⛺ **Camp Wight** (page 303), **Glamping the Wight Way** (page 303)

Yarmouth is the Isle of Wight's prettiest port, its seemingly too-small ferry slipway shoehorned between a castle and a large marina where the boardwalks always wobble to a steady stream of just-landed sailors. The one-way system for vehicles disembarking from the ferry encourages you to drive off to other parts of the Island, swerving

A RIVER RUNS THROUGH IT

Bisecting the two sides of this part of the Island is the **River Yar** (its proper name is the Western Yar but you'll rarely see or hear it referred to as such), which trundles for four miles from its sources high in the downs. The river offers a perfect chance to reconnect with nature and spot wildlife thanks to the hides, riverside clearings and benches where you can sit and take in views of woodland spreading away to the south, east and west as the watercourse winds northwards. Wherever you find yourself on the Yar, you're never more than an hour's walk from Yarmouth and several fine choices for food and drink.

around the town – don't make this mistake. Fortunately, for those on foot, the passenger terminal deposits you right into the town's Norman grid-like street system.

The Solent washes up along Yarmouth's north shores, while the estuary of the River Yar and its woodlands – Saltern Wood on the west shore, Mill Copse and Backet's Copse along the east – throw a protective arm and fetching backdrop around the west and south peripheries. The foreshore, too, is lined with hedgerows and pockets of alder trees. All in all, it makes for the softest of soft landings if you've just crossed the water from Lymington in the New Forest.

At first glance, Yarmouth seems to be just a slip of a town – indeed, with a population of fewer than 900, it is actually the second-smallest town in the United Kingdom (after Llanwrtyd in Powys). But size doesn't mean everything as Yarmouth is big on charm, its two squares and cobbled streets lined with houses and shops made from crushed rubble and flint. However, this is no toy town, for it is constantly busy, not just with ferry passengers but with Islanders dropping by for their shopping or to grab a coffee. Almost 900 years old, its modest town centre boasts an ornamental timber sign proudly bearing the original name of Erumue (which means 'muddy estuary' in Old English).

Although there is evidence of both Roman and earlier activity in the area, such as Bronze Age fish traps pulled out of the muddy estuary, the first proof of a fixed settlement at Yarmouth lies in a tax survey of AD991, and was confirmed the following century in the Domesday Book compiled for William the Conqueror. During the reign of Henry I, the Lord of the Isle of Wight, Baldwin de Redvers, sought to strengthen his island possessions and decided to create an accessible purpose-built town at Yarmouth – making it the Milton Keynes of its day – to which he granted an official Charter in 1135. A deepwater haven (where the marina now stands, to the west of the present-day town) made the port a busy place for the exchange of trade. By the start of the 13th century, Yarmouth had established itself as one of the three most important port towns along the south coast, together with Portsmouth and Southampton. The following centuries saw this stature embellished and recognised with the construction of defensive fortifications under

---

1 Yarmouth from the Solent. **2** The castle interior. **3** Wheatsheaf Lane. **4** Ferry journey across the Solent. **5** Yarmouth Tide Mill. ▶

SS

DAVE SMITH 1965/S

ROLF RICHARDSON/A

J M RITCHIE/S

J M RITCHIE/S

WHEN WIGHT WAS ROTTEN

Students of political history place Yarmouth in a notorious canon: for the best part of 300 years, it was considered a textbook example of a 'rotten borough', one that was able to elect an MP despite having few or no voters. Under a gentlemen's agreement, two MPs were nominated by a handful of locals in return for financial favours, to the detriment of some 95% of the town's population. This shady state of affairs continued well into the 19th century, before the 1832 Great Reform Act put an end to this brazenly corrupt practice. Not all parliamentary goings-on here have been steeped in shenanigans, however, and Yarmouth has given the UK four MPs who went on to become prime minister: Canning, Melbourne, Palmerston and Wellington.

Henry VIII. In the Victorian age, it was the go-to port for well-to-do arrivals who dreaded the mudflats of Ryde (page 104).

By the 1880s, the town was significant enough to be the middle leg of the Freshwater–Yarmouth–Newport Railway and it boasted a railway station until the 1950s. In what could generously be considered something of an oversight, the railway line never actually connected with the Lymington ferry, and as a result all arriving coal, livestock and passengers had to be transported for half a mile down the backstreets of Yarmouth to get to the train. Perhaps this was why the railway never really made any money (one year's accounts show a profit of just £6) and it was closed for good in September 1953.

A TOUR OF THE TOWN

If disembarking the ferry on foot, you'll first pass the hotchpotch of yachts, schooners and yawls that populate the marina. Tight by the pier is **Yarmouth Castle** (Quay St ✆ 01983 760678 ☉ Mar–Oct; English Heritage), which you'll likely have seen from the ferry. It was built on the orders of Henry VIII after the town was all but destroyed by the French, though completed in 1547 after his death. More of a gun platform and garrison than a conventional castle, it achieved its aim of deterring French incursions through the Solent. Today, it comes into its own in warm weather as a delightful place for a picnic with a sea view from the battlements and rampart lawns – on the way to the top you can skip through a brief historical exhibition.

From the marina, turn sharp left – or port if you're still in ferry mode – and you'll find a Norman plan of cobbled, narrow streets and two broad and handsome squares home to a handful of good cafés, pubs, inns, art galleries and food shops. Many buildings, whether private homes or businesses, boast distinctive 16- or 20-pane sash windows. Towering high above most, however, is the substantial **town hall**. Dating to 1763, its original red-brick ground-floor arches are now filled in with windows that stand guard either side of a formidably fortified wooden door.

Quay Street leads on to Pier Square, where your line of sight is drawn towards the older of the town's two **piers**. A Grade II-listed structure, it is the only surviving all-wooden pier in the UK and extends 610ft into the Solent. The timber may make for fetching photographs, but it is something of a nightmare to maintain – twice already this century appeals have raised hundreds of thousands of pounds to treat it for a variety of marine-based chomping predators, including shipworm, timberworm and a voracious ever-hungry crustacean muncher known as the gribble worm.

Pier Square merges into St James's Square, at the southern end of which is **St James's Church**. Another Grade II-listed building of great charm, the church dates to the 17th century though the full height of its western tower was added 100 years later, once its potential as a landmark for sailors was belatedly recognised. Like most buildings in Yarmouth, the church teeters above a narrow pavement and was built from a mixture of freestone, stone rubble and flint that is easy on the eye. Inside you'll find a richly pigmented six-light stained-glass window and a sepulchred chapel. Yarmouth's most famous inhabitant and one-time governor of the Island, Admiral Sir Robert Holmes (see box, page 48), is buried here, immortalised with a suitably swashbuckling marble statue. The church bells are almost certainly not original – legend has it that those were carried off to Cherbourg or Boulogne after the French launched one of their intermittent sackings of the town during the Middle Ages.

WALKS FROM YARMOUTH

Yarmouth is so small that you can buy a coffee, walk out of town, find a picturesque stretch of river or woodland, and drink it while it's still hot. One such spot is **Mill Copse**, just a ten-minute walk south from the ferry and a good place to see that bundle of animal magnetism that is the red squirrel. From the terminal, walk across the large car park visible on the south side of the roundabout and pick up the riverside

YARMOUTH'S MOST (IN)FAMOUS SON

Wandering around Yarmouth's genteel and handsome streets you'd be forgiven for thinking the town's most famous son would be a man of noble regard whose actions have stood the test of history. Instead, however, that honour goes to an individual who reverberates through history as a privateer, slave trader, local MP, friend to King Charles II and high-ranking naval officer during the Restoration period.

Sir Robert Holmes was – allegedly – pithily summed up by the poet Andrew Marvell, who is believed to have dismissed him as an 'Irish livery boy, a highwayman and the cursed beginner of the two Dutch wars'. Born in Ireland in 1622, Holmes was fighting for the king at the age of 20 in the English Civil War and by the time he was 40 had gained notoriety as a privateer, mercenary and commander of a seafaring squadron. He plied the west coast of Africa (around modern-day Guinea), dabbling in trade (mostly slaves) and seeking out sources of gold. His growing naval influence put the fear of God into the diarist Samuel Pepys (whose day job was a navy administrator) after they argued about the suitability of the crew of Holmes's ship. The threat of a duel to the death between the two never quite materialised and instead Holmes appeared to settle for picking fights

with the Dutch West India Company – he is widely credited with provoking two wars with the Dutch. Episodes within these conflicts and allegations of importuning and embezzlement saw him briefly imprisoned in the Tower of London, but eventually reprieved. In between this he found time to do some historical good by trialling a new pendulum clock, in pursuit of that Holy Grail for ship navigators of reckoning longitude. He was subsequently promoted to acting Rear Admiral of the Navy.

In 1666, the year of the Great Fire of London, he gave his own name to 'Holmes's Bonfire', in which he razed communities on two Dutch islands, acts which drove his stock in royal and national circles to new heights. Holmes purchased the governorship of the Isle of Wight in 1667 and a year later was convicted of murder but reprieved after acting as a second in a duel.

In the 1670s Holmes slowed down – a relative term – and he increasingly spent time on the Island where he was now MP, fortifying castles around the coast. He invested in property, including what today is the George Hotel in Yarmouth, and ensured his brother secured the rotten borough seat of Newtown. He died in 1792 after suffering from gout.

path, which accommodates both walkers and cyclists. Once past the old Tide Mill House you come to a gate and a path with options to turn right, left or straight across; Mill Copse is right ahead of you. Although barely 12 acres in size, this 400-year-old woodland has developed around the cyclical coppicing of hazel, in which oak, wild cherry and spindle have also thrived. What you see today is, in truth, a mere sliver of its former glory. By the 1960s, labour-intensive coppicing of hazel had become uneconomic and the Forestry Commission cleared the copse and replanted it with conifers and beech trees. Little of the original woodland survived and the future looked bleak. Since the 1990s, however, volunteers from the Wight Nature Fund (⊘ iwnhas. org/wight-nature-fund) have planted more than 300 hazel trees and the domineering conifers are being slowly removed. From spring to autumn you may encounter migrant hawker dragonflies and white admiral butterflies, and year-round you should be able to pick out goldcrests among the conifers and red squirrels scampering along branches. There is a hide close to the banks of the river where you can spot many species of bird, including godwit, redshank and lapwing.

From Mill Copse, a worthwhile detour en route back to Yarmouth follows the main bridleway running along the east shore of the Yar. After retracing your footsteps from the copse to the walkway by the River Yar (the walkway doubles as the Yarmouth–Freshwater cycle path), bear right so that you walk slightly inland between hedgerows along the paved path, following the edge of a large pond fringed with reeds. As you pass Off the Rails café (page 50), turn right along a narrow path over a stream and follow this for barely half a mile to **Thorley Copse**. Coots, moorhens and other waterbirds frequent the waters hereabouts and their inelegant splash landings are likely to be the only noise you hear. At the far eastern end of the copse, the footpath meets the B3401; turn left here for 200yds and then turn left again on to the cycle path to return to Yarmouth.

¶¶ FOOD & DRINK

With some good cafés, restaurants and an excellent deli, Yarmouth offers a textbook introduction to the Isle of Wight's prodigious food scene. I've learnt over the years to skimp on breakfast if I've arrived here on an early ferry as there are a couple of great options for a celebratory start-of-holiday brunch.

The Blue Crab High St, PO41 0PL ⊘ 01983 760014 ⊘ thebluecrab.co.uk. Small restaurant tucked away off the main squares but with a strong emphasis on local food – try the garlic mackerel fillets or roasted ray wing.
The Bugle The Sq, PO41 0NS ⊘ 01983 760272 ⊘ characterinns.co.uk/the-bugle-coaching-inn. This elongated pub sprawls along the eastern flank of St James's Square, the beams and

stones of its façade having eased themselves into one another over the centuries. A good choice for a real ale or fine wine among wood-panelled surroundings.

The Gossips Café The Sq, PO41 0NS ✆ 01983 760646 **f**. Adjacent to the pier, Gossips has the best sit-down views of the Solent. Wide-ranging menu includes Island sausages, salads and afternoon crab cream tea.

Off the Rails Station Rd, PO41 0QT ✆ 01983 761600 ⌂ offtherailsyarmouth.co.uk. Housed in Yarmouth's former railway station, this café-bistro may be furnished in homage to a yesteryear train carriage but the food is modern and excellent. The French owner and chef Philippe Blot offers giant gourmet burgers, Yarmouth crab and a good offering of veggie, vegan and gluten-free dishes. No children's menu, but you can order half-sized (and half-priced) portions. There's even an ice-cream menu for dogs to help them through hot summer days. While the food is on the pricey side, the quality means you won't feel short changed.

On the Rocks Bridge Rd, PO41 0PJ ✆ 01983 760505 ⌂ ontherocksyarmouth.com. A quirky restaurant serving steaks on hot volcanic rocks. This cooking technique means you can eat your meat rare as soon as it's served or watch it sizzle further before tucking in. Just don't pour sauces on the rocks – they'll cascade on to your lap!

PO41 Coffee House Quay St, PO41 0PB ✆ 01983 761105 **f**. This cosy café within a former post office serves palm oil-free cakes, meringues, excellent coffee and hot chocolate. Their coffee is processed at a young offenders' institution as part of a rehabilitation scheme.

A SLOW JOURNEY ACROSS THE SOLENT

The Isle of Wight forces you to slow down even before you reach it shores. Ferry journeys from the mainland trundle across the Solent at around 10 knots, meaning that the hurried pace of working life is slowly shed.

No-one knows this more than Andy Burtt, a captain on the Wight-class roll-on, roll-off ferries that ebb back and forward between Lymington in the New Forest and Yarmouth.

'The best time is when you start with the first ferry of the day and the light is breaking. You hear all the birds singing,' he says. Andy has seen deer ford the river as well as countless species of wading bird and seabird.

'Before I started work here, I sailed across the Irish Sea. When you docked in Northern Ireland there were just miles and miles of articulated lorries. But here, we tie up next to a castle. There's just something romantic about the whole experience.'

The bridge of the ferry, in most weathers, is a serenely relaxing place. For the first 20 minutes, as it departs Lymington, the ferry follows the bends of the River Lym, flicking like a slalom skier between navigational posts that ensure passage at all but the highest of spring tides. The journey then eases into clear water across the Western Solent all the way to Yarmouth. The ferry master uses local knowledge, radar and an electronic chart to navigate. Winter

In homage to the building's history, the original post box remains in situ and still functions, with daily collections.

Yarmouth Deli 1 The Sq, PO41 0NS ✆ 01983 761196. Excellent choice for a take-away snack or lunch. They'll make up a sandwich or you can buy homemade sausage and vegan rolls and local cheeses and breads.

🛍 SHOPPING

By and large, Yarmouth eschews seaside tat though maritime themes (think wood-carved yachts fit for mantelpieces) most definitely abound. It's worth a short stroll along the High Street (the small size and location of this lane, now displaced just to the east of the centre of town, indicates how trade has moved around over the centuries) where you find the Forresters Hall, the ground floor of which is occupied by the **Yarmouth Gallery** (⊘ yarmouthgallery. com), a showcase of local arts and crafts with a rolling display by a core of regular exhibitors.

Harwoods of Yarmouth (⊘ harwoods-yacht-chandlers.co.uk) on St James's Square was founded in 1893 as an ironmongery and forge and is now a sprawling chandlery (though you won't find many candles here – their term also refers to a shop specialising in nautical items for boats and ships). Today it is both an emporium of sea-going goods – from sou'westers to ship's braids – and another good repository for both town and Island craftsfolk.

storms can liven matters up and the ferry will not sail in winds much above 40 knots.

Passengers are looked after by nine crew, including at least two on the bridge (one person acting as a lookout for wayward yachts or other vessels) and a chief engineer to ensure the engines keep turning. Fog can be a challenge and, when it casts its murky net, requires three senior crew to be stationed on the deck.

Wight Link has recently invested £30m in a flagship hybrid vessel, the *Victoria of Wight*, which plies the Portsmouth–Fishbourne route further east. It's the first hybrid-energy ferry in England and generates electricity through kinetic energy, with warmth produced by the engine used to heat water on board.

In addition to replacing plastic straws and plates with more sustainable alternatives, Wight Link has committed to supporting wider environmental policies around the Solent, including installing oyster cages in the Solent (oyster farming is viewed as a relatively benign activity and can improve water quality as oysters filter out nitrogen and carbon dioxide). From spring to autumn, you may catch a ferry safari on the Lymington–Yarmouth route, during which Island wildlife organisations give free talks and point out bird and marine life as the ferries travel between the two ports. Check the Wightlink website (⊘ wightlink.co.uk) for details of upcoming talks.

A walk along the River Yar

✿ OS Explorer map 29; start: Yarmouth bus station, by ferry port ♥ SZ354897; 4 miles; easy

A low-lying, sometimes swampy world of marshes, mires, lagoons and tidal mudflats, the River Yar nudges its way south–north (the Island's lopsided shape means all river courses flow this way) almost from coast to coast – but not quite: the downs that provide the source of the river also prevent it from making a final dart to the south coast. At its mouth, the river is a remarkable spectacle – its huge estuary quickly constricts and tapers into a river before shrinking further into what could generously be called a brook or a stream. Nevertheless, a river this is – in fact, it's one of two Yars on the Island, not to be confused with the River Eastern Yar, which works its way from the southeast near Ventnor to Bembridge on the east coast.

This circular loop offers delightful walking amid reed beds and hedgerows that are bursting with birdsong in spring and summer. The meandering route is flat, pleasant and easy, following the eastern shoreline until you begin to bump into the chalk ridges near the south coast and returning via fields and farm lanes to Yarmouth. Cyclists can follow the route as far as the Causeway and then divert on towards Freshwater; the footpaths of the western banks are not really suitable for two wheels. Wheelchair access is straightforward all the way from Yarmouth down the east side of the river to the Causeway, but impossible on the western return thanks to gates and mud. The last stretch of the west side, once past Kings Manor Farm, often sees shin-deep water collect on the path as it approaches Yarmouth.

1 From the bus station, walk across the adjacent car park and pick up the path that runs along the east of the river. What is striking, once you leave the swing bridge by the marina behind, is just how quickly the modest bustle of Yarmouth falls away into a soothing melange of salt marsh, shingle spit and brackish reed beds and the occasional stretch of sand dunes. You become surrounded by nature – thick hedgerows and brambles, bulrushes, mudflats, salt marsh and reeds – while the river seems to operate as a lake for all kinds of wildfowl. As you wander along the banks you will see curlews and redshank, as well as flocks of goldcrests in the hedgerows. The wildlife of the river is almost entirely undisturbed by any waterway traffic and so more secretive species such as barn owls, greenshank and kingfishers can often be spotted. In winter the estuary is home to impressive flocks of dark-bellied geese, curlew and colourful teal and wigeon.

2 Continuing along the footpath, you will pass handsome buildings, some of them former customs houses or mills such as the impressive red-brick **Tide Mill House**, which dates to 1794. A bank of woodland rises up to the west and there's the occasional distant church spire to complete a classical rural picture. A couple of hundred yards further on from the mill, you pass through a delightful series of coppices and pint-sized woodlands where alders, ankle deep in bog-like, shallow mires, line the path.

3 About two miles from Yarmouth you come to a meeting of paths, with a small lane, known as the Causeway, that cuts west across the river. Turn right (west) to cross the shrivelling Yar with views of thick, swampy reed beds to the south. At this point you might feel as if you have stepped into *The Wind in the Willows*.

4 Some 200yds beyond the Causeway you pass one of the Island's most beautiful and often-overlooked churches, **All Saints**, standing on your right near the head of a tidal estuary of the Yar. The graveyard is extraordinarily large and sprawling. Some of the church quoins (dressed stones at the angles of a building) at its northwest and southwest edges have survived since Saxon times, while the north doorway opens from a small Victorian porch and has three rows of zigzagging stones facing outwards. A 13th-century giant arch projects from the west wall. The Red Lion pub (page 146) is just a few yards up the hill, round the bend and out of sight, but perfect for a mid-walk break.

5 From the church, the path to the left heads due north, passing Kings Manor Farm after half a mile. The final leg back to the coast can take longer than you expect, as the path strays away from the Yar, through **Saltern Wood**. Soon enough, though, the woodlands fade away and the path turns into Gasworks Lane, from where you can see the Solent beyond. A right-hand turn takes you briefly along the A3054 back to Yarmouth. As you cross the bridge back into town there's one last view of the reed-fringed Yar as it meanders all the way to the Causeway. ▶

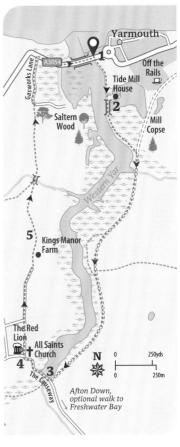

> **A walk along the River Yar** (continued)
>
> ▶Note that a version of this walk enables you to walk coast to coast, from Yarmouth all the way to Freshwater Bay, a distance of four miles one-way (you could then either retrace your steps or take the bus from the bay back to Yarmouth). To do so, once you reach the Causeway junction, keep straight ahead, south, along the east bank of the river. When you reach the B3399, dog-leg across the road and follow signs for Freshwater Bay. After 150yds, turn half-left following footpath F31. Continue along this path right up on to the top of Afton Down for fine views of the south coast. The cobbled beach of Freshwater Bay is below you.

The narrow streets of Wheatsheaf Lane and Jireh Place repay a brief nose around. Shops here include **Reflections** (1a Wheatsheaf Ln ⊘ reflectionsisleofwight.co.uk), which houses an extraordinary stockpile of fossils (some from the Island) and, just a few paces away, **The Book Room** on Jireh Place which is a good source of out-of-print paperbacks and first-edition collectibles.

WEST OF THE RIVER YAR

Yarmouth's western hinterland is unfalteringly bucolic. You can walk almost the whole length of the coastline (tides permitting) and wander between stretches of woodlands that open up into beaches or lead you to stumble upon an old military fort. Always, there are views west: the New Forest is close to hand but when the sea is calm you can enjoy clear sightlines of the chalk cliffs of Dorset arcing away in parallel with the curvature of the water.

2 FORT VICTORIA COUNTRY PARK

Westhill Ln, Freshwater PO41 0RR ⊘ fort-victoria.co.uk ⊙ park: year-round; café & attractions: seasonal, usually Feb–Oct

Given its location in the English Channel, the Isle of Wight has always proved attractive to seaborne raiders, from the Danes at the end of the 10th century to the frequent French attacks of the 14th century. Accordingly, it has been heavily militarised for hundreds of years; the first significant defences around the Island appeared during the time of Henry VIII, though the northwest has been defended since earlier in Tudor times. The area is also known as Sconce Point, from the Dutch word 'schans' for fortification.

Fort Victoria is a relative upstart, with the first garrison stationed here in 1855. Defences included 32-pound guns, a portcullis and a drawbridge. These were formidable on paper but advances in military capability and ship design – iron-clad hulls replaced wooden ones – meant the fort became redundant even as it was being built and spent the first decades of its life serving as a barracks and storehouse.

Fort Victoria's triangular, rather drab batteries, barracks and casemates today house a modest reptilarium, planetarium and model railway. But while the fort itself is certainly no thing of beauty, the surrounding country park surely is and there are plenty of places to picnic on the beach and banks behind it. As you stroll through this 54-acre reserve, you'll find a relatively young woodland, planted in the 19th century and featuring beech, sycamore and hawthorn shrubs, along with rather more exotic Corsican pines.

During the summer months, a resident country ranger gives guided wildlife tours in the adjacent woods and along the shoreline for a small fee. Turtle fossils and fossilised shark and ray teeth have been collected from the beach just a few yards behind the fort. The easiest approach for independent exploration is to follow the red squirrel markers that run up and down two parallel trails through the outer limits of the park and back, a distance of no more than 1½ miles. Eventually the squirrel paths converge on high ground by a small plaque to Robert Hooke, a pioneering 17th-century geologist. This spot offers uninterrupted views across the Solent towards Hurst Castle, built in 1554 on a narrow shingle spit of protruding Hampshire – it is just three-quarters of a mile away, but appears so close you feel you could almost skim a pebble across the water and it make landfall the other side.

Hooke hailed from Freshwater and was widely ridiculed by his contemporaries for his novel (at the time) theory that tectonic plates and geological movement had shaped the earth to look the way it did. Hooke described this stretch of cliff, almost opposite Hurst Castle, as made up of several layers of sands, clays and loams. Noticing that one layer was filled with several kinds of seashells, despite the fact it was 60ft above the high-water mark, he concluded that the earth had been shaped by earthquakes and volcanic activity. Perhaps there's something about the Isle of Wight that encourages people – then and now – to gaze and ponder and, in Hooke's case, stare into the abyss of time. Sadly for Hooke, he suffered the same brush off as Copernicus and

Darwin and Wallis: his theory was entirely ignored by his peers and the prevailing scientific consensus, although posthumously his ideas became mainstream.

Beyond the fort: the western hinterland

Other unmarked, smaller and rougher paths peel off to the west of the fort, in search of the coast; here and there, these further split into narrow routes that drop down to the sea. These little paths, serving rather like capillaries, are handy as this corner of the Island is not well served by footpaths (partly because they tend to crumble into the sea). The shoreline, mostly comprising sand with some rocks and boulder areas, not only offers good rock pools but also has a reputation as one of the Island's most underrated beachcombing locations. If you root around the shingle and rapidly eroding shoreline you have every chance of coming across a fossil or two. Mollusc shells are most evident but closer investigation may reward turtle shell and crocodile scutes (the thickened horny plate on the back of the animal), giving intriguing hints of the stature of fauna that once called the Isle of Wight home. The coast here is also an excellent place to watch the annual Round the Island Race in July (see box, page 85) as the boats make what appears to be a handbrake turn to avoid running aground at Hurst Castle. Inviting as the water may look here, fast-flowing currents make swimming dangerous, so do proceed with caution.

You can also follow the Coastal Path in a northeasterly direction from Fort Victoria towards Yarmouth, an attractive route boasting wonderful views across the ever-busy Solent to the New Forest. Along the way, in addition to fossil hunting on the beach at Fort Victoria, you will find a lovely mini-dune and salt marsh at the small hamlet of **Norton** just half a mile to the east. The mobile dune habitat here is dominated by marram grass with sea couch, sea beet and sea plantain.

Alternatively, to the south of the woods and barely a mile south of Fort Victoria, you approach the headland of Cliff End on which stands **Fort Albert**, another of the Victorian-era Palmerston forts that juts its chin out into the Solent (the wildest storms can see spray surmount the entire structure). The fort was a base for the deployment of some of the first torpedoes: in 1886 the wire-guided Brennan Torpedo, with a range of up to a mile, was installed here. Nowadays, this is a private collection of flats and it's only possible to snatch glimpses of the land on which it stands. The best views of this particular fort are actually from either the ferry from Lymington or from Headon Warren (page 134) to the south.

Beyond Fort Albert, the headland gives way to **Colwell Bay**, although, amid much private land, access is via the A3054 and the village of Colwell. Just before the small village common, a lane signposted to the west for the coast path leads down to the sloping shingle bay, which is picturesquely dotted with beach chalets. Despite the surrounding chalets and flats, the beach has an intangible feeling of being tucked away (perhaps this is because you don't actually see the shingle until you are almost upon it). High tide pushes everyone right up the beach but as it ebbs you can follow the water out to the point, where you feel you can almost reach over and touch Hurst Castle. The water close to shore is safe to swim in and the beach is deservedly popular with families.

3 GOLDEN HILL FORT & COUNTRY PARK

Norton Green, Freshwater PO40 9SJ ☉ park: year-round

Situated two miles south of Yarmouth, the 21-acre Golden Hill Country Park surrounds another of the Palmerston Follies that were built to protect the Solent from invasion from the French (see box, page 16). Positioned on high ground, it was designed to defend and support the coastal batteries. Winnie the Pooh's creator A A Milne was stationed here during World War I. After the armistice, the fort became home to thousands of demobbed soldiers, and has long since been converted to luxury flats and pretty much disappeared from public gaze, hidden behind large gates. Volunteers from the local charity Gift to Nature (⊘ gifttonature.org.uk) have cleared some of the scrub that overlies the wider site to reveal views toward Fort Victoria and Fort Albert, and at the time of writing they were formulating four walking trails through the country park, offering viewpoints and the prospect of spotting wildlife (including those famous red squirrels). Among the butterflies you might see are ringlet and brown argus, while the drumming of a green woodpecker may halt you in your tracks.

EAST OF THE RIVER YAR

The hinterland just to the east of Yarmouth is unlike anywhere else on the Isle of Wight: a tranquil and secretive coastline of low-sloping clay cliffs crowned with woodland and farmland, where the tucked-away

settlements have the feel of remote hill – and, it's sometimes whispered, hillbilly, or counter-culture – communities. Along with Ventnor (page 190), this is where some of those who turned on, tuned in and dropped out in the 1960s eventually washed up. A world of creeks, muddy inlets, unvisited coast and wildlife-rich woodlands, it can feel like a slice of the Island that time forgot.

4 BOULDNOR, HAMSTEAD & NINGWOOD

The first settlement you come to after heading east along the A3054 from Yarmouth, **Bouldnor** gives its name not only to a small hamlet but also the surrounding woodlands, a copse and the coastline. This is where you should go if you want to get off-grid on the Isle of Wight: there are no roads along the coast, just two entry and exit points for walkers (at either end of the village) and no facilities while you're here. Parking is extremely limited and doesn't actually get you that near to the coast, so the easiest way to explore is to set out from Yarmouth – either on foot, or by taking the bus and disembarking on the southern perimeter of the woodlands by the Horse and Groom pub. Once here, the best route is the Coastal Trail (page 23). A walk through this part of the island is detailed on page 60.

Sitting between the main road and the shoreline is **Bouldnor Copse**, which merges into a larger stretch of woodland, known as Bouldnor Forest. Whatever sylvan moniker you apply, this enchanting place is home to unusual birdlife, with glades and clay heaths open to the skies at its centre, and exuding a serenity that makes it a place apart from the busy shipping activity of the Solent. The heathland here is slowly being restored by the Hampshire and Isle of Wight Wildlife Trust which is removing scrub and conifer trees and allowing heather and dwarf gorse to return. Goldcrests and crossbills are just two birds to look out for, but summer months also bring one of the UK's more remarkable migrants to this part of the Island. If, when walking across the heathlands, you hear a mysterious, slightly spine-chilling whirring or 'churring', you are listening to the call of the nightjar. This medium-sized bird comes to the Island to breed from May to August but its ghostly call has given it many other names over the centuries, including 'goatsucker', as it was thought

◀ **1** Newtown Creek. **2** White-tailed eagles were re-introduced to the Island in 2019. **3** River Western Yar. **4** Black-headed gulls can regularly be seen at Shalfleet. **5** Red squirrel, Fort Victoria.

to steal milk from goats. Heard on a still, clear evening, this is a noise you will never forget.

The huge concrete building that abuts the recovering heathland is a World War II battery that supported heavy gun emplacements. Just

Hamstead to Yarmouth via Bouldnor Copse

✽ OS Explorer map 29; start: Horse and Groom pub (served by bus # 7) ♥ SZ399892; 7 miles; medium

The views along this delectable walk, from the grey-green shorescape of the mildewed mires around Newtown Creek to the rather dramatic collapsed cliffs of the north coast, are variously haunting and uplifting, on occasion both at the same time. The Coastal Path runs through here: along Newtown Creek, through the woodlands of Bouldnor Copse, across an unvisited landscape of clay heath and above the steep crumbling cliffs near Hamstead.

On a sunny day, as field edges yield to gloopy mires and shimmering salt marsh, you may conclude that mud can indeed look magnificent, while toppled trees lying on the shoreline, awaiting further decomposition by the next tide, add a sense of wild abandonment and desolation not usually associated with the Isle of Wight. The welcoming Horse and Groom (Ningwood PO30 4NW ℘ 01983 760672 ⊘ horse-and-groom.com) at the walk's start is a good place for refreshments – you can of course walk this route in reverse to end up at the pub and then hop on the bus back to Yarmouth.

1 From the Horse and Groom, take footpath S9 north. After 800yds you cross a footbridge and turn right with a stream to your right. Follow waymarkers through woodland until you reach the Coastal Path (S27) and bear left along this.

2 Follow the path past Pigeon Coo Farm. After 100yds, bear right, still following the coast path towards Lower Hamstead. The path continues unbroken for just over a mile until you reach Newtown Creek, where you can make a small diversion through a gate to reach the shoreline and a jetty overlooking **Newtown Harbour National Nature Reserve**. This is one of the Island's premier birdwatching sites and enjoys a haunting sea silence, broken only by gently ebbing water and cries of gulls.

3 Returning to the coast path, head west (straight ahead) for 300yds and then north (right) towards Hamstead Point, hugging the contours of the creeks and always following signs for the Coastal Path. A couple of footbridges and stretches of boardwalk navigate some of the boggier bits. After half a mile of heading due north, the coast path turns emphatically west at Hamstead Point. There are a few access points here where you can drop down to the beach offshore lies a submerged prehistoric settlement, the only one of its kind in the UK. While nothing is visible today as it is buried in the silt of a drowned oak and hazel forest under up to 35ft of saltwater, nevertheless, it's astonishing to think that 8,000 years ago people were

and explore the point and Hamstead Ledge before returning to the coast path. Note that you cannot follow the shoreline, even at low tide, back to Yarmouth; you must return to the coast path as it rises above Hamstead Ledge.

4 The path cuts west and inland above both the ledge and adjacent Hamstead Cliff, towards Hamstead village. The field walking here is often accompanied by birdsong piped from the mature hedgerows.

5 Skirting the northern side of Hamstead Farm, the path continues west and after 600yds darts to the south of West Hamstead Farm before reaching Sea View Road (always following the coast path signs). Bear left here, then right along West Close to pick up the footpath again. The landscape changes abruptly as you enter **Bouldnor Copse** (page 59) with its open spaces interrupted by clumps of gorse. You'll see several fenced-off areas, which are allowing native vegetation to return to the copse.

6 As you reach the western end of the copse, the path ducks back into woodland and across a short but sweet section of boardwalks. It then winds its way back to the A3054 via Victoria Road for a 600yd stretch of road walking to take you back to Yarmouth (be sure to walk on the pavement on the south side of the road).

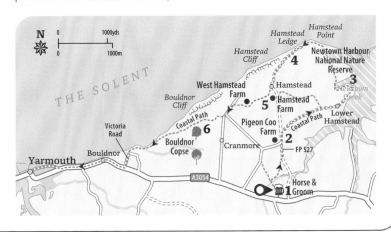

living off woodlands, by the shores of a huge swamp and marshland that connected the Island to the mainland.

To the east of the forest lies **Bouldnor Ledge**, another of the Island's excellent fossil-hunting beaches, with the early Oligocene beds (dating back 30 million years) on the shore home to prehistoric and entombed mammal, crocodile, turtle, crustacean and fish remains. Fossils range from very large sections of tree trunks to tiny gastropods, and molluscs, plants and seeds can be spotted simply lying on the foreshore. According to fossil enthusiasts Roy Shepherd and Robert Randell (their website ♂ discoveringfossils.co.uk is well worth visiting and is where they will announce if they are resuming guided fossil hunts), both expert and amateur palaeontologists have uncovered more visually dramatic finds here, such as turtle carapaces and sections of jaw, including teeth belonging to an *Elomeryx porcinus* (a small hippopotamus-like mammal).

Time a visit for a low or retreating tide as the majority of finds are made among the pebbles on the foreshore. Periods of stormy weather or during the winter, when the foreshore has been disturbed and new fossils exposed, also stack the odds of discovering something interesting in your favour. To access the beach, follow the Coastal Path east from Bouldnor Copse. Alternatively, you can reach it along Cranmore Avenue, turning north off the A3054 just past Isle of Wight Dairy Goats; continue on foot along Sea View Road towards the coast until you reach a large private residence. Alongside the seaward edge of the property is a public footpath leading directly to the beach after 400yds.

The tiny settlement of **Hamstead** lies a quarter of a mile south of Bouldnor Copse, although there isn't much more to see save a curious mismatch of architecture. The first houses were designed by architect John Nash in 1804, but after World War I the government issued land grants to returning soldiers who were able to build whatever homes they wished. The legacy is therefore mixed, with some houses in states of disrepair, others ageing with more grace and character, and modern properties springing up from the *Grand Designs* school of architecture.

Run by the Hampshire and Isle of Wight Wildlife Trust, little **Ningwood Common** is a nature reserve really worth visiting. Access to the reserve is along a circular permissive route; head north along Hamstead Road, just off the A3054, some 400yds east of Cranmore Avenue. The area's clay soils defeated post-war attempts to farm the land and it was left to nature to take over – to the subsequent benefit of wildlife lovers. Nightjars are often heard in summer but earlier, in April and May, visitors may catch the mellifluous tunes of the nightingale. Red squirrels are a safe bet, while a rarity to look out for is the (well-named) reddish buff moth, for which Ningwood is the only recorded UK site. The whole site has been sensitively managed by the Wildlife Trusts who are keen to ensure that it doesn't get overrun, though such is its isolation that it receives relatively few visitors. Access to the site is limited to a permissive circular path.

SHOPPING

Isle of Wight Dairy Goats The Green Barn, Main Rd, Bouldnor PO41 0XN ✆ 01983 761310 ⌖ thegreenbarn-isleofwightdairygoats.co.uk. Good little farm shop selling goats' cheese, kefir, goats' milk and a strong, tangy goats' milk fudge, all produced from their own herd, which features exotic-sounding breeds such as Toggenburg (originally from Switzerland) and Anglo-Nubian (their lop ears are inherited from the Middle Eastern half of the breed's origins).

5 SHALFLEET

Just four miles east of Yarmouth and on the #7 bus route, Shalfleet is a tiny hamlet with a mooring point for fishing boats and pleasure craft that dozes quietly as the world passes by. The name 'Shalfleet' means 'shallow stream' and the watercourse in question that passes through the village is the Caul Bourne. Victorian guides to the Island noted that Shalfleet was 'not too lively' and that remains the case today; it still has only one street – the A3054 – and the hamlet straddles this road with a traffic light at each end. The **church** stands at the heart of the village, opposite the pub and next to the village hall and the little green where the village fete takes place (usually on the August Bank Holiday). While people have worshipped here since the 12th century, and on this site for many hundreds of years before that, the dedication of the church has been forgotten. The parish, apparently feeling the want of a patron saint, rededicated the church to St Michael the Archangel in 1964, but he is not thought to be the saint first selected.

The church is a rare example of Purbeck stone being used on the Island. The oak pulpit, with its carved designs and a bookrest on brackets all round, is of the time of Charles I. The tower is the oldest part of the church and is striking for its massive structure, the walls being over 5ft thick. Built in the late 11th century, it may have predated the church and served from the start as a stronghold for local inhabitants when threatened by invaders or piratical marauders. It must have been almost invulnerable as there were no openings at all at ground level and access was gained only by climbing an external ladder and scrambling over the parapet. In 1800 the cupola was replaced by a wooden, tile-hung steeple, the subject of a well-known rhyme about Shalfleet people: 'Shalfleet poor and simple people – sold their bells to buy a steeple.' The steeple itself was removed in 1913.

Shalfleet Quay is located five minutes' walk from the church along Quay Lane and has been in use since medieval times, when the harbour was deeper and more swollen than it is today. At that time, Newtown Creek opened into a mighty harbour estuary used by larger vessels, while salt was made in pans on the marsh. Centuries of coastal ebb and flow, erosion and silting have changed all that. The quay you see before you was built in the 17th century, and what's left today is a delightful setting of meandering waterways that are guarded from the wider sea by large shingle banks and tidal mudflats while mature trees line the inlets and the pint-sized Newtown River.

There hardly ever seems to be anyone around the village boatyard, but there is always a handful of boats hauled up on dry land. The boats are coated with resin to keep them waterproof, a process known as caulking, which gives rise to the local name for a true Islander, a caulkhead (page 17).

Your main companions here will almost certainly be birds, including black-headed gulls jerkily flicking back and forwards in mid-air, and little egrets settling down among the reeds for a spot of fish catching. Water voles also do well on the banks of the creek, and indeed along all the Island rivers. They should be grateful that their arch-enemy the mink has not made the journey across the Solent.

The one time of year when water voles may be shaken out of their reverie is in July when the Rhythmtree Festival ($\hat{\partial}$ rhythmtree.co.uk) takes place. This enjoyable musical event features mainly Island performers and is oriented towards families, so campervans and tipi tents tend to be the order of the day.

6 NEWTOWN

Visible across the creek from Shalfleet Quay and 1½ miles east of Shalfleet village, the minuscule hamlet of Newtown stands at the heart of a National Trust-owned nature reserve. It is unusual in that it is a rare example of a medieval new town that failed economically due to a combination of plague, changing river flows and those ever-marauding French neighbours.

In the early and mid 14th century, Newtown was the most important port on the Isle of Wight – something that seems rather improbable to the modern-day visitor – with an oversized town hall the only surviving nod towards the community's former stature. Sackings by the French, particularly a visitation in 1377 that saw just about every building razed, started to tilt the angle of decline. Slower, less dramatic but harder to thwart or recover from, was the natural and inexorable process of increased siltation in the estuary, which saw larger, more lucrative trading vessels heading instead for deeper port waters at Yarmouth and Newport. While Newtown withered over the centuries, it escaped development and regeneration and many of its original green lanes and small paddocks have survived, along with a grid-like street pattern radiating out from the shore like those at Yarmouth and Newport.

The hamlet is just a short walk from Shalfleet, following a meandering route alongside creeks, inlets and coppices: cross the creek, go through woodland and take two left road turns to reach Town Lane. As you enter, you'll pass the **Old Town Hall** (National Trust), a red-brick house resting on large pillars and dating to 1659 (though the town gained borough status much earlier, in the 13th century). As Newtown's stature and importance waned, so did the fortunes of the hall, to the point that it became a town hall with no town. In fact, by the end of the 16th century, the 'town' had become one of the notorious 'rotten boroughs' (see box, page 46). This shoddy status was removed in 1832 when the seat was abolished by the Great Reform Act.

The town hall was rescued from physical collapse in the 1930s by the intervention of the eccentric Ferguson's Gang, a group of masked women who remained anonymous but devoted their time to raising funds to buy property for the National Trust. They would burst into Trust meetings and plant a sack of cash on the table, Robin Hood style, with strict instructions on how it should be spent.

Just up the road from the hall, the **church of the Holy Spirit** is the epitome of the rural idyll, with a symmetry to its Gothic porch and arched windows that gaze out upon a lush churchyard. Unlike the hamlet in which it stands, the church offers a relative injection of young blood, having only been built in 1835. Indeed, so lovely is the church that architectural historian Nikolaus Pevsner described it as 'the finest early 19th-century church on the Island'.

A short walk from the path to the west of the church leads through **Newtown National Nature Reserve** to the shoreline; road's end is a boardwalk to an attractively positioned bird hide. The lagoon-like waters of the inlets of Newtown Creek were once saltpans until breached by a fierce storm in 1954. In spring and summer the whole area is a delight, fringed with the blue tinge of sea aster and the purple of sea lavender. The adjacent coastal meadows are infilled with green-winged orchids and classic hay meadow species such as the superbly named corky-fruited water-dropwort, whose white flowers sit atop a bolt-upright stem that's 3ft in height, and, in a nod to one of the trades that once was active here, dyers greenweed (confusingly, yellow in colour), which was used for dyeing cloth. The latter is an important food crop for the marbled white butterfly and 20 or more species of moth. This is a good place to spot Mediterranean gulls, with their distinctive red beaks and white ring around their eyes. Hundreds of dark-bellied Brent geese overwinter here, along with teal and pintail ducks, while in summer after the hay is cut Belted Galloway cattle are put out for a late-season graze.

The waters here are replete with grey mullet, which seem to appeal to the young **white-tailed eagles** released over the past couple of years (page 276). The birds also go for bream and cuttlefish in these same waters. Your chances of seeing this gravity-defying leviathan of a bird wheeling away with aquatic prey wriggling in its talons are reasonably high.

The England Coast Path (a nationwide project) is being implemented on the Island and is expected to improve access around Newtown within the lifetime of this edition. The existing Island coast path route frustratingly keeps the hiker at arm's length from the coast at times, but the enhanced extensions will give access to more coast via the hay meadows behind the hides overlooking the creek and Newtown River. In the meantime, you can access more of the coast here via footpath CB16A (by the town hall car park) which leads around the south side of Newtown. The coastline is gorgeous – soft, green rolling hills tumbling to the foreshore, while the New Forest makes for a wooden-framed horizon across the Solent.

You can also explore the easterly side of the headland on which Newtown sits. From the car park in the village, head north along Town

Lane and take the sharp right-hand turn; keep going until you reach Walter's Copse. Where the lane starts to bear right, you'll see a path off to the left that goes through the woods, passing now-derelict buildings that were once part of an oyster farm, before emerging almost on top of a creek known, a little confusingly, as Clamerkin Lake. The sea wall here offers fine views further east along the coast amid the setting of the creek's sweeping arm, and once upon a time you could have continued along the sea wall all the way back to Shalfleet – but sadly it was breached in that 1954 storm, meaning you have to retrace your steps. You can still pick out fence posts here and there from the pre-storm farming landscape, but the cattle that once grazed here have long gone and the whole area has reverted to salt marsh.

THE HINTERLAND

The hinterland to the south of Shalfleet is curiously overlooked by visitors to the Island. While the majority use the Newport Road to move between Newport and Yarmouth and Freshwater, these trunk roads bypass villages such as **Calbourne** and **Newbridge** that sit blissfully off the tourist trail in the shadow of the downs. The area is also a good place to take on board the Island's phenomenal produce, with field upon field planted with crops such as sweetcorn, while cattle chew the cud on the rougher pasture. In order to savour the fruits of the land, the shop and café at **Tapnell Farm Park**, the farm shop at **Calbourne Water Mill** and the pizza restaurant at **West Wight Alpacas** should be on your list.

7 CALBOURNE & NEWBRIDGE

🏠 **Calbourne Water Mill** (page 303)

The village of **Calbourne** is first mentioned in the Domesday Book of 1086, which records two corn mills under one roof, plus a wheat mill and a malt mill, all of which drew on the modest River Cal Bourne that sprung from the downs to the south. The mills were passed down through local generations of families with the just one survivor today. **Calbourne Water Mill and Rural Museum** (Newport Rd, PO30 4JN 𝒜 01983 531227 ⊘ calbournewatermill.co.uk) comprises 35 acres of landscaped gardens. Domesticated farm animals abound, such as peacocks and geese, while moorhens dabble in the watercourses. The grounds extend into a small woodland, where among the oaks you may pick out red squirrels. The stream at the bottom of the hill (running behind the café) is home to eels; visitors can buy a bag of fish food and feed both these and the large fish found in the mill stream. Short easy climbs radiate out from the mill into the foothills of the downs and provide views across the west of the Island towards Alum Bay and north, where your eye is drawn all the way along the River Yar to Yarmouth.

It can be easy to forget this actually remains a working mill – flour is ground the traditional way here, using the 17th-century water and stone mills but using only the power of water. Two millers produce approximately 50 to 60 tons of flour and oats each year and in summer months you can watch them at work at 15.00 (Sun–Fri). You can buy the finished products in the farm gift shop. The site also includes a small museum of yesteryear farming life, featuring hay wains, wheatsheaves and the like as well as a pottery mill where you can purchase locally crafted bowls and vases. The café gets extremely popular but deservedly so, given the extraordinarily wide range of calorie-laden cakes and other bakes available.

The mill is quite separate from the village of Calbourne, which lies half a mile to the southeast and on the south side of busy Newport Road. Once you've left the traffic behind, you'll find one of the island's most delightful villages. The main street, Lynch Lane, winds gently downhill and leads to the 13th-century All Saints' Church. This is another Island church gem, built of Isle of Wight rubble and flint with lancet windows and the original font, made of Purbeck marble, still in place. In the south aisle you'll find a late 14th-century brass image of a knight with a loyal dog at his feet, a memorial to William Montague, the son of the Earl of Salisbury, who was killed while jousting with his father.

Descending in parallel to Lynch Lane is narrow Winkle Street, also known as Barrington Row, which features a fetching clutch of stone and thatched cottages and – a rare survival of its kind – a Grade II-listed **sheepwash**, found just south of the cricket pitch. First mentioned in 1640, the sheepwash is fed by a stream that squeezes under a stone bridge. This practice of using adapted sheepwashes (which use natural features rather than manmade tanks) such as this slowly became replaced by the use of parasite-controlling chemicals, which required

1 Winkle Street, Calbourne. **2** Ningwood Common. ▶

the more confined application of enclosed sheep dips. The last recorded washing of sheep at Calbourne took place in 1975.

Just over a mile north of Calbourne is the small hamlet of **Newbridge**, which sits on a gentle rise divided by the River Cal Bourne. From here, a landscape of undulating downlands opens up. One of the Island's many ghosts, a bearded man wearing a grey cloak, is said to linger around the crossroads. Today, ghosts aside, this is a docile, sleepy place, its properties of Island stone adorned with thatched roofs and home to the Island's sole remaining Wesleyan Methodist chapel, now a private residence.

This somnolent atmosphere throws a cloak upon the village's nefarious past. In 1830 Newbridge was described as a village with inhabitants that were 'but little removed from the vilest of the vile; that gin was to be bought in every house; that scarcely a virtuous person lived in the place'. This observation came from the Reverend Woolcock, a fire and brimstone preacher, in his book *History of the Bible Christians*, so it seems he would have no doubt had a particular axe to grind. Today, its inhabitants – presumably much reformed – must make for Calbourne should they wish to have a drink (at the Sun Inn; see below).

¶¶ FOOD & DRINK

Sun Inn Calbourne PO30 4JA ✆ 01983 531231 ⏱ sun-calbourne.co.uk. This popular pub is very much at the centre of its community. Hearty, classic homemade pub food, including roasts, curries and pies. The patio garden is a pleasant sun trap.

8 TAPNELL FARM PARK

🏠 **Tom's Eco Lodges** (page 303)

Newport Rd, PO41 0YJ ✆ 01983 758722 ⏱ tapnellfarmpark.com ⏰ Wed–Sun

Four miles west of Newbridge and Calbourne lies this enormously popular (and dog-friendly) farm park. Children can play on giant haystacks and sledge slides, enjoy a round of mini-golf, a splash in the aqua park or a lap on the go-karts, and pet not only goats and pigs but also more exotic animals such as alpacas, meerkats and wallabies. Food is available at The Cow, housed in a huge former barn (see opposite). Access is by bus #27 (summer only), which runs between Yarmouth and Newport and takes you to the entrance to the farm or footpaths via Compton Down from Freshwater (two miles) and Yarmouth (four miles).

Despite its family-friendly nature, Tapnell Farm also offers an insight into how land is managed on the Isle of Wight. The land at Tapnell (and the adjacent Afton Farm) has been owned by the Tourney family for generations and, until the start of the 2010s, was grazed by a dairy herd of 800 cows that produced 24,000 litres of milk every day. At that point, with milk prices volatile but invariably low, the family relocated the herd to Dorset and set about transforming the farm into a family attraction. 'We looked at every way to make the dairy farm work, but the milk price kept dropping,' says Tom Tourney, who now co-owns the farm along with members of his wider family.

Tapnell Farm goes the extra mile to reduce its carbon footprint: solar panels make the farm a net exporter of energy, while on-site sewage plants use good bacteria to break down human waste, and the resulting water is returned to the ground.

If you're in the mood to stretch your legs, you can follow the Tapnell Trail. This six-mile circular route runs through the grounds of Tapnell Farm to the River Yar Estuary, crossing by the Causeway near Freshwater and returning to the farm via a series of hedgerow-lined footpaths and rights of way that run along the bottom of East Afton and Wellow downs. Being mostly level, it's a good walk for children, with the lure of food at the farm on the return. Look out for buzzards above and keep an ear cocked for songbirds in the hedgerows. If all this were not enough to keep you on and around the farm for a day, you can even stay at the site's various accommodation options (page 303).

¶¶ FOOD & DRINK

The Cow Tapnell Farm, Newport Rd, PO41 0YJ ℘ 01983 758725 ⊘ thecowco.com. Set in a converted barn, The Cow at Tapnell Farm Park operates along the lines of a gastropub, with a seasonal menu ranging from burgers to beer-battered fish, using produce sourced from the Island. Outside you can even dine among 'cows': don't worry, these are merely several primary-coloured life-sized sculptures (even the most committed carnivore would surely be unsettled by munching beef while overlooked by real-life bovines).

9 WEST WIGHT ALPACAS

Main Rd, Wellow PO41 0SZ ℘ 01983 760900 ⊘ westwightalpacas.co.uk

'Llamas are just the most chilled animal to walk,' says Neil Payne, who owns West Wight Alpacas with his partner Michelle. 'They are more biddable, bred as beasts of burden on the Altiplano in South America.

You start walking with a llama and after about 30 seconds it gets it and the breeding just kicks in.'

This is all part of the joy of the walking experience the Paynes have created here with their 60 Suri alpacas and Argentine woolly llamas. Visitors can choose from an easy walk, escorting the animals (note that alpacas are a little edgier) around the farm and its immediate hinterland – though you may get the distinct impression it is they who are escorting you – or a slightly longer trek to the top of the farm. From here, the views stretch away across the Solent and deep into Hampshire.

Originally started as a hobby by Michelle in 2010, the farm's popularity has taken this modest couple by surprise. 'We get boyfriends and husbands dragged along here by their partners,' Neil explains, 'but the minute they start walking with the animals the penny drops – they come back saying it's the best thing they've done on their holiday!'

The animals are not just for walking – both are also reared for their fleeces. (The Incas described the coats as 'the fleece of the Gods'.) The yarn is sold or manufactured into socks and scarves by local knitters. 'It's hard-wearing,' says Neil, 'four times more insulating than wool and it doesn't have a prickle factor either.' They also run the on-site Llama Tree bistro and café and have plans to further expand their empire in the next couple of years to include Bactrian camels. 'Then we'd have the whole camelid family,' says Neil. 'They are very green animals to keep, very sustainable. Their impact on their environment is low – unlike Kashmir goats which eat up everything around them!'

¶¶ FOOD & DRINK

The Llama Tree Main Rd, Wellow PO41 0SZ ✆ 01983 760900 ⬚ westwightalpacas.co.uk/cafe-bistro. You'll find some of the best wood-fired pizzas in southern England here (don't worry, while there are meat options, llamas are definitely not on the menu). Mouth-watering sourdough topped with Island tomatoes or homemade pesto are the order of the day. You can even order dessert pizzas, topped with the likes of chocolate, blackberries and ice cream.

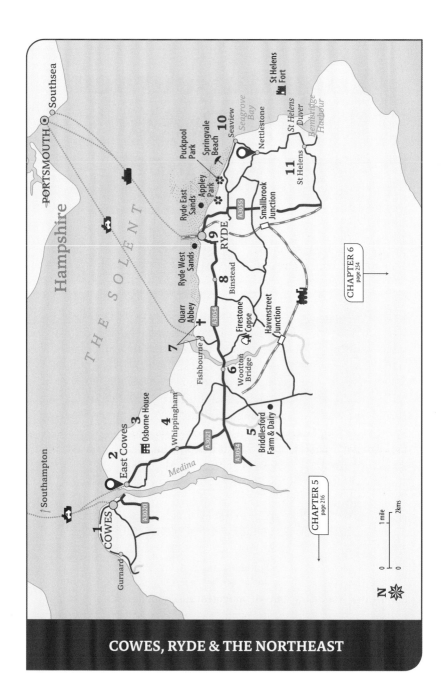

COWES, RYDE & THE NORTHEAST

2
COWES, RYDE & THE NORTHEAST

The hinterland around Cowes has some of the Island's most appealing 'slow' attractions. The coastline here rewards walking with elegiac views across the Solent against an ever-changing backdrop of ferries, yachts, cruise ships and cargo vessels, the last of these often embarking on journeys of up to 9,000 nautical miles and destined for a port in China. The area bursts into high activity in midsummer when **Cowes Week** takes place, but either side of this event life bubbles along in a manner that belies the area's underlying rural nature. This is mainly down to the vibrancy of both **Cowes** and the town of **Ryde**, which is emerging from its post-Victorian slumber with the reputation of a highly regarded and quirky arts hub.

You'll also find 'real' villages here – that is, communities with few second homes or cross-Solent commuters – such as **St Helens** and **Seaview**, where multi-generational Islanders and incomers have combined to create a viable local economy, a cat's cradle of interdependence between shops, small businesses, shoppers and visitors. The hinterland around the village of **Gurnard**, meanwhile, is a strong contender for the title of the Island's most underrated and under-visited location.

All these places, but particularly Seaview, enjoy a faded elegance that is as close to a *fin de siècle* experience as you will get on the Isle of Wight, but they still manage to be anything but crusty and dusty. In between Cowes and Ryde lies the eye-catching Benedictine structure of **Quarr Abbey**, still a working monastery, and architecturally impressive churches such as that at **Binstead**.

These villages and towns are set among a fetching landscape of gently undulating woodland and an indented and sometimes surprisingly rugged coastline, where the Island's sharp edges, ledges and watery shallows have a dark record of snaring unwary sailors.

This is also Royal country, the place where Queen Victoria was perhaps most amused. For it was just outside East Cowes that she and her beloved Prince Albert oversaw the construction of Osborne House which increasingly became their retreat from London. After Albert's death, it became a retreat in a more literal sense for the Queen, who lived out her days and finally passed away here. Her former abode and surrounding grounds are a magnificent spectacle and proof that the Island can do stately homes as well as any other part of the UK.

GETTING THERE & AROUND

PUBLIC TRANSPORT

Even on an island so well served by public transport, the northeast excels itself. **Bus** routes converge on Ryde and it can feel as though they visit every village as they join the dots between the larger centres. The #2 and #3 connect Ryde with Newport, while the #4 links Ryde and East Cowes, along with Binstead, Wootton Bridge and Osborne House. **Train** lovers are spoilt for choice with an appealing restored vintage railway line and a London Underground tube line that links Ryde to points south. And if things do feel a touch too slow, you can always take a spin on a **hovercraft** (see box, page 108), a design-classic transport mode as iconic as Concorde. Return trips from its Ryde terminus to Portsmouth are popular with visitors and will see you back on the Island within the hour.

WALKING & CYCLING

Cycling is easy as much of the area is flat (once you are out of East Cowes) and **walkers** can, as elsewhere, knit together most places of interest on foot, the only limits on distance and possibilities being your time and energy levels.

COWES & EAST COWES

Split by the River Medina, **Cowes** (on the west bank) and **East Cowes** are quite discrete entities. The 19th-century Romantic poet John Keats visited Cowes in 1819, took in the spectacle and observed how he had 'never beheld anything so graceful', which is quite a statement from a writer who eulogised autumn, nightingales and Grecian urns. If you land on the western bank of the Medina, where the pulsating Solent pulls away to the west, you may just catch a glimmer of what he meant.

Landfall at East Cowes, however, is less immediately uplifting as you are greeted by a rather unsightly jumble of narrow one-way streets and industrial estates. In fact, both 'Coweses' have a more industrial feel than you might expect: it's only really in Cowes Week that you will bump into stereotypical nautical coves in striped sweaters.

Unsurprisingly, Cowes is the place that is being referred to when you hear about Cowes Week. Here, by the mouth of the Medina, you'll find the Royal Yacht Squadron (one of the world's oldest yacht clubs, founded in 1815), along with the Royal London Yacht Club and the Island Yacht Club. There's also a large marina, Cowes Yacht Haven, where sails and masts bob up and down in tune with the river's ebbs and flows. Sailing is serious business here, not just a hobby, and both sides of the river feature shipyards, sailmakers and other marine-supporting small and medium-sized enterprises.

Their shared name reflects a mutual history and geography that goes back at least to the arrival of the Vikings of the 8th century, who are thought to have favoured the natural harbour and shelters at the mouth of the Medina for overwintering. The settlements were for a long time known as West and East Shamblord, before the names Eastcowe and Westcowe emerged in the early 14th century. The story – challenged by some linguists – goes that these were from the names of the two sandbanks either side of the Medina Estuary that resembled either cows or cow horns. West Cowes became simply 'Cowes' in 1895. The sandbanks are the location for a tidal game of cricket (see box, page 86), which must be one of the most unusual sporting events you will see anywhere on the planet. The Medina, meanwhile, gets its name from a Latinised form of its old Saxon name Medene, or 'middle river' (which could refer to it being the middle of the three Island rivers or simply its location, more or less in the middle of the Island).

The town's reputation for boat making emerged in the 17th century. J S White, the shipbuilding company that commissioned the giant hammerhead crane by the Medina (page 82), has a presence in town that dates to at least 1623 and the first large boats were built in the yards of Joseph Nye in East Cowes in 1696. Cowes developed as a port from the mid 17th century onwards, with quays on both sides of the Medina increasingly surrounded by warehouses and alleyways. The demographic of Cowes came to be dominated by mariners and merchants who traded with the newly settled American colonies and the town secured a niche as an important port where goods cleared customs before being landed on the mainland or shipped on to Europe. Shipbuilding on an industrial scale began here in the early 20th century and rather confounds the widespread assumption that this industry was confined to the Clyde in Scotland and the northern ports of England. In the first half of the 20th century, 25 naval destroyers as well as several submarines were built in Cowes.

Cowes and East Cowes can be easily explored on foot thanks to the **chain floating bridge ferry** that connects the two and at £1.50 (one-way) for a foot passenger (cars cost more) it's an extremely economical means of travel. The service across the Medina is one of just seven remaining chain ferries in the UK and the 800yd journey takes barely five minutes on the highest tides, the distance dropping by 260ft from high to low tide. In East Cowes, it's located 200yds south of the ferry dock; the departure point on the Cowes side is a little further from the centre of things, around 800yds from the mouth of the harbour.

1 COWES

🏠 **The Caledon Guest House** (page 304), **Onefifty Cowes** (page 304)

This is going to seem a curious observation to make about a port, but the first-time visitor can be surprised at just how adjacent Cowes is to the sea. The town hugs the coastline tight, its waterside paths frequently lapped by the Solent, which at high tide can seem like a bathtub full to the brim. The town, rather than being wary of the Solent, appears to welcome it with open arms. Cowes's layout is also as stereotypical as you could expect, with bold and impressive buildings – the work of royalty and yachting dignitaries – standing defiantly hard above the Solent; these give way to a warren of narrow, busy streets from which uneven alleyways break off and lead to marinas, dockyards and other seafaring industries. Saltwater really is in the blood of the town.

1 Cowes waterfront. **2** Sir Max Aitken Museum. ▶

GETTING TO COWES & EAST COWES FROM THE MAINLAND

Which Cowes should you arrive at? Services to both are operated by Red Funnel (⌂ redfunnel.co.uk) and the choice of transport can be a little confusing, so make sure you book the right one, especially if you are driving. A high-speed Red Jet foot passenger service scoots across the Solent from Southampton to (west) Cowes in just 25 minutes, while the ferry from Southampton (one hour) heads for East Cowes. This has more of a feel of an ocean liner and dwarves all the other ferries that trundle across the Solent. The service often seems to fill up, however, particularly from Friday to Monday and when there are any wind-related delays to other routes (the East Cowes route is usually the last to close to high winds). For more information on ferries, see page 20.

If you do take the wrong vessel (a mishap that can only befall foot passengers; motorists must take the East Cowes ferry), it's not actually the end of the world: thanks to the chain bridge ferry you can easily enough traverse the Medina from one side to the other.

Cowes Week has been held every year in early August since 1826 (with the exception of wartime and 2020) and typically sees around a thousand boats participating in up to 40 races per day. Begun by the Royal Yacht Club, the regatta involves many races and has long enjoyed the seal of royal approval, with members of the extended royal family having regularly taken part. Until World War I, big cutters and 'raters' were raced by gentlemen amateurs employing skippers and crew; in the wake of World War II there was a revival of big ocean-going yachts. The status of the week is reflected in its place among the trio of summer British social gatherings of the 'great and the good' (some would say, the 'wealthy and privileged'), alongside Glorious Goodwood and the beginning of the grouse shooting season.

Recent years have seen a move towards more inclusivity and among the 8,000 competitors who rock up each year you will find Olympic yachtsmen and women as well as weekend sailors. Add in the hundreds of boats that drop anchor to get the best waterside view, the live music, food stalls and marquees and exclusive cocktail parties and you have quite a spectacle.

Even if sailing is not your thing, there is plenty to do in and around the town, with fine waterside walks and good pubs. You'll most easily find Cowes's charms by wandering along its coastline, around The Parade by the mouth of the Medina and Bath Road, which extends into High

Street. At the bow of the town, so to speak, is the former Cowes Castle (closed to the public), which caps The Parade as it bumps into the Solent. The castle was one of Henry VIII's defence forts and dates to 1539. Much of the original structure was remodelled or demolished in the 18th century, and the Royal Yacht Squadron took over and restructured what remained in the 1850s. The 22 small brass cannons positioned in front of the castle by the sea wall are fired whenever races or particular vessels arrive or depart, which is more often than you might think.

The most striking building on The Parade is the emphatically Art Deco Osborne Court, whose geometric and streamlined façade now houses residential flats so can only be admired from afar. Just up the hill behind the castle is Northwood House, a Grade II-listed mansion house based on a classical design by John Nash that dates to 1842 and featuring two storeys with a nine-bay range, Tuscan columns (a plain, unadorned pillar) and a three-bay pediment. The house is open only for events and private functions, including the Isle of Wight Literary Festival every October, but it is set in the public space of Northwood Park, which is laid out as a Victorian pleasure garden, planted with mature specimen trees such as cork brought back by Cowes sailors returning from the High Seas.

At its southern end, The Parade curtails abruptly and Cowes quickly narrows into the tight contours of High Street, which retains much of its medieval layout and whose overhanging buildings seem to keep those passing by below in shadow even in summer. One of these buildings, a former sailmaker's loft, houses the **Sir Max Aitken Museum** (83 High St, PO31 7AJ ✆ 01983 293800 ⬧ sirmaxaitkenmuseum.org ☉ May–Sep Tue–Sat; see ad, page 119), an excellent museum that pays tribute to one of the town's most famous sons. John William Maxwell Aitken was born in Canada in 1910, the eldest son of Lord Beaverbrook, the owner of Express Newspapers. Cut from the same derring-do mould as Lawrence of Arabia and the author-explorer Gavin Maxwell, Sir Max lived life to the full, mainly on the sea, but also in the air and on the motor-racing track. The building boasts his personal collection of historic and nautical artefacts, some of which he acquired, others presented to him by a who's-who of political and high society.

Eyecatchers include the gaff (a pole to which a four-cornered sail is attached) from the Royal Cutter Yacht *Britannia*, dating from the 1920s – at 51ft long, it spans the length of the museum – and a naval dagger said to have been recovered from Hitler's bunker and handed to Beaverbrook by Stalin. Other curiosities offer insights into the everyday lifestyle of Sir Max and his circle: there's a miniature cannon which was used to announce the time for gin and tonic in the late afternoon (a pinch of gunpowder would be dropped on the cannon and an eyeglass would reflect the sun to heat the power to exploding point); and a gimballed table, whose surface moves with the waves and ensures that the said gin and tonic will not spill in a Force Eight gale.

Some 600yds from The Parade, a narrow alley leads towards the water and **Cowes Yacht Haven** (Vectis Yard, PO31 7BD ∂ cowesyachthaven. com). It's worth briefly sticking your nose into this large marina where typically more than 200 yachts are berthed or hauled out on to dry dock for repairs and TLC (the marina is on the site of a former working boat yard).

As far as points of interest go for the visitor, the aft of the town has plenty to offer. Adjacent to the chain bridge ferry is the unmissable **hammerhead crane** (Medina Rd, PO31 7LP; no access but easy to view from the adjacent Classic Boat Museum). This giant cantilever crane, whose horizontal jib and tapering front could be said to resemble a giant dystopian metallic mouse from a futuristic filmset, is an iconic piece of engineering. Towering 164ft high, it took its place on the Cowes skyline in 1912 and its cast-iron frame has gazed down sternly on the approaches to the Medina and the Solent ever since. It is the only surviving pre-World War II hammerhead crane in England. Designed in Scotland by Babcock and Wilcox, the crane was key to increasing the Cowes shipyard's capacity for producing naval warships and was used for the heavy-lifting tasks, such as lowering turbines and boilers into the vessels. The crane has been out of use since 2004, though a local trust is endeavouring to restore it and make it the centrepiece of an interpretation of Cowes's shipbuilding heritage. You can follow developments at ∂ coweshammerheadcrane.org.uk.

The crane stands next to an equally gargantuan former boat shed that houses the **Classic Boat Museum** (117a Medina Yard, Theitis Rd, PO31 7DJ ∂ classicboatmuseum.com). Here you will find more than 70 yachts, racing boats and lifeboats, including an Americas Cup test boat used by Sir Ben Ainslie in 2017. This is a pleasingly tactile museum where you can wander – sometimes squeeze – between the vessels, many of which look as though they were freshly varnished the night before. Occasionally you will spot an aficionado gently stroking a helm, as they might their pet cat or dog. Appropriately, the museum straddles the Medina, with its second building, the Classic Boat Gallery, based across the water in East Cowes (Columbine Building, Columbine Rd, East Cowes PO32 6EZ ℘ 01983 244101), which features model boats, photographs and uniforms of past racing competitors, though most visitors may find the contents of the boat shed satisfies most of their curiosity when it comes to the area's seafaring traditions.

Cowes Beach is a short pebble- and shell-covered strandline immediately to the west of the town, reached by heading anti-clockwise from The Parade for 600yds. The beach makes the perfect vantage point for the town's many sailing events. This is also *the* place to see the Round the Island Race (see box, page 85). While the beach is mainly stony, there is some sand below the low water mark and you can find shells, sea glass and other sea jewels among the pebbles.

The village of **Gurnard** lies two miles west of Cowes and enjoys a seaside setting popular with families, thanks to its beach, adjacent green and ice-cream options. Gurnard is easily reached by following

THE ART OF FUDGE: FAR FROM PLAIN SAILING

Rachel Powell and her husband Steve opened Slab (13 Bath Rd, PO31 7QN ℘ 01983 295400 ⟨ slabfudge.co.uk) in 2015. 'We were surprised there wasn't an "Island" fudge – after all, you expect to find fudge in seaside towns,' Rachel says.

Fudge making is far from plain sailing, for the base material is capricious: fudge, if it takes the mood can choose not to set, or it can set like concrete. 'It's a pretty science-based business,' says Rachel as she recalls how she taught herself to make fudge over the winter of 2014. 'You look at recipes online and you quickly realise most of them are awful – they burn the ingredients, or if they work the first time it all comes out wrong the second time.' After experimentation and endless tweaking

– cooking it a bit hotter, using less sugar, more butter – Rachel eventually settled on a recipe of her own.

Ever since then she has been kept busy working late into the night and cutting and packaging fudge at 05.00 ahead of selling at fairs, fetes and Cowes Week. Flavours include rum and raisin, gingerbread, lemon cheesecake (served with ice cream or double cream, this variety makes for an unusual but delicious dessert) and peanut butter.

The move into the shop was a logical next step and visitors can watch fudge being made in front of them. 'We opened the shop because we were storing the fudge in our house and it was full of boxes, the fudge was just taking over,' she laughs.

the promenade that runs all the way from The Parade in Cowes. There's a good café and the steady flow of tacking yachts offshore, making this a popular place to while away the time. To the east of the main Newport–Cowes road, you can't miss the signs for the **Wight Military and Heritage Museum** (Northwood Camp, 490 Newport Rd, PO31 8QU ☎ 01983 632039 ⌖ wmahm.org.uk). While the tanks and heavy guns will appeal more to the pure military buff, the museum volunteers have worked hard to welcome a wider audience who can admire the veteran Britten-Norman Islander short-haul aircraft or take an armoured car tour.

☖ FOOD & DRINK

The Butcher Shop 23 High St, PO31 7RY ☎ 01983 293129 ⌖ thebutchershop.uk. Specialists in a wide range of meats, including dry-aged beef hung to mature in a cabinet in the shop window.

The Food Hamper 116 High St, PO31 7AX ☎ 01983 295680 ▆ TheFoodHamper116 ☺ Mar–Dec. Offers a mouth-watering range of eggs, pies, breads, biscuits and chocolates. Ideal for an upmarket picnic of crab sandwiches or hot soup.

Gurnard Press 31 Worsley Rd, Gurnard PO31 8JW ☎ 01983 293182 ⌖ gurnardpress.co.uk. Creative pizza restaurant on the edge of the village. Menu succeeds in its efforts to be that little bit different and includes pizzas with figs and yellow courgettes. Also does take-away sandwiches and hot drinks (excellent coffee) – handy if you're on the adjacent Coastal Path or at Gurnard Beach.

Slab Artisan Fudge 13 Bath Rd, PO31 7QN ☎ 01983 295400 ⌖ slabfudge.co.uk. Sea-salted caramel, cookies and cream, lemon meringue… we are of course talking fudge, glorious fudge… and most recently, vegan fudge. In all, you can choose from 12 flavours. See box, page 83.

The Travellers Joy 85 Pallance Rd, Northwood PO31 8LS ☎ 01983 298024 ⌖ travellersjoycowes.co.uk. Out-of-the-way pub, set back between Gurnard and Cowes, which has a good feel about it. Hearty, filling food and a range of cask ales that leads to it being spoken of in hallowed terms by real ale drinkers. Beer garden, too.

The Waters Edge Beach Café Shore Rd, Gurnard PO31 8LD ☎ 01983 299929 ▆ WatersedgeIOW. Serves decent food all day – from baguettes to fish dishes – but my personal choice would be a for a lazy breakfast here on a sunny morning. Superb location overlooking the green and the sea.

Well Bread 53–54 High St, PO31 7RR ☎ 01983 281814. Rock cakes that could double as doorstoppers, and a delicious range of pastries and breads. Also offers sit-down meals and fillers, such as Welsh rarebit with focaccia.

⌨ SHOPPING

The Island book publisher **Medina Press** recently opened an excellent bookshop at 50 High Street (PO31 7RR 🖉 01983 300044 🖱 medinabookshop.com). This is the place to come for a definitive range of books on Island history as well as books by local authors.

Another Cowes business worth checking out online is **Rapanui** (🖱 rapanuiclothing. com), an eco-clothing producer that doesn't have a shop front. Rapanui is something of a pioneer when it comes to sustainable clothing and is aiming towards the concept of the 'closed loop', where fabrics for clothing are sourced sustainably and then repurposed and recycled, so that nothing in the chain is wasted. You can order online – choose from T-shirts, flannel shirts, plastic-free beach towels, T-shirt dresses, fishermen's jumpers and towel-change robes for surfers.

2 EAST COWES

With its jumble of warehouses and narrow streets squeezed into the watery confines at the bottom of a hill, East Cowes can feel more enclosed than its neighbour and is certainly less visually appealing. For much of its history, however, it has been at least as economically important and was an established customs clearance port in the 16th and 17th centuries. In the 18th century, shipbuilding took off and some of the great engineering names of yore made their name here, including Saunders Roe, Westland and the British Hovercraft Corporation (which was actually a reincarnation of Saunders Roe). High-profile buildings include the **Columbine Hangar** in Venture Quays. Now a heritage landmark, in 1977 the hangar doors of what was then the British

WATER RACES

Immediately following Cowes Week is one of the world's most famous and challenging sailing races: the **Fastnet Race**. It takes place every other year and boats race from Cowes, through the Needles Channel in the Solent and into the open waters of the Celtic Sea, round the Fastnet Lighthouse off the Irish coast, finishing in Plymouth, a distance of 700 nautical miles. In a popular year, more than 500 boats participate. The race's darkest hour came in 1979 when a huge storm overturned at least 75 boats and led to the deaths of 15 competitors and four rescuers.

Another famous sailing event is the **Round the Island Race,** which takes place early in the summer. Boats race west around the Island to and from Cowes, a distance of 50 nautical miles. The first race in 1931 had 25 entries but it now regularly attracts up to 1,800 boats. Winners usually circumnavigate the Island in around 2½ hours.

CRICKET'S WETTEST WICKET

It's hard to think of anything more idiosyncratically and quintessentially British than a cricket match played on a sandbar in the middle of one of the busiest shipping channels in the world.

Every year, when the spring tide is at its lowest (usually in either late August or September), the Brambles cricket match takes place on the Bramble Bank, just offshore from Cowes. The location moves slightly each year as the sandbar, by definition, changes shape a little with every tide. The contest dates from the 1950s and is between the Royal Southern Yacht Club and the Island Sailing Club: it is even briefer than a T20 match, with play possible for barely 40 minutes. Players are bare footed, with trousers rolled up to the knees. Jokes about batters being 'out for a ducking' abound. The teams take turns to win each year, the losers buying breakfast, or lunch, depending on when tides have permitted play. When an American TV crew dubbed the match 'the world's most pointless sporting contest', everyone involved took this to be the ultimate endorsement.

Hovercraft Corporation were painted with the world's largest image of the Union Flag (150ft x 39ft) to mark the Silver Jubilee, which can still be seen today.

East Cowes is also home to the engaging **East Cowes Heritage Centre** (8 Clarence Rd, PO32 6EP ⊘ isleofwightsociety.org.uk/heritage1.aspx), one of those unsung gems, run by volunteers and bursting with black-and-white photographs and tales of how the town evolved. Exploration won't take more than a few minutes but the detail is impressive and thoughtfully put together. The tale of Frank James, recorded at the centre, is typical: James's name was posthumously given to a nearby (now former) home for retired seamen, after he was killed by an elephant in Gabon in 1890 during an expedition that involved sailing his yacht, the *Lancashire Witch*, around the coasts of West Africa.

OSBORNE HOUSE TO WHIPPINGHAM

East Cowes occupies a self-contained area close to the riverside and gives way quickly to a rural hinterland of woodland and small villages, most of them set back slightly from the coast. The one downside is that the shoreline on this part of the Island can be frustratingly elusive and not always easy to access. Part of the reason for this is the substantial slice of land taken up by Osborne House. Access campaigners such as The Ramblers have long argued that the foreshore should be incorporated into the coastal footpath. For now, at least, English Heritage is not budging, so in order to access the beach, you'll have to pay at the front door. Nevertheless, footpaths and cycleways radiate out well beyond Osborne and allow endless hours of perusal of woods, hidden coves and waterways.

3 OSBORNE HOUSE
🏠 **Pavilion Cottage** (page 304)
York Av PO32 6JX; English Heritage

Queen Victoria described Osborne House as her and Albert's 'little paradise'. The queen clearly had a soft spot for the Island, having visited twice as a child, and the house you visit today was purpose built for the royal couple between 1845 and 1851 to provide the opulence and grandeur of a renaissance palazzo, glorious wildlife-friendly grounds and a little-visited shingle beach. Albert was sufficiently imaginative to liken the location of the proposed house position overlooking the Solent to that of a view of the Bay of Naples. He himself worked closely on the design of Osborne with the architect Thomas Cubitt, who had overseen the façade of Buckingham Palace.

The royal new build replaced a Georgian pile, also known as Osborne House, that had been bought from Lady Isabella Blachford, whose extended family had grown rich on the slave trade (which had been abolished by the time Victoria took over the property). After Prince Albert's death in 1861, the queen more or less retreated here permanently until her death in 1901. In the intervening years she formed a famously close friendship, to the great displeasure of the royal household, with her attendant Mohammed Abdul Karim (and which was wonderfully dramatised in Stephen Frears's comedy-drama *Victoria & Abdul* in 2017).

Much of the house can be visited and it really should be on your list because, both outside and in, this truly is a pile fit for a monarch. Before you enter, stand back and take in the wider spectacle of the exterior and its Italianate style, set among lawns edged by veteran oaks and yews. Cubitt was also responsible for the house's landmark twin belvedere towers. The pavilion (to the right as you look at the house) contained the royal couple's rooms while the main wing comprises three-quarters of the length of the house.

East Cowes to Ryde via Binstead

✳ OS Explorer map 29; start: East Cowes ferry port ♥ SZ502956; 8 miles; easy to medium

This walk through the quiet backwaters of woodlands and lanes that run between the coast and the main roads is a lovely option for travelling between East Cowes and Ryde. Along the way you encounter the villages of Whippingham, Wootton Bridge, Fishbourne and Binstead, with little for company other than churches and copses. The entire route is waymarked with the Coastal Trail signposts, though the name is a little misleading as private property keeps the Solent at arm's length for much of it. The initial steep climb out of East Cowes, following the busy A3021, can be skipped by taking bus #4 to the Campfield Road bus stop.

1 It's two miles from the port at East Cowes to Whippingham and this stretch involves road walking up the A3021, though fortunately there is a pavement all the way. By the junction with New Barn Road there is a plaque commemorating the conviction in 1899 of Henry House for 'furious driving'. House was deemed to have driven at a speed 'greater than 8mph' and was fined £3. This was the first motoring offence on the Island. Continue along the pavement until you reach Whippingham School.

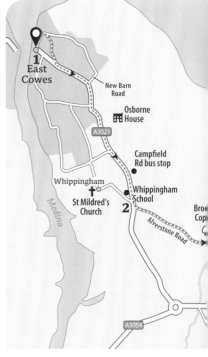

2 Just south of the school, bear left (east) along Alverstone Road. This quiet lane dips and lifts for 1½ miles as it meanders through woodlands such as Brocks Copse, before bringing you to the edge of Wootton Bridge.

3 Follow the Coastal Path signs closely through Wootton Bridge; there are several dog-legs that take you through a small housing estate, but the path is waymarked all the way here. You emerge on the main road, the A3054. Keep on the road as the bridge crosses the Old Mill Pond and Wootton Creek and climbs uphill.

4 After 400yds, the path leaves the main road, turning left at Ashlake Copse Lane. After another 400yds the road narrows into a track and briefly passes through a plantation before emerging on to Ashlake Copse Road. Continue ahead on the road for 400yds and then take the footpath to the right, which climbs slightly uphill. Turn left on to Fishbourne Lane and pass the ferry terminal (for services to Portsmouth). The Coastal Path signs lead you out of the village, but a quick detour down the lane immediately to the left after the ferry car park leads to the Fishbourne Inn, which is a fine stop for a refuel. Returning to the coast path, the route continues almost due east and passes the entrance to Quarr Abbey; from the path you enjoy views across the grounds to the Solent and the mainland.

5 The coast path continues eastwards and is clear and well signposted, if still set back from the Solent. Luckily, this stretch has two points from where you can access the coastline easily and where you will find a smattering of sand and views of the water: half a mile east of Quarr Abbey, along footpath R46; and just 400yds west of Binstead Church of the Holy Cross, on footpath R47 (both footpaths are left turns off the main path and are barely 400yds long). Shortly after the R47 turning, the coast path follows the lane in front of Binstead Church. ▶

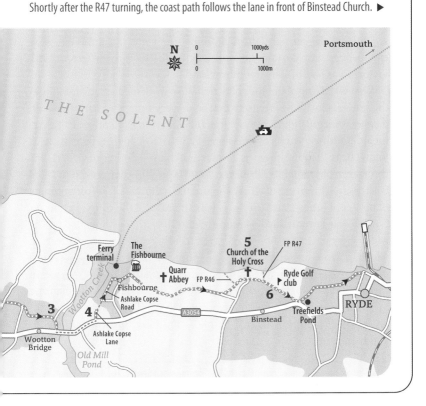

East Cowes to Ryde via Binstead (continued)

▶ **6** The route traverses Ryde Golf Club; as you reach the edge of Ryde itself, look out for the delightful Treefields Pond on your left where you are likely to see dragonflies from spring until early autumn. Although the pond looks natural, it is thought to have been created in the mid 19th century and used for watering cattle and horses; it is one of 26 ponds in the town. Finally, follow waymarked backstreets into the town to land you on the seafront at Ryde Esplanade.

Inside are sumptuous state rooms and opulently furnished corridors adorned with items of antiquity and great craftsmanship. This was, after all, where the queen, at the height of the British Empire, welcomed guests from across the world. Among them was King Cetshwayo, the exiled King of the Zulus who fled to England following defeat in the Anglo-Zulu War.

A set route leads you around the state and family rooms. They include the staggeringly adorned dining room which features cut-glass chandeliers, satin curtains and full-length mirrors and is where, in 1901, Victoria was laid in state upon her death before burial at Windsor.

What is striking about the collection of artwork on display throughout the house is just how intensely personal everything is – many items on display were gifts given by Victoria and Albert to each other. Paintings include 19th-century commissions by artists of high repute such as John Lucas. Among them is Lucas's touching painting of Albert, his three-year-old daughter, Princess Victoria, and his pet greyhound Eos. Perhaps most moving of all are the marble sculptures cast from moulds of plaster of limbs – arms, legs, feet and hands – of the couple's children.

After you have padded around the interior, it's worth exploring the wider grounds of the house and the recently renovated Italian terrace which is overrun with tulips (something of a Victorian obsession) in spring, as well as the summer bedding displays that thrive in the Mediterranean microclimate. Prince Albert oversaw the planting of many ornamental evergreens and oaks and you may also spot red squirrels, along with tree-trunk-loving birds such as nuthatches and treecreepers.

1 Swiss Cottage Garden, Osborne House. **2** St Mildred's, Whippingham. **3** Durbar Room, Osborne House. ▶

Beyond the flowers of the garden, you can make your way towards the shoreline. Take time to inspect the bathing machine where Queen Victoria got changed before she took to the water. Resembling a cross between a garden shed and a cowboy's wagon and adorned with wrought-iron scrolling, the machine was entered by the queen via wooden steps. She would then change (out of sight) and wait while the machine was pulled into the sea before stepping into the water, shielded by curtains from public view.

Osborne House was a genuine family home and all Victoria's children spent some of their childhood here. Just behind the house is Swiss Cottage, a whopper of a Wendy house where the royal infants would play. Many original toys remain and it is a rather charming place. Not all Victoria's children recalled Osborne House so fondly, however: on assuming the crown in 1902, Edward VII handed it over to the state. During World War II, the house served as a convalescent home for injured officers, including A A Milne and Robert Graves; the latter recorded in his autobiography, *Good-Bye to All That*, how he slept in the royal night nursery and played billiards.

4 WHIPPINGHAM

The village of Whippingham lies just over a mile to the south of East Cowes and immediately to the west of Osborne House. Although the village was incorporated into the royal estate created by Victoria and Albert, a settlement has existed here on the east bank of the Medina since at least Domesday times, when the hamlet was recorded as 'Wippa' (which is possibly the name of a Jutish chieftain). Under Albert's supervision, the village enjoyed a makeover that saw a school remodelled (it was one of the first schools in England to enjoy flush toilets and sinks with running water), a forge built, and a farm established and orchards planted to feed both the estate and its labourers. Bus #4 from East Cowes drops you at The Forge stop for access to the village, its impressive church and heritage trail.

The land to the west of the village, just south of the Folly Inn on the banks of the Medina, has been home to a couple of important factories. In 1910 it became the location of the Saunders Aircraft Company's factory in where the superbly named Bat Boat, Europe's first amphibious aircraft, was tested and flown. Between 1916 and 1918, 80 such aircraft were built and launched straight out over the Medina, where presumably, they either flew or sank. In 1921, Fred Goatley, an employee at the factory, became manager of the Folly Plywood factory, where he designed many boats that proved incredibly helpful for commandos during World War II, including folding assault boats, canoes and nimble torpedo boats.

You can't miss the tower of **St Mildred's Church**, with its five soaring pinnacles (said to resemble a castle on the Rhine), which was Victoria and Albert's place of worship. Architecturally, this is a building of great merit, Grade I listed and first redesigned by John Nash (who had demolished an earlier church on the site) in the early 19th century and later by Prince Albert himself. You enter through a churchyard lined with a guard of honour of yew trees.

Inside, rose windows project light on to hundreds of intricate stone bosses, and tiles in red and cream have been chiselled out of the masonry on the walls and ceiling. Queen Victoria's prayer chair awaits perusal and there is a side chapel dedicated to the Mountbatten family to admire. This chapel contains a richly ornamental Bible and a vast marble sarcophagus that houses the remains of Princess Beatrice (Victoria and Albert's youngest child) and her husband Prince Henry. On the inside wall of this chapel hangs a small crucifix and inscribed plaque dedicated to the Romanovs, the Russian royal family who holidayed on the Island (see box, page 94). The plaque is out of sight but, if you ask, a volunteer may be obliging and open up the chapel for you. Despite all these qualities, the church still managed to meet with Victoria's displeasure: when she attended a service here she was sufficiently unimpressed that she gave £10 for the organist to pay for some much-needed music lessons.

"Architecturally, this is a building of great merit, Grade I listed and first redesigned by John Nash in the early 19th century."

A pleasing way to explore the village is to take the waymarked **Whippingham Heritage Trail** (two miles) which runs mainly on the west side of the A3021. There's a useful interpretation board for the short walk located just by the bus stop for Alverstone Road, opposite the school. It's also worth following footpath N122 here (waymarked for Newport Quay), which runs south alongside the Medina River from the Folly Inn and leads to a secluded riverbank that's a haven for wildlife: you may see oystercatchers, herons and egrets, plus migrating Brent geese in winter.

THE WIGHT RUSSIANS

Royalty has always been drawn to the Isle of Wight but arguably the most unlikely blue-blooded visitors came from Russia. Perhaps the tsars appreciated a seafaring culture similar to that which prevailed at home in St Petersburg (which Peter the Great declared should be a window on the west). The whole, slightly unlikely tale is recounted in *Isle and Empires* by Stephan Roman (despite his name, he has no royal links though his own grandparents escaped the Russian Revolution by the skin of their teeth).

According to Roman, the Russian connection to Cowes was forged in 1698 when Peter the Great appointed a man from the town as his chief naval carpenter. The Imperial links flourished mainly in the 19th century when successive tsars visited the Island. Most royal sojourns centred on Osborne House, the abode of Queen Victoria, or with the Russian royal yacht *Shtandart* weighing anchor in the Solent. The last tsar, Nicholas II, was also entertained at nearby Barton Manor, above East Cowes, by Edward VII.

The most endearing tale in Roman's book is an account of an away day in Cowes undertaken in 1909 by the Romanov grand duchesses, Olga and Tanya. Aged 14 and 12, their sheltered life as royal children meant they had little experience of life beyond the gates of Russian royal palaces. Cowes was to prove something of a shock. An entourage followed the two girls at a distance as they took the chain ferry across the Medina and bought postcards, perfume and hairbrushes in the High Street. The atmosphere changed when they hailed another group of Russians in town in their own language. Local ears pricked up, one thing led to another and soon it seemed as though half the town was assembled, trying to grab a view of what were rumoured to be the tsar and tsarina themselves. After several attempts to escape the crush of curious people, who at times encircled the girls and even cheered them, the pair were whisked by police down a narrow passageway and back on to the ferry.

The sojourns came to an abrupt halt when the Russian Revolution brought the Romanov dynasty to a brutal end with the execution of the tsar, his wife (Alexandra, also known as Alix, Queen Victoria's granddaughter) and children in 1918.

You'll find a small memorial and inscription to the Romanovs in St Mildred's in Whippingham; a more substantial memorial cross was erected in Jubilee Park in East Cowes in July 2018 to mark the centenary of the murder of the royal family.

FOOD & DRINK

The Folly Inn Folly Ln, PO32 6NB ✆ 01983 297171 ⬨ greeneking-pubs.co.uk/pubs/isle-of-wight/folly. With its timbered roof and covered terrace abutting the bank of the Medina, the Folly Inn would not look out of place in Henley-upon-Thames. Many of the clientele wouldn't either, as it is popular with yachties and other sailors who have moored either in East Cowes, just downstream, or at the pontoon linked to the riverbank. Food is decent – pies, fish, chocolatey desserts – though as it's part of a pub chain you are left wistfully wishing, given the pub's delightful setting, for a little more originality. In the interest of balance, it should be said that the views do enable you to cut the pub a little slack.

SOUTHEAST TO BINSTEAD

An area that roads make it all too easy to whisk through en route to somewhere else, the undulating landscape between Cowes and Ryde is home to watery creeks, farmland and attractive, wildlife-rich copses. It's a good place for walking or even taking a vintage train back into the Island's past.

5 BRIDDLESFORD FARM & DAIRY

⊘ briddlesford.co.uk ⊙ daily

This fascinating working farm is worth lingering at, not least for its excellent farm shop and café (page 96). The farm is home to 120 milking cows, 200 head of cattle and a small informal museum which skims through the history of the farm.

The family-run farm began in 1923 when the great-grandfather of Louise Griffin, who runs the farm shop today, set up with just 15 cows (the animals you see today are the direct descendants of that original cohort). 'The dairy industry has been through difficult times,' says Louise, recalling how the farm shop developed. 'We had to make a decision about what to do – but we couldn't sell our cows, they are descended from my great-grandfather's, they're our history.' The farm shop opened in 2005 and sells 150 products from across the Island, from meat, quince, petit pains (a type of squash shaped like an overweight frisbee) and jams to the five cheeses made on site. All the milk on sale comes from the farm.

Engagement with the public is a key part of their approach today, and Welly Wednesdays (during school holidays), when children can explore the farm, and open days, when the barn is open to visitors and you can ask questions of staff, are hugely popular. 'It's really about telling the public what we do,' says Louise. 'We don't give our animals names but it's a good idea – sometimes you think some people don't realise meat comes from a real animal.'

An easy walk of just 1½ miles connects Wootton Bridge to this lovely farm shop. An amble there and back will take little over an hour, allowing plenty of time to break the stroll and dawdle over tea and cake at the farm's excellent café. To get there, take the footpath that heads south immediately to the west of the bridge in Wootton Bridge. This meanders for a mile through fields and woods, with occasional views of the creek where you may spot a cattle egret or a heron. The path crosses the steam railway line and almost immediately reaches Woodhouse Farm. Turn right here; in 400yds you'll reach the hamlet of Littletown. Turn left down the bridleway of Littletown Lane to reach Briddlesford Road and you'll see the farm directly opposite. Cross with care as this is an extremely fast road.

¶¶ FOOD & DRINK

Bluebells Café Briddlesford Rd, PO33 4RY ✆ 01983 882885 ⌚ briddlesford.co.uk. The farm's café, whose bright interior is augmented by huge windows, features generous sandwiches, jacket potatoes and more substantial meals such as halloumi burgers and schnitzel, as well as a fine range of cakes.

6 WOOTTON BRIDGE

🏠 **Grange Farm** (page 304)

Straddling Wootton Creek, the village of Wootton Bridge infills the hinterland either side of the water and, away from the main road, is essentially residential. Cars zip across the modest traverse of the eponymous bridge in seconds; you can walk along the sheltered pedestrian-only 'chicane' and take in a serene and rather timeless view up and down Wootton Creek to the north and the Old Mill Pond to the south of the bridge. The houses around the Sloop Inn by the bridge are thought to be more than 250 years old, but the village's history is much older than that: the Romans landed cargo along the creek, King Canute is said to have come ashore here, and the monks from nearby Quarr Abbey, who owned the mill, operated a fishery here from the 12th century until the Dissolution of the Monasteries in the 16th century.

The scenic charms of Wootton Bridge extend into the village periphery. Heading east along the A3054 in the direction of Ryde, 200yds after crossing the village bridge a right turn uphill along the logically named Firestone Copse Road will lead you, after 600yds, to **Firestone Copse**. This is a charming small woodland, managed by the Forestry Commission, where hazel has been coppiced to allow flowers space to thrive in the light of open glades. The network of paths through the copse includes a wheelchair-accessible path.

ISLAND RAILWAYS

Up until the 1950s, railways provided virtually the whole of the Island's transport needs, from school travel, commuting and holiday traffic to the movement of farm produce from the field to factories and ports. At this time, the Island boasted 55 miles of railway line. The 'main line' from Ryde Pier Head to Ventnor was the busiest, partly because it served the principal holiday resorts of Sandown and Shanklin. The short 2¾-mile branch from Brading to Bembridge was opened in 1882 and came about as a result of plans to reclaim Brading marshes. The railway used a dam embankment for part of its length through the drained land. At the other extreme, the rural lines to Freshwater and Ventnor West were never profitable and epitomised the 'sleepy country branch lines' that were caught in the crosshairs of the Beeching cuts. After the war, little time was wasted closing the loss-making lines. The tracks to Ventnor West, Bembridge and between Newport and Sandown were all closed in the 1950s.

Just inland from the village is the **Isle of Wight Steam Railway** (⌀ iwsteamrailway.co.uk ☉ May–Sep daily, Oct, Dec & Mar–Apr train operating days only, check website). Access is on Station Road, half a mile south of Wootton Bridge. A trip on this restored steam railway represents a glorious step back into yesteryear. The railway occupies about five miles of the old Ryde & Newport Line, which originally opened in 1875; it also connects to the Ryde–Shanklin Island Line railway at Smallbrook Junction (you can buy tickets that are valid for both services). Most people take the ten-mile round trip that passes through (and stops at) Smallbrook Junction and Havenstreet as it gives you the most time on the train. For the most part, the views are dominated by farmland, with snatched glimpses of the downs to the south. The Havenstreet Junction stop (you can also board here) is home to the railway's Train Story, a small museum (which opens when trains run) where you can admire rare rolling stock and Victorian and Edwardian carriages. Kids will have fun dressing up as guards or drivers.

A pleasing way to pass a few hours would be to combine a trip on the train with a visit to **Rosemary Vineyard** (Smallbrook Ln, PO33 4BE ✆ 01983 811084 ⌀ rosemaryvineyard.co.uk). Set back a mile or so to the south of Ryde, the vineyard is open for tours and has a well-stocked shop where you can buy or sample a spicy white muscatel and oak-flavoured red sourced from Alsatian grapes. It's an easy post-tipple wander back to Smallbrook Junction afterwards.

7 FISHBOURNE & QUARR ABBEY

⌂ The Fishbourne (page 304)

The village of **Fishbourne** splits its personality between the large ferry port and a picturesque village green, which encircles an ageing oak. The hamlet's name originates from the location of a fish house that served Quarr Abbey, and where fish were salted, cured and stored. Immediately beyond the green, a narrow cul-de-sac opens on to the shores of the Solent.

Beyond Fishbourne, the landscape pattern of fields, woodlands and glimpses of the sea continues until you reach **Quarr Abbey** (Quarr Rd, PO33 4ES ⊘ quarrabbey.org). Completed in 1914, the abbey stands centre stage in an estate of 200 acres and is home to a small community of Benedictine monks. The striking belfry has an onion dome reminiscent of both Eastern Orthodox churches and Moorish architecture and

"Beyond Fishbourne, the landscape pattern of fields, woodlands and glimpses of the sea continues until you reach Quarr Abbey."

can be picked out above the woodland west of Ryde for miles around – you'll also see it if you arrive by ferry on the Portsmouth to Fishbourne route. More than a quarter of the estate is open (and free) to the public.

The abbey is set among grounds that feature smallholdings, animal pens, allotments, herb gardens and woodlands. As you admire the enclosures that are home to a mixture of Saddleback and Tamworth pigs, you may even find yourself standing next to one of the brothers, though there is every chance they will be in their working farm clothes (or bee-keeping suits).

Two sets of thick doors lead into the main church (it's said that one visitor gave up at the first set and complained: 'it's not worth going in, it's only a cupboard!'). The abbey was designed by architect (and Benedictine monk) Dom Paul Bellot, who was heavily influenced by his travels in southern Spain and loosely based the abbey's structure of symmetrical brickwork on the mosque at Cordoba. Built from 1,984,250 Flemish bricks, the abbey has a harmonious terracotta and biscuit-brown appearance. Subtly tinted glass means that the natural light gets greater and the bricks become richer in colour as you walk deeper into

◀ **1** Wootton Bridge. **2** Holy Cross Church, Binstead. **3** Quarr Abbey. **4** Isle of Wight Steam Railway.

the church. The innovative dome and belfry that cap the church caused the Island builders some consternation: they'd never built anything like it before and needed persuading to remove the supporting scaffolding when it was completed, for fear of the thing collapsing. Ravens can often be seen flapping down to land on its ledges, something that Benedictine monks find pleasing, for it's said that a tame raven hopped off with a slice of poisoned bread that a jealous monk had prepared for St Benedict.

Walk around the back of the abbey and you come to the small cemetery, planted with thick-set crosses that mark the burial spots of monks of the Quarr. At the back of the abbey is the tiny, rather austere Pilgrim's Chapel, with its four side altars intended for private prayer (the chapel is also a back-up option for general prayer should the cost of heating the main church become too expensive). The grounds beyond the chapel can be explored along trails that lead to hides where you can watch out for red squirrels (if you have children, ask for a free explorer's kit at the tea shop).

Today's Benedictine monks are the successors to an earlier community on the site, which goes back to the 12th century – the original religious order was a Cistercian one which founded an abbey here in 1132 but was dissolved by Henry VIII. To see the crumbling remnants, walk 200yds east of today's abbey along the coastal trail, past the abbey lodge and a house built in a part-restored church (both now private properties). You can't enter the ruins, which are located in a grazing meadow, but the surrounding woodland cover pulls back to reveal views of the chapter house and the kitchen, as well as a wide vista of the Solent. A magnificent three-trunked oak tree, reckoned to be 400 years old, stands on the far side of the field; its middle trunk still planted in medieval stone that was once part of the infirmary. Beneath your feet on the path, awaiting excavation at some point in the future, are more remains of the original Cistercian church.

You can access the Quarr Estate on bus #4, on foot along the coastal trail and on two wheels along the Taste Round the Island Trail (which here is numbered cycle trail #22).

¶¶ FOOD & DRINK

The Fishbourne 111 Fishbourne Ln, PO33 4EU ✆ 01983 882823 ⬡ thefishbourne.co.uk. This lovely country pub dates to the early 1900s and can be found by woodlands on the banks of Wootton Creek. Food features local produce and the pub routinely makes it into

The Good Pub Guide and picks up AA awards year after year. Emphasis is on upmarket pub favourites – fish, sausages – as well as daily specials. At least one local ale is usually on tap. Book ahead for a seat on the sun-drenched patio.

Tea Garden and Farm Shop Quarr Abbey, PO33 4ES ✆ 01983 882420 ⊘ quarrabbey.org. The abbey's tea shop really should not be missed, for it draws heavily on the produce grown within the estate, as well as offering a good range of sandwiches, soups and hot drinks. Look out for menu options that feature some of the 300 orchard trees, a variety of beetroot known as Chioggia pink, yellow French beans and nine varieties of tomatoes, such as Mr Stripey (red and yellow) and Yellow Stuffer (pepper-shaped, with an easily hollowed-out centre, perfect as the name suggests for stuffing).

8 BINSTEAD

Although the village of Binstead merges into the outskirts of Ryde, its church is quintessentially rural. Standing high and lonely, **Holy Cross Church** dates to the 11th century and its location, outside the centre of the village, suggests it had close associations with Quarr Abbey. Like the original 12th-century abbey, the church would have been built with limestone from quarries at Quarr and Binstead. The limestone was also used to build Winchester Cathedral and Romsey Abbey as well as parts of the Tower of London.

Look out for the sheela na gig (a lewdly carved gargoyle intended to ward off evil spirits) on the stone gateway. The bellcote contains a pre-Reformation bell thought to have come from the original Cistercian abbey at Quarr.

The graveyard here is oddly fetching, overlooked by huge mature trees and hosting some impressive tombstones. The pick of these is that of Thomas Sivell, who was mistaken for a smuggler and shot by a customs officer in 1785. According to the epitaph on his tomb, poor Sivell is spending eternity in a state of permanent indignation, for it reads: 'All you that pass pray look and see/ How soon my life was took from me/ By those officers as you hear/ They spilled my Blood that was so dear.'

¶¶ FOOD & DRINK

The Fleming Arms Binstead Hill, PO33 3RD ✆ 01983 243555 ⊘ theflemingarmsiow.co.uk. Eclectic menu ranging from tapas and cod with saffron potatoes to coconut curries, all of which are a notch above standard pub fare. The owners also run The Pantry (⊙ Wed–Sun), a small farm shop squeezed inside the pub, and which sells Island produce as well as their own seasonally grown vegetables.

RYDE & THE NORTHEAST COAST

Ryde has welcomed seaside holidaymakers for generations and its open spaces, public gardens, sandy beaches and seaside stalls merge with the hustle and bustle of the Island's largest transport interchange to create a truly distinctive coastal resort. The town manages to cling – by its fingertips in places – on to the *fin de siècle* air of its heyday while nurturing a palpable artistic vibe of a more modern vintage. Beyond an appealing centre, you'll find quiet streets comprising thick-stone, whitewashed buildings and long gardens, which contribute to the town's overall feeling of openness. Eventually these peter out into shoreline and woodland.

An elegiac whiff wafts along the northeastern shores of the Island. You can promenade along the sea defences, drink in views of yachts, ferries and cargo ships bobbing up and down in the Solent, and pop into independent hotels and local shops with barely a national chain to be seen. The coastal mudflats are wonderful for birdwatching: the Solent estuarine ecosystem, comprising mudflats and eelgrass, is an internationally important area for wintering waterfowl. Life seems to wash slowly over you, just as the ebbing tide laps over the rocky shoreline at **Seaview**, just two miles east of Ryde but an utterly serene contrast.

9 RYDE

🏠 **The Auction House** (page 304)

Architecturally, Ryde has a bit of everything. As a 2011 Ryde Conservation Area report compiled by the Island council succinctly puts it: 'The [conservation] area encompasses vernacular and designed architecture of the 17th, 18th and 19th centuries, 19th century industrial architecture, tourist-related structures and 20th century suburban development.'

A brief history

In 1341, the original fishing village of Lower Ryde was one of the three ports by which you could enter and leave the Island. Around this time, 'La Ryde' was recorded as an outlier of the medieval manor of Ashey, within the medieval parish of Newchurch (the word 'ryde' or 'rithe' means a small stream).

◀ **1** Ryde. **2** Seaview. **3** Alan Hersey Nature Reserve. **4** Goodleaf Tree Climbing.

ON THE BUSES

One of the striking things about the Isle of Wight is the bus service, with Islanders – despite their grumblings – patently better catered for than many other rural parts of the UK. The legacy goes back a long way and you can learn the history of the bus network and admire some vintage gems from a bygone era at the **Isle of Wight Bus Museum** (Park Rd, Ryde PO33 2BE ✆ 01983 567796 ⌂ iwbusmuseum.org.uk ☺ Easter–Oct).

The uncharitable of course, might say that on an Island so often portrayed as stuck in a time warp (which is an untrue characterisation), many of these vehicles – some of which date to 1927 – would not look out of place on today's roads. With their cream and Granny Smith green liveries and often absurdly oversized external iron radiators, the veteran buses are undoubtedly photogenic. Most were built by the great manufacturers of the day, based in Bedford and Bristol, and often custom built because the narrow roads of the Island required small vehicles. Even then, some roads still had to be lowered in order for the new arrivals to squeeze under bridges. Around 30 vehicles are now shoehorned into the former bus depot that houses the museum, and, as is so often the case with such collections, they have been immaculately and lovingly restored. There's also some good humour: a horse-drawn carriage is accompanied by the specifications 'maximum speed: gallop; engine type: carnivorous'. Another bus enjoyed a second life taking backpackers overland to Nepal up until 1997. This is one of those museums that can make anyone, not just a bus devotee, linger longer than they might expect. Vintage days out on the buses are often held, which are great fun; check the website for details.

A packway was built in 1574 to move goods up the hill from the shore. Upper Ryde developed on this higher ground as a medieval open field system with farmsteads that, by the 16th century, were being divided and enclosed. By the late 18th century what had been essentially two separate medieval communities, Upper Ryde (top of the hill) and Lower Ryde (bottom of the hill, by the sea), had come together, united in 1780 by what would later be called Union Street.

Wealthy visitors were beginning to be drawn to Ryde by this point, bringing with them an increased social standing for the town among mainland citizens. This allure must have been powerful to the point of being magnetic, for visitors from the mainland had to travel from their ship in a wherry (a boat with a long overhanging bow) over Ryde's mud- and sandbanks, and then carried ashore by cart, a practice described by Henry Fielding in his *Journal of a Voyage to Lisbon*. This stodgy, perilous constraint on visitors was largely addressed by the construction of the pier in 1814 and the extensions that followed in 1824 and 1842. In 1860 the pier was widened to accommodate a horse-drawn tramway and in 1880 a double-track railway line added. Ryde's popularity and prestige were heightened further by its subsequent proximity to Queen Victoria's Osborne House (page 87).

The surrounding sandbanks hide their own grisly tales. Prior to the establishment of a burial ground in Ryde, the majority of the deceased were either buried at Binstead or Newchurch as the burial ground at St Thomas's Chapel was severely limited. Those were the lucky ones. In 1782, following the sinking of the *Royal George*, the bodies of many of the 900 who died or were washed ashore at Ryde were buried on the sandbanks in an area that was to become the Strand. Not all arrivals and departures were so dramatic: a few years later, in 1787, to less distress but greater historical significance, the First Fleet set sail from Ryde for Australia.

Exploring the town

Ryde's bustle and the focus of activity for the visitor is the seafront Esplanade, from where Union Street with its hanging baskets rises inland and uphill. Across the town, from the high point of Union Street and the sea-level perspective of the Esplanade, you enjoy views across the Solent to the mainland. The best views of the town itself are from the pier, looking inland, with the spires of All Saints' Church and Holy Trinity Church, and the former Royal York Hotel clearly visible.

One of the keystone seafront buildings is the Grade II-listed Pavilion, constructed in 1926 by McFarlanes of Glasgow and featuring decorative cast ironwork and pagoda-like turrets and, nowadays, home to a bowling alley, bar and grill. It's heyday as a music venue saw the Rolling Stones play here. You'll see similar finery in the balustrades of the pier.

The Esplanade itself is a chaotic jumble of buildings of varying scale, decorative stucco and traditional shop fronts: tall, low, fat, narrow, with everything from Tudor beams to Georgian townhouses and filigree balconies. Some are home to vibrant businesses, while others would appear to be living on borrowed time (it's fair to say that some parts of town are more in need of restoration than others). Along the Esplanade you should definitely nose around the Olde Ryde Sweet Shop at number 4, its former life as a Victorian pharmacy betrayed by the

TICKET TO RYDE

As recently as Victorian times, important visitors to Ryde had to be carried across the mudflats to the town. Not only will you keep your feet dry today but you are spoilt for choice as to how to arrive, for Ryde must enjoy some of the best transport links of any small town in the country.

Think of the area around Ryde Esplanade as Island Grand Central: here you'll find a ferry service, the hovercraft, the northerly terminus of the only surviving public train line on the island, and a bus station from where routes radiate out across almost the entire Island.

The **FastCat** service to Portsmouth (⟨⊘⟩ wightlink.co.uk/ports/ryde-pier-head), which takes foot passengers only, operates from Ryde Pier Head. (You may still encounter cars on the approach as the pier is the only one in the UK that allows vehicular traffic – to a passenger car park; driving along the reinforced planks of the pier's former tramway can give the unsettling impression that you are actually on a railway line.) The adjacent beach is where foot passengers can board the **hovercraft** (⟨⊘⟩ hovertravel.co.uk) to Southsea Common at Portsmouth. Just the other side of the fence from the beach is the **train line** (⟨⊘⟩ southwesternrailway.com/destinations-and-offers/island-line), with services to Brading, Sandown, Shanklin and other points south. Meanwhile, a steady stream of buses pulls in and out. Key routes of use are the #2, which heads for Sandown; #4, which serves East Cowes via Binstead and Osborne House; #8, which heads for Bembridge; #9 to Newport; and #3 to Ventnor (this takes a long 90 minutes). The #8 also serves Newport but this travels via the east coast and, at one hour 40 minutes, is scenic but not one to take in a hurry.

original wooden shelves and snugly fitting wooden drawers that once stored medicine and cures for 19th-century agues. Close by at number 7, Chocolate Apothecary is of similar historical merit (page 110).

Other high-profile buildings include the former Ryde Town Hall and Theatre on Lind Street, a heritage landmark featuring Doric pillars, urns and a four-way clock face embellished with arched and recessed cornices. The building desperately needs saving and at the time of writing sadly looked utterly battered. That said, despite the peeling paint the course stone cut in the shape of bricks still shines through. A short walk away is the half-restored Art Deco Royal York Hotel on George Street which, if it is ever completed as either hotel or flats, will be a magnificent choice for accommodation, with its sweeping spiral staircase, glass skylight and curved windows. On Union Street you'll find the stuccoed if tired-looking Royal Victoria Arcade (Grade II* listed), constructed in 1835.

Thanks to the high tidal range along this stretch of the Solent, **Ryde Pier** juts out into the water more than most piers (at 1,740ft, or nearly half a mile, it is the second longest pier in England, after Southend) and this means you can follow the tide out and have a nose around the pier's sandy foundations. At the far end is the 'sponge garden', where the joists, pillars and foundations of the pier are smothered in sea life. Here you will find extensive beds of eelgrass and mudflats, along with beadlet anemones and pipefish (resembling seahorses) sheltering within that eelgrass. You may also see marine sticklebacks and tiny daisy anemones which close up when you approach, along with larger dahlia anemones. 'It looks tropical, people say they have never seen anything like it,' says Ian Boyd of Arc Consulting (⏣ arc-consulting.co.uk). Ryde is included in the UNESCO biosphere designation conferred upon parts of the Island in 2019 – it can come as a surprise to learn that urban areas can be included in biospheres. 'The point of the designation is that it shows how humans can coexist with the natural world and Ryde seafront is a good example of how the two rub along,' says Ian, who was instrumental in compiling the winning case for biosphere status.

The pier is also a good place for wildlife watching. Migratory birds drop by in spring while in winter you will pick out sanderlings and ringed plovers, large numbers of Brent geese, redshanks, turnstones, oystercatchers and flocks of wading birds such as black-tailed godwits, curlews and dunlins. It's possible to see some of the avian and marine wildlife at close hand by joining a walk at low tide with the annual Under the Pier (⏣ underthepier.space) event, though any low tide in autumn affords the chance to wander out under the structure.

A brief stroll to the southeast of the town centre is rewarded with the chance to admire the exteriors of some finely proportioned Regency and Victorian housing. Starting at the top of Union Street, head east and peruse Cross, Melville, Trinity and Dove streets and Vernon Square, which overlooks a private Victorian walled garden. The buildings (none of which open to the public) are mainly two or three storeys in height, constructed in stone or buff-coloured brick or rendered in stucco. Classically fronted Regency terraces sit beside Italianate-style façades, often within generous gardens. Their unifying linear street pattern enables clear views across Ryde with occasional glimpses of the sea.

Along with diverse housing of significant architectural merit, Ryde has an unusually high concentration of artists and not only hosts

HOVERTRAVEL: QUICK, QUICK, SLOW

The hovercraft seemingly levitates its way across the Solent from Southsea Common to Ryde in just ten minutes. The service was launched in 1965 and originally it was on-demand, with no scheduled timetable. The service is thought to be unique in Europe, and many first-time travellers to the Island are surprised to find it is still around.

The hovercraft 'flies' above the surface thanks to two large centrifugal fans, powered by air-cooled diesel engines, that draw in air that becomes trapped beneath the hull in a flexible 'skirt' (the large inflated rubber 'hull'). The vessel hugs the waves and in choppier seas it feels as if it is on an undulating conveyor belt, tightly hugging the contouring swell of the Solent. The lack of contact with the water gives the hovercraft the ability to move in any direction, easily sliding sideways or even, if necessary, backwards with little resistance.

Since the vessel moves above the water – even if only by 5ft – its regulation comes under the jurisdiction of the Civil Aviation Authority, which issues licences to the captain of the hovercraft (applying the same rationale, the location from where the captain commands the vessel is referred to as a cockpit rather than a bridge). With 22,500 hours under his belt, Captain Peter Mulhern is thought to have traversed the Solent more often than anyone else alive. 'You have to be nimble and quick to counteract all the elements – crosswinds, tides, waves,' he says. 'You look ahead, to see where the gaps are in the waves. Every crossing is different. The vessels can usually sail in any winds up to Force 8.' Hovercraft crews are tight-knit – Peter worked his way up to captain after starting as a crew hand.

Advocates of hover travel are keen to point out that the hovercraft is in fact 'slower', in the sense of being less environmentally polluting, than you might think. Since the craft sits above the water surface, marine life is left to its own devices, undisturbed by the hull. The same case is made for those huge turbine fans, which, elevated behind the vessel, avoid any displacement of water.

the **Ryde Carnival** (⌀ rydecarnival.com) – the oldest carnival in the UK, dating back to the Jubilee of Queen Victoria in 1887 – but also **Ryde Arts** (⌀ rydearts.org), a year-round programme of exhibitions and events. The town's artistic bent is driving an application for Cittaslow (⌀ cittaslow.org) status, an international accolade accorded to communities of fewer than 50,000 residents which can demonstrate a critical mass of low-impact activities, ranging from community engagement to local produce, that can be visited on foot or by public transport. The movement emerged from the slow food phenomenon and more than 260 towns around the world have achieved the status.

Appley Park

⟡ friendsofappley.co.uk

The beautifully laid out woodlands of Appley Park unfold to the east of Ryde, above an extension of the town's promenade. Their design shows the hand of Sir Humphry Repton and represent the remaining segment of a much wider parkland he devised in 1796. Here you will find strands of ancient woodlands where some of the oaks have been in place for at least 400 years. Nearby, hard upon the seafront, stands the folly of Appley Tower, built in 1875. It's a striking building, which appears to have been built by an architect who was set the challenge of squeezing the most features into the smallest space. The result is something that resembles an oversized castle from a game of chess, with a ship's funnel attached: the tower boasts a turret, crenellated parapet, an oriel window overlooking the sea and an external staircase with much of the exterior cased in attractive dressed stone. Tours of the interior take place rarely, usually once a year on 22 June, which is loosely dedicated by the council as 'Appley Day', when fete-style activities take place in the park.

The woods also offer the chance to – in safety – climb an age-old oak. 'If you want to really appreciate a tree, then climbing one and dangling 50ft above the ground is a good way to do that,' says Paul McCathie, owner of **Goodleaf Tree Climbing** (⟡ goodleaf.co.uk). The tree in question is a magnificent 200-year-old English oak in Appley Park, standing just back from the sands. After a safety demonstration on how to pull yourself up using a harness, you're free to go. 'You pull yourself under your own steam,' says Paul. 'You're by yourself, unlike rock climbing where you are belayed to someone else. You have the tree to yourself.' Paul encourages anyone with an anxiety about heights to consider giving tree climbing a go. 'There's no pressure, you go at your own pace, you can set the goal where you want it – that can be just the first branch off the ground.

"The result is something that resembles an oversized castle from a game of chess, with a ship's funnel attached."

Just to the east of Appley Park is the small but family-friendly **Puckpool Park**, home to another of the Island coastal batteries, this one built in 1861. The remains are substantial and can be viewed from outside; it stands adjacent to more conventional family attractions such as swings, mini-golf and a tea house.

FOOD & DRINK

Chocolate Apothecary 7 Esplanade, PO33 2DY ☏ 01983 718292 ⌂ chocolateapothecary.
co.uk. Great coffee, cakes and petits fours in a sumptuous building that was once a
fishmongers. The atmospheric café oozes with original features, including Minton tiles
from 1861, delicate coving and Art Deco lamps of wrought iron and glazed green glass. The
handsome glass-topped wooden tables (infilled with coffee beans) offer a good vantage
point to gaze out across the Esplanade while rattan fans hanging from the ceiling throw in a
whiff of southeast Asia for good measure.

The Island Bakers Ryde Farmers' Market, Co-Op car park, Anglesey St, PO33 2SX
⌂ theislandbakers.com ☺ 08.30–12.30 Sat. Excellent local breads – sourdough, focaccia
and pastries; see box, opposite.

Number 64 64 George St, PO33 2AJ ☏ 01983 614071 ⌂ no64ryde.com ☺ Tue–Sat.
Right on the corner of George and Cross streets, this is another of Ryde's fine clutch of cafés.
Imaginative specials include Thai coconut and butternut squash soup.

The Wonky Goat 30 Union St, PO33 2DT ☏ 01983 716930 ⌂ thewonkygoat.co.uk. Snug
café selling the usual but good cakes and paninis along with charcuterie sharing boards and
fine coffee.

SHOPPING

Ryde has plenty of artistic talents whose work is well worth perusing. For sheer originality and
audacity, it is hard to beat the porcelain pottery created by **Sue Paraskeva** at her studio (22a
Green St, PO33 2QT ☏ 07968 336485 ⌂ sueparaskeva.co.uk; visits by appointment). Shallow
bowls and cups appear clamped together, like a bunch of mussels on the seashore, while
larger vessels have rakish splits or indented, uneven sides to them. This is achieved by the
simple process of throwing the softly moulded cup (before it hardens) on to the floor. These
are then fired in a natural gas kiln, which adds a haunting blue-white hue to the pottery.

Another artist, **Abi Wheeler** (114 High St, PO33 2HW ⌂ abiwheeler.com; visits by
appointment), grew up on the Isle of Wight and feels that the separation from the mainland,
in those distant days before the internet, helped to nurture distinctive and original talent
across the Island. Abi's work focuses on tactile materials such as hand-stitched quilts.

Bou Chic 2a Melville St, PO33 2AE ☏ 01983 614587 ⌂ bouchic.co.uk. A Ryde shop to its
core, stuffed with quirky, fashionable coats, jumpers, socks, bobble hats and crockery.

Pure Wight Soy Candles 60a Union St, PO33 2LG ☏ 01983 568344
⌂ purewightsoycandles.com. Run by Jenny Bull, a former aromatherapist. A wide range of
candles, scented with essential oils, and ceramic house tea lights, which use the waxy flakes
from soy beans and so represents a good use of a resource that would otherwise go to waste.
The soy wax also burns more cleanly and for longer than traditional candles.

THE ISLAND BAKERS

One of the most mouth-watering displays of pastry awaits at the **Ryde Farmers' Market**, held every Saturday in the Co-Op car park on Anglesey Street (☉ usually 08.30–12.30). The Island Bakers are John and Helen Fahy who produce chocolate swirls, croissants and almond brioche, while their trailer also sags with sourdough and baguettes. Recent innovations include pasties such as cinnamon buns, salted caramel cookies and IW honey and almond cakes.

John begins work most days at 02.00, though in the summer season he starts at 23.00 to meet demand. All bread is leavened and, unlike supermarket bread that takes just two hours to produce, the process takes three days. John sources his flour on the Island from Flourish Flour, produced by Matt Bowman in Cowes (Matt doesn't have a shop front but you are likely to find his flour among listed ingredients in many of the Island's slow-food places to eat), and is also an advocate of the Real Bread Campaign, which asserts that bread must be made without the use of artificial additives or processing aids. 'Supermarkets can sell a sourdough roll that isn't actually sourdough,' he says. 'Everything we make here takes time, I think it's important that the bread tastes of the grain. It's something to be proud of, it never gets boring.'

The couple have taken a roundabout journey to the Isle of Wight, where Helen has family connections. They met while working in the royal kitchens of Buckingham Palace and later both taught at Gordon Ramsay's cookery school. They are now happily settled on the Island. 'We both worked in London but there is a work-life balance that you need,' says John. 'When we finish work we can go on to a beach with the children. I like to sail. I can't think of a better place to be.'

John and Helen also sell their bakes around the Island and you will find their wares at Farmer Jack's, Brighstone Village Shop, The Deli at Yarmouth, the Food Hamper in Cowes, London House in Ventnor and The Farm Shop in Bembridge. They also sell their breads at Newport Farmers' Market (St Thomas's Square) on Fridays.

Ryde Bookshop 135 High St, PO33 2RJ ✆ 01983 565227 ⊘ ryde-bookshop.co.uk. A good independent choice for picking up books on local history and literature. As with many such bookshops, it's something of a Tardis and extends to the rear and upwards. Well worth a browse.

THE NORTHEAST COAST

The northeast shores of the Island have their own distinctive feel, discrete from the bustle of Ryde and Cowes. Always, there is a backdrop of classic yachts (as well as ferries and cargo ships) bobbing up and down in the Solent and pop into independent hotels and local shops where there is barely a national chain to be seen. Life seems to wash slowly over you in this part of the Island, just as the ebbing tide laps over the rocky shoreline at **Seaview**, a village only two miles east of Ryde but which provides an utterly serene contrast.

10 Seaview

🏠 **The Boathouse** (page 304), **Northbank Hotel** (page 304), **Seaview Hotel** (page 304)
⋏ **Priory Bay Yurts** (page 304)

It is really worth heaving yourself out of bed early one morning and strolling along the shoreline at Seaview, to understand why such an apparently unoriginal and self-evident name actually fits the village wonderfully well. As dawn eases its way through the twilight, look for bats flitting in and out from the nearby eaves of the graceful flint-built buildings that characterise the village. In the clear, still dawn half-light, these airborne mammals can seem surreal, rather like broken umbrellas being jerked up and down by an invisible hand. Lines of cormorants fly east along the Solent from their overnight roosts, honking geese following in their slipstream. It's a timeless scene – if you had to date it you might feel you have stepped back 100 years – and all that seems to be missing is a lady twirling a filigree-trim parasol while carrying a poodle under her arm, escorted by a wheezing, portly gentleman taking the sea air on doctor's orders.

A non-stop walk around Seaview takes perhaps ten minutes (you have little more to explore than an anti-clockwise loop starting on the High Street, which leads down to the Esplanade from where you turn back uphill along Seafield Road), but it would be easy to dawdle a whole day here, spending time in either of the two good hotels, the handful of cafés and two excellent shops, all of which are centred on or just immediately off, the High Street. Some visitors come for a week and get no further than here on the Island.

The coast path runs around the edge of Seaview, often tracking a sea wall that keeps the Solent at bay, and there are uninterrupted views of Ryde East Sands and the shingle-sand mixture of Springvale Beach. The defences, for now at least, keep the sea from overwashing the smattering of new and rather exposed houses that sit hard above the beach. Follow the coast path a few hundred yards west from Seaview and you'll come to the **Alan Hersey Nature Reserve** (∂ herseynaturereserve.org.uk/birds), named after a former local councillor who passionately cared for the local environment. The woodland is small but runs inland alongside a reed-fringed lake and is an enchanting place, especially on an early still morning when, if you tread quietly, you may catch a green woodpecker foraging on the ground. To the dismay of today's local wildlife lovers there's a proposal – vigorously opposed – to convert the reserve into a yacht park.

A narrow coastal road and sea wall separate the reserve from the adjacent **Seaview duver**. A duver (pronounced to rhyme with 'cover') is a geological feature comprising a spit of sand and shingle and this one spreads out in rectangular fashion on the seaward side of the sea wall. Both the reserve and duver are part of a Special Protection Area, an environmental accolade awarded to species-rich places, and you will almost certainly see herons and little egrets. In addition, nine species of bat have been recorded here. The duver provides an important habitat for sandwich, roseate and little and common terns, along with wintering ringed plover, teal and black-tailed godwit. Had you been here in 1887 you would have had something more grisly to gaze upon, for that year the steamer *Bembridge* struck a whale near St Helens Fort (page 118). The unfortunate cetacean was exhibited in a tent on the beach at Seaview.

The village of **Nettlestone** sits on higher ground inland, less than a mile to the southeast of Seaview. While it has no sights as such – the B3330 passes through its heart and sees its fair share of traffic – like its neighbour, this village feels as if it has a gentle, easy-going rhythm. If you want something to do, visit the Mermaid Bar at the Isle of Wight Distillery (formerly the Wishing Well pub) on the village's northwestern fringe, where you can indulge in a tasting tour of the new gin distillery (page 114).

¶¶ FOOD & DRINK

The Boathouse Springvale Rd, PO34 5AW ✆ 01983 810616 ⬦ theboathouseiow.co.uk. This pub with rooms enjoys a graceful setting overlooking Ryde East Sands, at the end of the coastal strip that links Seaview to Puckpool Park. Food is of a good standard and ranges from ciabattas with Island cheddar and caramelised red onion marmalade to main meals of sea bass, plus the likes of summer berry pavlovas for pudding.

Lily's Café 15 High St, PO34 5ES ✆ 01983 617367 ◼f LilysCoffeeShop. Bright and breezy café at the top of High Street, serving excellent Island roasted coffee, sandwiches and pizzas, and a good range of cakes to provide calorific refuelling when you come off the beach.

A walk between Nettlestone & Seaview

✷ OS Explorer map 29; start: the Mermaid Bar at the Isle of Wight Distillery, Pondwell Hill, Nettlestone PO33 1PX; ♥ SZ619912; 3½ miles; easy

T his is a low-key but appealing circular route around and between the adjacent villages of Nettlestone and Seaview that combines wildlife-watching opportunities with pleasing vistas of the sea. Bus #8 will drop you at the start point, the Mermaid Bar (you will still hear this stop referred to by its former incarnation, the Wishing Well pub).

1 From the pub, walk downhill for 200yds and bear right along a footpath where the road turns left. Soon afterwards, this path bears left to meet a track coming in from the right. Keep ahead for 400yds until you reach a T-junction of paths. Turn left to cross a stream before turning immediately left along a field edge; here you have a good chance of spotting a buzzard or a kestrel. The path then winds its way slightly uphill as it climbs towards Nettlestone.

2 Cross the B3330 with care and dog-leg into Priory Drive (which in turn curves immediately to the right; don't walk down Caws Avenue). Keep ahead, with housing on your left, until you all but bump into the Priory Bay Hotel. Bear left along the path, which leads after 600yds into Ferniclose Road. This turns into Gully Road and drops you down on Seagrove Bay. This is a vast stretch of deep golden sand and at any time other than high tide you can walk along the beach all the way to Seaview. If the tide is up, you'll have to follow the waymarked alternative coast path (you'll find this just a few yards back up from the slipway), which runs along Pier Road for three-quarters of a mile and brings you on to High Street at Seaview.

3 Walk down High Street to the sea and then turn left. Just past the yacht club, take the wobbly, uneven footpath (R91) which makes a dart for the sea and provides superb views towards Ryde.

4 Continue along the sea wall for 400yds until Salterns Road comes in from the left. Turn up the road for 300yds and then bear right into Pond Lane. Follow this to the entrance to a holiday park. The path from here is easy to miss – it skirts to the immediate left of the park entrance

The Mermaid Bar Isle of Wight Distillery, Pondwell Hill, Nettlestone PO33 1PX ✆ 01983 613653 ⬡ isleofwightdistillery.com. Mission control for the Island's first gin distillery (see box, page 116), this venue operates both as a gin joint and a pub. The menu features simple, wholesome pub fare – think Italian stone-baked pizzas, local cheese and fish, and brioche burgers. The small team also offer gin tasting and talks, and you can sample other liver-ticklers in the distillery range, including a salty vodka and a Navy-strength rum (a percentage of each sale goes towards the restoration of HMS *Victory*). The terrace is one of as you approach and climbs up the modest incline of Nettlestone Hill before turning right along R114, which runs parallel to, but is shielded from, the B3330 and gives views down the Barnsley Valley to the Solent. Where the path rejoins the pavement, follow it back to the Mermaid Bar, which is clearly visible uphill.

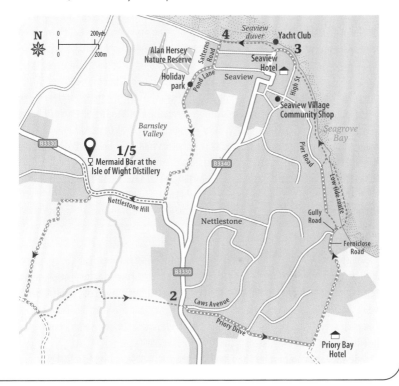

the Island's unsung prime spots for a drink with a view, with vistas sweeping down across the Barnsley Valley to the Solent; when the long nights draw in you can retreat to a sofa by the log fire.

Seaview Hotel High St, PO34 5EX ✆ 01983 612711 ⏱ seaviewhotel.co.uk. With its cosy lounge and friendly bar, the Seaview Hotel is the social hub of the village and has established a reputation for fine food. Independently owned and blissfully chain free, it exudes charm from the minute you step across the terrace and through the front door into

GIVE ME BEER, GIVE ME WINE, GIVE ME GIN

What do you get if you cross a vineyard with a brewery? The answer, perhaps uniquely, and typically for the Isle of Wight, is a gin and whisky distillery. The Island's first distillery, home to Mermaid Gin, is the dream of Conrad Gauntlett, who founded Rosemary's Vineyard in Ryde (page 97) and his lifelong friend and brewer Xavier Baker of Goddard's Brewery.

As with many such enterprises, the gin started as a cash-flow sideline while the whisky was laid down. The whisky, incidentally, uses local barley from Goddard's Brewery and, having been washed, is now maturing in charred white wine and bourbon barrels (though there is no date yet for the release of the first malt).

For now, the gin remains the focus – it features ten botanicals, three of which come from the Island: Boadicea hops (added for bitterness), elderflower and rock samphire. The last of these is collected from the southern shores of the Island and give the gin its distinctive smell and taste. 'A local name for rock samphire is "the mermaid's kiss"', explains Ginnie Taylor, the distillery's marketing manager. 'It has a pungent smell and it was said that shipwrecked sailors knew that if they could smell it then they were close to shore and near to safety.

Mission control for the enterprise is the Mermaid Bar at the Isle of Wight Distillery (page 114), which has taken over the old Wishing Well pub, on the B3330, on the northwest of the village of Nettlestone. You can drop by, take a tour, enjoy a sample and, should you find it hard to drag yourself away, conduct your own research at the bar.

the conservatory. Dinner at the Seaview is something of a treat. You can choose between the main restaurant, the Pump Bar and Aquitania, the last of these placing a strong emphasis on fish. The bar is often bustling and offers top-class classics such as fish and chips and burgers, while the excellent main restaurant is the only one on the Island to boast a Bib Gourmand. Three courses are typically priced at £28 and can include hake and mussels with a curry velouté, plaice with prawn tortellini, and locally shot woodpigeon.

Seaview Village Community Shop High St, PO34 5ES ✆ 01983 616487. The Isle of Wight's first community shop opened in the winter of 2017. Stocked with Island produce, the shop has quickly become a focal point of the village. The shop stocks a wide range of goods, from basics like bread and jam to local cheeses and more exotic treats, such as colourful pasta and biscotti from Italy.

11 St Helens

Boasting what is claimed to be the second largest village green in England, St Helens essentially comprises several lines of houses running alongside the open space, which is uncluttered bar a football pitch and a cricket pitch. The original village church was built on the seafront 800 years ago and you will still find its remains here. The old church's location says much about the past importance and size of the village: the once much larger parish included a Cluniac priory (a 12th-century monastic order that stubbornly refused to be subservient to local feudal lords) to the north (now the Priory Hotel), while its straggling edges extended to the periphery of what is now Ryde.

The sloping green stretches for around half a mile east to west and a quarter of a mile north to south, interspersed with minor access roads. You'll find a well-stocked bookshop, **The Goose** (Lower Green Rd, PO33 1TS ✐ 01983 874063 ⌖ thegoosebooks.com), on its southern perimeter, while just around the corner is the studio and gallery of artist **Becky Samuelson** (Kempsford, Hilbre Rd, P033 1PJ ✐ 01983 873351 ⌖ beckysamuelsonfinearts.co.uk). Becky's paintings capture landscapes you are bound to encounter during a visit to the island, such as wildflowers along field edges and rockpools. 'Sometimes I think there must be more artists per square inch on the Isle of Wight than anywhere else,' she says. 'We all share the same wonderful light. The geology is so different that you go to another part of the Island and you have a completely different landscape to paint.' Unlike many artists, Becky flits between oils, watercolours and acrylics. 'I find it interesting to have all the options and opportunities they present.'

To reach the sea from St Helens, you head east along the green until you pick up signs for 'the Duver' (logically enough, this is accessed along Duver Road). A short walk downhill along the lane and the top of St Helens Common leads to sandy grasslands that back the duver (there are coast path signposts to guide you). On the way, if you cast your eye on the ground, you may see the black-and-yellow-striped Argiope spider, which springs itself on unwary summer grasshoppers. The sea laps up against **St Helens Duver**, which lines the northwest banks of the mouth of the River Eastern Yar and features pebbly sand that gives way inland to watery meadows. The north end of the bay is bookended by the tall, slender remains of St Helens Church. Built around 1220, the church eventually became unsafe and was closed for use in 1703 and bricked up. The original tower still remains and has been a well-known seamark for centuries. The new church was built further inland in the 18th century. In 1805, Admiral Lord Nelson's fleet gathered off St Helens to limber up before setting sail for Cadiz and the Battle of Trafalgar. It is commonly accepted that Nelson's last view of England was of St Helens, a fact recently commemorated by a plaque now pinned to the old church tower.

The rockpools exposed within the limestone ledges at low tide are among the best on the Island and you have every chance of seeing dogfish purses, whelk egg cases, cuttlefish shells and shore crabs.

Just offshore and ankle deep in the Solent is **St Helens Fort**, built between 1867 and 1880 to protect Portsmouth from French invasion. The fort is privately owned with no public access to it but has its own artesian well for drinking water. Once a year, at the lowest tide of the summer, there is a mass walk from the beach out to the fort and back, when the causeway, upon which the original materials to build the fort were carried out from the shore, can be walked upon.

₩ FOOD & DRINK

Ganders Restaurant Upper Green Rd, PO33 1UQ ✆ 01983 872014 ♖ ganders.co.uk. A relaxed atmosphere belies the high quality of dishes served here. A small but varied range of options drawn from locally produced and sourced ingredients, from pies to seafood paellas and local ice cream. Enjoys a picturesque setting, on the higher side of the sloping village green.

THE CALEDON GUEST HOUSE

Situated in beautiful Cowes, we offer the perfect mix of a boutique-style hotel with the friendly, welcoming service of a B&B. With comfortable, spacious bedrooms and a delicious breakfast freshly cooked using local produce.

59 Mill Hill Road   ✉ thecaledon@gmail.com
Cowes, IoW   ☐☐   ♖ the-caledon.co.uk
PO31 7EG   ✆ 01983 293599

SIR MAX AITKEN MUSEUM

*Explore this unique museum in
Cowes, home to three centuries of
yachting and maritime history.*

This magnificent 18th century building, once a Ratsey & Lapthorn sailmakers loft, was converted and restored by Sir Max Aitken in the late 1940s. Sir Max flew in the Battle of Britain and after the war he developed a keen interest in yachting. He founded the London International Boat Show and co-founded the Cowes Torquay Powerboat Race. In 1979, Sir Max created the museum to preserve his remarkable collection of nautical memorabilia, which has become a tribute to his exceptional life and achievements.

83 High Street
Cowes
Isle of Wight PO31 7AJ

🖉 sirmaxaitkenmuseum.org
🖉 01983 293800
✉ sirmaxaitkenmuseum@gmail.com

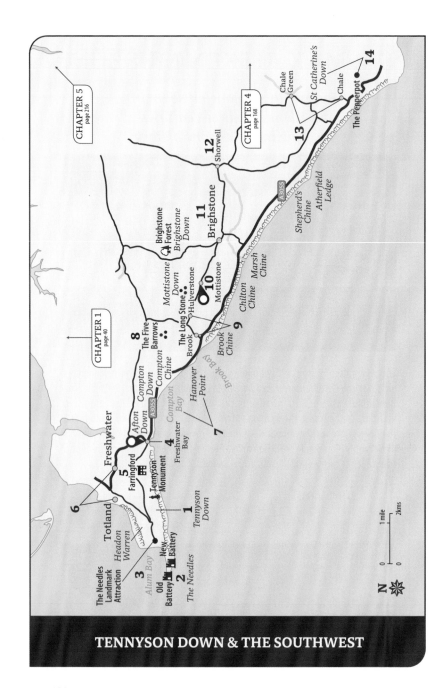

TENNYSON DOWN & THE SOUTHWEST

3
TENNYSON DOWN & THE SOUTHWEST

'An earthquake poised in mid-explosion' is how the late Poet Laureate Sir John Betjeman described West Wight – a term covering much of the area in this chapter. Stand high above the Needles, the incisor-shaped chalk pinnacles that punch up from the Solent on the Island's western extremity, and you'll realise he was on to something. Shudderingly steep chalk cliffs, whaleback hills, golden beaches and surfer-friendly seas… the southwest corner of the Isle of Wight delivers the images that promote the Island's charms far and wide on postcards and tourist brochures.

This 'earthquake' landscape is centred on the extraordinary drama of **Tennyson Down**, which resembles a vast, natural ski jump rearing up from sea level, though West Wight spreads further, extending to the west, east and north. Explore the area and you will see valleys, coast and undulating downland all bunching up against one another. Look one way and the land rises like a breaking wave, while in another direction the drama continues as the Island plummets abruptly into the English Channel, collapsing into narrow gullies, known as chines, that rush to the sea. Here, the waters turn the colour of milk chocolate as wave after wave thumps into those chalk cliffs. Everything appears disjointed, as if tossed about by huge tectonic convulsions.

Yet this great natural spectacle stands in vivid contrast to the manmade sights of the area. For some visitors, the military history and Victoriana, candy-floss stalls, the nodding donkey appearance of a chairlift – when set against the spectacle of the Needles – leave the landscape aesthetically smudged. Put this point to an Islander, however, and you will generally elicit a puzzled look. For most of them, the natural beauty and kiss-me-quick atmosphere are two sides of the same coin and have rubbed along together in harmony for more than a century.

It's no surprise that the southwest of the Island is one of the most popular destinations for visitors. The region features must-see sights

> **ℹ TOURIST INFORMATION**
>
> There is no tourist office in the area but you can pick up literature at most sights, such as Farringford House (page 139) and Dimbola (page 136), which operate as de facto, informal centres (though don't expect staffed information points). Noticeboards along the downs can be weather-beaten but are generally helpful, with maps pointing out what you are looking at and information detailing features of historical interest.

such as the crumbling coastline above **Compton Bay**, the roller-coaster ridges of **Afton and Compton downs** and glorious **Freshwater Bay**, encircled by cliffs and distinguished by a bulging tide. Yet this corner of the Island can also feel remote and ancient. Walk or heave yourself up by mountain bike along the chalk backbone of **Mottistone Down** and **Brighstone Forest** and you will stumble upon important Neolithic standing stones and Bronze Age long barrows, and be accompanied by rare birdsong, such as that of the haunting nightjar.

In between, among the foothills and folds of these downs and set back from the sea, are some of the Island's most charming villages, such as **Brighstone**, **Brook** and **Hulverstone**, where you can wander along ancient holloways and nose around architecturally impressive churches. The sea too is arguably at its most glorious and accessible along the southwest coast, thanks to the coast path that consistently provides exhilarating views.

Wildlife lovers are kept on their toes here with peregrine falcons regular visitors to Tennyson Down and Farringford House. In spring and summer, the lower cliffs at Freshwater are one of the few remaining breeding sites in southern England for guillemots.

GETTING THERE & AROUND
WALKING & CYCLING

A hike up Tennyson Down is not just the best walk in this corner of the Isle of Wight but arguably the most spectacular hike on the entire Island. From the brow, you will notice the **Coastal Path** sidling its way above the beaches of the south coast, all the way past Freshwater Bay, Compton Bay and funnelling downhill toward Chale, some 12 miles east. Elsewhere, footpaths invitingly trace through woodlands and forest of the higher downs and coastal margins. These include the Freshwater Way which weaves along the eastern banks of the River Western Yar, from Freshwater Bay north to Yarmouth, and the Tennyson Trail which contours along the downland ridges from west to east; meanwhile, the aforementioned Coastal Path provides more or less unmitigated access to the Island's edges.

For cyclists, the opportunities on this side of the Island are superb. The upper reaches of the River Yar offer easy, level riding, with the chance to drink in views of the downs, while the more energetic can enjoy some

DARK & CLEAR SKIES ABOVE

Despite the area's popularity, the triangle between Freshwater Bay, Compton Down and – a little further east – Niton (page 174) is the focus of a bid to attain Dark Skies Park status. This would see street lights turned off late in the evening and the impact of light pollution taken into account with any new housing or business developments. A lack of light will benefit wildlife, which can be confused by bright white lights, and enhance the tranquillity of the area. In the absence of light pollution, the thousands of stars revealed at night would also attract stargazers and provide the opportunity for night-time wildlife rambles and activities such as bat detecting. The hope is that this status will be conferred before the mid 2020s.

If your visit coincides with clear night-time skies, you should seriously consider briefly forsaking that snug pub and instead drinking in the heavens above. Any of the car parks along the Military Road are good options: from here you not only have the sky to behold but also the inky, undulating sea and contrasting white chalk cliffs to enjoy. You could even take a short walk up Tennyson Down (bring a torch) and head for the first bench above Freshwater Bay (beyond here, the cliffs become sheer and, in the dark, self-evidently hazardous). Here, on a still night, it seems as if the entire firmament is filled with twinkling lights; as your sense of hearing takes over from sight, the gushing, sloshing and lapping of the sea float up from below.

Dark Sky status has of course been awarded to other parts of the UK but playful weather will often, literally, dampen expectations and dilute the experience. In the Isle of Wight, optimism that the dark skies can be more co-operative appears well founded. I spoke to Joel Bateman of the AONB, about the perils of the unco-operative British weather and how it might thwart Dark Sky ambitions. 'The advantage we have over some other areas of the UK that have Dark Sky status is that our weather is generally better than elsewhere in the UK,' he said, struggling to keep the grin off his face. 'Having statistically less cloud and rain helps.'

You can follow developments at the appropriately named Dark Wight Skies website (⊘ darkwightskies.com).

thrilling off-road cycling along the **Tennyson Trail** which is around 12 miles long and stretches all the way from Carisbrooke to Alum Bay (but doesn't actually go up Tennyson Down). The Tennyson Trail actually represents the dramatic crescendo of the **Chalk Extreme Trail**, which heads up over Compton Down along a steep and rutted path and levels off before descending through the Freshwater Bay Golf Club. For cycle rentals, see page 28.

PUBLIC TRANSPORT

The area is well served by **buses**. The key routes are the #7 and #12 between Newport and Alum Bay, both of which call at Freshwater, Totland and the Needles (#12 also stops at Brighstone). The FYT bus (⊘ fytbus.org.uk) also operates three routes in this area, connecting Freshwater, Yarmouth and Totland. The summer-only Island Coaster (⊘ islandbuses.info) stops at Freshwater Bay and the Needles on its coast-to-coast route. One bus service is in effect a tourist attraction in its own right and really should not be missed. The open-top Needles Breezer (⊘ islandbuses.info/needles-breezer-probably-best-bus-ride-britain) runs from March to November and trundles between many points of interest in this chapter, including the Dimbola Museum, Alum Bay and the Old and New Batteries.

FROM TENNYSON DOWN TO FRESHWATER BAY

Just about every visitor to the island will gravitate to the extraordinary beauty of Tennyson Down, which in turn is something of a gateway to other adjacent and equally special places of interest. At sea level you'll find Freshwater Bay's vast shingle banks and sea stacks. On rather higher ground, Tennyson Down – and the Island itself – slips away to the crumbling chalk pinnacles of the Needles. Here, amid shudderingly high cliffs and eye-popping sea stacks, you'll encounter important military history at the Old and New Batteries. The area is also historically of great cultural importance for it was called home by both Alfred, Lord Tennyson and the pioneering woman photographer Julia Margaret Cameron. Their exquisite former abodes are open for nosing around. By way of contrast, but of arguably equal cultural significance, this is also where Jimi Hendrix famously, if briefly, laid his hat.

RINGFENCING THE DEAD

Near the eastern edge of the down, about 800yds from Freshwater Bay along the Coastal Path, just as the ascent stars to kick in, you can discern the lumps and bumps of a long mortuary enclosure (φ SZ 336855). Aligned east–west over an area of 258ft² and surrounded by a bank 16ft wide and 9.8 inches high, this oval earthwork is, as the name suggests, associated with human burials. The limited excavation carried out dates it to around 2800–2200BC, in the early or middle Neolithic periods. Such sites are very rare in the UK, with only around 35 recorded across the country (mostly concentrated in Essex and Suffolk) – the one here is the only recorded example on the Isle of Wight, and the most southerly in the UK.

Entrance is thought to have been from the south – that is, from where the cliff edge is today but where the downs, at one time, would have extended further out into the sea. Just who was buried here is unclear, but they would have been held in high esteem, perhaps a tribal elder or leader. Owen Cambridge, of the former Archaeology Discovery Centre at Fort Victoria, believes that burials here would have been deeply symbolic, representing the ascent of the deceased to another, higher place. 'There may well have been an audience of hundreds, positioned down [at sea level] at Freshwater,' he says. 'The rising downs and chamber would have been out of sight, in the clouds.'

1 TENNYSON DOWN

The southwestern corner of the Island is dominated by the stirring contours of Tennyson Down, named after the eponymous former Poet Laureate, Alfred, Lord Tennyson, who lived at nearby Farringford House for 40 years. Beginning at sea level immediately to the west of Freshwater Bay, the down rises inexorably for a mile to a 482ft-high brow before descending gently and levelling off as it heads towards its dramatic crescendo in the form of the Needles, the westernmost point of the Island. Along the downs' entirety, its southern flanks are guillotined by the sheerest cliffs imaginable, where kestrels hover close by.

Exploring the down can feel like navigating the deck of a ship that is cresting a wave, for while the land rises remorselessly up from Freshwater Bay, it also tilts this way and that. Ravens lurch upwards, sideways in kite-like manoeuvres; in great contrast, the northern flanks slip away into bucolic pockets of scrub and deciduous woodlands of oak, sycamore, beech holly and hazel, where thorny scrub has been left unchecked to mature into hedgerows and woodland. The downland is extremely varied with little coppices here and there and thick clumps of heather and gorse, which break up what could otherwise be a uniform landscape of cattle-nibbled grass. You will occasionally see horseriders galloping its broad bridleways.

The initial goal when walking Tennyson Down is to reach the **Tennyson Monument**, a plinth topped with a marble Celtic cross found at the summit of the down. The monument, erected in 1897, is

A walk up Tennyson Down

❀ OS Explorer map 29; start: footpath behind Dimbola Museum & Galleries, House Terrace Ln, Freshwater Bay PO40 9QE ♀ SZ346856; 3¼ miles (one-way); medium, with a steepish initial climb

The hike up Tennyson Down is *the* classic Island walk and is accordingly much-loved by visitors. For big horizons, wide open spaces, wildlife and spectacular coastal drama, it has very few equals in the UK. Steer clear of sheer cliff edges.

1 From the Dimbola Museum, turn left along Gate Lane and take the first left along the footpath signposted for Tennyson Down. Bear half right to begin the ascent, which is moderately steep, over open ground.

2 After about half a mile you reach a line of trees and hedgerows and a conveniently located bench, from where you can enjoy the first outstanding views to the east across Freshwater Bay, the Military Road and as far as St Catherine's Down, some 12 miles distant.

3 Continue uphill for a further 1¼ miles, passing the amorphous bumps on the seaward side that represent a mortuary enclosure (see box, page 125) to reach the **Tennyson Monument**. The view is now truly 360 degrees, taking in multiple horizons with hills and downland piggybacking their way into the distance. The New Forest bulges up against the Solent and the

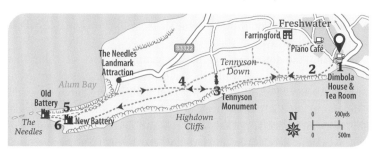

both an unofficial beacon for sailors and a tribute to the poet. Some elegiac lines from Tennyson's poem, *Crossing the Bar*, are inscribed on the base:

> Sunset and evening star,
> And one clear call for me!
> And may there be no moaning of the bar,
> When I put out to sea.

port of Yarmouth is suddenly so small you may have to narrow your eyes to find it. When you do, you are likely to also spot the ferries chugging back and forth to Lymington. To the east, the chines and bays of the south coast rise up abruptly to the undulating downs; turn your gaze west and the sheer scale of Tennyson Down becomes apparent, with the land sweeping away for a further two miles before dipping out of sight. Everywhere you look is criss-crossed with inviting-looking footpaths that may whet your appetite for further hikes on another day. To the south, there is nothing but open water. Highdown Cliff drops some 328ft vertically to the sea here, so keep any little people on a tight leash.

4 Continue westwards from the monument, either following the broad bridleway or wandering as you choose – just keep heading west. As the down descends it becomes more of a heathland, dotted with gorse and small coppices. Paths fork and merge, offering the choice of following the south, middle or north parts of the downs as the mood takes (they all eventually converge amid pockets of scrub and gorse at a line of hedgerows, which you pass through by a gate).

5 In one last crescendo, the downland's trailing edges sweep upwards once more and, eventually, you see some private houses emerge. Bear to the left (south) of these to go through a series of gates. Suddenly, the Isle of Wight comes to a grinding halt before you, collapsing on its southern haunches into sheer white cliffs that taper to a pin-shaped headland which, in turn, collapses into **the Needles**. Despite the crowds that flock to nearby Alum Bay and the military batteries, here you are likely to be accompanied only by the occasional raven hopping behind you at a distance, sizing up your packed lunch – or possibly you – with a beady eye.

6 Having reached the end of the road, you can either retrace your steps to Freshwater Bay or follow the headland paths a little north to reach the New and Old Batteries (page 129). If you don't fancy the walk back to Freshwater, simply follow the road that winds downhill from the batteries to reach The Needles Landmark Attraction above Alum Bay, where you can pick up the #7 bus to Yarmouth or Newport, or the Needles Breezer back to Dimbola Museum & Galleries.

The 'bar' in question is a treacherous sandbar, which, along with its adjacent shallow waters, ferry masters must navigate on their journey to the mainland. It lies in the Solent, to the north of the downs, and can be seen easily at low tide. You can almost imagine spotting Tennyson here too, his ghost pacing the sweeping downs, wrapped in his signature cape and sporting his trademark broad-brimmed hat. Never short of an apt turn of phrase, Tennyson described the air found upon the downs as being worth 'sixpence a pint'.

The memorial is just 1½ miles from Freshwater Bay but the down tapers westwards for nearly two more miles as it merrily roller-coasters its way to the horizon. At the down's furthest reaches lie the three sea stacks of the Needles. The Needles are actually the western crescendo of the band of chalk that runs like a backbone through the heart of the Island, from Culver Cliff above Sandown Bay (24 miles east). Hauntingly, the chalk ridge doesn't actually stop at the Needles but continues, submerged, to the Isle of Purbeck in Dorset, which you can just about pick out on a clear day. At one time the ridge even extended to Old Harry Rocks, some 20 miles across the water. When this ridge was breached and drowned, around 7,000 years ago, the Solent River was formed, creating the Island. There is said to be much drama underground, too – if only you could see it. A mortuary enclosure has been identified (see box, page 125) and even more inaccessible is a series of caves at the base of the cliffs, which are the preserve of specialist wet-caving expedition clubs. These include Neptune's Cave (200ft deep), Bat Cave (90ft deep) and Roe's Hall (believed to be 600ft high).

2 THE NEEDLES

Rising to around 100ft at the Island's most westerly point, these three strikingly vertical sea stacks are arguably the Isle of Wight's most iconic landmark. The result of the heavy folding of chalk, the stacks of hard chalk that remain are extremely resistant to erosion. They attained their current appearance during a storm in 1764 when a larger fourth column, known as Lot's Wife, collapsed, leaving behind the pinnacles we see today. Remarkably, a 110ft-tall lighthouse stands proud, at the base of the westernmost pinnacle; a helipad was added in 1987 to allow emergency access. The lighthouse replaced an earlier attempt at a beacon, which was built on Tennyson Down but suffered from the same fate as other earlier warning lights on the Island, in that it was positioned too high and often enveloped in fog (page 167). The current lighthouse is under constant threat of following the chalk coat tails of the Island into the sea and requires constant monitoring and occasional underpinning with reinforced concrete.

Even if you've come to the Needles to take in the natural beauty, you can't fail to notice the leftover footprint of the military in the form of **The Needles Old Battery and New Battery** (National Trust). A rather surreal combination of Victorian coastal defences and a secret rocket site, the batteries are worth exploring and their appeal reaches beyond just that of the hard-core military buff. (Note that the railings below the New Battery provide the best unimpeded and free view of the Needles.)

The **Old Battery** dates to the 1860s and is another one of the Island's Palmerston Follies, built to defend Portsmouth's naval ships against French incursions that never materialised (see box, page 16). The guns you see today were actually retrieved from the seabed of Scratchell's Bay some 300ft below – in 1903 the guns were deemed to be no longer useful and so were simply shoved over the cliffs and largely forgotten about. They stayed on the seabed until the 1980s when the National Trust arranged for their recovery and they were hauled up and returned to the Parade Ground. You can get a good view of the Needles from the end of the Parade Ground, where there is also a wheelchair-accessible viewing platform. For an even closer and dizzying view, go deep through the downs and head along the underground tunnel beneath the perimeter fence. Although the Old Battery was superseded by the New Battery, it had an important part to play in both world wars and the stories of some of the soldiers based here are now on display; you can also enjoy access through the underground tunnel to the searchlight emplacement.

Further up the headland on High Down above the Old Battery, you reach the **New Battery**, which was built in the 1890s. The rationale for constructing a new battery was the need to accommodate a generation of heavier guns – the fear was that were they to be positioned in the original battery, their weight might cause the cliffs to collapse. The headland is a thrillingly elemental place and a not-so-gentle reminder that the elements can even damage the landscapes of southern Britain. In November 2019, wind gusts of 109.4mph pummelled the Needles – winds above 90mph are infrequent but far from rare.

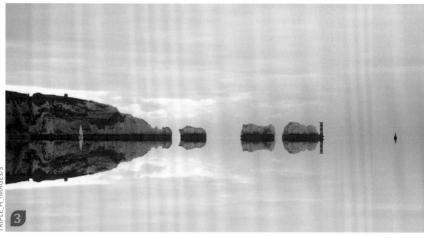

This was the site of a top-secret UK operation in the 1950s and 1970s that tested space rockets. The Black Knight was the earlier of the two rockets and was designed to test the effect on a ballistic missile of re-entry into the earth's atmosphere. The Black Arrow was designed to put a satellite in orbit. Neither was actually fired on the Island, though the first test runs of the rocket engines were conducted here. In the underground rooms of the New Battery, which were the nerve centre of this slightly improbable-sounding operation, there are models of the two rockets and of *Prospero*, which was the first satellite launched by the UK (on a Black Arrow rocket) in 1971. Some of the rooms have been recreated as they would have looked when the top-secret tests were being carried out.

3 ALUM BAY

The Needles and their adjacent headland collapse to the north into Alum Bay, where more geological drama awaits. Even the name hints at the geological origins, for 'Alum' refers to pyrites and their by-products. Gone are the whiter-than-white chalk cliffs with their gloss finish, replaced by crumbling walls of multi-coloured sands – 21 swirling bands of sands and clays have been identified here, twisted and exposed by deeply ancient folds and contortions of the earth's crust.

The striations on the cliff face represent some 150 million years of geology, though the precise timescales of the contortions that created what you see today will probably remain forever a secret. The cliffs have been wrestled into what is known as a syncline, a kind of 'inside-out' geology where the youngest rocks are actually embedded the deepest in the folds of rock (typically an exposed cliff or mountain reveals younger rocks at the surface, the older rocks at its heart).

Some 70 million years ago, the seabed was pushed up to a point where it became exposed and eroded before another, unfathomably vast, combination of geological upheaval and rising seas saw it dragged beneath the water once again. Over time, the rocks settled in shallower seas where sands and clays were then laid down. Some ten million years later, movement in the bedrock caused these sediments to be pushed nearly vertically to form the multi-coloured cliffs that are visible today. Another visually striking consequence of such contortions is that the layers of rock are more vertical than horizontal.

◀ **1** Tennyson Monument. **2** Headon Warren. **3** The Needles.

The sands are made of three minerals – quartz, felspar and mica. In their pure state they are white, with richer colours produced through contamination by other minerals and by oxidisation such as red-iron oxide and yellow limonite. You'll see striking variations of red, yellow, black, green and white within the cliffs; only blue is noticeably absent.

Since at least the Victorian era, generations of visitors have come and collected or bought these sands in distinctive glass jars. Once upon a time you would have gathered the sands yourself; today you'll have to pay for it at **The Needles Landmark Attraction** (New Rd, Alum Bay PO39 0JD ⌀ theneedles.co.uk ☺ all year but weather-dependent), a confection of amusement stalls and Victorian entertainment which sits at the top of the cliffs. Staff, aware of the need for a more sustainable and environmental approach these days, scour the beach in the autumn to collect the sand that has fallen from the cliffs in landslips.

"There's a striking contrast between the bustle of entertainment and the thrilling natural beauty of the landscape."

There's a striking contrast between the bustle of entertainment and the thrilling natural beauty of the landscape in which the attraction stands and it all adds up to a slightly disorienting experience, one where nature meets Victoriana. One of the most striking features of the Isle of Wight is how magnificent landscapes stand shoulder to shoulder with popular and traditional seaside attractions and the Needles (along with Sandown Bay; page 255) is where the collision of these two worlds is most powerfully felt. Where else could you take in a superb coastal seascape, walk through time beneath cliffs that span 150 million years of geology, then visit a sweet factory and take – the ultimate memory maker – a chairlift down to Alum Bay?

You may find the most appealing element to the attraction is this chairlift, which funnels its lines and guy wires through what resembles a nodding donkey from a coal pit head and then wobbles its passengers precipitously down to the bay. The vertical height is 167ft but, with just a metal barrier keeping you in your seat (the chairs are exposed to the elements rather than sealed pods), this can feel higher. The actual distance travelled is some 820ft and this gives you plenty of time to take in the view. The Needles fill the frame and, hunkering below the vast cliffs of Tennyson Down, the bay itself is extremely picturesque, with its shallow waters performing a passable imitation of the Caribbean on a sunny day. Down on the beach, don't forget to look upwards at the startlingly collapsed cliff face you have just descended (you may be

THE ISLE OF WIGHT – ON A PAR WITH THE OKAVANGO DELTA?

Around 141,000 inhabitants call the Isle of Wight home, which sounds like quite a lot of people. Yet in 2019 the Island's communities and landscapes were awarded UNESCO Biosphere Reserve status, an elite designation that places them, in a technical and administrative sense at least, on a par with the Okavango Delta in Botswana, Uluru in Australia and Mount Vesuvius in Italy. Just six other such reserves exist in the United Kingdom.

While it's a bit of a stretch to say the Island is the equal of such world-famous places, the accolade does suggest that the Isle of Wight is taking similar steps to those areas when it comes to environmental innovation. UNESCO, the cultural arm of the United Nations, praised the combination of community engagement and economic activity, which it deemed sympathetic to the Island's diverse range of landscapes.

Key to biosphere status is the way in which a local population interacts with that environment. A biosphere is not an uninhabited area; to fulfil the criteria, people *must* live in the area. In practice, this means that economic activity on the Island – which ranges from ecotourism to a strong manufacturing sector and local supply chains in marine industries, aerospace, plus a healthy level of self-employment and micro-businesses – does not operate in isolation from the natural environment in which it is based. 'Nowhere is perfect, nor can it be,' says Ian Boyd of Arc Consulting, who was the driving force behind the campaign for the Island's biosphere status. 'What makes the Isle of Wight a credible biosphere reserve is how we work together to face the challenges that are ahead of us. Biosphere reserves provide a framework for projects that improve people's lives and protect the environment in a sustainable way. We have shown UNESCO that we have the right mix to meet the social and economic needs of our populations while ensuring the needs of wildlife are also met.'

The biosphere has a core and a buffer zone. The richest biodiversity is found in the core zone and this covers most of the coast, along with the estuarine landscape around Shalfleet and Newtown in the north; the buffer zone features more human activity and covers much of the hinterland of West Wight, the Arreton Valley and the downlands north of Ventnor.

Essentially, this all means that independent, outside environmental observers have recognised the Island's special mix of some of the best wildlife sites in England, set among a landscape of national and international importance and rich culture and heritage.

forgiven for crossing your fingers that the cliff will still be there for your return lift back up; reassuringly, the cliff is constantly monitored for any significant movement). Back at the top, you can grab a tea and cake at Marconi's Tearooms.

In the shadow of the Needles lies little-visited **Headon Warren**, which offers arguably the best view from land of the Needles' chalk pyramids. A combination of downs, lowland heath and a headland protruding west into Alum Bay, this exquisite corner (part of a wider Site of Special Scientific Interest that takes in a chunk of Tennyson Down) exudes appeal for walkers, nature lovers and archaeologists alike. If you consider yourself all three, you've hit the jackpot. To reach the warren take the small lane immediately north of The Needles Landmark Attraction (this does not involve paying to enter the site) and, after 200yds, turn right through a gate following footpath T17 gently uphill. The walk to its modest summit takes about 20 minutes.

Headon Warren is well named, for during the 15th century it was a warren where rabbits were farmed for food and fur. But its history goes back much further, evidence for which you'll stumble upon in the form of the huge and impressive earthwork at the top of the ridge. This structure represents the remains of a Bronze Age burial mound dating to 1500BC and there's general agreement that it was the burial place of an important local chieftain. The site has long been plundered; it was certainly unpicked after Henry III issued a charter in 1237 that required such structures to be ransacked in search of treasure. Footpaths bisect the modest rise and allow you to explore the earthwork, always with a backdrop of the Needles.

The sandy soils support gorse, while the holes you see in the flanks of the warren have been dug out by insects including mining wasps and tiger beetles; the heath also provides breeding opportunities for the Dartford warbler.

After returning to the access road to the warren, a short extension of 400yds will give you a close-up view of Alum Bay. Turn right down the paved path which descends gently beneath the chairlift. At the time of writing the wooden staircase that drops down to the shores of Alum Bay was unsafe and closed off, so do not go past the 'no entry' sign, even if you see people on the beach (they will have reached it via the chairlift). From the path end, however, you can peer up and appreciate the vast, slithering, shiny, steep chalk cliffs that make up the Needles.

FRESHWATER BAY & AROUND

Freshwater Bay refers to both the graceful, arc-shaped cove where the Isle of Wight meets the sea and the small community that radiates out to the northwest of the beach, and which in turn merges into Freshwater village.

4 FRESHWATER BAY

🏠 **The Bay Boutique Bed and Breakfast** (page 304)

Freshwater Bay always seems too small to hold the water that fills it to the brim on the rising tide. A pebble beach bookended by chalk cliffs and a steep drop off just offshore, in stormy weather it's a magnificent place to watch waves and swells muscle up on to the beach before they retreat, creating a shimmering and crackling effect as water particles reverberate on the flint, cobbles and pebbles. Two sea stacks add drama to what is already a particularly photogenic setting: Mermaid Rock became a stack only in 1959, when the sea and gales finally tugged it loose from the southern headlands of the bay. In November 2020, the elements dealt it another glancing blow, when a sizeable chunk fell into the sea. Stag Rock (which stands closer to the beach) is said to be so named after a stag leapt on to it to escape a pursuing dog (this sounds implausible, not least because of the absence of deer on the Island). Sadly, the prevailing view is that the days of both stacks are numbered – indeed, a third stack, Arch Rock, fell into the sea in 1992.

The cliffs either side of the bay are good for picnics. Paths lead up the lower flanks of Tennyson Down to the west, while the Coastal Path ascends quickly to the east to provide unfolding views of the downs lined up for inspection. For an even better vista, cross the A3055 behind the beach and follow signposts through Freshwater Golf Course on to Afton Down. It's easy to find a spot to sit when you reach the top of the gentle brow, to drink in the milky waters of the seascape in front of you.

It's possible to kayak or snorkel around the eastern edges of the bay where there are several sea caves. The nearest of these to the beach is walkable at low tide, if you follow the tide out. Alternatively, you can kayak westwards below Tennyson Down past Watcombe Bay where there are several more caves to nose around. In each case it's strongly recommended you use local guides (page 29), and even the most experienced kayaker or swimmer should consult these for knowledge about currents and other risks before heading out. It's easy to keep paddling west below Tennyson Down to see just one more cave and then find yourself a fair distance from Freshwater Bay.

On dry land, the bay's architectural merit reflects the money poured into the area by wealthy and well-connected Victorian visitors. Gate Lane, which heads west from the bay, boasts several substantial three-storey houses commissioned by Queen Victoria for sea captains and high-ranking naval officers. These properties cast a Siren-like spell on just about anyone with a literary inclination or appetite for high office. Among those who pulled back the curtains here to gaze out at sea were D H Lawrence and Henry Sewell, the first prime minister of New Zealand. Hazelhurst, now converted into an apartment block in Gate Lane, housed (not at the same time) the authors Anne Thackeray Ritchie, Mary Coleridge and Virginia Woolf, as well as the children's book illustrator Kate Greenaway. The poet and historian Sir Henry Newbolt also stayed here, with his lover Ella Coltman, though they also found time to pop up the road to Farringford to hold séances with Tennyson. Coastguard Lane, opposite the Albion Hotel, played host to W H Auden, the former prime minister Clement Attlee, and the writers and playwrights Christopher Isherwood and George Bernard Shaw, while on Victoria Road you'll find Tower House, where Edward VII conducted his affair with the socialite Lillie Langtry.

At the western end of Gate Lane stands **St Agnes Church** (PO40 9PY), the only thatched church on the Island. This and the wooden bell turret and small lancet windows lend the church exterior a picturesque olde-worlde charm, a sense that initially seems to be confirmed by the '1622' inscribed on a thick-set date stone along the exterior walls. Despite this, St Agnes is a relatively modern creation that was only consecrated in 1908. The 17th-century stone is believed to show the date of the nearby derelict farmhouse whose walls were pilfered to build the church. The same farm, on Hooke Hill, was the birthplace of the natural philosopher, architect and polymath Robert Hooke (page 55).

A short stroll from the church is the former home of the photographer Julia Margaret Cameron (1815–79), now **Dimbola Museum & Galleries** (Terrace Ln, PO40 9QE ✆ 01983 756814 ♂ dimbola.co.uk ◷ Apr–Sep

1 Freshwater Bay. **2** Rockpooling, Freshwater Bay. **3** Compton Bay. **4** Dinosaur foot fossil, Compton Bay. ▶

Tue–Sat; check website for winter times; tea shop all year). The building was originally two cottages that Cameron had linked by a Gothic tower (the base of which is the modern-day public entrance); Cameron would regularly entertain her arts friends from London who were eager to breathe the Island's creative airs (Virginia Woolf was her great-niece). Today this fine little museum pays homage to her work and includes many of her portraits (she was well known for leaning over a balcony and inviting passers-by to have their photograph taken), as well as some of her photographic equipment, including a formidable dry plate camera. You might idly wonder if the weight of contemporary cameras was a reason Julia gravitated to portraits; this would have been easier than heaving such an unwieldy beast up Tennyson Down in search of landscape images. On other floors and wings you'll find changing

ROCK 'N' ROLL ON THE ISLE OF WIGHT

Easy as it is to characterise the Isle of Wight as an oh-so-genteel holiday destination, the Island most definitely has a more radical, alternative side – and the bust of Jimi Hendrix in the gardens of Dimbola is the dead giveaway. The rock legend gave his last public performance on the Island at the Isle of Wight Festival in August 1970; he died three weeks later.

Held on Afton Down, immediately behind Freshwater Bay, the Isle of Wight Festival 1970 was the last of three consecutive annual rock music jamborees to take place on the Island. Incredulously, it has become widely acknowledged as the largest musical event of its time, greater even than the attendance at Woodstock, with a throng of up to 700,000 thought to have dropped in and tuned out. The event was organised and promoted by enterprising local brothers, Ron, Ray and Bill Foulk, though it's fair to say not everyone supported their proposal. Then, as now,

the Isle of Wight was a favourite retirement destination of the well-heeled British and a haven for yachties, who had a diametrically different view of life from the marauding hippies they feared were poised to descend like locusts upon the Island. Nevertheless, East Afton Down Farm was given permission by local authorities to host the event, the thinking being the site was unsuitable and would deter visitors. Instead, it meant many could simply sit on the flanks of the down, overlooking the stage. Hendrix's performance is recorded on *Isle of Wight*, a live album released posthumously in 1971.

The 1970 festival went out with so much of a bang that, amid local objections, funding problems and competing demands for headline acts, it was consigned to history – until its revival in 2002. Since then, it's been held every year, with the exception of 2020, when the Covid-19 pandemic was at its height.

exhibitions that focus mainly on up-and-coming female photographers and a permanent exhibition on the Isle of Wight Festival, which was held just up the road on Afton Down (see box, opposite page).

¶¶ FOOD & DRINK

Dimbola Tea Room Dimbola Museum & Galleries, Terrace Ln, PO40 9QE **f**. The tea room at Dimbola has been wonderfully refurbished very much in the image of Julia Margaret Cameron: quirky and eclectic. Home bakes prevail, including an exquisitely stylish pistachio rose cake, but it's the setting that is just as likely to grab your attention, with paintings and drawings by local artists on the walls and your food served on mismatched vintage china. The new terrace is the perfect place to enjoy a coffee and take in the views of Freshwater Bay.

The Piano Café Gate Ln, PO40 9PY ✆ 01983 472874 ⚭ thepianocafe.co.uk. Bright café enjoying a prime position at the foot of Tennyson Down and so perfect after any coastal sojourn. Breakfasts are excellent and include toasted local sourdough bread, sweet potato hash or eggs with peppers. Evening meals have a similar vibe and include bruschetta, mezze and fresh calamari, plus a Piano Vegetarian Platter, a mouth-watering mix of hummus, falafel and Island blue and soft cheeses. The café is named for Queen Victoria's piano tuner who once ran a piano business here. Tennyson would occasionally amble down the road from Farringford to buy sheet music.

5 THE FARRINGFORD ESTATE

🏠 **Farringford Cottages** (page 304)

Bedbury Ln, Freshwater Bay PO40 9PE ✆ 01983 752500 ⚭ farringford.co.uk ⊙ Easter–Oct Wed–Sat; pre-booked tours only. See ad, page 167.

From 1853 until his death in 1892, the Island's most famous resident, Alfred, Lord Tennyson, made his home at **Farringford House**. Painstakingly restored to its former 19th-century Georgian glory in 2017, this magnificent Grade I-listed building is an extraordinary, turreted neo-Gothic country pile and sits within sumptuously leafy grounds of what is, effectively, parkland with mature trees, farmland and a good deal of wildlife. Before you enter, take a while to admire the house from afar, where features you might pick out include the castellated parapets that give the impression of battlements.

The interior is well worth exploring with the excellent audio tour, which lead you up spiral staircases, and into the pantry and the opulent library. You may never see anywhere else such an intensely rich azure blue as that found on the walls of the reception room: it would not look out of place on the glazed tiles of a minaret in Samarkand. Elsewhere you will see a staircase that Tennyson used when he wished to escape his more dull visitors (he would either ride out the time on a balcony, or scuttle away into the grounds) and you navigate past paintings and marble and bronze statuettes that attest to the sophisticated tastes (and substantial budget) of the poet and his loyal and stoic wife Emily.

As well as describing what you are looking at, the audio tour does a wonderful job of conveying Tennyson the human being. While he was painfully aware of his status as 'Top Poet' (as Lynne Truss deliciously named him), you are also left with the impression that here was an enlightened father who was somewhat ahead of his time and distanced from the Victorian stereotype: a doting dad who blew bubbles with his two sons, played badminton with them and took them on walks on the downs.

After Tennyson's death the house continued in the possession of the family until 1945. A rather chequered era then unfolded with the building reincarnated as a hotel – it was owned first by Thomas Cook (the travel firm founder) and later Sir Fred Pontin (of the holiday camp empire). In the post-war period, some historic pieces of exquisite furniture – crafted from surrounding trees – were deemed superfluous and, to the horror of onlookers, who included some of the original craftsmen, hurled on a bonfire by new owners, their value unappreciated. Farringford remained a hotel until 2010 when the new owners bought it with a view to embarking on the restoration you see today.

The **wider estate** comprises 33 acres of lawns, fields and gardens and these wider grounds and farmland are being managed in a sympathetic way that echoes the landscape Tennyson would have known. White park cattle, the same breed as stocked the land during Tennyson's time, chew the cud while the woodland behind the house has been thinned and planted with primroses, which are thought to have been a favourite of the poet's. A huge cedar of Lebanon, once sketched by Edward Lear, continues to stand proud outside the rear windows of the house, while the conspicuous, scarlet-flowered rhododendron around the grounds is thought to have been planted by Tennyson shortly after he moved in.

The **walled garden** is thoughtfully managed with consideration to the landscape in which it is set, paying homage to the one that Tennyson knew and tended. Sadly, the original was razed and replaced by holiday homes. In 2016 these buildings were removed and work began on restoring the walled garden to a condition that Tennyson may have

TENNYSON'S LOVE FOR THE ISLE OF WIGHT

Lord Tennyson was a landscape poet – views and settings were of great importance to him, and he would have found the Isle of Wight extraordinarily varied in comparison to the gently rolling hills and flatlands of his Lincolnshire childhood. Having also lived in Epping Forest, Cheltenham and Mornington Crescent in London, it is perhaps unsurprising that he found his greatest inspiration on the Island, where he arrived in 1853.

When Tennyson heard Farringford was on the market, he visited the house and, although he noted it looked 'rather wretched with wet leaves trampled into the lawn', he was impressed at how it was surrounded by trees. Seclusion was another appeal, for he was thoroughly fed up with the attention that fame bought him, with literary admirers beating a path to his door in London. He liked the estate enough to suggest that his wife Emily should travel over and give him her opinion. Freshwater was an isolated place in the 1850s, and, having missed the steamer from Lymington, the Tennysons made their crossing of the Solent in a rowing boat. On a number of subsequent trips to the island the poet had to resort to pulling Emily in a small carriage along the final stretch to the house.

Farringford was home to the Tennysons for 40 years. They rented at first before buying it with royalties from the popularity of his poem, *Maud*. The couple wasted no time in renovating and significantly upgrading the house, sorting out foul-smelling drains, arranging for bay windows to be fitted and later extending the library to accommodate the poet's overflowing book collection.

The house provided the perfect medium for Tennyson to write his poetry and *The Charge of the Light Brigade* was composed here in 1854. Not only was the setting conducive to creativity and the written word, the ambience and acoustics of the building enhanced the spoken word rather as an auditorium might. During Tennyson's lifetime, poetry was often intended to be spoken aloud as much as it was read and most evenings he would read his day's work to stolidly enduring Emily. One can almost hear, down the years, Tennyson's voice booming out as he read from *Maud*.

And ye meanwhile far over moor and fell

Beat to the noiseless music of the night!

Has our whole earth gone nearer to the glow

Of your soft splendours that you look so bright?

A compulsive walker, Tennyson enjoyed daily jaunts behind the house to High Down (later renamed Tennyson Down) and also opened up old paths in the patch of tangled woodland here known locally as 'the wilderness', with the pleasing side-effect of improving public access to the downs.

recognised. Historical records proved invaluable, in particular the journals of Emily Tennyson, and gave the estate's walled garden manager,

Ellen Penstone-Smith, a licence to plant flowers that are referenced in them, as did poems such as *Maud*.

A contemporary etching provided a guide for the replica summer house, covered with jasmine, roses and other scented plants. 'Walled gardens were quite formal,' says Ellen, 'But Tennyson was ahead of his time and wanted something wilder and adventurous. In one letter, he referred to a "carelessly ordered garden" on a "ridge of a noble down", which is widely assumed to have meant Farringford.'

There are, of course, challenges: in Tennyson's time, mature elm trees sheltered the garden from the strong westerlies, and ever since those succumbed to disease the wind is funnelled off the downs and through the garden (though the walls act as a buffer, tipping the stronger gusts 'over the crossbar').

From spring to autumn, the garden is a haven for pollinators and boasts striking colours – yellows, greens, purples – of passion flowers,

THE VICTORIAN A-LISTERS

'Everybody is either a genius, or a poet, or a painter, or peculiar in some way', wrote author Anne Thackeray Ritchie on a visit to Freshwater in 1865. Another common refrain from visitors in the second half of the 19th century was, 'is there nobody commonplace?' As the residence of the Poet Laureate at the time, Freshwater appealed to 'great brains' – creative types were drawn here to pay homage to Tennyson and wax lyrical about the Island's natural majesty, or simply to rub shoulders with other luminaries in the hope that the stardust might be shared all around. Intellectuals also descended, with lofty ambitions to infer deep meaning from the landscape. They formed what was known at the time as the Freshwater Circle.

Among those beating a path to Tennyson's door were the pre-Raphaelite painter William Holman Hunt, Prince Albert (Queen Victoria's consort), author Lewis Carroll, artist Edward Lear and Charles Kingsley, the priest, social reformer and author of *The Water Babies*. Henry Wadsworth Longfellow (author of *Hiawatha*) brought a party of ten for tea. Carroll left chastened, however, having been given the cold shoulder by Tennyson, who failed to see the joke when Carroll lampooned his poetry. Perhaps the most exotic visitor was Queen Emma of the Sandwich Islands (now known as Hawaii), who had a special chair carved for her at Farringford in 1865. And this particular A-list merely covers those who visited Tennyson. The tradition also continued half a mile down the road, where photographer Julia Margaret Cameron entertained luminaries such as Charles Darwin and Virginia Woolf (her great-niece) at her home, Dimbola (page 136).

lilies and larkspurs that match the scheme in the house. Keep an eye out for wildlife: red squirrels often bounce along the walls and buzzards perch in trees in the adjacent skyline.

6 FRESHWATER & TOTLAND

Set back from Freshwater Bay, **Freshwater** may be a village but, with a population of around 5,000, it is much larger than the town of Yarmouth a few miles further north – a curiosity that has long defied explanation. The best part of a mile from the coast and Freshwater Bay, the village centre is nonetheless a good place for daily provisions if you're staying nearby, as it's home to some good independent shops and cafés. The most pleasant way to reach the village from the coast is along the signposted walking route, the Freshwater Way, which begins from the car park behind Freshwater Bay and winds its way along streams that feed into the River Yar, with woodlands, mires and reed beds for company.

To the west, Freshwater village soon merges into **Totland**, a built-up residential area to be negotiated en route to the sea. Italian inventor Guglielmo Marconi, who lived on the Island in the late 1890s and early 1900s, sent the first wireless transmission from the Broadway Inn (now a post office) in Totland. Like its northerly near-neighbour at Colwell, Totland Beach is a good choice for swimming but you may just be stopped in your tracks by the simple serenity of the bay. Though it can undeniably be busy in midsummer, at other times of year it enjoys a singular nature, with beach huts neatly lined adding a parti-coloured timelessness, a few fishermen whiling away the hours and a backdrop of overhanging woodland where soil imperceptibly gives way to sand. There's a sea wall too and high tides invariably see the bay filled to the brim. Were you to construct an ideal day, it might involve sitting on the wall as high tide laps your ankles, against a backdrop of a setting sun.

ᵒ FOOD & DRINK

The Freshwater Coffee House 5 School Green Rd, Freshwater PO40 9AJ ✆ 01983 754095 ⌂ freshwatercoffeehouse.co.uk. Good coffee is almost taken for granted nowadays, but Stefan Powell and his small team know how to make an excellent cup of joe – extra hot if you wish. Breakfasts include freshly baked croissants while a little later in the day you can tuck into paninis or a pancake stack with apples, chocolate and whipped cream. While the drinks and food are excellent, the most impressive thing about this café is how it has become

A walk on Afton & Compton downs

❄ OS Explorer map 29; start: eastern end of Freshwater Bay ♥ SZ346856; 5 miles (6 miles with diversion to Compton Beach); medium

If you've wandered up Tennyson Down then you cannot fail to have noticed the whaleback hills and ridges that sweep away to the east. Rising sharply from Freshwater Bay, this expanse of downland actually enjoys several names as you move through it, from Afton Down to East Afton, Compton, Tapnell, Wellow and Shalcombe downs. The remarkable plethora of names given to the downs can be confusing: they are all, in reality, part of the same lump of land. Collectively, they knit together into nearly three miles of undulating, sweeping brows (which makes them roughly the same length as Tennyson Down) until they pause for breath briefly, tumbling down into a shute (the Island name for a narrow, dipping valley) above the village of Brook. Beyond there, the downs resume their journey eastwards, though under different aliases again.

After a short, steel climb, walking along the top of the downs is easy thanks to an innovative 'Donate-a-Gate' scheme promoted by the island branch of the Ramblers (page 24). The latter part of the return route shadows the cliffs; be careful of sheer drops just above Freshwater Bay.

1 The easiest way to access Afton Down is to follow signs for the golf club, located immediately above Freshwater Bay. There is a right of way past the clubhouse and footpath fingerposts direct you east and uphill; be mindful of golfers as you walk. The path winds across the course for half a mile before leaving it behind as you move seamlessly on to Compton Down. The walking here is outstanding, with views to open water on both sides and the Island stretching away to a vanishing point in the west. The cliffs to the south change colour, too, from white to golden sandstone.

2 After a couple of miles, you come to an assembly of tumuli, or burial mounds, known as The Five Barrows (page 148). After inspecting them, continue downhill (east) for some 300yds before taking the first path to the right, which involves half-turning back on yourself and walking southwest.

3 The path meanders downhill through woodlands before emerging above the National Trust-owned Compton Farm. Walk through the grounds of the farm, along the right of way, and

part of the community since opening in 2018. This is due in no small part to the 'extra-curricular' effort Stefan puts in – events held here include everything from storytelling and Lego swaps to open mic popular themed nights, all of which will hopefully restart once the Island has recovered from the impact of Covid-19.

then, with care, cross the A3055 (known as the Military Road; see box, page 146) before heading along the obvious footpath towards Compton Chine for 200yds. An ice-cream van is present in the car park above Compton Beach in just about all seasons (you may have spotted this tantalising prospect from up on high, around The Five Barrows). To reach it, head left above the chine, with the coast on your right, for three-quarters of a mile. Generations of families and surfers have queued here for a 99. After you've got your ice cream, retrace your steps to where you turned left and continue ahead.

4 Whether or not you have succumbed to ice-cream temptation, to head back to Freshwater Bay, follow the Coastal Path past Compton Chine via a bridge across a small stream. You are now walking underneath the high downs on which you were rambling just a short while before.

5 As the path meets the A3055, it starts to climb. Continue through a gate to walk by the side of the road (keep to the seaward side of the road). While the cliffs seem sheer from a distance, the hills here in fact slope gently to the sea and there are several paths to follow (pick one to suit your head for heights) as you return to Freshwater Bay. The best bet with children is to keep to the highest ground, where there is a footpath running in close parallel to the road.

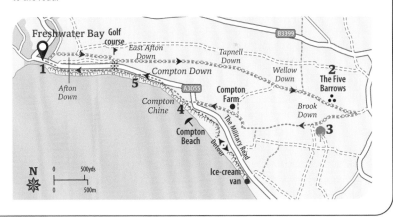

Rabbit Hole Patissiere and Chocolate Shop 55 School Green Rd, Freshwater PO40 9AS. Views across the green from this rather good café that is tucked away at the eastern edge of the village. Here you can snaffle excellent locally made truffles to take-away or settle down in the small tea room and munch on equally delicious cakes and sip a good range of teas.

The Red Lion Church Pl, Freshwater PO40 9BP ☏ 01983 754925 ⌂ redlion-freshwater. co.uk. This tucked-away, welcoming pub is a ten-minute walk from the centre of Freshwater, next to All Saints' Church (page 53), and consequently has the feel of a truly rural pub. Hearty food is served alongside a good range of wines and beer.

SHOPPING

Mrs Middleton 49 School Green Rd, Freshwater PO40 9AS ☏ 07973 212723 ⌂ mrsmiddleton.com. You may spend more time here than you think as this is no house-clearance secondhand bookshop: the owners pride themselves on unearthing books that are hard to find. So, as well as possibly stumbling upon a collectible, should you want something to read about a part of the Island you've visited, this may well be the place to find it.

THE MILITARY ROAD'S LAST STAND?

Following the southwest coast for 10½ miles from Freshwater Bay to Chale, the A3055 cuts high above the sea, seemingly chiselled out of the side of Compton Down. Known as the Military Road, it is so named as it was built during Napoleonic times to transport troops from one side of the Island to the other and to bolster the south coast against invasion – troops would be deployed along the clifftop and, higher up, along the ridgeline of the downs, which continued the long history of the downs serving as an important watchpoint against invaders.

The Military Road may be a magnificent tourist spectacle but it's somewhat controversial locally, on account of it living on borrowed time. As coastal erosion bites into the cliffs, the sea gets ever closer and has already forced both the road – at eye-watering cost – and the coastal footpath to divert sharply inland. Parts of the road run anything from 60ft to just 15ft from the cliff edge (two stretches, between Brook Bay and Hanover Point and below Afton Down, are particularly adjacent).

This has led to a grim local joke where a visitor asks an Islander 'how far is the road from the sea?' and is met with the answer 'about seven years'. No timescale has been placed on the road's demise but when the time comes this may become one of the strangest footpaths in the country, a road with no cars – something that has already happened further along the A3055 by the Undercliff at Ventnor (page 174).

One consequence would mean that villages such as Brighstone and Brook, part of an area known historically as 'Back of the Wight', would have no main road to link them with the rest of the Island: they would, until somebody comes up with a plan B, return to their medieval links of inland drovers' routes (which nowadays are the series of B and other minor roads that weave between the villages and over the downs, through small gaps such as Shorwell Shute). Proposals are regularly put forward by the Island council to buy the road more time by pile-driving reinforced rods deep into the rock, but sceptical locals sigh and simply note that they have heard it all before.

7 COMPTON BAY & HANOVER POINT

This is a simply magnificent slice of coast, with the beach at **Compton Bay** stretching for a good half mile. Surfers love Compton Bay and you will often see hardy souls riding the rollers on a late afternoon in deep midwinter. The bay gets its fair share of stormy weather, but even a strong breeze and a high tide is enough to nibble away at its cliffs. At low tide this is a simply magnificent stretch of sand, pancake flat and, open to the western horizon, it comes into its own against a setting sun. Towards the bay's easterly end, **Hanover Point** juts its craggy features into the sea.

The palpable impermanence of the coastline at Hanover Point means that surfers are not the only ones drawn to the bay. The sandstones and mudstones have eroded here, exposing 8,000 years of geology for you to take in – accordingly fossil hunters consider this to be one giant Jurassic playpark. Some 20 species of dinosaur have been found along this shoreline, dating back 125 million years. Just to the east of the Compton Bay car park, near the bottom of the cliffs, you'll find foot casts of a three-toed Iguanodon. The casts are not signposted but, at 2ft in width, are unmistakeable for anything else; you may well locate them by noticing other goggling beach goers who have beaten you to it.

More recent (relatively speaking) but equally haunting relics are found on slightly higher ground. The rock at the top of the cliffs around the point is often exposed by eroded topsoil. Usually brown in colour, it is up to 5,000 years old; look deeper and you'll see a distinctively darker layer that is up to 8,000 years old. In each layer you may well find pine nuts and pieces of wood. Both are proof that our Neolithic and Bronze Age ancestors managed or grew hazelnut forests here (at that time, the point where land meets sea would have been as much as half a mile further out), with which they fed wild boar or pigs. Although they appear to be robust, the nuts are amazingly well preserved rather than fossilised. If you take one home (please only do this with nuts you find on the ground that have been worked free from the soil by the elements), simply leave it on the mantelpiece for a few months and one day it will have disappeared, replaced by a small pile of dust.

Despite all the drama at play, the Coastal Path here is at its very flattest and offers easy walking. You could walk east from Hanover Point to Chilton Chine and back – a distance of 3½ miles – in a couple of hours or so. Along the way, cutting into Brook Bay, is **Brook Chine**, another

CHINES

The Military Road (see box, page 146) also shadows a series of chalk gullies, known locally as chines. A dominant feature of the south and southwest of the Island, chines are created by the streams that flow from the downs and cut through the soft cliffs. Essentially, these are relatively short river valleys with walls of hard chalk, which act as culverts, pushing softer mudstones and clays into the sea. Chines provide access to the sea, which is elsewhere hard to reach. From Freshwater to Brighstone, a distance of more than five miles, there are just two gaps, at Grange Chine and Brook Chine. They tend to be steep, hard to access and were historically beloved by smugglers.

All this makes for a dynamic landscape rich in wildlife. 'The landscape is always changing,' says Joel Bateman of the Isle of Wight AONB, 'which is why you get so many interesting animals making chines their home for a short while. Wasps and other insects settle in until the next storm or landslip changes everything.' In May and June you can spot the Glanville fritillary butterfly, an orange-brown flutterer for which the Island is the only UK stronghold. Wildflowers include pink rock sea spurrey, while the chines are excellent places to witness the arrival of migrant songbirds such as wheatear and several warbler species. In need of a good meal after the cross-Channel hop, they can dine well on the chines' abundant insects.

good spot to hunt out those large three-toed dinosaur foot casts. The National Trust, which owns sections of the coast here, asks that visitors only gather fossils from the beach, rather than work them loose from the exposed cliff faces.

8 THE FIVE BARROWS

While few signs remain of where Bronze Age people lived on the Island, many can be found of where they died. The Five Barrows is one such example, and these extraordinary ringed graves can be picked out from sea level in much of West Wight.

The thing you need to know about the Five Barrows is that there are actually nine of them (how they came to be known as Five Barrows is as lost in the mists of time as the provenance of the humps themselves), of which seven are visible today. They are located 538ft above sea level, where Brook Down meets Shalcombe Down, just west of the B3399. The barrows would have originally appeared as black-and-white concentric rings (this colouration was created by digging out a circle to expose the chalk, and then throwing soil around the circumference, before repeating this process with an outer ring), but what you see today is a large hollow resembling a small quarry, interspersed with grassy mounds. Close up, they are actually quite easy to miss if you're coming from the east – the Tennyson Trail runs immediately below them, but if you were to approach from the east without the knowledge that they were there you could possibly walk past unawares. To reach them, however, all you need to do is clamber up the flanks of the down from the path for some 20yds. When you see the trig point

THE NEOLITHIC ISLE OF WIGHT

While a great deal is made – justifiably – of the Isle of Wight's importance as a place for dinosaurs, less emphasis is laid on the Island's prehistoric human presence. Despite this, the Island has an archaeological heritage of significance, even if it remains unheralded, and a visit offers the chance to skip along its ancient timeline. 'We know the archaeology is out there,' says Owen Cambridge of the Island's former Archaeology Discovery Centre, which sadly closed in 2019. Owen is awestruck every time he climbs up Brook Down. 'You often hear of places where our ancestors built processional ways to bury their dead. But there was no need to build one on the Isle of Wight. I think we're standing on a natural one,' he says, sweeping his hands west towards the slopes of Tennyson Down and east towards Mottistone Down, where you can just make out the Long Stone (page 156). 'You have a 360-degree panorama of the Island. This would clearly have been important to our ancestors.'

Standing among the Five Barrows, should you look to the farmland fields to the southeast you will notice how some of them have circular boundaries, a feature that is frequently a sign of pre-Roman, especially Bronze Age, farming (more recent field boundaries, particularly those of the enclosures of the 18th and 19th centuries, tend to be ruler-straight). Owen suggests it is no great leap to connect the burial mounds of Five Barrows with the fertile soils of the inhabited landscapes below.

Other parts of the Island, including the coast east and southwest of Yarmouth, have yielded Roman field systems, axes, flints and pottery dating back to the Neolithic times as well as more recent discoveries. You are encouraged to scour beaches yourself and see what turns up. Older artefacts include a Palaeolithic hand axe and timber stumps dating to the Mesolithic period, some 8,000 years ago. 'They were used to make log boats, so there was boat building on the Island then, just as there is today,' says Owen. The closure of the Archaeology Discovery Centre in 2019 left a dinosaur-tooth-sized gap in the opportunities to see some of the Island's key finds. Some pieces have been transferred to the Shipwreck Museum at Arreton Barns (page 241) but others appear to be gathering dust, awaiting a new home.

you'll know you are in the right place. If you do manage to walk past, don't worry as the approach from the west is obvious – a short goat track leads diagonally up to them; at most you will have plodded an additional 300yds.

THE REAL WAR HORSE

In *War Horse*, Michael Morpurgo's novel turned Hollywood and West End blockbuster, horse Joey is purchased to serve in World War I, surviving one extraordinary adventure after another. Morpurgo has said that his tale was inspired by stories gathered from veterans in his local pub, but the fields and coast around Brook were once home to an even more tenacious war horse, the presciently named Warrior. Raised and trained on the Isle of Wight and exercised in Sidling Paul fields in Brook, Warrior was led into numerous battles during World War I by General 'Galloper' Jack Seely, a friend of Winston Churchill who served in two Liberal governments as an MP before 1914.

Warrior was dubbed the 'horse the Germans couldn't kill' by newspapers at the time, having survived some of the war's most arduous conflicts, including battles at Ypres (1915), the Somme (1916) and Passchendaele (1917), where he became stuck in the mud. At the Battle of Moreuil Wood in 1918, Warrior became lame and Seely was gassed. Upon his return to the Island, Warrior was received as something of a local hero.

While we might be forgiven for thinking Warrior's ordeals were improbable, his charmed life and narrow escapes are well documented. It's a remarkable tale of survival: eight million other horses and mules did not return from the front. In 2014, he was posthumously awarded the PDSA Dickin Medal, recognised as the Victoria Cross for animals.

You can follow the trail of Warrior in the local area along the thoughtfully constructed Warrior Trail (visitisleofwight.co.uk/things-to-do/walking/warrior-trail), a six-mile circular route that takes around three hours to cover. Beginning at the Five Barrows (page 148), the route traverses the downland and coast including Brook Bay, where Warrior first learned to brave the oncoming waves and was trained to confront the dangers of battle in the surf. One question may occur to you as you walk: why does the trail not include Warrior's final resting place? According to local rambler David Howarth, who leads guided walks along the trail, the answer is garnished with brutal realism. 'When you learn that Warrior died in 1941, you may have already begun to answer your own question,' he tells me, clearing his throat and shuffling his feet. 'This is the bit where I warn the children on any walk I'm leading... the country was well into World War II by then, rations were short and Warrior was eating a large bucket of food a day. People were going hungry. It couldn't be justified... David prefers at this point to leave his audience to join the dots together themselves.

9 BROOK & HULVERSTONE

Squeezed into folds of downland as the Island tips towards the English Channel are these two quintessential English villages. Straddling the B3399, **Hulverstone** amounts to a smattering of houses and a pub (see below), while **Brook** is best known for its church of St Mary the Virgin, which actually stands a mile north of the village. Constructed in 1864, its triangular west wall oddly brings to mind a Swiss chalet. Inside, that same wall is decorated by a long and sobering list of shipwrecks and rescuers; over the years, much of the restoration of the church has used reclaimed wood from ill-fated ships.

The building high on the brow above Brook is the Grade II-listed Brook Hill House, which was built for Sir Charles Seely and only completed the year before his death in 1915. The architect was Sir Aston Webb, who designed the frontage of Buckingham Palace as well as Admiralty Arch in London. Built from Island coursed rubble and ironstone, the house is an L-shaped affair, described by Historic England as 'of the Egyptian or Assyrian style', of tapering columns, a flat roof, tall stone chimneystacks and a one-storey wing on either flank. Seely's grandson, David Seely, later recalled how Sir Charles had been told by his doctor 'that it wasn't doing him much good to live down in the valley at Brook and he ought to build himself a house which was up above the mists which tended to form over the stream which runs down there'. Today the house is a private residence, divided into luxurious apartments.

An uplifting jaunt on foot can be made from Brook to Hulverstone via Hulverstone Plantation, which lies immediately northeast and upwards from Brook; head northwest along Badger Lane before turning east towards Hulverstone via the B3399. There is no great visual drama to this route but it has a simple, ineffable charm: after this sojourn of barely two flat miles, with big skies and far-reaching horizons to both east and west, invariably accompanied by birdsong, you could put the world to rights in the Sun Inn.

¶¶ FOOD & DRINK

The Sun Inn Hulverstone PO30 4EH ✆ 01983 741124 ⌖ characterinns.co.uk/the-sun-inn
⊙ year-round Wed–Sun. This family-owned 16th-century thatched pub offers creative, eye-catching food – crab doughnuts anyone? – along with stews drawing on local lamb and pork. In summer you can dine in the garden with views as rural and bucolic as they come, including a backdrop of Tennyson Down. In winter, snuggle up by the fire.

BACK O' THE WIGHT

Historically, the hinterland in the shadow of Chillerton and St Catherine's downs forms the easternmost limits of an area known as 'Back o' the Wight', a term covering the land set back from the sea all the way from Chale and Chale Green west towards Compton Bay. From the Middle Ages through to Victorian times, this was a place of traditional trades, home to blacksmiths, shoemakers and chimney sweeps. It was also regarded a financially poor part of the Island and shipwrecks were sometimes seized upon as a welcome source of income and, even though there is little documented evidence, wrecking (the deliberate luring of ships to their rocky doom) may well have taken place. Given the harshness of daily life, it is likely that such a prospect would have been too tempting to resist. This uneven and eventful history is hard to imagine today, for the sprinkling of hamlets strung out along this hinterland are, almost without exception, the epitome of the rural idyll, blessed with good pubs, historical and architectural interest, and gateways to fine walks.

The area is enclosed to the north by yet more of the Island's ever-rolling downlands, in this case Chessel, Westover and Brighstone downs. They pick up the geological baton, so to speak, from Shalcombe Down and hurtle eastwards for the best part of three miles, high above the communities of Brook (page 151), Mottistone, Brighstone and Shorwell. These downlands and their accompanying heaths and commons are magical, wildlife-rich places. Forget the bland, sweeping monocrops you see in much of England's agricultural heartlands; here any risk of monotony is disrupted by the layer of flint laid down during the last ice age that pokes up randomly through the grass. This has in turn encouraged acid-loving plants such as gorse and heath bedstraw. Grazing cattle and nibbling rabbits prevent the scrub taking over the grassy flanks. Linnets and yellowhammers nest in the gorse while whitethroat and wheatear (the males of the latter are identified by their 'robber' mask patterning) can also be spotted, hopping between gorse and rocky outcrops. This ensemble of downs is also home to 30 species of butterfly, including adonis blue, chalkhill blue and dark green

---

1 Mottistone Gardens and Estate. **2** The Pepperpot, St Catherine's Down. **3** The Long Stone. **4** Brighstone. ▶

fritillary. Look out too for the beautiful small copper butterfly and another flutterer, the well-camouflaged grayling.

Heathland was an important habitat here in medieval times when it was utilised for grazing farm animals, with heather used for thatch and gorse for bedding. Across the UK, a combination of agricultural improvement and neglect has seen 82% of heathland cover lost over the past 100 years or so. The picture is a little more positive on the Isle of Wight, where substantial chunks of heathland remain and are carpeted with heather and gorse. A conservation scheme managed by the Island charity, Gift to Nature, now seeks to restore it by reintroducing livestock, whose grazing can turn depleted grasslands into wildlife-rich landscapes by creating, for example, habitats for the Dartford warbler to breed. On a summer evening, these downs are another location where you have a sporting chance of hearing that haunting *churr* of the nightjar.

10 MOTTISTONE

The village of Mottistone features the impressive **church of St Peter and Paul** (fivechurches.org.uk). The church's location on a low knoll makes it appear to levitate slightly above the village. The graveyard here is wildlife rich, with the grasses left uncut until late summer to allow plants and flowers, such as ox-eye daisies and orchids, to seed. Chain mail – an unusual flourish – hangs over the porch while the chancel roof timbers come from a shipwreck. The village is almost absurdly bucolic. Different types of stone have been used on the buildings and in the churchyard, and accordingly many have species of lichens growing on them. Swallows dart around at low level in their hunt for insects, and many small birds such as wrens, blue tits, great tits and robins nest close by. Autumn is a good time to see red squirrels collecting walnuts on the village green.

Mottistone Gardens & Estate

PO30 4ED ☺ gardens Mar–Sep; National Trust

Although first mentioned in the Domesday Book in 1086 – making it one of the original Domesday manors – the building you see today is an L-shaped survivor, dating mainly to the late 15th and early 16th centuries, though some internal structures confirm that it dates back to Saxon times. Remarkably, given that a house of one kind or another, and of such significance and repute, has commanded an enviable piece of land for the best part of 1,400 years, little is known about its history until more recent times. The back of the manor was engulfed up to the eaves by a landslide in 1703 and remained partially buried for more than 200 years. Those parts that were accessible became used as a farmhouse.

The restoration of the manor was led by the first Baron Mottistone, or 'Galloping' Jack Seely, who had ridden the war horse Warrior (see box, page 150) into battle during World War I. Seely began the slow process of bringing the old family house back to life in 1926. It was a family affair, as Seely's architect son, John, was brought in to draw up the restructuring and rebuilding plans. From a small wooden shack (still standing today) in the grounds of the manor's tea garden, they not only drew up plans for the house and gardens but also outlined bomb-hit buildings for rebuilding, such as the church of St John in Clerkenwell in London.

The restoration of the two-storey manor required a degree of remodelling but proved remarkably faithful to the original, with mullioned windows inserted and the rubble stone cleaned and rendered. Stone slate tiles and gables over the attic were replaced (the original Saxon and then medieval building would have been thatched). At the time of writing, you could only admire the manor from outside, though the National Trust opens it to the public a couple of days each year; it's worth checking online as there are plans to start tours of parts of the building within the lifetime of this edition. These escorted visits will be worth it, for inside the house is more like a castle, with stairs, timber frames, thick-set walls, latticed windows and doors spanning several hundred years all thrown together. The house is set among six acres of beautifully managed gardens, with reams of foaming, draping wisteria separating the front of the house from the village. House and grounds form part of a wider, 78-acre Mottistone Estate; the informal boundary between the two is delineated by banks of sycamore trees and a handful of giant cypresses, which wear their shaggy branches like a crumpled absinthe-green velvet coat.

The ornamental displays are nowhere near as ancient as the house but were bedded in the 1960s by the flamboyant Lady Vivien Nicholson who lived at Mottistone on and off from 1947 until her death in 1991. She was inspired by her Sicilian upbringing and the Isle of Wight's mild climate to combine terracing with fruiting trees and herbaceous borders of bright orange lilies and blue catmint. The gardens are among the most southerly owned by the National Trust, which has adopted a Mediterranean-style planting approach to landscaping. Central to this is a no-watering policy, which both reflects a typical Mediterranean climate and the Trust's wider climate-change adaptation measure of reducing water use. The growth of drought-resistant plants is encouraged and yuccas, bananas and palms are now almost as common as roses, agapanthus and herbaceous borders.

The Long Stone

High above the village is Mottistone Common, where you will find the Neolithic site known as the Long Stone. As can often be the case on the Island, the name is deliciously misleading, for what awaits your attention is actually two stones, which in turn are thought to be part of a much more substantial burial chamber. To reach the stone, cross the road by St Peter and Paul Church and follow footpath BS43 and waymarkers uphill for three-quarters of a mile. This is a delightful, sunken lane, though it has an unrelenting steep gradient. The path ends abruptly as you emerge on downland in front of the Long Stone.

The stone(s) comprise two huge blocks: one, an iron sandstone pillar, stands 12ft tall; the other, 9ft by 4ft, slumbers horizontally. They dominate the surrounding downland and it's thought they date back 5,000 years and are aligned with the winter solstice so that the sunlight would run through the pencil-thin gap between the two. Their actual provenance, even their original location, remains uncertain as archaeologists believe they may even have been moved to their current position from elsewhere on the Island in Saxon times. The more credulous, however, will cleave to the tale that the taller of the pillars was thrown here by St Catherine, from the down that bears her name, in a Devil's wager. The Devil's smaller stone fell short and he lost the bet – according to legend, his defeat is said to symbolise the triumph of good over evil. Regardless of origin, the stones were certainly dislodged in the 19th century by Lord Dillon, a local squire who was curious to see what lay beneath them. Sadly, he unearthed nothing for his efforts.

The meaning of the stones was eventually unpicked a century after Dillon had finished rooting around by Jacquetta Hawkes, the first woman in the UK to take a degree in archaeology and anthropology (and who later helped found the Campaign for Nuclear Disarmament). After marrying author J B Priestley, the pair moved to Brook Hill House (page 151), not far from the Mottistone Estate, and she began to excavate the Long Stone in 1956.

While the stones' alignment with the sun may well be correct, Hawkes overturned the prevailing assumption that they were the same stone, broken in half: they had always been two, which, with a lintel, formed a dramatic entrance to a corbelled chambered tomb. The entrance appears to have represented a boundary between two binary worlds – the one that lay within the tomb and the one outside it. Hawkes further established that the stones are what remains of a 6,000-year-old Neolithic communal long barrow for burying the dead: at almost 100ft long, 30ft wide and 7ft high, this would have been both substantial and rare, given that long barrows in this part of England that aren't on chalk or limestone are uncommon. Rather gruesomely, various schools of thought suggest that, as with such tombs elsewhere in the UK, bodies may first have been laid out for birds and animals to feed on, then the bones buried in chambers and the soil heaped up into a mound.

If you get down on your hands and knees, tell-tale holes in the ground may indicate the lairs of burrowing insects. Two unusual ones which are now fairly widespread again on the common are the mining bee and the beewolf, which is actually a digger wasp. Other insects to look out for are the bright green tiger beetle and the common field grasshopper.

11 BRIGHSTONE

⌂ **Homelea B&B** (page 304) 🏠 **Weirside Cottage** (page 304)

The most substantial of the south coast's conveyor belt of picturesque villages, Brighstone is an agreeable miscellany of mill ponds, thatched houses and streams.

Squeezed among the thatched cottages in North Street (just to the north of the village shop) is the tiny **Brighstone Village Museum** (North St, PO30 4AX; free) which brings to life the traditions of the local people, the old school, fishing and the brave lifeboat men of years past. Next door is a private house, **Myrtle Cottage**, which from 1862 was home for 20 years to pioneer fossil hunter Reverend William Fox, who entertained many of the most eminent geologists of his day. He liked to exasperate his church-going flock with references and religious metaphors linked to his love of hunting out 'old dragons'. He had more old dragons – dinosaurs – named after him than any other Englishman, including the Island's own species of Iguanodon, *Hypsilophodon foxi*.

From the Long Stone along Mottistone Down, Brighstone Down & Brighstone Forest

❀ OS Explorer map 29; start: St Peter and Paul Church, Mottistone ♀ SZ405841; 5 miles; medium

This fine walk offers top-of-the-world views as it undulates along Mottistone and Brighstone downs and Brighstone Forest. You may lose count of the number of hovering kestrels you see, gracing the air above the Galloway cattle that lazily graze on steep-sided ridges. The flanks of the downs are dominated by heathland that creates a hauntingly magical landscape at any time of year and is perfect for walking and cycling. Brighstone Forest, dominated by beech and conifers, is actually the largest forested area on the Island, just beating the competing claim of Parkhurst Forest by a handful of acres.

1 From the opposite side of the road to the church, follow footpath BS43 north and uphill through woodlands for three-quarters of a mile to emerge at the Long Stone (page 156).

2 Bear left along the clear path that runs alongside the Long Stone and turn right through a gate, heading uphill with the edge of a wood on your left. After some 500yds you exit the wood through another gate and bear half-left uphill, contouring northeast below the sweep of Mottistone Down.

3 Where the path meets the Tennyson Trail, turn sharp right to walk uphill along the spine of the down. Pass a series of hummocks, thought to be burial mounds, and continue due east 1¹/₃ miles across Mottistone Down with superb views east towards the beckoning woods of Brighstone Down and, away to the south, of Mottistone and Brighstone, all framed by the coast.

4 The path drops down to a small car park on Lynch Lane. Turn left here (this is another of those distinctive Island shutes, or narrow valleys) and continue down the road for 300yds to a junction of paths.

5 Ignore the first footpath on the right for Brighstone Forest and instead take the adjacent second, less-substantial path which heads gently uphill, east through the forest.

Downland streams, with their clear fresh water, meet at Brighstone Mill (now a private residence), just to the south of the village centre, and form an intriguing network of mill ponds and sluices. These energetic waters pass under the branches of a mystical ancient oak known locally as the **Dragon Tree** before tumbling over a spectacular waterfall en route to the sea. The tree boasts several extraordinarily large tentacle-like branches and earned a certain back-from-the-grave reputation after

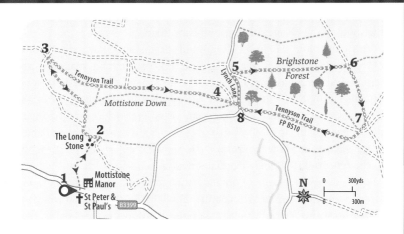

6 The wood is often dense and characterised by a mixture of regimented beech plantations liberally interspersed with free-standing broadleaved and conifer specimens. It won't take long from the road before the sounds of the outside world become muffled. After three-quarters of a mile, you'll come to a path; bear left for 50yds before turning right in a small clearing along footpath BS8, which runs slightly uphill through the forest and then drops down in the direction of the sea.

7 After half a mile, a main path (the Tennyson Trail) comes in from the left; bear right to follow this and continue for 150yds, ignoring paths to your left and right, until you reach a T-junction at the edge of the forest. Here, turn right (west) along footpath BS10, signposted for Freshwater.

8 The path descends to the road, where you dog-leg across to the right to reach the small car park once again. From here, climb back up to Mottistone Down and retrace your steps to the church at Mottistone.

it was blown down in a storm, only for these vast branches to re-root and bring the tree back to life (the date for this appears to have been lost from living memory). Well before that, a more archetypical medieval narrative tells of a dragon that visited horrors upon the local good folk, devouring all the children of Brighstone. Enter, stage right, the doughty St Tarquin of Vectis. Recently returned from the Crusades, Tarquin had undergone an epiphany and was transformed from a pillaging privateer to a pious soul. He speared the dragon, causing it to metamorphose into a tree – but not before he himself received a mortal blow. In 2019 the tree came third in the Woodland Trust's UK-wide Tree of the Year competition. You'll find the waterfall and tree along footpath BS23, to the south of the village shop, just off New Road.

The cows you see in fields around Brighstone may come from **Marshgreen Farm** (⊘ wightwagyu.co.uk), owned and managed by Jeremy Fisk who has developed a niche for Wagyu beef. The farm was established in 1866 with pedigree Jersey cows from Queen Victoria's herd at Osborne House and in recent years Jeremy has merged their descendants with Japanese Wagyu cows to create a hybrid meat available in the village shop (see opposite).

Though Brighstone may be quaint and olde-worlde, even this village cannot escape the plague of graffiti – though in this case it is of a riper vintage and dates to the 17th century. You'll find it if you head west for 400yds past the Three Bishops pub, opposite Moortown Lane. On the wall to the left is an etching of a galleon – just who did it and why is unclear but Owen Cambridge, a former Island archaeologist, believes this was no bored Tudor teenager. 'People like to say it's a sign that smuggling took place here,' says Owen, 'but that doesn't make sense – the last thing smugglers would do is announce their presence.' Instead, Owen believes it represents an ancient signpost for sailors docking at nearby Marsh Chine or Chilton Chine who sought fresh water. To see what he means, walk up Moortown Lane (opposite the galleon graffiti): after 800yds, you pass footpath BS83 on the left and, just beyond here, opposite footpath BS94 (signposted for Shorwell), is an old barn covered in graffiti. These include references to Christmas Day 1701, depictions of galleons and foot soldiers. The source of fresh water lies in a field just north of here, so not far from where sailors would have passed. It's worth walking a little further up this road (where it becomes Lynch Lane) to seek out a large sandstone outcrop. Looking rather solitary in a field opposite Old Rock Cottage, it appears to have been dropped from the sky. The pockmarks on the surface are holes drilled out by solitary honeybees.

Any thirsty sailor would not have had far to walk from the coast, which lies half a mile south of Brighstone, You can access it – as they would surely have done – via Marsh Chine, Grange Chine and Chilton Chine, all of which open out on to modestly sized stretches of shoreline and are accessible along footpaths from the village.

THE BRIGHSTONE COIN HOARD

Dinosaur fossils are not the only finds of interest to fall out of the Island's cliffs. In 2011, a ceramic pot containing 700 Roman coins was discovered on the coast south of Brighstone by fossil collector Mick Smith.

Dating from AD253–274, the coins were made of a copper alloy and are associated with a time when Britannia, Gaul and Germania formed the Gallic Empire, a breakaway from the central empire. They are of a kind of coin referred to as radiates, after a design of crown worn by the emperor. The coins retain their shape and clearly depict emperors, including Claudius II. It's unclear if the flagon, made from clay from the New Forest, was stored for safety and the owner never returned to recover them or if they were part of some ritual. Another theory is that at the time they were in use, Roman emperors had debased coins to the extent that bronze coins had no bronze in them: in which case, the coins were actually worthless. Perhaps the owner stored them away just in case they ever did come back into any value.

The find was declared as treasure trove and, although Mr Smith was entitled to a reward, he waived the money on condition the coins went on public display. Brading Roman Villa (page 269) paid the separate reward due to the landowner where the coins were found and they were placed on permanent display at Brading Roman Villa. The museum possesses another three hoards and, in all, some 35 such hoards have been discovered over the years across the Island.

Alongside the hoard is a zoomorphic brooch uncovered by a detectorist at Shalfleet which dates to the late 2nd century AD. The brooch is barely a fingernail in width but a magnifying lens allows you to discern its intricate detail, which features a bulbous head, a hooked beak and a rib running through its centre. Two sets of tiny pinpricks run down the side of each wing, inlaid with red enamel. Its provenance is uncertain but the detail suggests it was not a common piece of apparel but instead worn by someone with money, status, or both.

¶¶ FOOD & DRINK

Three Bishops Main Rd, PO30 4AH ℘ 01983 740226 ♂ ourlocal.pub/pubs/three-bishops-brighstone. Set rather conveniently in the middle of the village, this has the feel of a locals' pub, with regular music and solid, filling meals rather than any great nods towards gentrification.

SHOPPING

Brighstone Village Shop Main Rd, PO30 4AH ℘ 01983 740843 ♂ brighstonevillageshop. co.uk. If you fancy a picnic on the adjacent beaches at Marsh Chine, Grange Chine and Chilton Chine, you can buy all you need at this family-run shop and then wander the short distance down to the coast along footpaths and quiet lanes. You'll find the forecourt stacked with chopped logs, coal, squash and flower beds made from railway sleepers. Inside, the shop is well stocked with everything from tinned fruit to flour and everyday washing-up items. Local produce, however, prevails. 'We're just a busy, bustling village shop,' says proprietor David Hollis. 'I like to think this is a friendly place, that it's a centre of the community. If you want something, we can get it. We provide as much Island produce as we can. Farmers have looked to diversify and we want to help them do that.' True to his word, David stocks local beef from Newbarn Farm, Wight Waygu beef from Jeremy Fisk's farm, bread from three bakeries and honey from local hives in the hamlet.

12 SHORWELL

🏠 **Westcourt Farm** (page 304)

Home to thatched houses with latticed windows and short, winding lanes overhung with trees, Shorwell reinforces the area's reputation for postcard-worthy villages. Named after the local watercourse that runs through it, the Shor Well, the village (locals pronounce it 'Shorrel') and wider parish have more than 20 Grade II-listed buildings, and thatched houses, crow-stepped gables and neat gardens abound.

Shorwell also boasts not one but three manor houses, the Grade I-listed **Wolverton Manor** on the south side of the village, **Northcourt House**, to the north, and the equally geographically well-named **Westcourt Farm and Manor** to the west. All offer various opportunities for inspection (see box, opposite). The icing on this gateaux of village delights, so to speak, is the Crown Inn, as quintessential a village pub as you'll come across, with a thatched roof and the Shor Well trickling through its garden (page 164).

Standing at the centre of Shorwell is **St Peter's Church**, its elevated graveyard buttressed by a 7ft-high flint wall, the outer-lying gravestones seemingly poised to teeter over into the lane. Overhanging the north door of the church is a 15th-century painting of the life and times of St Christopher, a fresco that is widely regarded as a masterpiece. Among the scenes depicted are his martyrdom and an image of the saint carrying the Christ child across a stretch of water (while this depiction is traditional, in this instance it appears that the artist chose to paint a far wider passage of water than usual, which may possibly be the Solent).

The village was nudged out of its reverie in 2004 with the discovery of the Shorwell Helmet, one of just six Anglo-Saxon helmets ever found in England. Dating to the 6th century, the iron helmet was found in some 400 pieces; despite this, according to archaeologists its rarity

TO THE MANOR BORN

For the best part of 1,000 years, Shorwell has caught the eye of the rich and powerful; by the time of the Domesday Book, parts of Shorwell were already being divided up into manors held in demesne (land appropriated for private use to exploit as desired) by the king of the day and the Norman landowners who enjoyed his patronage. Various lords of the Island and of Carisbrooke Castle also assumed ownership; much later Henry VII and Henry VIII took a strong interest in the lands.

With such royal patronage, it seems unsurprising that three grand manor houses emerged. **Wolverton Manor** (Pound Ln, PO30 3JS ⊘ wolvertonmanor.co.uk) can be admired while walking along footpath SW4; it's a typical Jacobean house, built in a classical 'E' shape and originally set upon a small islet (the moat still exists and is overlooked by a grove of cobnut trees). The house you see today is the second on the site and was built by Sir John Hammond, physician to James I. The green sandstones – quarried at Quarr Abbey on the north coast (page 99) – and mixture of mullioned and large-glazed sash windows make for a handsome exterior. Inside, the showstopper is the Chinese Chippendale staircase. The house is the centrepiece of the estate but the working farm is also of interest and contribute to the manor's wider historical importance. The thatched shearing farm is considered to be among the finest of its kind in England.

Westcourt (Walkers Ln, PO30 3LA ✆ 01983 740233 ⊘ westcourt-farm. co.uk) is an old Elizabethan Manor also connected to a farm and covers some 200 acres. Ownership of the Westcourt manor lands was long held in the hands of associates of William Fitzosbern, a kinsman of William the Conqueror. In the early 16th century the east end of the present-day house was built (you can see the initials of the owner, Sir John Lisle, carved on the spandrels of the porch) but the main part of the present manor house emerged towards the end of the Elizabethan reign, around 1579, with final changes added in the 17th century. Its appearance is striking: built with ghostly pale Isle of Wight rubble, capped with gables, fitted with triple-mullioned windows and topped with a roof of age-old tiles that slightly dip and rise, as though they have been kneaded into place.

The third village manor house, **Northcourt** (Main Rd, PO30 3JG ⊘ northcourthouse. co.uk), is the most secluded, hidden within pockets of woods just to the north of the village centre. The largest Jacobean house on the Island, it dates to 1615 and is a fine stone structure: its zigzag roofline and high bay windows make it arguably the most aesthetically pleasing of the manor trio.

All three houses are accessible to varying degrees. Wolverton holds a folk and blues music festival in May and an annual garden and horticultural fair in September (check ⊘ visitisleofwight.co.uk for dates). It can also be visited by appointment. Parts of Westcourt, meanwhile, have been converted into a B&B, while Northcourt is available for large-group self-catering rental.

places alongside a counterpart at Sutton Hoo in terms of significance. The helmet was found in a shallow grave near the village by a metal-detecting club that was exploring a wider Anglo-Saxon cemetery that had long been destroyed by ploughing. It was originally dismissed as merely being part of an iron vessel but once the British Museum got its hands on it, however, the find's true identity as a utilitarian fighting helmet was revealed – though the museum has yet to put it on public display.

Shorwell is so self-contained and tucked away amid the southern folds of the downs that it's remarkably easy to forget that the village lies just a mile or so from the coast. To reach the sea on foot, walk west on the lane past Wolverton Manor towards Yafford, then turn left (south) along Doctor's Lane and walk past Wolverton Farm. After half a mile this turns into the waymarked Shepherd's Trail which crosses the Military Road and drops you down to the coast by Shepherd's Chine. Here the panorama opens up across Brighstone Bay, all the way to Chale in the east and Tennyson Down away to the west.

¶¶ FOOD & DRINK

The Crown Inn Walkers Ln, Shorwell PO30 3JZ ✐ 01983 740293 ⊘ characterinns.co.uk/the-crown-inn. A really fine pub in one of the Island's most picturesque villages. Although the menu emphasises pub perennials such as burgers and grills, everything is of a high standard and stylishly presented. The garden is hard to beat and features a trout stream in the form of the original Shor Well, as well as a duck sanctuary (which are, just to be clear, safe from the chef).

🛍 SHOPPING

Shorwell Village Stores Main Rd, Shorwell PO30 3JL ✐ 01983 740843 ⊘ shorwellvillagestore.co.uk. A good place to pick up fresh bread and bits and pieces for a picnic, as well as local jams, biscuits, village honey and other foods. Also serves bacon rolls. Really well-run shop at the heart of its community.

13 CHALE GREEN & CHALE

🏠 **Gotten Manor** (page 304) 🏠 **The Mission** (page 304), **The Scout Hall** (page 304)

Chale Green is a quiet hamlet with houses set back around a green; with adjacent coppicing and small pockets of unnamed woodland, everything here is very easy on the eye. It's the kind of place you can simply stumble upon while heading east from Shorwell.

The village is a good base for a fine walk up on to St Catherine's Down. Use footpath C1 to clamber up to the down from the northeast edge of the village green: it's barely a mile to the ridge and will take around 20 minutes. The route is easy: just keep on the main path, which soon climbs steeply before levelling out. Up on top you will come across the Hoy Monument, which looks rather like an unadorned Doric column with an Atlas stone (technically, it's a ball finial) placed on top. The obelisk commemorates the 1814 visit of Alexander I of Russia to Britain (the tsar never actually made it across the Solent, only travelling as far as Portsmouth, but he was a popular figure in Britain at the time for his anti-Napoleon stance). The 72ft column was erected thanks to the endeavours of the entrepreneur Michael Hoy, a Russian merchant who made his money in St Petersburg before buying land on the Isle of Wight.

The tiny community of **Chale** lies 1½ miles to the south of Chale Green, bunched around the A3055, and represents the eastern full stop on the coastal flatlands that extend all the way from Compton Bay. Chale is another small village dominated by its church, St Andrew's, which stands hard on the main junction of roads and is impossible to miss. The church is a grey flintstone structure that stands out against an uncluttered backdrop of fields and rolling downs. Views from the Coastal Path (just across the road) are popular with photographers seeking sunset images, for the southern plains and coastal contours of the Island unfold unimpeded all the way to Tennyson Down. For the best views of the setting sun, follow the coast path west from the church and you gain access above Walpen Chine and, after three-quarters of a mile, reach Whale Chine, where Tennyson Down truly fills the frame. For a contrast, look east from here and the A3055 becomes a tree-covered funnel as it abruptly narrows and twists its way uphill towards Blackgang Chine (page 182); the village name 'Chale' is thought to refer to the chine.

¶¶ FOOD & DRINK

The Wight Mouse Inn Church Pl, Chale PO38 2HA ☎ 01983 730431 ⬦ wightmouse. co.uk. A cavernous pub with an equally large beer garden that mixes standard pub fare with a consistently good specials board drawing more on local food. Has some of the most far-reaching views of any pub garden on the Island; you can take in much of the south coast as you dine and drink.

14 ST CATHERINE'S DOWN & THE PEPPERPOT

The best view of the surrounding landscape is from the oratory on **St Catherine's Down**, accessed by a short but steep walk from the car park (itself scenically positioned) immediately to the northeast of Blackgang Chine, on the A3055 (the down lies across the road, so be careful while crossing as cars come down the hill at speed and there are blind bends).

The oratory is also known locally – for obvious reasons when you see it – as the **Pepperpot**. Perched high on St Catherine's Hill, the oratory overlooks Chale Bay and its round stone base abuts, rather incongruously, some large transmission aerials. The grasslands around the oratory are a fine place for a picnic. To the immediate west and south of the oratory the land falls away into a series of gorse-filled dips and hollows that are full of birdsong in spring.

Although the Pepperpot looks as if it may have once been a hermitage or a similar place of retreat, the oratory's origins in fact lie as a medieval lighthouse (albeit with a degree of religious input) and date to the 14th century. In 1313, the ship *St Mary of Bayonne* was blown off-course and ran aground on the notorious Atherfield Ledge, which stretches out to sea more or less due south from the oratory. Among the goods salvaged by the crew was a cargo of white wine destined for a French monastery. Naturally, this was sold by the sailors to local people, with many barrels finding their way into the cellars of Walter de Godeton, Lord of the Manor of Chale. All this was, needless to say, highly illegal. De Godeton may have got away with it were it not for the fact the ship came from Gascony, then part of the kingdom of the ruling English king, Edward II. The incident was brought to the king's notice and de Godeton was summoned to an ecclesiastical court and heavily fined. Unfortunately for de Godeton, the Pope got wind of the affair and, to avoid excommunication, de Godeton was ordered to build an oratory and beacon on Chale Down (now St Catherine's Hill) as penance. A priest tended the light to guide ships and say prayers for the souls of the drowned – all at de Godeton's expense. Since the building was, in essence, a bell tower with a beacon alongside, it is unclear how effective it proved and the priest probably spent more times saying prayers for those lost at sea than saving souls or raising the alarm.

The building was abandoned following the dissolution of the monasteries under Henry VIII, and fell into disrepair. The octagonal tower was spared, surviving only because of its importance as a seamark.

In 1785 plans for a more substantial and effective lighthouse on the site were drawn up but the beacon was never completed for the simple reason it would have proved useless more often than not: the hill is often shrouded in mist. In 1838, work began on a new, third lighthouse on St Catherine's Point (page 175).

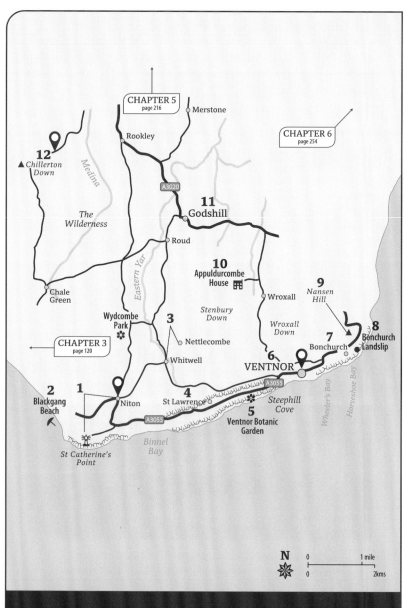

CHAPTER 5
page 216

CHAPTER 6
page 254

12
▲ Chillerton
Down

Merstone

Rookley

Medina

The
Wilderness

A3020

11
Godshill

Roud

10
Appuldurcombe
House

9
*Nansen
Hill*

Eastern Yar

Chale
Green

*Stenbury
Down*

Wroxall

8
Bonchurch
Landslip

Wydcombe
Park

3

*Wroxall
Down*

7
Bonchurch

CHAPTER 3
page 120

Nettlecombe

Whitwell

6
VENTNOR

Wheeler's Bay

Horseshoe Bay

2
Blackgang
Beach

1

Niton

4
St Lawrence

A3055

*Steephill
Cove*

5
Ventnor Botanic
Garden

A3055

*Binnel
Bay*

*St Catherine's
Point*

N

0   1 mile

0   2kms

THE SOUTH

4
THE SOUTH

The Isle of Wight has its own beautiful south. This is the part of the Island where downs and hills collide, bumping into one another to create valleys that resemble punchbowls. Should you glance at the Ordnance Survey map for the Island, the south seems to resemble a giant amphitheatre with bookends of hills rising on all sides. Ultimately, these ridgelines collapse into tiny, tucked-away bays, some of them home to communities of fishing families. The hub of the coast here focuses on **Ventnor**, a quirky town that has managed to plant its tenacious roots among the steep inclines on the Island's southern extremity. Away from the coast, you'll find handsome villages and great walking and cycling opportunities. While the downs require more effort in order to explore their ridgelines than their counterparts further west, when you do make it up here – to Ventnor Downs, Wroxall Down or Nansen Hill – you will find some of the loveliest but least-visited uplands of the Island, with waves of undulating folds and vertiginous valleys that are reminiscent of Dorset. Were that not enough, the area enjoys a thrilling sense of being a place apart – and not just by dint of the geological barriers that separate it from the rest of the Island. Access to the south involves a steep climb up roads or paths from the north, west and east. Perhaps more than anywhere else on the Island, this is where you come for true solitude: look out from the coast here and the contrast with the bustle of the Solent is striking – the major shipping lanes bypass this area, so only seabirds are likely to cut across the view as you gaze out to sea.

The south is also a geological curiosity, dominated along much of its coastline by the Undercliff, an elongated hotchpotch of clays, soils and rock that, thanks to the relentless efforts of the sea and rain, seem to have collectively given up the ghost and collapsed into the water. The Undercliff's tumbling ledges repay exploration all the way from Niton to the edge of Shanklin – this is a landscape where you can walk along

TOURIST INFORMATION

There's no official staffed tourist information point in the south of the Island but the Ventnor and District Local History Museum (page 193) and Ventnor Botanic Garden (page 188) have a useful assortment of leaflets and Island-wide information.

roads where cars no longer drive, or squeeze through clefts in cliffs so narrow that even the leanest of readers may have to breathe in deeply to proceed. Elsewhere you can drop down to shorelines that you can enjoy all to yourself and where you really are far from the crowds of Shanklin and Sandown. The downs also act as a weather curtain, buffering Ventnor and its surroundings from the chillier temperatures that northerly and easterly winds can bring. The beaches here can be up to 5°C warmer than those elsewhere on the Island.

A little further inland, you will find more of the Island's quintessentially charming villages. **Godshill** in particular, with its thatched cottages and formidable array of tea gardens, can feel like a walk-through pastiche of the homely rural idyll. Rivers – some of them in reality merely supersized brooks and streams – weave their way between these communities and offer the chance to pass under the gaze of a stately home, catch sight of a kingfisher, or linger by a brook as the sun shines through the branches of a willow tree. There are few better areas on the Island to go slow.

GETTING THERE & AROUND

WALKING & CYCLING

The region's major walking trails include the **Yar River Trail**, which follows the Eastern Yar (often called the East Yar or just 'the Yar' – not to be confused with the River Western Yar near Yarmouth), heading northeast from Niton all the way to Bembridge and St Helens on the northeast coast, and the **Wroxall Stream Trail** (islandrivers.org.uk/explore/walks/yar-trail/explore-the-wroxall-stream-link), which meanders for eight miles from Ventnor to Godshill, via Wroxall, and is waymarked for its entire length. As elsewhere on the Island's downs, once you have slogged your way up (invariably from sea level) to the ridgeline, you can bounce along on undulating whalebacks to your heart's content. The Coastal Path runs through the area too, and is at its most physically demanding here, threading its way through the vagaries of the Undercliff, along skyline ridges and sometimes, either side of Ventnor, hard by the sea, all but daring the tides to overwash it.

For cyclists, the approaches to Ventnor, either from Shanklin in the east, or Chale and Blackgang in the west (both via the A3055), are formidable and involve ascents of 500ft or so in less than a mile. The **Taste Round the Island Trail** (page 25) follows this main road but also explores the car-free Undercliff and knitting together villages such as Wroxall, Whitwell and Niton. For families, the **Red Squirrel Route** (page 26) runs immediately behind Godshill and offers an easy, level 3½-mile cycle to Wroxall. Running for a while along the same paths is the **Sunshine Trail**, a 12-mile loop that takes in Wroxall and Godshill and extends to Sandown. You can download a detailed route from the website of Routefifty7 (⊘ routefifty7.com/cycling/sunshine). For the more energetic, the **Chalk Extreme Trail** (page 26) comes to the fore in this part of the Island too and straddles much of the higher points of the downs, all the way from Chale Green to Wroxall, before heading for points north. Time, perhaps, to hire one of the many electric bikes on the Island (page 28). There are no cycle-hire outlets located within the area covered by this chapter but a couple of companies will drop off and collect bikes from Godshill and other locations (page 28). It's also worth asking at your accommodation as a number of B&Bs and hotels now offer electric, along with regular, bikes for hire.

PUBLIC TRANSPORT

Southern Vectis **buses** (page 21) covers the south of the Island comprehensively. The key route is the #3 bus, which runs from Newport to Ventnor (and on to Ryde). This is a coastal route and the extremely scenic nature of the journey can, for visitors, make it feel rather like a subsidised bus tour. Bear in mind, however, that the journey time from Ventnor to Ryde is 50 minutes, so allow time if you're heading for the hovercraft. The #6 also links Ventnor to Newport and is handy as it passes through Chillerton, Chale, Whitwell and Niton.

ALONG THE UNDERCLIFF TO NITON & ON TO ST LAWRENCE

You often see brown tourist signs for 'The Undercliff' around the south coast of the Island but you'll search in vain for a village or fairground-style attraction of that name. Instead, the Undercliff is the moniker given to an eight-mile stretch of collapsed cliffs and land edges that tumble into the English Channel either side of Ventnor.

The explanation for the Undercliff lies in geology. Parts of the downs that run around the southeast corner of the Island are topped with angular flint gravel; below this is a layer of chalk (chances are you'll stub your foot on protruding lumps as you walk along the tops of Luccombe and Ventnor downs). The next layer below the chalk is green sandstone, and below that lies gault clay, also known locally as Blue Slipper which, unfortunately, happens to be something of a geological weakling. From time to time the pressure of chalk and sandstone becomes too much for the weaker gault clay and gravity and weight reassert their dominance, causing the cliffs to buckle and collapse.

Despite this cliff-edge turbulence, much of the Undercliff is accessible thanks to a combination of the Coastal Path and smaller tracks, some of them truly ancient, which thread their serpentine way through the undulating landscape of exposed stone and rock. Paths into and around the Undercliff can be of great antiquity and include the Cripple Path, by St Catherine's Point, which is barely 200yds long (page 183) and links the Undercliff portion of Niton with the village parish church. Another, St Rhadegund's Path, snakes uphill from the A3055 to meet the Ventnor Road half a mile south of Whitwell and continues to the door of St Mary and St Rhadegund's Church.

Over the years, the collapsing Undercliff has claimed several roads and lanes. A stretch of the original A3055 between Blackgang and Niton disappeared into the sea in 1928 and another part of this ill-fated road has been closed between Ventnor and Niton since a landslip in 2014. Eight houses were evacuated after this latest drama but, while engineers say that knitting the road back together is possible, the £2 million price tag means that no-one is holding their breath. To drive or take the bus between Niton and Ventnor – a distance of three linear miles – you must now travel for almost five miles, inland via Whitwell.

Architecturally, the Undercliff is of substantial interest, as it features several examples of cottage orné, an eclectic architectural style that wholeheartedly embraced, above all, ornate timberwork: this translates

---

1 Bluebells carpeting Boniface Down. **2** A Victorian water pump, Whitwell. **3** Blackgang Beach, near Niton. ▶

THE ROAD WITH (ALMOST) NO CARS

The old A3055 – known as Undercliff Drive – is accessible on foot from Niton in the west and Ventnor in the east. The route described here heads west, from Ventnor; the distance between the two points is three miles. Walking its length is really worthwhile, not least because at either end you can refuel in pleasing fashion at The Buddle Inn in Niton or Ventnor Botanic Garden. The route is equally enjoyable on two wheels as on two legs, as Kevan Ansell of Routefifty7 cycle hire (page 28) attests: 'It's just magical. I cycle here from Shanklin and it is one of my favourite places to cycle on the Island.'

Beginning at Ventnor Botanic Garden, walk for 1¾ miles west along the A3055 and, after passing the turn off north (and uphill) for St Lawrence, you reach road end: here the paved lane becomes, briefly, a tapering narrow path that is accessible only to walkers and cyclists.

The road has effectively been cut in two by a landslip that's visible on the seaward side. A few yards later it opens up into a 'proper' road once more. From here, it's simply a matter of keeping ahead until you reach Niton and The Buddle Inn.

This is a magnificent and absurdly isolated corner of the Island and you have to pinch yourself that this is southern Britain. Walking along Undercliff Drive, alongside densely packed woods with the exposed chalk cliffs and escarpments high above, unseen waves sloshing far below, you realise just how completely wild this landscape is. Exploration also makes for an oddly eerie and bizarre experience. Despite knowing to the contrary, you can't help feeling that any moment a speeding lorry will turn the corner and whizz towards you. Instead, buzzards float above you, utterly unbothered by your presence.

in practice to exposed or embedded beams and woodwork that can resemble – depending on how tightly you narrow your eyes – Tudor, Georgian or even Edwardian façades, along with the occasional thatched roof, Swiss chalet and designed grounds. The best examples can be found in St Lawrence. More prosaically, long-forgotten and closed-off access roads, now moss-covered and unmaintained, peel off here and there towards the sea. Some of these are marked with daunting, official signs that forbid entry at risk of life and limb; some appear merely overgrown and pot-holed while others sink into the crumbling cliff face.

1 NITON & ST CATHERINE'S POINT

Castlehaven Retreat (page 304), **St Catherine's Lighthouse Cottages** (page 305)

In January 1901, Guglielmo Marconi transmitted radio signals from Knowles Farm on the coast below the village of **Niton** to the Lizard

Radio Telegraph Station in Cornwall, 186 miles away. Sometimes when you pass through Niton it can feel you need a similar means of communication for, although a small community (population: 2,000), the village feels rather spread out, thanks to both a circuitous one-way system and a fabulously collapsed section of cliff. The latter means the village, while evidently busy, is disarticulated, with an upper part where you find a pub and the village store and a lower, more residential area, with a second pub and access to the sea on foot.

The main sights of interest actually lie just outside the village, but do drop by the village church, St John the Baptist, before exploring further afield. Set back from the Blackgang Road on, unsurprisingly, Church Street, it hides bashfully behind mature trees and is worth visiting to admire the table-top tombs in the churchyard, which were a handy hiding place for both smugglers and their contraband. Just to the west of the church, by the side of Blackgang Road, you'll find a waymarker pinpointing the source of the River Eastern Yar. Rather than flowing the short distance to the south coast (which lies just a mile away), the river, perhaps in defiantly quirky Island style, opts instead to head northeast, all the way to Bembridge, fed by a network of small tributaries and spring-lines (the smallest of watercourses, which spring from the ground and merge with one another) and draining 20% of the Island along the way. This epic journey means it is, with a formidable length of 12 miles, the Island's longest river.

A wide, lozenge-shaped slab of grassland, **St Catherine's Point** is almost stereotypically scenic. The approach along the access land from Niton, half a mile to the north, slaloms downhill, providing the picture-postcard image of a lighthouse engaged in a defiant stand-off with the sea. The surrounding flatlands do not extend too far, however, and before long they bubble upwards into a collapsed and seemingly heaving heap of rocks, sands, outcrops and escarpments (some exposed to the elements, some wooded). Positioned just half a mile to the east of Blackgang Beach, the spectacle of grasslands and sands is as juxtaposed as chalk and cheese.

This headland is the location of the third attempt to build a lighthouse on this part of the Island and the first to be even partially successful. It's said that when cows on the downs first saw the new lighthouse, they stampeded – perhaps this was in astonishment at the belated achievement. The beacon was established in 1837 after yet another

A walk along the Yar Valley Trail from Niton to Godshill

✻ OS Explorer map 29; start: the source of the River Eastern Yar (page 170) ♥ SZ508762; 5 miles; easy

A spring near Niton is the source of the River Eastern Yar and following its journey northeast to Godshill offers a chance to enjoy Island views from a different perspective from those from the roads and coastline.

The Eastern Yar flows through fertile and accordingly highly cultivated farmland. The water here comes straight out of the gravel ridge and creates some very special habitats, including pools and marshes that support a tremendous variety of wildlife, including dragonflies and insect-feeding migrant birds such as chiffchaff. Water voles are commonly recorded along its length too, though they are so bashful that you will be lucky to spot one. As you walk along, look out for the remains of some of yesterday's uses: the sheepwash in Whitwell (on Sheepwash Lane) and withy beds planted for basketry along several stretches the river.

While there are lots of twists and turns along the way, the route is reassuringly waymarked in its entirety, with a 'YVT' motif, resembling a pair of swashbuckling cutlasses and inspired by traditional stonemasons' marks. It's possible to turn this short walk into a multi-day hike along the entire 18½ miles of the trail, which winds all the way to St Helens on the northeast coast. For full details, visit the trail website (⊘ islandrivers.org.uk/explore/walks/yar-trail/explore-the-yar-river-trail).

1 From the source of the River Eastern Yar (it's decidedly modest but marked, about 200yds west of Niton's church), walk along the main road, past the church, to cross Niton High Street, with the White Lion pub on your right. Dog-leg across the road to pick up the waymarked trail at School Lane and follow the waymarkers out of the village to Allotment Road and Ashknowle Lane, heading towards Whitwell.

2 After 1¼ miles, you reach Whitwell. Pilgrims bound for France in medieval times followed the trail along Ashknowle Lane to receive healing waters at Whitwell's holy well; the stream was a good supply of clean drinking water and iron cups were fastened to the arm of the pump for villagers to drink from. The route runs behind the church of St Mary and St Rhadegund. Where Ashknowle Lane ends, turn left in front of the church and downhill on to Whitwell High Street (if you want to inspect the original well, it lies directly across the road from the church, a few paces down footpath NT13). Just after the White Horse pub, turn left into Bannock Road and then right on to Slay Lane before following the footpath out of the village. After Whitwell, the trail follows the Eastern Yar through fens and marshes that bloom with plants such as speedwell and wild garlic from spring to autumn. The path keeps to the left (west) of the river. Around two-thirds of a mile out of Whitwell the path reaches Southford Lane.

3 Turn right along the lane and, immediately after crossing a small stream, turn left along the footpath, now on the east side of the river. You pass disused mills at Southford and Ford, dating from the 18th century; both had closed by the end of World War I. The path switches to the west side at Ford Farm along footpath 112 before crossing once again to the east bank as you continue to head north to reach the minuscule hamlet of Roud.

4 The path reaches Roud Road and dog-legs to switch to the west bank of the river again. Continue north, with the river on your right, for two-thirds of a mile until you meet a road named Beacon Alley. Turn left and, after 100yds, turn right up Bagwitch Lane. After 150yds, take the footpath on the right, passing to the south of Mill Cottage (there's a cattery and ▶

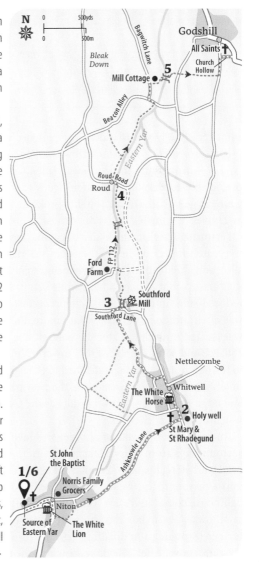

A walk along the Yar Valley Trail from Niton to Godshill (continued)

▶kennels here). You pass the remains of the ruined Bridge Mill and its adjacent cottage, which dates from at least 1759; the metal gears you see around the cottage are from the early 19th century.

5 Follow the path over the River Eastern Yar to reach Whitwell Road. Cross over and continue along a footpath across a large field to Church Hill. Turn left along the lane then, after 180yds, turn right down Church Hollow into Godshill.

shipwreck finally saw Islanders lose patience with the uselessness of its predecessor on St Catherine's Down, 1¾ miles to the northwest (page 167). Returning from the Caribbean laden with rum, coconuts and, less predictably, turtles, the *Clarendon* struck rocks at the foot of Blackgang Chine in gale-force winds. The ship broke up in heavy seas with the loss of 23 lives (the turtles' fate is not recorded).

Featuring a stylish three-tier octagonal tower, it seemed as though the search for the right lighthouse in the right place had finally been successful. Yet teething problems meant that the south coast lighthouse saga was to continue for a little while yet: in 1875 the height had to be reduced substantially as – like its predecessors up the road – its light was often shrouded in mist. What's more, the original fog signal house was located on a cliff nearer the sea but, due to erosion, was at risk of collapse and so was replaced by a tower – similar but smaller in stature to the lighthouse column – attached to the lighthouse in the 1930s. This finally settled the matter and for the best part of 90 years these little and large structures – known locally as the Cow and Calf – have kept a watchful eye over the coast.

An easy walk of a couple of miles will take in the lighthouse and its surroundings from Niton. Starting from The Buddle Inn (page 180), head west along the lane and follow it as it bears left downhill and turns into a private road (walkers are allowed). After a third of a mile, the lighthouse comes into view. The lane passes the lighthouse and finishes at Knowles Farm but the footpath continues westwards for a little further through an undulating coastal strip with exceptional views of the cliffs above. After 300yds or so, where the path finally meets the sea, simply bear left and follow the coastal tracks east with views along the coastline towards Reeth Bay. A stile lifts you over the lighthouse walls and you can continue across fields for half a mile to a woodland and the small Castlehaven caravan park. The minuscule patch of grass (you can

THE LOSS OF SS *MENDI*

It's easy to romanticise shipwrecks while you admire a skilfully carved ship's head that has been retrieved from the depths. The reality is of course inevitably more brutal and casualties that foundered around the Island range from the exploration of the 'New World' and what were then called the East Indies to those of a more recent vintage. The sinking of the SS *Mendi* represents one of the most shameful episodes in British seafaring history.

The SS *Mendi* was a steamship which sailed from Cape Town in 1917 and, after 34 days at sea, was heading around the Isle of Wight to drop the men on board in France. These were not soldiers but labourers bound for the Western Front to build trenches and railway lines. At 05.00 on 21 February, some ten nautical miles south of St Catherine's Point, the *Mendi* hit a cargo ship, SS *Darro*, in thick fog. The *Darro* had failed to sound its foghorn and ploughed into the *Mendi*, gouging a 20ft hole in her starboard bow. Most of the men, who were sleeping in bunks right where the hole was tripped in the boat, stood little chance. In all 646 people died, the vast majority of them black South Africans; survival rates were somewhat higher among the white passengers.

The tale becomes, if it is possible, even more harrowing. Reports say that the pastor Isaac Wauchope Dyobha, recognising the ship was sinking, began a grisly dance, known as 'the death drill', even as the waters overwhelmed the ship. As he and the doomed men drummed their feet on the deck, his words were recorded and include these lines:

> You are going to die, but that is what you came to do. Brothers, we are drilling the drill of death. I, a Xhosa, say you are all my brothers, Zulus, Swazis, Pondos, Basutos, we die like brothers. We are the sons of Africa.

The actions of the crew of the *Darro* have long been the subject of suspicion. While other ships in the area were alerted and came to assist, the *Darro*, which was still seaworthy, did nothing but simply stood by. The reasons why have never been established but some historians and many South Africans have maintained that the captain, Harry Stump, did not act because of the men's skin colour, though others have said that in fog he may have been disoriented. There is no record of Stump expressing remorse. A cracked porthole from the ship, along with other items, are on display at the Shipwreck Centre and Maritime Museum at Arreton (page 241). The disaster was hushed up and only unfolded once the ship had, by chance, been located by local diver Martin Woodward (see box, page 242).

traverse it in perhaps four strides) just behind the caravan site overlooks Reeth Bay and is officially, if improbably, a village green. No-one seems to know exactly when or how this triangle of land attained its status but in recent years the local community has restored the green, clearing away the sea-blown rubble, which has enabled coastal flowers such as sea pink and silver weed to recolonise its edges. Set hard by the bay, this is a good location for a picnic. To get back to The Buddle Inn, take the lane uphill by the caravan site and then, shortly after it bears right, follow the steps on the left uphill back to the pub.

¶¶ FOOD & DRINK

The Buddle Inn St Catherine's Rd, Niton PO38 2NE ✆ 01983 730243 ⌂ characterinns. co.uk/the-buddle-inn. This excellent 16th-century pub has a history of smuggling, and it's easy to imagine ne'er do-wells hauling their booty up the cliff faces before sinking a pint with their ill-gotten gains in a snug corner, one eye keenly alert for customs inspectors. The menu is extensive and mixes traditional mains with inventive local dishes such as Island pheasant stew with chestnut dumplings. In an ideal world you'd visit this pub on a sunny early summer evening when you can sit on the flower-decked patio-terrace that has won awards as the best Island pub garden. The pub interior is wonderfully atmospheric and equally welcoming on a cold winter's night when the inglenook beams, flagstone floors and, most importantly, roaring fires come into their own.

Castlehaven Beach Café Castlehaven Ln, Niton Undercliff PO38 2ND ⌂ thetruefoodkitchen.com ☺ Apr–Sep but check website for good-weather opening outside these months. Operating out of a static caravan kitchen (run by the owners of the Tramezzini restaurant in Ventnor) on the Castlehaven caravan site, with outdoor table dining. The excellent Mediterranean food ranges from tuna with mango salsa to lemongrass panna cotta and panko banana bao buns (a kind of Chinese bread roll).

Norris Family Grocers Newport Rd, Niton PO38 2DB ✆ 01983 730275 ⌂ norrisstores. co.uk. Well-stocked family-run local shop, which works hard to promote local produce such as Island cheeses, breads and booze. This is a great place to put together a picnic or shop if you are self-catering.

Stonelands On Undercliff Drive, just after the road junction with St Catherine's Road, keep an eye out on the left for the honesty farm shop operated by the Stonelands Project (⌂ stonelandsiow.wixsite.com/niton), selling locally grown vegetables and fruit, including squash, lettuce and chillies. The project has a strong religious element and seeks to offer young people in difficulty the opportunity to work in agriculture.

The White Lion High St, Niton PO38 2AT ✆ 01983 719402 ⌂ whitelioniow.co.uk. Looks the part, both externally with an age-old whitewashed (but freshly painted) façade of thick-set stone, a rickety porch and, inside, heaving timbers that are starting to bend at the knees. Popular with locals and run by the Holmes family, this is a pub at the heart of its community. Food to match, including hearty pies.

2 BLACKGANG BEACH

Niton is also the gateway to the magic of Blackgang Beach, which is a strong contender for the most beautiful – if rarely visited – of all the Island's beaches (note that if you try and get here via Blackgang Chine you won't get very far – the only access to it is through Niton).

The reason for the beach's low profile is clear enough: it is inaccessible to all but the most determined and reached by a steep, sometimes awkward (but never dangerous) path. The reward is a glorious beach of ochre-coloured, fine-grained pebbles (your feet sink ever so slightly as you cross the beach) that lies under a magnificent sandstone escarpment that looks like a vast slab of honeycomb.

The beach is delightfully isolated – you won't find an ice-cream van here – and it is not too fanciful to think that the beach could pass for an iconic image of a remote coastline such as those found in Australia. The western end of the beach is known as Rocken End and is an established naturist beach but you are under no obligation to follow suit (this stretch is also quite pebbly and must surely make for uncomfortable reclining; naturists in the know presumably pack an extra-thick towel). Note that, when you get on to the beach along the right-hand path, you should not turn left, as the sand soon turns to Blue Slipper mud (page 172) and you may get stuck.

From Niton to the beach is a good mile's walk in each direction. To get there, head south from Niton and, where the A3055 turns sharp left, head straight on into St Catherine's Road and then take the first right along Old Blackgang Road for 800yds. This ends in a small car park; the walk from here to the beach takes around 15 minutes but can feel much longer, especially if it has been raining recently. Take the first gate in the car park and follow the grassy path for 150yds into a glade where you turn right downhill and through a gate. For a south-facing path (and so exposed to direct sunlight), the descent can be surprisingly muddy and slippery for much of the year. Be prepared to slither and slide, and grab hold of branches. Altruistic local people occasionally fix ropes to some trees to help you keep your balance but these aids do seem to come and go. Just after you go over a second stile the paths diverge above a small pond. The left-hand path leads to a part of the beach covered in vast boulders from the collapsed cliff and offers fine views of nature at work at high tide. Take the right-hand path to continue to slither your way to the beach.

Blackgang Chine (PO38 2HN ℘ 01983 730330 ⌀ blackgangchine. com) lies just half a mile to the west along the coast from its namesake beach, but is inaccessible on foot from the shoreline. Perhaps the most spectacular of the Island chines, this broad incision in the landscape sees the high coast and foreshore abruptly slump into the sea. The only downside is that you will have to pay to see it: ask anyone who grew up on the Island and the chances are that they visited Blackgang Chine as a child. The UK's first theme park, this is a resolutely entertainment-based ensemble of Victoriana set amid what was once a magnificently desolate and wild gorge. The park was opened in 1843 by Alexander Dabell, a lace maker from Nottingham. The origins of the venture were serendipitous: in 1842 a huge fin whale was stranded near the Needles and, alert to the fascination this would exert on potential paying visitors, Dabell made sure he bought the whale – all of it – at auction. He sold off the blubber and put the skeleton on display and it remains on display today. When news later spread that a spring arising in the chine offered health benefits to ailing Victorians, the enduring popularity of the place was assured. Over the subsequent 170 years, the gardens have been developed into an eccentric and eclectic collection of displays about the local history, fantasy animated shows, cowboy towns, dinosaurs and rides for most ages. Like some of the other Victoriana on the Island, it's something of a Marmite experience. Should you be disinclined to spend a day at a theme park, public access either side of and above the chine is easy, allowing you glimpses of its natural beauty.

3 NETTLECOMBE & WHITWELL

⌂ **Kingsmede** (page 304) ⌂ **Nettlecombe Farm** (page 304)

With their thatched cottages set among rolling hills and farmland, the village of **Whitwell** and adjacent hamlet of **Nettlecombe** are both very easy on the eye. Whitwell Church is dedicated to both St Mary and St Rhadegund, a rare example of an English church named for this Thuringian princess and Frankish queen. The church originally comprised two separate chapels, one (St Rhadegund) for inhabitants of Whitwell, the other (St Mary's) for those trekking in from outlying

Godshill and St Lawrence. Nowadays, the Jacobean pulpit serves both communities. Restoration work during the 19th century uncovered an expert wood carving of a pair of hands in the roof (today you'll find them on the south wall, near the Lady Chapel).

As you wander around both Whitwell and Nettlecombe, you'll notice an unusually high number of what appear at first glance to be fire hydrants. These are in fact red cast-iron water pumps and were installed in the 1880s by a foresighted Islander, William Spindler (page 186). Having moved to the Island to improve his health, Spindler sought to enhance that of others by funding a waterworks to supply safe drinking water to villagers. Their design is impressive and features a lion's head, from which the water would flow. The fact they were even needed is ironic since Whitwell was for centuries venerated as a source of healing waters. 'White' is an Old English word meaning 'clear' or 'pure' and accordingly the village is assumed to have taken its name from a spring of safe drinking water that was also possessed of properties to heal the infirm. There are even suggestions that pilgrims stopped here on the early parts of journeys to sites in France, Spain and even the Holy Lands of the Middle East. Having

"As you wander around, you'll notice an unusually high number of what appear at first glance to be fire hydrants."

landed along the coast around St Catherine's Point, they would ascend to Whitwell along the Cripple Path (today this is footpath NT117, accessed from Undercliff Drive, half a mile to the east of The Buddle Inn; the name comes from the Old English word for a narrow passage and does not have any link to a concept of infirmity). The original well is located opposite the church, on footpath NT13, and today is a modest spring marked by an large overhanging stone inscription and covered with wire mesh to stop toddlers and small birds falling in.

The hamlet of Nettlecombe is centred upon Nettlecombe Farm (page 184) and its smattering of outlying cottages. You move from one village to the other as you meander up Nettlecombe Lane. The road narrows and climbs and on the left the old Whitwell railway station has been reincarnated as holiday lets. Today, it can seem improbable that such a somnolent location as Nettlecombe ever merited a railway halt but before World War II the area was busy with smallholders and agricultural workers tilling the fields. The farms are still there – some parts, such as stables and milk parlours are now also holiday homes –

but the landscape looks much as it would have done then, with fields demarcated by hedgerows. 'We have a little of everything here,' says Emma Theunissen, who works at Nettlecombe Farm. 'With a short walk we have views of the sea, there's always a magical light, it's the perfect place for a childhood. We feel like we live in a mini-country that we have to our own.'

An alternative, more rustic route up to Nettlecombe from Whitwell involves taking footpath NT13 opposite the church (which goes past the original village well). The path enters woods where you follow NT5, with lakes on your left, to reach the farm, where footpaths are open to the public (but please respect the privacy of residents). The total distance is a little under a mile. At the point at which you join footpath NT5, you are actually walking through fields that cover the original, now deserted, village of Nettlecombe. The jumble of grassy mounds that arise from the pasture represent the foundation platforms of buildings, while shards of pottery exposed by ploughing indicate the village was active from medieval times through to the Elizabethan era, something confirmed by Assize Rolls (early court records) which date it to at least 1271. Frustratingly, the site has never been excavated and little is known about what lies below or even why the original village was abandoned. Many such villages were depopulated as a result of the various waves of Black Death that dropped by over the centuries, or because villagers were relocated by emparkment (that is, evicted by rich landowners). Yet neither explanation is thought to apply to Nettlecombe and instead one supposition is that, situated on lower ground in a valley, villagers simply moved uphill to release land for grazing and to seek protection from the waters that would cascade downhill during heavy rains.

If you fancy stretching your legs further, you can keep going uphill beyond Nettlecombe Farm along footpaths that lift you all the way up on to Stenbury Down for more exquisite views of coast, downland and valleys; these really are some of the very best views to be enjoyed on the Island and the paths up high see surprisingly very few visitors. From Nettlecombe Farm to the ridgeline of Stenbury Down, by its distinctive transmitter mast, is 1½ miles. Take footpath NT3 behind the farm (with the lakes to your right) and then NT19 which rises slightly uphill, before turning left after 400yds into NT119, which contours in satisfying fashion above the farm and becomes NT1. This in turn sweeps uphill to the ridge via a couple of stiles, a flight of wooden steps and gates. On the brow you can turn left along GL51 and walk the 600yds or so towards the mast. To the northeast is Culver Down and Sandown Bay; to the north, the land sags into the wrinkled folds of Arreton Down; look east and you are taking in the Ventnor Downs, from left to right: Shanklin Down, the back side of Nansen Hill, St Boniface Down and Wroxall Down. Let your imagination go and you can almost see the joins where nature has knitted and hung this sweeping landscape together. Perhaps most surprising of all is the view when you turn to the west: there, the coastal plains run clearly all the way from Chale to Compton Bay, Freshwater and, some 18 miles distant but pin-clear on a day when the clouds are co-operative, Tennyson Down.

Wydcombe Park

National Trust

One of the Island's most delightful but unsung slivers of nature can be found just 1½ miles north of Whitwell. Although this is a National Trust site, you wouldn't really know it as the Trust has a very low-key presence here. This is not a park in the formal sense, instead it essentially comprises a combination of cattle-grazed heathland reminiscent of Dorset and beech woods; the two combine in a way that is extremely wildlife friendly. You are highly likely to see red squirrels, nuthatches, treecreepers and long-tailed tits. Please respect the owners of the smattering of private houses that are adjacent to the footpaths in the dell at the heart of the park. You can reach the park by walking a mile north of Niton along the Newport Road and then taking the signposted footpath NT86 northwest for half a mile. There's also just enough space for a couple of vehicles to be parked, with consideration, near the footpath.

¶¶ FOOD & DRINK

The White Horse High St, Whitwell PO38 2PZ ✐ 01983 730375 ♻ whitehorseiow.co.uk. Good food in a popular pub that, dating to 1454, is widely regarded as the oldest on the Island. Menu ranges from rustic bread to local seafood and burgers. Note the tiles that have replaced a much-missed thatched roof: after two fires either side of the Millennium, the owners bowed to the inevitable and opted for a less flammable exterior. A beer garden, children's play area and age-old farming equipment repurposed as décor complete something approaching the perfect pub.

4 ST LAWRENCE

A fetching village comprising a tight-knit lattice of narrow lanes lined with 19th-century houses, St Lawrence is tucked away above Undercliff Drive, to the south of Nettlecombe and west of Ventnor. Approaching it from the old A3055, it feels as though you are exploring *terra nova*, so hidden away does it feel from civilisation; were it not for the signposted footpath uphill to the village and church, you could easily miss the village altogether, even though it sits just a couple of hundred yards to the north of the road. For drivers, the community is connected to the outside world by a paved road, St Lawrence Shute, a spur of the Whitwell road and, more easily, along Undercliff Drive from Ventnor.

Squeezed in between the narrow lanes is the tiny Grade II-listed **church of St Lawrence**. This diminutive church is of 13th-century origin, though it was restored nearly 100 years ago. When first built it was 20ft long and 12ft wide, and for centuries was regarded as the smallest church in England. Even its modern-day proportions have swollen to a mere 45ft x 15ft. The interior is a mixture of whitewashed, austere walls and of the exquisite, with a 15th-century baptismal font, a painted royal coat of arms dating to 1663, 18th-century coat pegs and pre-Raphaelite stained-glass windows.

As well as passing the occasional cottage orné, you may glimpse sturdy Victorian-era brick-built houses as you walk along the road, some of them still inhabited, others easing into decay and ruin (most are still occupied, so please respect owners' privacy). They seem rather out of place, set back from the woods, and are the slightly surreal legacy of a German developer – and optimist – William Spindler. Taking the view that to create a flourishing business you should set up next door to someone doing things successfully, Spindler (a chemist by trade) aimed to develop the village of St Lawrence as a holiday rival to Ventnor. The idea never quite took off, possibly because, despite his altruistic efforts in Whitwell (page 183), history portrays Spindler as a hectoring, somewhat gauche individual with a singular talent for getting people's backs up. Issuing 'improving' pamphlets in which he lectured local villagers for being lazy probably didn't help his cause.

Located deep in the Undercliff, to the west of St Lawrence, you'll find **Binnel Studios** (Old Park Rd, PO38 1XR ⊘ binnelstudios.com ☉ by appointment), a collection of artists working in the Island's former glassworks' building. For such a tucked-away place, the quality of work here may take you by surprise as the artists are often internationally renowned rather than decent hobbyists. They include painter Celia Wilkinson, whose distinctive abstract brushwork focuses on elemental Island landscapes, and Matthew Chambers, whose concentric wheel-shaped pottery has been purchased by the V&A and exhibited in New York. Another is Jane Cox (see box, below) who produces ceramic work, often with calligraphic features, as well as Art Deco concoctions, prints and collages. The artists hold an open studios event each year, usually over

BINNEL BAY: A WINDOW FOR ARTISTIC INSPIRATION

Around Binnel Bay perhaps more than anywhere else on the Island, you get that sense of being 'away from it all', and so it comes as little surprise to find a community of artists drawing on the landscape, light and solitude on offer. 'Binnel Bay is an exceptionally stunning place,' says ceramicist Jane Cox. 'It is one of the wildest, rockiest bays on the island, a romantic escape and great for dreaming and collecting driftwood.'

The bay, and more widely the Island, proved a revelation for Jane after she found it increasingly hard to stir the creative juices in London. 'I lived and worked in busy London and I was beginning to get burned out and overloaded,' she recalls. 'The move here brought focus to my work and improved my work-life balance. My studio is ten minutes down a beautiful coastal track, past luscious semi-tropical vegetation, and it puts me in the right mood to make my work and the long hours of patient meticulous concentration that's required. I punctuate my working days with frequent walks to the beach, to catch a red sunset or the fleeting glimpse of a sea eagle hunting prey over the bay.'

Inspiration for her work comes from outside the front door. 'This part of the Island has a very temperate microclimate,' says Jane. 'Outside my studio door are some amazing tree and plant species which delight and inspire new work, giant leaves of the Tetrapanax Rex plant, spikey towering fronds of numerous palms, a whole array of sculptural tree ferns and, for colour, giant tree peonies, hollyhocks and clematis, and the spikey flowers of acanthus and echium.'

This lush landscape provides a fertile environment for creativity, too. 'The combination of the exotic and ever-changing landscape and weather, the Island's tranquillity and uniqueness... all these attract creative types,' she says. They may even identify with the Island's smuggling past and draw inspiration from its often harsh rocky coastline. 'I think this attracts artists who are often by necessity very like this themselves – not always well off, living by their wits and using resources economically to get by and survive,' Jane adds. 'People here make things happen, come what may.'

the August Bank Holiday. Otherwise, note that visits are by appointment: all the artists work independently and at times may be away exhibiting on the mainland or abroad, so it's always best to contact a few days in advance. **Binnel Bay** itself is accessible, though like Blackgang Beach (page 181) a little tenacity is required to get there. The path from the studios is clear: it's a bit of a scramble, though much briefer than Blackgang, and there's a useful rope with which to steady yourself. You're rewarded with a superb pebbly beach, with plenty of stones containing remnants of fossils.

VENTNOR & AROUND

Ventnor is hemmed in by high downs to the north and by the Undercliff on either side, so you get the sense of a town that is geographically a place apart. This is a quirky town, landscaped by the Victorians in a manner that makes for a slightly make-believe environment, where grand houses appear to have been chiselled into near-sheer hillsides. These in turn overlook a huge bay and a promenade that bustles with ice-cream stalls and traditional seaside entertainments. The main draws of the town are not only this promenade and its fine adjacent coastline but also the exotic floral delights of the botanic garden.

Exploring Ventnor can feel rather like descending a particularly wayward roller-coaster, or navigating a painting by M C Escher, with roads and footpaths somehow combining to make the entire town hang together amid the southern foothills of the Island downs. Today it's an absorbing town to explore as it is now embarking upon a transition from a centre of genteel retirement to a creative and artistic hub.

5 VENTNOR BOTANIC GARDEN

🏠 **Ventnor Botanic Garden** (page 305)

Undercliff Dr, Ventnor PO38 1UL ⌂ botanic.co.uk

On the Undercliff, midway between St Lawrence and Ventnor, these popular gardens make the most of their hospitable climate that keeps them typically 5°C warmer than the rest of the Island. This is due to Ventnor's south-facing aspect, the moderating influence of the sea and the protection afforded against northerly winds by the chalk downs that tower above the town. More than 6,000 species of plant are grown here, fighting for space alongside more substantial mature and exotic specimens. Lush plants, many of them exotics – Mediterranean and subtropical – thrive in a broadly frost-free environment. These include a series of champion trees, so named as they are believed to be the largest recorded specimens of their kind. Among their number is a spectacular Alpine cider gum that fans out some 49ft high.

FOOD MILES & METRES

When it comes to the concept of Slow food, you often hear the term 'food miles' banded around, to reflect the carbon footprint of the food on your dish. At Edulis, the restaurant at Ventnor Botanic Garden, the chef and the kitchen team talk of 'food metres'. Much of the food here is really as local and as seasonal as it is possible to be and the kitchen always has at least two plant-based dishes on the menu which are grown on site, such as with apples from the arbour or pumpkins from the plantation.

Salads are snipped fresh daily and the menu constantly changes as the kitchen uses what is emerging from the ground, from mushrooms, hops, squashes, olives and potatoes to radishes, kohlrabi (a member of the cabbage family with a crisp crunchy texture), Romanesco and beef tomatoes. At this point, the rationale for naming the restaurant Edulis becomes apparent: the term means 'edible' in Latin and in this case the message is clear: eat the garden.

'We love to grow our own food, we are very climate aware and zero food miles supports our ethos,' says Ventnor Botanic Garden ambassador Jack Cavanagh. 'Everything is seasonal and that shapes what the gardeners deliver to the kitchen and what goes on the menu. It's then up to the chefs and catering team to create a menu around the produce – the garden dictates the menu rather than the chef.'

That task is made a little easier since the crops clearly thrive in their own microclimate bubble, thanks to the sheltering effect of Ventor Downs and the garden's location in an ancient landslide. The garden rarely ever sees frost and it doesn't stick around long when it does.

The emphasis on local sourcing brings with it a requirement for innovation in order to ensure variety – in some instances, particular plants may be available for just one week, several months after the seeds are planted.

Unusual flavours from botanic ingredients include winter's bark – shavings from the bark of the tree, collected in a way not too dissimilar to the process of collecting cinnamon – which is fiery hot and used in coffees, cakes and soups. Evergreen magnolia buds are blended into sugar or used to flavour gin.

The garden staff are also tuned into the concept of 'ethnobotany', the study of human relationships and interactions with plants. 'Eating food fresh as you can get has many well-known benefits,' he says. In this way, it seems the original history of the garden's site, to help make people better, continues, though perhaps in ways its founders never imagined.

The gardens in which these trees are set are jaw-droppingly beautiful, with striking and varying colour schemes unfolding and fading from early spring to late autumn. In spring, the blossom and vase-shaped leaves of magnolia trees can you make you feel as though you are wandering through an open-air cream bubble bath. A real crowd-pleaser is the flowering of the giant echiums – bell-shaped flowers with tall spires – in May and June, which has been likened to a floral firework display. All year round you can see the showy red and yellow spikes of kniphofia, a plant also known as 'red hot poker'.

The uplifting nature of a visit here belies the rather sadder origins of the garden and buildings, which were once home to the Royal National Hospital for Diseases of the Chest. Ventnor's warm airs were considered to be a curative for tuberculosis; among those who took the air here was the perennially ailing Karl Marx. The hospital developed in the 1860s after Dr Arthur Hill Hassal visited Ventnor to recuperate from an illness and drew some enlightened conclusions about the role the microclimate could play in alleviating the scourge of the day. The formal botanic garden was opened in 1972.

♉ FOOD & DRINK

Edulis Botanic Garden & **Plantation Room Café** Ventnor Botanic Garden, Undercliff Dr, Ventnor PO38 1UL ✆ 01983 855397 ⌖ botanic.co.uk. Two superb places to eat can be found at the botanic garden and both allow you to sit back and imagine you are closer to the Mediterranean than the North Sea. Edulis is the more upmarket and is among the very best fine-dining experiences to be had on the Island; food here is seasoned and made with ingredients – herbs, salads and fruits – fresh from the garden (see box, page 189). The more informal Plantation Room Café, meanwhile, is an ideal pit stop for those walking or cycling the south coast. In both places, and the shop, you can buy the garden beers – Botanic Ale and a separate pale ale – brewed from hops grown on site. The hops are only truly ripe for one day a year and in late August the garden botanists keep an almost hourly vigil before picking them. If your visit coincides with this harvest, you are welcome to join in.

6 VENTNOR

🏠 **St Maur** (page 304)

Until barely 200 years ago, the area now known as Ventnor comprised only a few fishermen's cottages and a mill but the seaside location, seclusion and balmy temperatures saw it promoted as a health-giving location and development as a seaside resort began in earnest from

VENTNOR'S WORLD LEADERS

Most holiday destinations, if they look hard enough, can exhume public figures and world leaders who once bought an ice cream or looked at their resort through a train window – but Ventnor appears to be in an eclectic class of its own.

A sickly child named Winston Churchill was brought to Ventnor in the late 19th century, with his nanny Mrs Everest, to help him recuperate in the town's airs, but the future wartime prime minister was far from the only VIP to draw breath here. Mahatma Gandhi visited the Island while on holiday during his law studies in London in 1890 and his autobiography describes a walk on the downs above Ventnor with the unchaperoned 25-year-old daughter of his landlady. Although Gandhi was anything but a slow walker, he struggled to keep pace with the woman who 'was flying almost like a bird and chatting all the while'. She then dashed down the hill in high heels, leaving Gandhi trailing in her wake. In between this excitement, the sole surviving photograph of him in England was taken, during a visit to the Isle of Wight Vegetarian Society.

Karl Marx, the German inspirer of communist ideology, visited the Isle of Wight not once but three times, staying in Ventnor in 1882 and 1883 in an endeavour to improve his health. Marx suffered from neuralgia and liver problems aggravated by insomnia but still took regular daily strolls through and around the town, dosed up to the eyeballs with morphine. A plaque at Chimnetz, 1 St Boniface Gardens, notes his residency there. Marx once circumnavigated the Island by boat and even took time to write to his fellow socialist philosopher Engels, describing the Island's beauty. Engels was persuaded and he too later visited, as did his compatriot and author Ivan Turgenev. The latter composed *Fathers and Sons* here, a novel that finessed the philosophy of nihilism, an absolutist form of political ideology that is widely believed to have inspired communism.

Haile Selassie, the deposed Ethiopian emperor, fled to Britain as a refugee in 1936 and visited Ventnor two years later. His abrupt impoverishment meant he could only afford to stay at the Beach Hotel on the seafront, snootily dismissed in the refined circles of the time as merely being the third-best hotel in town. He spent most of his time walking, though a photograph in the town museum shows him clambering out of a boat on the beach.

around 1830. Before long, the town was referred to as Mayfair-by-the Sea, with millionaires swanning around hotels that boasted the new wonders of the age such as hydraulic lifts and palm courts. The town remained popular well into the 20th century and in 1952 demand was high enough to justify 45 trains a day from Ryde to Ventnor. It didn't last – the emergence of the overseas package holiday phenomenon saw

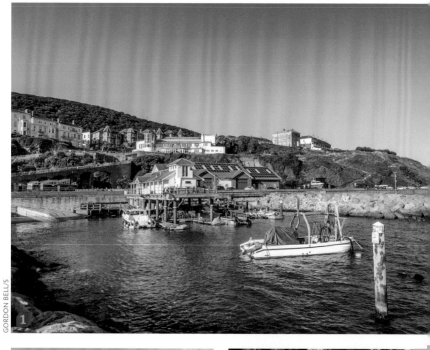

to that – and the town's slow decline was mirrored by the closure of its railway station in 1961, 100 years after it opened.

Ventnor is shoehorned into the contours of the towering downs that overlook it from the north. The town divides, very roughly, into three distinct areas: terraces of houses gaze down from on high; the next tier down comprises the town centre, with a one-way road system centred on the High Street with its array of independent shops; below here, Shore Hill descends steeply in a zigzag past the Winter Gardens and the Cascade Garden to the Esplanade and the beach. The helter-skelter nature of the town would seem to make it the perfect landscape for an annual cheese-rolling competition from downs to sea.

Here and there you will see grand mansions, classic Victorian townhouses, Mediterranean palms and other Italianate features. Properties are built mainly in the local greensand stone but there are plenty made of brick and of flint (in Victorian times, flint was considered second-rate but it was cheaper; you'll notice many houses have sandstone frontages but their back and sides are pockmarked with chunks of flint). The sea is constantly imposing its presence on the town and, in an attempt to resist erosion, 30,000 tons of Mendip limestone have been deposited along the shore, starting to the west of town, and extending into a mile-long sea wall to the east.

Before heading for the Esplanade, it's definitely worth popping into the **Ventnor and District Local History Museum** (11 Spring Hill, PO38 1PE ✆ 01983 855407 ⊕ ventnorheritage.org.uk), which is another one of those little gems, packed with nuggets of information about the town's past. You'll see just how much the town has changed over the years as its development is captured by the works of local artists on display. Shipwreck tales also abound – spare a thought for one of the unluckiest (or foolhardy) victims, Richard Tatton-Groves, who drowned after returning to the stricken *Underley* in 1871 to retrieve a pet bird. The other 30 passengers and crew survived.

The Esplanade rewards a stroll along its half mile of sea views and mix of traditional ice-cream stalls and modern bay-view apartments. To reach it, you descend from the town centre past the Cascade Garden, an ornamental public space that combines a rock garden with floral bedding; with its yucca plants and mosses, it has the feel of a lush

◀ **1** Ventnor. **2** Steephill Cove. **3** Bonchurch Landslip. **4** Ventnor Fringe Festival.

grotto. The garden was created in the late 19th century, utilising the waterfall which originally descended from the mill when Ventnor was still a hamlet.

The beach's sand is soft and there are several cafés and restaurants close by at which to pause. The 6ft needle standing upright by the beach is a gnomon, the spire that casts a shadow on a sundial. It was given to the town by Sir Thomas Brisbane (a governor of New South Wales who gave his name to the eponymous Australian city). A marker used to stand on the opposite side of the Esplanade and at midday the gnomon would cast a shadow upon it.

A little further west along the Esplanade is a conspicuous resin-coated beach hut, the original hut built by the Blake family, who made their money from the 1830s by hiring out beach chairs and bathing machines. These machines were works of wonder and were deployed in ranks along the water's edge during Victorian times. The emotionally rigid visitors of the time would have been scandalised at the sight of anyone exposing flesh or, heaven forbid, swimming in the water. Instead, single-sex machines had to be hired, along with an attendant.

This small town (the population is just 6,000) also has a distinct vibe. Every July, the town runs its mini-version of the Edinburgh Fringe Festival, the Ventnor Fringe Festival (⏁ vfringe.co.uk), which includes an eclectic range of entertainment from pop-up street comedy to puppet shows in a launderette. More than a hundred shows take place over six days and several acts then head up to Edinburgh for the Fringe Festival. Ventnor also runs a carnival every September, featuring a torchlit procession, floats and music, which dates back to 1889, making it the second-oldest carnival in the UK.

"Stay a while and you may hear a local mantra: 'Keep Ventnor Weird'. That's not to be taken too literally..."

Stay a while and you may hear a local mantra: 'Keep Ventnor Weird'. That's not to be taken too literally; it really just means that those mining Ventnor's artistic seam are keen for the town to resist any attempts at gentrification. 'I think that our remoteness from everything mitigates against that risk,' says Jack Whitewood, who manages the **Ventnor Exchange** (11 Church St, PO38 1SW ⏁ ventnorexchange.co.uk), a creative hub that also features a theatre and a craft beer bar. Ventnor has always been creative, says Jack, otherwise no-one would have attempted to build huge villas on impossibly angled slopes, or invested in dozens of those cumbersome bathing machines.

Look out, while you're here, for Ventnor's wall lizards, which are thought to be yet another introduction by the Victorians. The species is extremely rare in Britain, though common on the Channel Islands. If you want to spot them (they tend to be green-backed in Ventnor), pick a hot, sunny afternoon and investigate the town's older, south-facing stone walls. The public car park at La Falaise, west of the Esplanade, is an easily accessible site for the lizards.

Although small in size, **Ventnor Park**, lying just to the west of the town, may be less heralded than the adjacent botanic garden but the grounds regularly win national and regional Britain in Bloom awards and are a dizzying collage of exotic Mediterranean pines and sturdy British specimens. One magnificent oak resembles a candelabra, with branches reaching upwards like imploring fingers from the palm of a hand. A little further west, you'll pass the signposted footpath that leads down to Steephill Cove. The track runs alongside Ventnor Cricket Club which is popular with touring teams from the mainland, partly on account of its unusual geography: the boundary edge is higher than the wicket, so a fielder at third man (or long on) will be able to gaze down on proceedings and – presumably – has a better chance of intercepting any balls destined for six.

The descent to **Steephill Cove** is down a zigzag of uneven steps but it's worth persevering with (the only other way into the cove is by boat). You can easily spend a day here – some people base their entire holiday at the cove and, given its seclusion and the fact everything you need is at hand, it's easy to see why. At sea level and just above the sloping sandy, pebble-dotted beach and breakwater boulders that are somehow cobbled together to form a loosely curved promenade, you will find fishermen, a handful of cottages, brightly coloured canopied deckchairs, beach huts and hauled-up lobster pots. There won't be a slot machine, car or burger in sight. Resident fishermen have been practising their tradition since the 1400s and still bring fresh crab and lobster ashore daily (weather permitting); the legacy is a handful of good eating options that can save you from lugging your own food down the steep steps to the bay.

Another very much an 'in the know' place, **Wheelers Bay** lies to the southeast of Ventnor. As scenic as its counterpart to the west, Steephill Cove, Wheelers Bay has also been carved out of the crumbling Island rock by the English Channel and is backed by a wind-blown woodland that climbs steeply away inland. The sea wall has been fortified here – and indeed all the way east to Bonchurch – to keep the ever-hungry sea at bay, though the side effect is that a large chunk of beach, typically exposed at low tide, is now infilled with, in effect, a corniche of concrete. A walk from here to Bonchurch and Horseshoe Bay (page 201) and back along the sea wall, which doubles as the Coastal Path (roughly half a mile in each direction), with a stop at The Seapot for food, is one of the Island's great, leisurely pleasures. The bay is named after the Wheeler family, who arrived in 1842 at what was then known as Hudson Bay, and who set about handling the importation of trade and distributing it inland.

Don't leave Ventnor without taking in the magnificent **spray-paint mural** on the High Street near the eastern edge of town, which features a sea creature morphing into the Isle of Wight, the Needles by its feet. The three-storey work was created by Phlegm, a painter of world-renown in street artist circles. It's an unforgettable spectacle and should finally dispel any lingering misconceptions you might have that Ventnor is simply somewhere people go to retire.

⑪ FOOD & DRINK

5 a day 34 High St, PO38 1RZ ℘ 07891 083806 ∎. Local greengrocer offering exactly what the title suggests. Sources fresh fruit at good prices, despite adjacent competing supermarket interests.

Cantina 20 High St, PO38 1RZ ℘ 01983 855988 ⊘ cantinaventnor.co.uk. Vibrant, small restaurant with tapas-style plates and a quirky menu of larger dishes that works well, such as spicy crab with macaroni cheese. Excellent coffee and breakfasts (such as avocado on delicious sourdough bread) too.

The Crab & Lobster Tap Grove Rd, PO38 1TH ℘ 01983 852311 ⊘ crabandlobstertapventnor.co.uk. A cosy boozer, this was the only inn in Ventnor for 200 years and its longevity is a tribute to its atmosphere and location, set back about four hairpin turns above the waterfront. As well as cask ales, they also serve food, essentially high standard but homemade bar meals, such as a fine fish pie.

The Kitchen at London House 40 High St, PO38 1RZ ℘ 01983 638856 ∎. Mouth-watering selection of pastries such as Victoria fruit slices, along with sandwiches, pasties and jacket potatoes. A good place to assemble a picnic before wandering around the downs.

The Seapot Wheelers Bay PO38 1HP ℘ 01983 857787 ∎ seapotcafe. This is the sort of gem you hoped to find when you first planned a visit to the Isle of Wight. Locally run, small in size but huge in passion and flavour. Expect seafood platters, crab sandwiches and Mediterranean dishes with olives and flatbreads, as well as scones and jam.

The Spyglass Inn Esplanade, PO38 1JX ✆ 01983 855338 ⏣ thespyglass.com. If you're going to have a traditional Ventnor experience, go the whole hog and eat or drink at The Spyglass. You'll be greeted by a ship's head and a pirate mannequin, but it's all good fun and the food is reasonable. Certainly best on a sunny day when you can sit on the terrace, overlooking the sea. Beneath your feet, hidden away under the floorboards, are the old Victorian saltwater baths.

The Tea House 40 High St, PO38 1RZ ✆ 01983 856478 ⏣ theteahouseventnor.co.uk. This is an excellent place to boost energy levels after clambering over Ventnor Downs. Main meals range from soups to brunches but you may also yield to the wide selection of cakes which include slices of *speculaas*, a Dutch bake that squeezes almond pastry between cinnamon and nutmeg.

Ventnor Exchange 11 Church St, PO38 1SW ⏣ ventnorexchange.co.uk ⊙ 11.00–23.00 Tue–Sun. Contemporary bar inside the town theatre with an emphasis on craft beers – there's up to 70 available, sourced from Belgium to Japan. Snack platters are available too, featuring olives and Island cheeses.

Ventnor Haven Fishery The Pier, East St, PO38 1JR ✆ 01983 852176. Crab? Lobster? Fish and chips? A sea view? You can tick all four boxes at Ventnor Haven Fishery. The Blake family have been fishing the seas off Ventnor Bay for decades and their boats sail daily into the bay, which means the fish and shellfish you buy from the Haven is local and fresh, most likely caught the same morning, and can range from cod to turbot. More creative dishes are available too, including crab samosa, apple fritters, sweet potato fries and dauphinois potatoes made with cream from Briddlesford Farm. Order at the small take-away window.

Wheeler's Crab Shed Love Ln, Steephill Cove PO38 1UG ✆ 01983 852177 ⊙ Easter–Oct. Features the catch of the day including daily specials, fresh mackerel and popular crab pasties. There is also an adjacent café for teas, coffee and cakes.

SHOPPING

Ventnor has no shortage of independent shops, selling everything from locally made scents and soaps to antiques. Most of these are clustered around Pier and High streets.

Blue Labelle 7 Pier St ✆ 01983 700878 ⏣ bluelabelle.co.uk. A scents and essential oils shop established by Pascale Edwards-Labelle in 2011. The majority of Pascale's products are certified as organic at source. These include geranium, bergamot, ylang ylang and rosehip oil.

Burfield Fine Furniture and Antiques 38 High St, PO38 1RZ ✆ 01983 853909 ⏣ burfieldsantiquesandart.co.uk. A good stock of collectables, from period antiques to 21st-century fine art, as well as local pottery and other crafts.

A SALTY TALE

When you visit Ventnor you may see a lonely individual dipping buckets into the sea – but Simon Davis is not panning for gold but harvesting salt.

Simon is founder of Wight Salt (✆ 07786 095439 🖱 wightsalt.co.uk). Having returned in 2015 to the Island where he grew up, Simon admits he was scratching around for a way to augment income from his day job as a professional musician, playing jazz, piano and leading recitals. 'I've got an entrepreneurial streak and I just wondered why no-one was making sea salt. I looked into it a bit more closely and decided there was no reason why it couldn't be an Island "thing" like garlic or tomatoes. My father was a smallholder and collecting the salt is in effect harvesting the sea, so perhaps it was in my blood.'

To gather the salt, Simon pulls on his wellies and wades into the waters off Ventnor, dunking buckets into the sea. 'The coast gets washed by three tides there and that creates a special mix and blend of the trace elements and minerals,' he says. 'It's actually similar to those found in the Caribbean. The salt tastes sweeter.'

So how does Simon process the salt? He admits he has, in the tradition of Islanders, taken an innovative and eclectic approach. 'In Spain and France they have salt pans where the sun just burns the water away,' he says. 'Even though we get a lot of sun here, we don't have that option.' Instead,

Lesley's Nutshell 25 Pier St, PO38 1SX ✆ 07411 315279 ⬛ ⊙ Wed–Sat. Organic and wholefood shop also selling a phenomenally eclectic range of gifts, from children's umbrellas to biodegradable glitter and Scandinavian Dala horses, as well as Fair Trade products. The fact all such products appear to do a roaring trade offers quite an insight into the soul of Ventnor's inhabitants.

7 BONCHURCH VILLAGE

The tiny village of Bonchurch is remarkably easy to overlook, tucked away among the folds and hairpin turns of Bonchurch Landslip (page 202) and smothered with a dense canopy of mature trees. Approaching from Shanklin along the A3055, you need to take Bonchurch Shute, which snakes down into the village. From Ventnor, bear right along St Boniface Road by the hairpin bend at the eastern edge of town.

Rather like Freshwater, Bonchurch drew the great, the good and the benevolent from Victorian and Edwardian times, beguiling them with sylvan charms and opportunities for the seclusion and repose so crucial to set the cogs of great brains whirring. Their number included Henry de Vere Stacpoole, author of *The Blue Lagoon* and *The Pearl Fishers*, who he approached sea-salt producers from somewhere a little further north: the Isle of Skye. On their advice he invested in a polycrub (a super-strong, storm-resistant, insulated polytunnel) in which he pours the sea water into 25-litre tubs to a shallow depth of just one inch. 'Between April and September there is enough warmth and sun to heat the polycrub [like a greenhouse] and boil the water away in three to seven days,' he says. 'I don't use steam heating to boil it off, it's all solar powered.'

The salt is then used for a range of products, from sprays to jars of food salt. The flavour is monitored by regular testing – friends and family are given salt to try on their Sunday roasts. 'I'm not really into novelty flavourings or products for the sake of it, there has to be a point to it,' says Simon. 'It's really about tasting the waves, cooking with the sea. The activity has quite a primal feeling to it, I'm not doing anything unnatural to the salt. With table salt from the supermarket you are eating a highly processed food that has been mined. Sea salt has the clue in its name, it's natural and comes from the sea. This is all about going back to the Island's roots.'

Simon sells his products across the Island – you'll find them at Farmer Jack's (page 246) and Quarr Abbey (page 101), as well as online. In Ventnor you can buy them at Lesley's Nutshell, Cantina, 5 a day and the Kitchen at London House.

moved to the village in 1920. Before him, Charles Dickens holidayed here and wrote *David Copperfield* while staying at Winterbourne House (see box, page 202). The legacy of the well-to-do incomers is everywhere today, in the shape of fine houses with grand verandas, thatched roofs and lush gardens.

For several hundred years before this, Bonchurch had been a low-key place, home to fisherfolk who supplemented meagre incomes with farm and estate work and the occasional spot of smuggling. Nowadays, Bonchurch is a thoroughly fascinating, vibrant village, home to craftspeople and residents who have forged a palpable community spirit. It's the sort of place where an old forge may now house a motorcycle repair shop, while just a few paces away you'll come across a gatepost topped with an exquisitely carved stone acorn and elsewhere you will pick out finely carved latticed chimneys, or fleur de lys decorating the guttering.

The village straddles, roughly, three ridges. The centre, Village Road, is where you will find the duck pond, which was once home to oyster beds and was augmented by Stacpoole who donated it to the village. Its rectangular shape, ornamental features and duck houses are easy on the

A walk above Ventnor

✽ OS Explorer map 29; start: the signposted footpath for the Wroxall Stream Trail, by the former Ventnor railway station at the top of Grove Rd. ♀ SZ562776; 4 miles; medium

Quite simply, this is a superb short walk that comes with a kick. The steep ascent of Ventnor Downs is worth it for the reward of increasingly spectacular views over much of the island. Ventnor Downs are home to a population of around 30 Old English feral goats, which happily graze away at the holm oaks, a non-native species that has inhibited local wildlife (they were an adornment planted by the Victorians). The top of the downs is a fine place for humans to graze too, and a picnic here, halfway along the route, is one of life's pleasures. Also bear in mind that at the bottom of Grove Road, as you return to Ventnor at the end of the walk, you pass the serendipitously located Crab and Lobster Tap pub.

The route described here is circular and returns to Ventnor. Should you wish to head further inland instead, it's worth noting that the first half of this walk follows the Wroxall Stream Trail (page 170).

1 From the signposted gate by the old railway station, walk steeply uphill along a narrow footpath. Luckily the gradient eases off after 300yds (for a while) and takes you through a glorious valley in the shadow of the humps of Ventnor Downs. The valley soon begins to rise again, slowly then more steeply, and you walk pretty much up its middle before the path zigzags its way up to the transmitter masts.

2 There's a convenient bench in front of the transmitter masts from where you can take in the view to the west – as Mahatma Gandhi must have done – with glimpses of Ventnor away to the southwest and the rolling features of St Catherine's Down filling the horizon. Beneath you, the remarkable punchbowl appearance of the valley you have just traversed becomes apparent. Right in front of the masts, bear left along footpath V1a (the path closest to the fence) and contour around what is now St Boniface Down. After a third of a mile you emerge

eye. Just to the east of the pond you'll find a stone pyramid embedded into the wall. Dating to 1733, this is regarded as an early advertisement, compiled by the village stonemasons who wished to show off their skills as well as the quality and versatility of the stone available locally.

If you walk 100yds west of the pond, you'll come to the 101 steps, which climb straight as a die and at an angle of 50 degrees to deposit you by a lane called The Pitts, where many grand houses are set back from the narrow cul-de-sac. Below Village Road, Shore Road descends on to Down Lane, a minor road on the ridgeline that provides service access to the masts and to a small car park.

3 Bear left along Down Lane. Wroxall is visible far way to the north at the bottom of another gorgeously picturesque punchbowl-shaped valley. After 200yds, you'll see a sign for the Wroxall Stream Trail and Wroxall pointing east and downhill along footpath V8. If you want to follow the trail all the way to Godshill, take this path and follow the directions on the Island Rivers website (page 32).

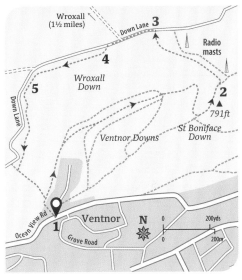

4 To stick with this route, however, turn your back to Wroxall and pick out any of the small footpaths that lead through the scrub on the south side of the access track. They all quickly converge on the main path; here, turn right to contour west along Wroxall Down (with Ventnor now away to your left). This makes for easy, superlative walking: the aesthetics of the curving path, which is laid out ahead of you for half a mile, are easy on the eye.

5 The path meets Down Lane again by a gate. Here, bear half-left downhill, with woodlands to your right. Part of the descent is very steep but quickly drops you back on the path just above Ventnor. Turn right on the path to return, still heading downhill, to the starting point.

in serpentine fashion to the sea at Horseshoe Bay, where you will find a pottery and views along the coast towards the edge of Ventnor. An excellent local map and pamphlet about the village, produced by the late resident, architect and artist Oliver Cox (and father of local artist Jane Cox) is available from the post office in Ventnor and Ventnor Heritage Centre. The maps were Oliver's last work and were devised with a view to raising money for the village community. These were based upon notes and historical research carried out by his own father, and Oliver

BONCHURCH'S GREAT EXPECTATIONS

Charles Dickens visited the Isle of Wight on three occasions: in 1838, 1849 and 1860. His second sojourn involved a long summer in Bonchurch village, where he entertained Tennyson and other literary luminaries, including William Makepeace Thackery and Thomas Carlyle, the philosopher author of *The French Revolution: A History*, which Dickens used as a source for *A Tale of Two Cities*. According to research and a study of archive letters and local history by Alan Cartwright, less heralded local people may have inspired some of Dickens's most notable characters.

Dickens is reported to have written Chapter 13 of *David Copperfield* when he arrived at Winterbourne Villa, the grand property near St Boniface Old Church where he stayed in the summer of 1849. Alan believes that the character Mr Dick is based on Samuel Dick who lived in Uppermount, Bonchurch. In addition, Alan is convinced that Miss Haversham, the dust-encrusted jilted spinster who weaves a spell around Pip and Estella in *Great Expectations*, is based on Samuel Dick's daughter, Margaret Catherine Dick. Margaret was jilted on the morning of her wedding in 1860 and left her family home to live a reclusive life in the village's Madeira Hall. Perhaps for reasons of decorum, Dickens named the character after Margaret's neighbour Catherine Haviland.

Drawing on their research, Alan has developed a blue-plaque literary walk around Bonchurch and Ventnor taking in

added illustrations, sketches and architectural elevations of some of the most interesting properties in the village. There is also an excellent local website (⌂ bonchurchvillage.co.uk) which covers the full absorbing history of the village.

⊙ FOOD & DRINK

The Bonchurch Inn Bonchurch Shute, PO38 1NU ℘ 01983 852611 ⌂ bonchurch-inn. co.uk. This fine pub – a former coach house and part of an old stableyard complex – has a real 1930s feel to its interior, with vintage panelling and hints of its past as a spit-and-sawdust place. The food is excellent, ranging from crab and salmon bruschetta to vegan Penang curry, and there are local ales on offer.

Smugglers Haven 76 Leeson Rd, PO38 1QD ℘ 01983 856627 ◼ ⊙ usually Apr–Oct. A well-positioned café with a conservatory design that gives views over downland, landslip and sea. Offers sandwiches, hot drinks and cream teas.

8 BONCHURCH LANDSLIP

A large area of woods and jumbled paths, Bonchurch Landslip lies 1½ miles east of Ventnor and its tentacles of layered tiers of rock, trees, clays,

Dickens-related places of interest. These properties include Haviland Cottage on Madeira Road (Catherine Haviland's former abode, which Alan now operates as a self-catering property); Winterbourne Villa, where Dickens stayed, on Madeira Road; Hillside Cottage on Bonchurch Shute where John Leech, who illustrated *A Christmas Carol*, sojourned; Madeira Hall, where Margaret Dick retreated after being left at the altar; and Margaret's grave in Ventnor cemetery (the entrance is at the southern end of Newport Road, just above the junction with Steephill Down Road). The route also includes East Dene, near Winterbourne House, which was the childhood home of the rather tiresome, self-declared decadent Victorian poet Algernon Swinburne (something of a mini-me Lord Byron), who is buried in the 'new' St Boniface Parish Church. His interment in 1909 caused scandal as his reputation followed him to the grave and villagers rolled up their petticoats and stiffened their collars in dismay that such a licentious and libertine soul should ever be laid to rest there. The poet Dame Edith Sitwell, then a lovelorn young woman, travelled from Bournemouth to tip a libation on his grave. As many of these houses are now private properties, the route is thoughtfully devised so that you observe the buildings from afar and avoid intruding upon owners. You can download it at ⊘ havilandcottage.com/dickens.

paths and steps hold the village of the same name in a firm embrace. Featuring some remarkable landforms, cliffs, boulders and steep steps, the landslip (managed by Gift to Nature ⊘ gifttonature.org.uk), is one of the most unheralded landscapes on the Island and should not be missed. This is where, in effect, a part of the Undercliff simply gives up the ghost and falls apart. The only downside is that, while the landslip is in no way perilous, its narrow, uneven, often slippery paths and steep steps make access almost impossible for people with limited mobility. The easiest way to reach and enter the landslip is from the car park on the south side of the A3055 at the base of Nansen Hill, east of Ventnor. Bus #3 also stops here.

The present terrain derives largely from major landslides in 1810 and 1818 but the landslip is believed to have existed in some form for thousands of years. A contemporary account of the 19th-century landslips describes a 'scene of devastation, which seemed to have been occasioned by some convulsion of nature'. The lower slips comprise mixed clay and sandy habitats, which once would have supported a complex mix of acid- and chalk-loving plant species though much of this has long fallen into the sea. The lowest surviving areas of the landslip are almost impossible to access because of the continued land movement. The landslip was developed as a picturesque woodland walk in Victorian times, one that incorporated natural features that can still be seen today.

Ash, oak and beech have thrived in the woodland that has emerged in the landslip over the past 200 years, with some specimens of all three species now approaching veteran status. The ash trees are the primary reason the area has been designated a Site of Special Scientific Interest. The word 'unique' can be overused but the official SSSI listing notes just how special and rare the landslip is, for it records how the 'Bonchurch landslip woodland would not seem to have any close parallel'. As you wander around the upper and middle levels, you may spot pyramidal and bee orchids as well as heather, all competing for light and space within a lush landscape of ferns and lichens.

"As you wander around the upper and middle levels, you may spot pyramidal and bee orchids as well as heather."

It can be hard to resist the temptation to delve deeper into the landslip and it's perfectly safe to do so as the paths are numbered; the main hazards are that it can be slippery after rain and the terrain, perhaps unsurprisingly, can be higgledy-piggledy. The best option for exploration is to take the right-hand (westernmost) entrance into the landslip from the bus stop/car park area. In great contrast to the chaotic wilderness that awaits below, the upper layer of the landslip remains a formal public garden with rhododendrons and clearings that open up views of the sea.

Look out for the small sliver of open woodland immediately to the southwest of the car park. Walk for just a couple of minutes and you'll find a couple of benches where you can gaze out to sea before – or after – exploring the footpaths. Below this viewpoint, paths clamber up, down and along the landslip to create a terraced effect.

The descent into the landslip heads southwest from the benches and follows footpath V65c. You'll soon be confronted by a natural gap known as the **Devil's Chimney** where steep steps squeeze you through a tiny fissure in the cliffs and lead to an even narrower passage known as **The Chink** (if you're carrying a rucksack, you may need to take it off your back). Soon after, you meet the Coastal Path at a T-junction. Turn right (west) along this; the walk continues underneath thick canopies of trees which occasionally give way to vantage points such as the **Wishing Seat** or Wishing Stone, a large moss-covered rock.

Half a mile beyond the rock a tiny church emerges out of the jumbled landscape of tilting rocks, coastline and stop–start woods: **St Boniface Old Church**, on the eastern edge of Bonchurch village. Rebuilt, according to an entry notice, in 1070, the church dates to the Norman Conquest and replaced an even earlier Saxon church on the site (the Isle of Wight was one of the last places in Britain to embrace Christianity). Oozing medievalism, it is entered through an arched doorway of thick planks that leads to a chill interior, light only grudgingly allowed to squeeze through the tiny 13th-century windows. Once your eyes adjust, look out for the impressive 17th-century Flemish altar cross made from black oak. On the north wall you can make out a medieval wall painting, which may possibly be of the Last Judgement. The churchyard looks almost stereotypical, with weathered tombstones at half mast and flowers and grasses encroaching from all sides to create a hemmed-in, secluded resting place.

On the return to the start of the walk described here, just before the car park and bus stop, you can refresh yourself at Smugglers Haven (page 202).

9 NANSEN HILL

If you still have any puff left after exploring Bonchurch Landslip, you can scurry across the A3055 and climb Nansen Hill for superb views across much of the Island. Access is the same bus stop as for Bonchurch Landslip; cross the road with care as cars do sweep around the bend here at speed.

You begin the climb up the hill from the gate directly across the road from the Bonchurch Landslip car park. It's an ascent with bite, super-steep and rising some 300ft in height in barely 300yds. Keep going until you reach the gate beneath the coppice on the horizon. From here, the gradient calms down and you follow a broad, gentler path between gorse to the brow.

Nansen Hill is popular not only for the panorama from this brow but also for its wildlife. From spring through to autumn the chalk grasslands are magnificent for butterflies and orchids. Most years see a good spread of autumn gentian at the top of the slopes (the Island also has 80% of the UK population of the extremely rare early gentian) while you may spot the Glanville fritillary butterfly (chequered orange and brown), which flutters around the Island at the northern limit of its range, favouring the coastal landslips around Bonchurch.

As the incline relents, you follow a broad sweep of cattle-grazed downland for a quarter of a mile to reach the broad summit where the Ventnor Downs, Shanklin Down, Luccombe Down and St Boniface Down all collide (at 791ft, St Boniface Down is the highest point on the Island). The scenery here is outstanding: to the north the entire sweep of Sandown Bay arcs away until it blurs into the base of Culver Down, right across to the distant Yarborough monument some six miles northeast. The ground falls away in dramatic geometric sweeps and where the ridges of these various downs meet, they seem to create a series of giant, comfy sofas, with – at the risk of overextending the metaphor – crumpled folds of sloping and undulating valleys (representing seat cushions) hemmed in by long ridges (the sofa arms).

Local wildlife experts assert that this stretch of escarpment around Nansen Hill is the first place in the UK to welcome spring and the last to bid autumn goodbye (swallows, house martins, even willow warblers, are visible and audible here well into October). Nansen Hill's elevation also means that it is a brilliant place to see migrant birds on the move – thousands of the aforementioned hirundines pass overhead in the spring and autumn, as well as the occasional osprey and honey buzzard. In the spring the spectacular bluebell display up here really is one of the great sights (perhaps surprisingly, bluebells are a globally restricted plant, essentially an Atlantic coast speciality). You can also look out for a good population of Devil's-bit scabious and autumn gentian, while common spotted orchids can be found on the wave-cut grass ridges, known as terracettes, on the higher north-facing slopes.

"Local wildlife experts assert that this stretch is the first place in the UK to welcome spring and the last to bid autumn goodbye."

The fenced-off grounds at the top of Nansen Hill (where it merges into Bonchurch Down to the west) protect a series of transmitter masts as well as the former World War II RAF radar station. The radar station played a key wartime role: built in 1938, it monitored both ship and aircraft movements during the D-Day landings as well as tracking V1 flying bombs, or doodlebugs, and was bombed twice. The station was converted into a luxury home by the architect Sarah Cheeseman and interior designer Howard Carter. You'll pass it on any circumnavigation of the hill and it may bring to mind the lair of a James Bond villain. A walk around the perimeter of the station allows for yet more stirring views.

From Nansen Hill, it's best to walk clockwise around the radar station, keeping the fence on your right to return, after a mile, to the same place. This gives the most far-reaching views, first inland and then out to the east coast and allows you to gaze almost right across the Island in all directions. The raised humps that you see in clusters are burial mounds dating to the Bronze Age, which were situated here, it is thought, to enable the deceased to guard their living descendants.

THE SOUTHERN HINTERLAND

⌂ **The Chequers Inn** (page 304)

Like the back of a wave, the downlands behind Ventnor ripple inland, taking in farmland, escorting streams and rivers on their embryonic journeys towards the east and north coasts, and accommodating sparsely populated villages such as Rookley and Chillerton. These two communities are really little more than hamlets and, like the more substantial village of Wroxall, are of little real interest to the visitor. However, they are located within areas that are most definitely worth exploring and so you may find yourself passing through them regularly. In contrast, the village of **Godshill**, bursting at the seams with tea shops and honey-stoned architecture, is for many visitors the archetype of an Isle of Wight village.

10 APPULDURCOMBE HOUSE

Appuldurcombe Rd, Wroxall PO38 3EW; English Heritage

Along the westerly edges of the large, missable, village of Wroxall is the Grade I-listed Appuldurcombe House, widely recognised in its heyday as a masterpiece of 18th-century English Baroque architecture. Sadly, the same could not be said of it today. Despite being regarded for 150 years as the finest house on the Isle of Wight, it had fallen into disrepair by World War II. Accidental bombing by the Luftwaffe, who were aiming for coastal batteries, all but finished the place off. Complete collapse was only averted thanks to the intervention of the Ministry of Works, which had the foresight in the post-war period to preserve the house as an architectural ruin.

Today's visitor encounters a slightly surreal spectacle: a stately home version of the ruins of Fountains Abbey or Whitby Abbey, set in 11 acres of pleasingly landscaped Grade II-listed grounds originally shaped by Capability Brown, with mature yew and oak trees and rolling lawns hemmed in by wrought-iron fences.

The route from the car park approaches the house from the rear and you are greeted with the bare skeleton of once-grand rooms and wings, now open to the elements. Walk around to the front and you see the vestiges of how the building must once have looked, where the grand hall and what is thought to have been a bedroom have been shored up against the weather. The impressive pediment surrounding the front entrance remains but the vases and statues that once adorned it are long gone.

The house was built as the seat of the Worsley family, who were a classic example of a gentry family making a fortune out of royal favour in Georgian times. In reality, the rot set in even as the house was being built, for its ruinous cost stretched the family to the limit and they eventually ran out of cash to pay for the building to be fully completed. It was only when the house was taken on by the Earl of Yarborough at the start of the 19th century that the finishing touches were applied. The Worsley's misfortune extended to their private lives, for the 7th baronet Sir Richard Worsley was involved in an excruciating court case in 1782 in which his young wife and heiress Seymour Fleming admitted to having 27 lovers. Fleming inspired a character of loose morals, Lady Teazle, in Richard Sheridan's play *School for Scandal* in 1777. Were that not enough, she went so far herself as to commission a steamy poem in her defence which, lapped up by a public with an appetite for the salacious, became a bestseller of its time. Two lines are probably sufficient to convey the gist of its central theme: 'Oh, had you seen me on his breast relin'd/ Lips glu'd to lips, and limbs with limbs entwin'd.'

The family name is also attached to a waymarked trail (⊘ visitisleofwight.co.uk/dbimgs/9.Worsley%20Trail.pdf) that runs for 13 miles from Brighstone to Sandown. Following the trail as it skirts around the house provides a good opportunity to admire the woodlands and downs that lie within and immediately beyond the boundaries of the Appuldurcombe Estate. This can be incorporated into a short but enjoyable circumnavigation of around three miles that will take a

◀ **1** Appuldurcombe House. **2** Godshill village.

couple of hours at most. From the car park, follow the footpath sign for Freemantle Gate, which you reach after half a mile. The Freemantle Lodge Gate is Grade II listed and its stark, striking design features ornamental dressings and cast-iron gates. Turn left (west) here along the Worsley Trail and after half a mile turn south at a meeting of paths; you're now walking along the lower flanks of Appuldurcombe Down, below the radio station. The path seamlessly rises up on to Stenbury Down (the second set of masts you pass are the same you reach on the Stenbury Down walk from Nettlecombe Farm). South of these masts, turn sharp left (east) downhill after 300yds and descend past Little Span Farm to reach Rew Lane. Turn left here and, a few yards further on, where the lane turns right, keep ahead on the footpath past Span Lodge to return to Appuldurcombe.

The **Isle of Wight Donkey Sanctuary** (Lower Winston Farm, St Johns Rd, PO38 3AA 🕿 01983 852693 👣 iowdonkeysanctuary.org) lies close to Appuldurcombe House, just north of Wroxall. This is a good choice for children as the sanctuary is home to more than 100 donkeys and almost 30 ponies, all of whom were either rescued or had been abandoned. You can meet the donkeys, and groom and walk them.

11 GODSHILL

🏠 **Godshill Park Farm & Cottages** (page 304), **Koala Cottage** (page 304)

Were you to design a quintessential rural village from the 1950s, you'd end up with something like Godshill. A single street winds its way between thatched cottages, most of which house pubs, souvenir shops or producers of local food and drink; wisteria seems to have become entwined around every sash window. This village portrait is augmented by wishing wells, a model village and tea gardens, some of which feature, rather randomly, statuettes of nymphs that rear up over hedges and walls or gaze down upon your cream tea. To complete the picture, you need only look up to the High Street to see a photogenic age-old church gazing down on the entire happy scene.

For some observers, Godshill's decidedly twee ambience is the village's undoing, the charge being that over the years it has shamelessly metamorphosed into a cliché of a village living in a timewarp. The litmus test in such circumstances is whether the main car park has a disproportionate number of bays for coach parties: this is indeed the case in Godshill. Should you pick the wrong time to visit then Godshill can feel, along with Sandown and Shanklin, like some kind of Mission Control for the tourism of yesteryear. That said, you really should not dismiss the village – just come early or late in the day, or outside the summer holidays, and you'll see that Godshill wears its charms more subtly.

The first recorded spelling of the village is Godeshulle and it is believed to have evolved from one of the ancient parishes that existed before the compilation of the Domesday Book. The hill on which the church stands was once a place of pagan worship and legend records that the church was originally intended to be built at the foot of the hill. On three successive nights the stones were removed, unseen, to the site of the present church. Work was restarted on the first two subsequent mornings but on the third day it was assumed that a higher power (or perhaps a lower one) wished the church to be built on the hill, hence the name Godshill.

All Saints' Church is accessed from Church Hollow, the short meandering lane on the bend at the western end of the village. From the higgledy-piggledy graveyard you realise that Godshill is not only architecturally snug but, settled among undulating hills, geographically cosy too. The church repays exploration inside with grotesque springers and corbels arranged between the roof beams. Dating to 1350, All Saints is also known as the Lily Cross Church on account of a medieval wall that you'll find in the south chapel. The painting depicts Christ crucified on a lily and is thought to be one of just two such paintings in Europe; it seems the lily was chosen to reflect the purity of the Virgin Mary. The painting is in remarkably good condition given that it was whitewashed at least twice to save it from destruction, first during the Reformation and later in Puritan times.

The porch has a plaque dedicated to a local man, Richard Gard, which describes him as a generous parishioner known for his good deeds. In her excellent *The Little Book of the Isle of Wight*, the historian, writer and 11th-generation Islander Jan Toms records a different version, noting that others had dismissed Gard as a cheat and a rogue, who stole his neighbours' cattle and placed hot loaves on their horns to make them supple, so that, rather incredulously, their shape could be changed to make identification harder.

You could be forgiven for thinking Godshill has been somnolent ever since its inception before the Norman conquest but this serenity was shattered in unlikely fashion in August 1968 when the first Isle of Wight

ALL THINGS RARE & BEAUTIFUL

The hinterland around the hamlet of Rookley, just two miles northwest of Godshill, is particularly bucolic – something which belies the area's 18th-century notoriety as an epicentre of smuggling (although six miles from the south coast, it seems the village was an easy place to lug booty to and from the chines around Blackgang and then distribute it around the Island) – and offers a couple of special places to explore on foot. These are rarely visited, yet exquisite and bursting with wildlife. **Bohemia Bog** (∂ gifttonature. uk/our-projects/bohemia-bog) lies just behind the Chequers Inn and is reminiscent of a New Forest wetland. This is what is called a transition mire – a tiny, rather vulnerable peatland that is perched on the side of the hill. Bohemia Bog is one of the richest wetlands on the Island

and the only Island site for the beautiful little insectivorous plant pale butterwort (as well as populations of sundews, cotton grass and the stunning golden asphodel, all very rare here). Bus #3 passes the pub en route between Newport and Ryde.

Nearby is **Munsley Bog** (∂ gifttonature. org.uk/discover/out-in-the-country/ munsley-bog), located on the northeast side of the A3020 Newport Road immediately north of Godshill. This is a different kind of peaty wetland called a valley mire, and is one of the last places on the Island where you can find a little shrub called bog myrtle. The site offers a lovely display of heath spotted orchids in the summer. You can reach Munsley Bog by bus #2 or #3 – just ask to be dropped off at the Dubbers or Yarborough Close stops.

Festival was held at nearby Ford Farm. On a stage constructed from two trailers, 10,000 fervent fans watched acts such as Jefferson Airplane and T-Rex perform. Even though it lasted just the one day, it is revered as being the first great UK rock festival. Of appeal to a rather younger audience is the Model Village (High St, PO38 3HH ∂ 01983 840270 ∂ modelvillagegodshill.co.uk), which sets out its attractions amid an ornate garden landscape of topiary, neatly arrayed mature trees and a miniature lake. With model churches, bathing huts and buses, this experience is, in a literal sense, the Isle of Wight in miniature.

¶ FOOD & DRINK

The Chequers Inn Niton Rd, Rookley PO38 3NZ ∂ 01983 840314 ∂ chequersinn-iow. co.uk. Another of the Island's clutch of well-run, rural, family-owned village pubs. Hearty food ranges from pub perennials to creative Island-focused dishes such as chicken with Isle of Wight sweetcorn and black garlic from the Garlic Farm. Include the real ales and a garden for parents to let the kids play in and you have something of a gem. The fact there is a pub here at all is down to the current owners, local farming couple Sue and Richard Holmes, who bought the pub in 1988 after then-owners Whitbread sought to close it on the grounds it was not viable. Their actions meant a pub that dates to at least 1799 continues to quench thirsts and fill stomachs to this day. The pub sits just to the south of the village, a couple of miles northwest of Godshill.

The Cider Barn High St, PO38 3HZ ✆ 01983 840680. The old Wesleyan chapel is home to the village cider shop, where, along with some hard-hitting scrumpy, you can pick up an impressively eclectic range of fruit and flower wines and liqueurs, including cowslip wine (rather dry) and birch wine (which lands a pleasant bitter aftertaste), pineapple rum and blackberry brandy.

Isle of Wight Farm Shop Newport Rd, PO38 3LY ✆ 01983 840191 ⌂ brownriggfarmmeats.co.uk. Well-stocked farm shop set in a low-slung, cabin-like building. Sells Isle of Wight beef, lamb and pork from Cheverton Farm and the Isle of Wight Meat Co at Shorwell. Fruit and veg from Ash Hill Farm at Atherfield. Located on the A3020 between Rookley and Godshill; bus #3 goes past the front door, though be careful as this is one of the few stretches of Island road that can be hairy for cyclists and walkers.

Tansy's Pantry Church Hollow, PO38 3HH ✆ 01983 840921 ⌂ tansyspantry.co.uk ◷ Tue–Sat. Excellent vegan café offering creative dishes. Try vish & chips, featuring deep-fried banana blossom with mushy peas and chips, or a mouth-watering cheese-free lime cheesecake.

The Taverners High St, PO38 3HZ ✆ 01983 840707 ⌂ thetavernersgodshill.co.uk. To its credit, given it could simply open its doors and fill every table with coach parties, this pub serves food a couple of notches above standard pub fare, changing its menu according to what has been reared, caught, shot or hunted on the Island. Also bakes its own bread daily. Strong on meats, including 21-day dry rump steak.

Worsley's Tea Rooms & Bistro High St, PO38 3HZ ✆ 01983 840290 ⓕ. This tea room inside a 16th-century thatched building at the bottom of the rocky outcrop that supports All Saints' Church is a good choice to visit after you've walked up to the church. As well as filling baguettes and an Isle of Wight ploughman's (Gallybagger and Isle of Wight cheeses) they do excellent cakes – the cardamom and pistachio is a personal favourite – and fine coffee served on vintage china.

12 CHILLERTON DOWN

Situated 3½ miles northwest of Godshill, the tip of the mast on Chillerton Down rises steeply to 748ft above sea level and rewards a walk to its base with exceptional views. The mast is something of an Island landmark as you can see it from as far as Tennyson Down in the west, as well as from Sandown Bay to the east and Cowes to the north. The outward views from its base, at 548ft, are correspondingly special: looking south

A walk through the Wilderness: from Chillerton to Godshill

✻ OS Explorer map 29; start: Kervil Dairy, just south of Chillerton ♀ SZ486838; 4 miles; easy to moderate

The Wilderness is the name is given to an expanse of farmland that straddles the upper catchment area of the River Medina. Quite how the moniker emerged is unclear but one school of thought proposes that it simply relates to the fact there are very few roads of any stature out here; for centuries this was simply given over to the business of food production. This is a good walk for gaining a glimpse of the Island's beating farmland heart,

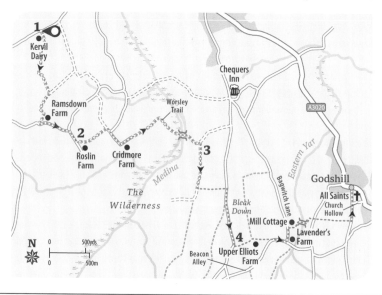

you can see Chale Bay which, thanks to the notorious Atherfield Ledge, lies submerged and out of sight. The mast is fenced off; to reach the viewpoint on its southern flank, follow the bridleway G13 from the lay-by 200yds south of Chillerton Farm (♀ SZ481829). Bus #6 conveniently stops near here every two or three hours on its route between Newport with hedgerows full of birdsong, and is a side of the Island very few visitors get to see. Just as importantly, you can conclude this walk in the relative 'wilds' of the Island with a meal or a cake at Tansy's Pantry (page 213) in Godshill. The #6 bus drops off in Chillerton while #2 and #3 pass through Godshill between Newport, Sandown and Ryde. Note the last leg of this walk overlaps with the mapped Yar Valley Trail (page 176).

1 From the dairy, follow Hollow Lane for three-quarters of a mile, gradually moving uphill. The views are initially slow to reveal their charms but as you gain height you appreciate the extraordinarily steep dune-like contours of the farmland around Chillerton. At Ramsdown Farm, turn left (east) to pick up the waymarked Worsley Trail.

2 Follow the trail as it zigzags east via Roslin and Cridmore farms; after 1½ miles, you'll come to a footbridge – follow this across the Medina. The river is decidedly modest in proportion here, perhaps 4ft in width and ankle deep. As an alternative to the footbridge, you can just about hop across and still keep your feet dry using the adjacent ford that gives access to cattle, and then continue straight ahead.

3 After 400yds, keep to the Worsley Trail as it bears south. Follow the trail as it turns sharp left (east) after another 500yds, to reach Niton Road. Turn right (south) down the road, following it for 600yds along the side of Bleak Down.

4 As the road swings southwest, take the footpath on the left that runs to the north of Upper Elliotts Farm and Lavender's Farm, where the path merges with a minor lane called Beacon Alley. After 100yds, turn left north up Bagwitch Lane (Lavender's Farm is to your right) and then immediately right (signposted as the Worsley Trail) to pass Mill Cottage and cross the River Yar. Then cross the Whitwell Road with care and follow the trail up Church Hill and turn right into Church Hollow and Godshill.

and Ventnor. Follow G13 west to a gate and then bear right around and above the old quarry. When you reach the perimeter fence of the transmitter mast, turn right along the fence line, head through a kissing gate, and you'll reach a wooden bench for soaking up the view.

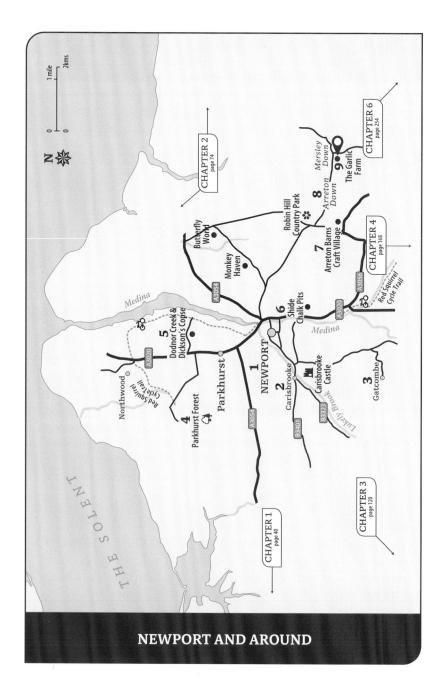

NEWPORT AND AROUND

THE SOLENT

N

0   1 mile
0   2kms

CHAPTER 2
page 74

CHAPTER 1
page 40

CHAPTER 3
page 120

CHAPTER 4
page 168

CHAPTER 6
page 254

Medina

Butterfly World

Monkey Haven

Robin Hill Country Park

Arreton Down

Mersley Down

The Garlic Farm

9

8

7   Arreton Barns Craft Village

6   Shide Chalk Pits

Medina

A3054

A3056

A3020

Red Squirrel Cycle Trail

Dodnor Creek & Dickson's Copse

5

A3020

Northwood

Red Squirrel Cycle Trail

4   Parkhurst Forest

Parkhurst

A3054

1   NEWPORT

2   Carisbrooke

Carisbrooke Castle

B3401

B3323

Lukely Brook

3   Gatcombe

5
NEWPORT & AROUND

The 'capital' of the Isle of Wight is positioned at its geographical heart, halfway between the Island's east and west edges, near the headwaters of the River Medina, and bordered to the south and east by gently undulating hills. The town has more appeal than the approaches via dual carriageways and flyovers (all very out of character for the Island) might suggest; persevere and you'll find that **Newport** has a good deal of history to be explored, an excellent arts complex (page 223) and good places to eat, drink and stay. Nowadays, the town extends into what was once the distinct and separate village of **Carisbrooke**. Home to an important castle, this is where King Charles I was detained before being dispatched for trial and execution in London.

The conurbation quickly gives way to a landscape more in keeping with the Island: the bucolic hinterland of the **Arreton Valley**, where the emphasis is heavily on Island produce in the form of farms and farm shops. Alongside livestock, wheat and other conventional crops, the area is also home to one of the Island's more pungent products – garlic – and a visit to the entertaining **Garlic Farm** should be on everyone's list. If there is one church on the Island you should not miss, it is the architecturally supreme **St George's** in Arreton.

The geographical heart of the Island is also an undulating region through which the chalk downlands pass on their traverse between the east and west coasts. The downs east of Newport rear up from the valley farmland floor more softly than their liminal counterparts and offer excellent walks and views that enable you to command the horizon after less arduous ascents. This is also a good area for appreciating the finer details of nature's handiwork: you'll come across small, unheralded pockets of countryside, with fauna and flora thriving in some rather surprising locations such as disused quarries (page 239) and roadside verges (page 246).

TOURIST INFORMATION

Visit Isle of Wight Newport Bus Centre, Church St, Newport PO30 1JZ ⌗ visitisleofwight. com.

GETTING THERE & AROUND

WALKING & CYCLING

As befits an agricultural hinterland, exploration by feet or wheels is easy, with quiet lanes that see little motorised traffic. For walkers, the 11-mile **Bembridge Trail** runs from Newport to Bembridge on the coast and takes in the Arreton Valley along the way, while other footpaths knit together places of interest such as Robin Hill, Arreton and the Garlic Farm.

Cyclists can also utilise the quiet lanes that peel off south from Mersley and Arreton downs (page 250), while the **Red Squirrel Trail** loops southeast from Newport along field edges towards the coast. The trail has a useful northern spur along the west bank of the Medina that offers hassle-free access to Parkhurst Forest. Both cyclists and walkers should, however, be wary of all stretches of the A3020 and A3056, along with the Downs Road near Arreton, which seem to attract motorists driving at speed.

For **cycle hire**, see page 28. Routefifty7 will arrange for you to pick up bicycles outside the Barley Mow pub (PO30 1HS) at Shide Corner on the Red Squirrel Trail, just south of Newport, which enables you to avoid the town-centre traffic.

PUBLIC TRANSPORT

Newport bus station is located in Orchard Street in the town centre. **Buses** radiate from here to all corners of the Island. Key routes are the #1 to Cowes, #2 to Ryde (via Sandown and Brading), #3 to Ryde (via Ventnor), #5 to East Cowes, #6 to Ventnor and #7 to Yarmouth, Freshwater and Alum Bay. For full details, see page 21.

NEWPORT & CARISBROOKE

With a population of 25,000, Newport is home to almost one in six Island residents and is comfortably the largest town. Deserving of more than a cursory glance, you'll find a Roman villa here, important art galleries and fine food and drink. The village of Carisbrooke is a far smaller settlement where all routes lead to its magnificent castle. This is also a gateway to Lukely Brook, one of the Island's classically diminutive and understated wildlife spots.

1 NEWPORT

⌂ **Newport Quay** (page 305), **One Holyrood** (page 305) ▲ **Kids Love Yurts** (page 305)

Newport is not, at first impression, a place of beauty, for which you need to thank the town planners of the 1970s who decided to build a flyover over the Medina. Don't be deterred, though, for what remains of old Newport, in the form of the quayside and fine townhouses, is definitely worth exploring. You are likely to navigate Newport at some point during your time on the Island as most bus routes go through it and, if driving across the north of the Island, there seems no way to avoid the interminable road junctions that surround the town.

Newport is well named, for the original 12th-century settlement was indeed a new port, designed and built on a grid pattern by Richard de Redvers, the Lord of Carisbrooke (and the Island). De Redvers appreciated how, although situated seven miles upstream from the coast, a new town on the Medina would be an important transport hub and could grow under the shadow of the newly assembled Carisbrooke Castle. Work began in 1180 but the town was sacked, as were Newtown and Yarmouth, by the French in the 14th century. Newport recovered in a way that Newtown never did and was prospering as a merchant town by the 17th century. What you see today – behind some dismal 20th-century city-centre shopping architecture – is the skeleton of an 18th-century brick market town. Despite its obvious vulnerability to attack, Newport was never a walled town and the layout of its centre still reflects the original medieval street pattern.

Yet despite few natural disasters of note and no invaders for the best part of 600 years, surprisingly little of medieval Newport remains. You will, however, find remnants of the Tudor-era town centred upon Sts Thomas' Square, which provided an open space for assembly and trade, a corn market and a long-gone fish and flesh shambles (an archaic name for a slaughterhouse). **Newport Minster** dominates the square, and while there has been a church on this site since the 12th century, the latest incarnation was completed in 1857.

A TALE OF TWO THOMASES

Curiously, the minster positioned on Sts Thomas' Square is dedicated to Saints Thomas (plural). The original church was dedicated to St Thomas Becket, the Archbishop of Canterbury (who was famously done in, back in 1170). Come the reign of Henry VIII, however, the Reformation saw the dissolution of monastic orders and Becket deemed a traitor rather than a martyr. In his place, Thomas the Apostle, also known as Doubting Thomas and more popular with the king, found his name attached to the minster. In 1854, during substantial rebuilding of the church, Prince Albert took the diplomatic approach of dedicating it to both Thomases and it is now formally called the Minster Church of Saints Thomas. In so doing, Albert deftly swerved around the thorny issue of just where to put any pesky apostrophes, a quandary with which the public space in which it stands (variously called either St or Sts Thomas' Square), is still grappling.

Internally, the church belies a rather humdrum exterior with several outstanding examples of craftsmanship to admire. Among the most eye-catching features is the Maiden's Window, a Gothic Revival work in the Lady Chapel dating to the 1860s. The cost of it was met by money raised, as described at the time, 'by the young ladies of Newport', hence the name. Just as impressive is the monument to Princess Elizabeth, the second daughter of King Charles I, which was created by the sculptor Carlo Marochetti with Carrera marble and is widely regarded as a masterpiece. Elizabeth was just 14 when she died (of natural causes, unlike her father) at Carisbrooke Castle (page 226). She was buried in the church but her grave remained unmarked and the actual spot was forgotten over the years. In 1753 workmen had to lift the floor and stumbled upon the tomb; Queen Victoria commissioned Marochetti to create the memorial a century later.

As you gaze at the pulpit (a fine example of 17th-century Flemish woodcarving), spare a thought for church minister William Martin, who was dismissed in 1653 for mumbling. The Puritan regime of the time felt that a stronger projection was required to ensure the brethren received the benefit of public ministry. Meanwhile, the font dates to at least the 1630s, disappeared in the 1850s, only to turn up in 2004 when it was retrieved from a garden where it had been used, its origins and significance apparently unrecognised, as a bird bath.

A handful of shops and cafés encircle the minster and include **Gods Providence House** (page 225), which dates to 1701 and stands on the site of a former building where it is thought that the plague was brought to an end in the 16th century, hence the name. Pushing up against the periphery of the square, Watchbell Lane retains important architectural features too. This narrow alleyway curves away from Quay Street and is lined with a smattering of half-timbered buildings. The lane's name arises from the fact this is where a hand bell was housed to warn residents of the curfew and remind people to put out their fires for night-time safety, a wise precaution as most buildings were thatched.

Immediately to the northeast of the square, just across the High Street, stands the Guildhall which is home to the **Museum of Island History** (High St, PO30 1TY 🖉 01983 823433 🖱 iow.gov.uk/Council/ OtherServices/MuseumofIslandHistory/Museum-of-Island-History ◷ Tue–Fri). The museum offers a succinct though knowledgeable tour of the Island's past, from the Romans to the all-too-frequent shipwrecks. Architecturally, the Guildhall is of some merit. Designed by John Nash, it was built in 1816 and features Greek Ionic columns, pediments, three round-headed arches and recessed sash windows, all capped with a Victorian clock tower.

St James's Street runs north–south through the centre of town and, near the junction with Lugley Street, you can see (only from the outside) the **former Grammar School**, built in 1619, where Charles I initially stood trial while he was a prisoner at Carisbrooke Castle.

Walking in a southerly direction along St James's Street will take you, after a third of a mile, into an area known as **Nodehill**, a name that dates from 1377. This is where many of the French invaders of that same year were ambushed, killed and buried (a 'noddy' is a body). If you continue in this direction a little further, you will come across Nodehill Middle School (now a sixth-form college) which became the UK's first lending library when built in 1904. Walking back towards the centre, and just off a lane called Church Litten, you'll find **Church Litten Park**. This was initially a cemetery used during the plague of 1583, when it was located outside the town centre. In the park you will discover a monument to Valentine Gray, a child chimney sweep who died in 1822 (see box, page 222). The stone gateway dates back to Tudor times.

From Church Litten, head south along Medina Avenue for 400yds before turning right into Cypress Avenue to reach **Newport Roman Villa** (Cypress Rd, PO30 1HA 🖉 01983 823433 🖱 iow.gov.uk/Visitors/ Where-to-go/Newport-Roman-Villa/Intro). The villa was discovered in

THE LITTLE SWEEP

The lifeless, beaten body of John Valentine Gray (usually referred to by his second name) was discovered in 1822 in the outhouse in Newport's Pyle Street where he routinely slept. He was just ten years old and his all too brief life as an apprenticed chimney sweep was one familiar to many children of the time. Although the work was dangerous by definition, Valentine died at the hands of his master, Benjamin Davis, rather than from falling to his death, being immured in a chimney or choking from soot inhalation. Davis and his wife were found guilty of manslaughter.

At the very least, Valentine's death slightly nudged the Overton window among society about what was acceptable with regard to child labour. In 1834, the Chimney Sweeps' Act was passed outlawing the apprenticeship of children below the age of ten, though the law proved difficult to enforce. It's thought Valentine's dreadful story reached the ears of Charles Kingsley, who drew on the tale to write his novel *The Water Babies*, which was published in 1863 and whose central character Tom is a chimney sweep. Only in 1875 was a meaningful law passed which outlawed the practice and demanded that the police enforce it. A memorial to Valentine can be found in the recreation area of Church Litten in Newport, where he was buried.

1926 by accident: an owner of a house was digging a hole in the ground to accommodate a garage when he came across substantial walls dating back to the late 3rd century. While not on the scale of Brading Roman Villa (page 269), the ruins are worth a visit for the homely picture they paint; as much as anything else you may be struck by the fact the villa is located in a residential street, just as, presumably, it may have been when it was built (although the boundary wall that separates it from its neighbours features wood panelling sourced from a DIY store rather than a Roman-era quarry). Parts of the complex, including surviving walls, are outside and exposed to the elements; inside is a bath suite, snippets of mosaic flooring and underfloor heating.

Back towards the River Medina, the broad, sweeping slopes of **Quay Street** are one of the few places in Newport where you can visualise how galloping horse-drawn coaches might once have transported dignitaries into town after they had disembarked from the river. Quay Street boasts some fine architecture, including 18th-century chequered purple and red-brick houses with wooden eaves, cast-iron balconies and sturdy doors that open hard on to the street. These are interspersed with early 19th-century three-storeyed houses, with grey headers, yellow-brick dressings, low pitch gables and slate roofs. Many have distinctive façades infilled with recessed sash windows looking on to the street, glazing bars intact on the second floors, and flat-brick arches. Today, these properties are almost entirely given over to private dwellings and offices but they make a pleasant escort on your way to the Medina and the smattering of Arts and Crafts buildings on its quayside.

Home to two art galleries, a theatre and a mighty fine café, **Quay Arts**, perched on the edge of the River Medina in Sea Street, is one of the Island's artistic focal points. Depending on the time you visit, the centre either appears afloat amid the waters of high tide or marooned in a valley of mud, thanks to the tidal ebbs and flows of the waterway. That Quay Arts exists at all is thanks to those who had the foresight to save the buildings that house it from demolition in the 1970s. At that time, when a dual carriageway was being built over the river, the site was just a collection of derelict factory buildings. A key aim of Quay Arts is to make its galleries, shows and talks accessible and locally themed. 'Local resonance is very important,' says Paul Armfield (⊘ paularmfield.com), a local writer and musician and the former manager of Quay Arts. 'The Island has a very defined sense of place and belonging. When you create that sense of local connection in what Quay Arts does, you attract a part of the public who might not otherwise come. Being an Island allows us to look slightly askance at things – there is no doubt that we have a different perspective from the mainland.'

The land where Quay Arts now stands used to be home to the Mew Langton Brewery, which laid claim in the 1880s to the invention of the screw-top can of beer that prevented drink going stale while being shipped to India. The tracks and winch you can see by Quay Arts were those used to transport the beer barrels on to barges floating on the Medina.

"Home to seven artists' studios, the building is something of an artistic hub for the Island and some of the artists do open to visitors."

Just a five-minute walk downriver along the Medina (on the east bank) and clearly visible from Quay Arts stands a former grain store, now restored to house **Jubilee Stores** (⊘ quayarts.org/about-us/jubilee-stores). Home to seven artists' studios, the building is something of an artistic hub for the Island. Though it is not formally open to the public, some of the artists do open to visitors by appointment. Look for their work around the Island (some is on sale in the shop at Quay Arts) and keep an eye out for Open Studios Week (⊘ isleofwightarts.

THE ISLE OF WIGHT'S EARTHQUAKE MAN

Natural disasters on this relatively geologically stable Island are few and far between. So it might be surprising to learn that Newport was home to John Milne (1850–1913), who history records as the father of seismology and who developed some of the earliest seismographs to detect earthquake activity. He also drew up the first codes of engineering practice for earthquake-resistant buildings.

Milne's training as a geologist included a stint at the Camborne School of Mines in tin-rich Cornwall before he took up the post of lecturer in geology and mining at the new Imperial College of Engineering in Tokyo (he experienced his first earthquake the day he arrived in the country in 1876). But it was another major tremor in 1880, known as the Tokyo–Yokohama earthquake, that got Milne really thinking about the extent to which it was possible to quantify their strength and impacts and, consequently, mitigate their damage by advance preparation. Like many others to this day, he failed in the pursuit of the Holy Grail: an ability to even remotely predict when an earthquake might strike. But, with a colleague, Milne designed what became known as the Gray–Milne seismograph, which recorded the time of an earthquake and its epicentre.

On his return to the UK in 1895, he moved into a house on Shide Hill, on the southern edge of Newport, with his Japanese wife Toné. He continued to work, finessing his seismographs with ever-improving technology, and built an observatory in the coach house in the grounds of his home, which accommodated what became known as the Milne Horizontal Seismograph. Milne was generous with his knowledge and invited Islanders to help process information from 30 similar stations around the world. The data they gathered was published in what were called *Shide Circulars*. He lived on the Island until his death in 1913.

Perhaps Milne knew more than we think, for he showed that low-level, Magnitude 3 earthquakes have happened from time to time on the Island. Even a M-5 is thought to have struck Newport in 1750, while the M-9 Lisbon earthquake of 1755 caused a tsunami to roll up the English Channel and lap parts of the Island with rather modest 3ft waves.

Milne was not the only Islander to ponder upon what lies beneath the Wight crust. Another geologist, Robert Hooke, endured professional disdain for daring to suggest that tectonic movements had shaped the earth's continents (page 55). Perhaps it's the sea air and all that thinking time spent gazing out to the horizon.

A permanent exhibition of Milne's life and times is on display at the Carisbrooke Castle Museum (page 228).

com/our-events/open-studios) in July. The venue does, however, offer regular classes in pottery, jewellery-making and printmaking. Among the resident artists is the tireless Ian Whitmore, who works on projects with schools and local groups across the Island in between working on his own distinctive cyanotypes (hand-cut prints), which feature striking cyan blue (hence the name) images of the sea.

🍴 FOOD & DRINK

Caffé Isola 85a St James's St, PO30 1LG ✆ 01983 524800 ⌂ islandroasted.co.uk/caffe-isola. Caffé Isola has grown into something of a coffee emporium: bustling with customers on the ground floor, with a more sedate, quieter vibe on the second floor. The artisan coffee shop produces its own Island Roasted Coffee and one of the commercial roasters operates here, so you can watch the team roast and pack its retail coffees while you sip your own. There's also a decent array of paninis and cakes.

Gods Providence House 12 Sts Thomas' Sq, PO30 1SL ✆ 01983 522085 ⌂ godsprovidencehouse.com. Wonderfully atmospheric tea room in a Grade II-listed building which serves up a fine teacake along with pies and sandwiches.

Newport Farmers Market Sts Thomas' Sq ⌂ islandfarmersmarket.co.uk ◷ early morning–14.00 Fri. A small but good range of breads, chocolates, meats, cheeses and pies are usually available here every Friday.

Peach 89 St James's St, PO30 1LB ⌂ peach-veganzerowaste.co.uk. A small, airy café in the heart of Newport with a vegan kitchen and zero-waste policy; choose from the likes of vegan sausage rolls, peanut butter cake and fine coffee. Everything sold in the café, such as vases, jars and toothbrushes, is sustainable and, says Stephanie Norris, who runs the café with her partner Guy Page, can 'be returned to the earth once you have finished with them'.

Quay Arts Sea St, PO30 5BD ✆ 01983 822490 ⌂ quayarts.org. Food in the art centre's café is excellent and ranges from butternut squash and chickpea vegan burgers to frittatas with kale salad. The list of local ales (from Goddard's Brewery), craft beers and wines is lengthy and good.

Walled Garden Café 14 Holyrood St, PO30 5AU ✆ 01983 716768 ⌂ thewalledgardencafe. co.uk. All-day breakfasts and a great emphasis on 'nammets' (generously filled sandwiches; page 17). Rear garden courtyard that is easy on the eye and where the owners grow potatoes, tomatoes and other salad items that end up on the menu.

🛍 SHOPPING

Gift to Nature 12 Holyrood St, PO30 5AU ✆ 01983 641972 ⌂ gifttonature.org.uk/shop-2 ◷ Tue–Sun. A small shop selling eco-friendly products and wildlife items such as packets of pollinating plants. All proceeds go the charity of the same name, which manages many wildlife sites across the Island.

Quay Arts Sea St, PO30 5BD ✆ 01983 822490 ⌂ quayarts.org. The gift shop at the Island arts centre is really worth seeking out as you'll find an excellent range of Island-wide crafts for sale, including paintings, pottery and jewellery.

2 CARISBROOKE

Lying less than a mile to the southwest of Newport town centre, the small village of Carisbrooke oversees the transition from the Island's urban heart to rural settlement. The boundary between Carisbrooke and Newport has long been occluded by development but, although the two are now conjoined, the village retains its own identity. The red-brick architecture apparent in Newport is here too and the village undulates over the foothills of the downs. Most of the village interest lies to the southeast of the junction of Carisbrooke High Street and Clatterford Road, in the centre.

Carisbrooke Castle

Castle Hill, PO30 1XY; English Heritage

With crenulated ramparts, forbidding walls, a portcullis and a tale of Royal incarceration, Carisbrooke Castle is every inch the classic fortress, right down to its Saxon foundations.

A fortification of some kind has stood at Carisbrooke since well before the Norman Conquest. The first recorded tenants were in fact dead ones, as testified by records of an Anglo-Saxon cemetery. The Anglo-Saxons then established a burh, or fortified settlement, here to withstand Viking incursions. These earth banks and stone walls formed a core structure on which subsequent developments were built, though the original timber buildings have, like that early pagan cemetery, long disappeared.

The bulk of what you see today centres on an enormous motte-and-bailey castle from the early 12th century, built upon more earthworks, along with a keep dating to around 1100. Inside this is a central courtyard dominated by a much-altered Great Hall, to which is attached the Great Chamber along with two chapels, a bowling green and an inner bailey. Much of this was built on the order of Baldwin de Redvers, a supporter of Henry I and one of the early grandly titled Lords of the Isle of Wight.

The gravest threat to the castle came in 1377 when it was subjected to attack by the French. Emboldened by having already emphatically torched Yarmouth and Newtown, the invaders pounded inland to the castle and laid siege. This time, though, the French met sterner resistance:

1 Carisbrooke Castle. 2 Carisbrooke Priory. 3 A Glanville fritillary – the Island is the only UK stronghold of this butterfly. 4 Sts Thomas' Square, Newport. ▶

their leader was killed by an arrow fired by the Lord of Stenbury and eventually an impasse was reached. After negotiations with the castle commander Sir Hugh Tyrell, matters were settled when a bribe was paid to the French to withdraw. Later, the castle became less a fortress to be defended – Henry VIII laid a greater emphasis on coastal defences – and more a residence for governors of the Island. Later residents included Princess Beatrice, Queen Victoria's youngest daughter.

The castle is a thrilling spectacle, entered across a steep drawbridge that bestrides a deep, dry moat and through a keep where a forbidding portcullis dangles, ready to halt any approaching hordes in their tracks. Your eye will probably be drawn first to the ramparts, which were an indulgence of George Carey, a cousin of Queen Elizabeth I who persuaded her to cough up for their construction in 1583. These exposed battlements are accessed by uneven steps made of Isle of Wight rubble. Some overlook sheer drops (perfect you might think, for tipping boiling oil and brimstone on to invading hordes) and can feel, in an age where risk assessments are everywhere, quite exposed. Keep little 'uns on a leash. The ramparts look as though they may have been drawn up by a young child: not quite geometrical enough to be described as a square. Collectively a mile long, they offer an exhilarating unbroken circumnavigation of the castle. As you thread your way around you may get a sense of why this location was chosen for a castle: the views from the walls take in a wide valley that gives way to rolling countryside and it would have been hard for any enemy to spring itself upon the castle defenders without being noticed.

Within the courtyard, and looking like another of the Island's architecturally sumptuous manor houses, the Great Hall takes centre stage. This is where King Charles I, the most famous (if reluctant) inhabitant of the castle, was held for 14 long months, before being taken to London to be tried and executed in 1649. The hall now forms part of the **Carisbrooke Castle Museum** (⊘ carisbrookecastlemuseum.org. uk), where Charles I's chambers are found, reached by a 17th-century staircase. You can nose around the bedroom where Charles whiled away the days, plotting his ill-fated escape attempts. With its wood panelling, four-poster bed and silk sheets, this was a form of imprisonment that contemporary detainees could only dream of.

Charles's first attempt at escape foundered when he became wedged in the bars of the bedchamber window (see box, opposite); sadly, the unco-operative window was removed during castle renovations in the 1850s and a stained-glass window has taken its place. Also on display are two secret, coded letters, sent by Charles to local Royalist sympathisers. Charles was not the only royal to be held against their will around that time. His daughter Princess Elizabeth (page 220) was also imprisoned and died here aged just 14; the story goes she caught a chill while playing bowls in the castle grounds. One of Charles's sons, the future Duke of Gloucester, was also held captive here, before later being exiled to France.

THE KING & HIS CASTLE

After months of being held captive and trying to bargain for his freedom via political deals, King Charles I hotfooted it from Hampton Court to the shores of the Solent in November 1647. He mistakenly believed Robert Hammond, the Governor of the Isle of Wight, to be sympathetic. Instead, Charles was confined to Carisbrooke Castle while Parliament worked out what to do next. Initially Charles was allowed considerable freedom, driving about the Island in his coach and attending church at St Blasius in Shanklin. He was far from inactive, seeking to bargain further with various parties, including a failed deal with the Scots to free him in return for political and religious favours.

His most infamous – and humiliating – attempt at escape came on the night of 20 March 1648. His chambermaid Mary smuggled out secret messages to sympathisers, and horses and a boat were laid on to complete the getaway. With the help of his page, Henry Firebrace, Charles planned to lower himself by a length of rope from his bedchamber window, which overlooked the courtyard of the castle. There was one flaw in the plan, and unfortunately, it was a fatal one: Charles had told Firebrace that he had checked that his head would fit between the window bars, 'and he was sure, where that would pass, the body would follow'. But when he attempted to clamber out, he got stuck as Firebrace later recalled: 'His Majesty... too late, found himself mistaken, he sticking fast between his breast and shoulders, and not able to get forwards or backwards... Whilst he stuck, I heard him groane, but could not come to help him.'

Undeterred, Charles embarked on another scheme that, while not quite so reminiscent of Laurel and Hardy, was equally humbling. In this instance, on 28 May of the same year, sympathisers had loosened the troublesome bars of his window with nitric acid, and his guards had been bribed. Though perhaps they had not been paid enough, for two of them betrayed Charles. Eventually, the authorities lost patience with the restless king and, following further negotiations in Newport, he was moved back to the mainland and, via Windsor Castle, to his doom.

The king's quarters may be the main reason to visit the museum but elsewhere within it there is a huge medieval fireplace dating to the late 14th century, and an enjoyably eclectic display of chain mail and crossbow bolts, along with a substantial toy collection to fascinate young children. The walls are adorned with fine art and include watercolours by J M W Turner, while the archaeology section features a substantial display of artefacts including a 12th-century gaming disc found in a local well and there is also a well-presented interpretation of the Island's social, ecclesiastical and medieval history.

There is also much of interest within the castle grounds, including watching donkeys drawing up water on a 16th-century treadwheel. The Princess Beatrice Garden has been designed to recall the original garden retreat of Queen Victoria's daughter and is considered Edwardian in design, with a water feature and blue, red and gold plants that mirror Beatrice's heraldic crest. The native trees and flowers come into their own in spring and summer, though the bare and stark branches add an austere quality in deep winter. The Chapel of St Nicholas now serves as a memorial to the Island's war dead and was rebuilt to mark the 250th anniversary of Charles I's execution. The wooden choir aisles are made from wood from HMS *Nettle*, one of the last wooden warships and which briefly saw service in the 1850s.

Staff from English Heritage work hard to bring the castle history to life, so look out for guided visits and well-rehearsed events, such as ghost tours during Halloween. Like any self-respecting castle, Carisbrooke is assumed to be thoroughly haunted and you can keep an eye out for the three separate ghosts that are enthusiastically promoted by staff: a grey lady in a long cloak who walks her four dogs around the moat; a face visible if you peer down the well, thought to be of a woman who fell in and drowned; and a third woman, another dog walker whose canine is said to be extremely obedient.

Adjacent to the castle are two other important sites that are entwined with Carisbrooke's history. To the northeast lies **Mountjoy Cemetery** (Whitcombe Rd, PO30 1DW), a grand old Victorian graveyard which opened in 1858. The cemetery also contains 16 war graves and offers views across the Medina towards a horizon infilled with the treeline of Parkhurst Forest. The cemetery was built upon meadow and farmland and, the graves aside, this remains the underlying grassy habitat, unimproved and free of fertilisers for more than 100 years. Overgrown in parts (a friends' group is steadily reining in the ivy and brambles), it is magical for wildlife: at least 15 species of butterfly enjoy the habitat, including the Glanville fritillary, common blue and grizzled skipper. Plants also thrive here, including pyramid orchids, crocuses, snowdrops, yarrow, common mouse-ear and spear thistle, while dogwood, sycamore and maples provide more substantial cover.

To the immediate southeast of the castle and also accessed off Whitcombe Road is **Carisbrooke Priory** (39 Whitcombe Rd, PO30 1YS ✐ 01983 523354 ◌ carisbrookepriory.org.uk ◷ Tue–Fri). While the priory looks as old as any of the Island manor houses, it is in fact a comparatively recent creation, built in 1865–66 by the Pugin-influenced

EXPLORING LUKELY BROOK

The area around Carisbrooke Castle is historically important and at one time was home to 14 mills, along with breweries and tanneries. Powered by the local waters, the 18th and 19th centuries saw the heyday of this bustle, which was centred on Lukely Brook. Sadly, few physical remnants of that time remain – the structure of Clatterford Mill, which stood in the shadow of the castle and produced writing paper in the 19th century, has long been removed. You can walk along the brook (◌ islandrivers.org. uk/the-rivers/newport-rivers/lukely-brook) from behind the castle – just follow Miller's Lane inland (this is the lane used to access the castle car park) and you'll immediately see the watercourse.

The brook – 'Lukely' is thought to mean 'stream of the shining way' – forms the northern boundary of medieval Newport and, although nearly seven miles from the sea and almost narrow enough at times to leap across, is subject to tides (though visually this can be quite subtle). Its headwaters lie some 800yds southwest of the castle, near Plaish Farm. A footpath alongside the brook wends its way here, its fringes opening on to meadows.

Island Rivers, a local organisation (◌ islandrivers.org.uk), is trying to improve the quality of the brook's water which has long suffered from the encroachment of development and alteration to its course and flow. The return of nature along the brook is something of a conservation success story. Island Rivers is particularly proud of the return of a small fish called the bullhead, known locally as the Millers Thumb and just two inches in length. Unfortunately, its perfect camouflage (a grainy riverbed brown) makes it all but impossible for the passing walker to spot. You may find it comforting to simply know that it is there. To explore the mill heritage of Newport and its hinterland further, you can follow the eight-mile Mill Trail (◌ islandrivers.org.uk/wp-content/uploads/2015/09/MillTrail2013_web.pdf), which joins the dots between the sites of the old mills and tanneries.

architect Gilbert Blount. The priory housed Catholic Dominican nuns who emerged from the 13th-century southern French Order of the Preachers. Now Grade II listed, the Gothic building rises for two storeys in coursed rubble and is capped with triangular dormers and cusped arches. The priory grounds are entered beneath a striking 13ft-high stone rubble gateway with a pointed arch, buttresses and a rectangular gable featuring a coat of arms.

The nuns vacated the priory in 1993 – among other reasons, they struggled to fund increasingly necessary renovations – and it is now cared for by the Carisbrooke Priory Trust, which continues the religious purpose of the building but allows public access to the house and gardens. The house's lounges and drawing rooms are of lesser interest than the gardens, which extend for two acres and feature an orchard and manicured lawns. The grounds belong to an organisation called the Quiet Garden Trust (quietgarden.org) and, in a nod to the monastic life that prevailed for so long here, are intended to be a place of – ostensibly religious – contemplation. While humans can be obliging in their silence, in spring it becomes clear that the birdlife hasn't read the script and the avian songsters can be truly exultant. Along with the adjacent cemetery, this must be one of the most underrated but exceptional places to hear courting birds. There is also a small gift shop, where the emphasis is on books (hence the name 'Carisbooks'), along with local pottery and artwork. There's a tea room too, selling hot drinks, soup and other modest but good meals.

¶ FOOD & DRINK

The Blacksmiths Calbourne Rd, PO30 5SS 01983 529263 blacksmithsiow.co.uk. Located just to the west of Carisbrooke, on the B3401 towards Calbourne, this 400-year-old pub has a reputation for good food. Mains range from duck to whole plaice served with samphire, though the signature dish is the chef's Newport Pie, which features slow-roasted lamb inside a shortcrust pastry. Desserts feature a generous Island cheeseboard. A great choice year-round, though it comes into its own in summer when you can eat in the beer garden or terrace at the rear with views drifting away to the Solent to the north.

3 GATCOMBE

Just over two miles south of Carisbrooke, the hamlet of Gatcombe really amounts to little more than a smattering of houses and smallholdings. It is, however, home to the fetching Norman **church of St Olave's**. The

13th-century church was originally built as the chapel for the Estur family of Gatcombe House and it still enjoys a wonderful symmetry: set on a gentle slope, its narrow proportions and protruding vestry and entrance porch lend it a curiously sphinx-like appearance, while some chillingly grotesque gargoyles, including a chubby-faced monkey, various winged monsters and a devil leer down at you. The splendid chancel windows are by an assortment of pre-Raphaelites including Dante Gabriel Rossetti and one by William Morris that depicts an angel on a wheel. The simple window by the south door dates to 1430 and is thought to be the oldest stained-glass window on the Island. Inside is a sturdy lead-lined Purbeck marble font dating back almost to the origins of the church, as well as a life-sized carved recumbent oak effigy, assumed to be of an esteemed Estur family member, accompanied by a carving of a loyal dog. The tower dates to the 15th century and boasts three large 17th-century bells that are reached by a spiral staircase.

THE LADY & THE KNIGHT

Any self-respecting isolated church has a ghostly tale to tell and St Olave's of Gatcombe is no exception. In this case the mystery focuses on the supposed grave of a Crusader and the inordinate attention paid to it in the early 19th century by a local girl, Lucy Lightfoot. Lucy had often been drawn to the effigy (which really does exist) in the church which, so the tale goes, was of Edward Estur (who is a real historical figure), a Crusader who died in the Holy Land in 1303. On the morning of 13 June 1831, a total solar eclipse of the sun triggered a violent storm and Lucy rushed into the church in the darkness to seek refuge. She was never seen again. When her desperate family looked for her in the church, they found that a rare jewel had disappeared from the hilt of the effigy's sword while beside the tomb was a large pile of dust. Only one conclusion could be drawn: Lucy, besotted with the Crusader, had plucked the stone from the sword and somehow slipped through time to be united with her true love.

There's just the one flaw with the story: it is utterly untrue and not a single part of it stands up to even the most cursory scrutiny. Not only did Lucy never exist but there also wasn't an eclipse of the sun in Britain on that day either. James Evans, a vicar at the church, confessed in the 1960s to concocting the entire tale in 1959 and expressed amazement at how his whopping fib was so eagerly seized upon by the parish's more credulous citizens. Evans's penchant for shaggy dog tales didn't stop there: he also spread the word that the carving of the loyal mutt by the effigy awakes from its slumber every 100 years on a full moon and trots, tail wagging, up and down the church path.

Just half a mile or so to the northeast of the village are the **Gatcombe withy beds**, a handful of acres of low-lying land dominated by willows, which are regularly coppiced. The wood is popular with Island fisherfolk for making lobster pots. To reach them, turn right (with your back to the church entrance) along the lane and at the first road junction turn right. After 150yds turn left along a track: this grassy track edges around some private buildings, through a wooden gate in a hedge and crosses two bridges to reach woodland. The withy beds are on your left. The tower you see here represents the forlorn remains of the Whitecroft Hospital, a Victorian asylum.

NORTH OF NEWPORT

The area immediately to the north of Newport makes for a neat segment to explore, bounded by the town itself to the south, the River Medina to the east and the outer limits of Cowes to the north. Parkhurst Forest is the focus here, a wildlife-friendly and picturesque mix of conifers (Scots' and Corsican pines) and native broadleaves (including some huge, mature oak trees) and home to that russet-tinged bundle of charm, the red squirrel.

4 PARKHURST FOREST

🏠 **Tiny Homes Holidays** (page 305)

Let's be candid: the clutter on any approach to the forest from the south is unpromising. Apart from the two adjacent Island prisons and their related service industries, the busy spokes of the A3054 and A3020 ringfence the woodland. Wander around the 975 acres of Parkhurst Forest, though, and that bustle quickly melts away and you are left alone in the company of ancient woodland, heathland and more recent plantations. The landscape is similar to that found in the New Forest and is another reminder that until the end of the last ice age, when sea-level rises got in the way, the two areas were part of the same landmass.

Another similarity links the two: like the New Forest, Parkhurst is not a 'forest' in the traditional sense. James I hunted here in the early 17th century, pursuing deer and other quarry through a mixture of open rides and woodland cover. The conifer canopy in particular is the Island's mission control for the red squirrel, as these medium-sized rodents prefer the menu of low-calorie seeds offered by the pine cones.

This is a working forest and conifers are grown and cut for the timber trade so you may encounter the occasional recently created clearing. Non-native trees are slowly being removed from the woodland, encouraging the greater spread of broadleaved trees and the creation of light-exposed rides and clearings where native flowers can thrive.

There is only one waymarked route in the forest (to a hide) so you are really left to your own devices to strike out from the car park and explore different elements of the wood. The bridleways – commonly used by horseriders – are the easiest way to navigate round. Given that every junction of footpaths can look the same, unless you are an expert in the navigational art of dead reckoning, you may feel a little like Theseus in need of a ball of yarn to find your way back to where you began.

Some of the oldest patches of the forest lie well to the north of the car park. If you follow the bridleways more or less north for a mile from here, almost to where the treeline peters out on the approaches to Gurnard, you come across large patches of what is termed 'neglected wood pasture', an increasingly rare kind of woodland in the UK. The word 'neglected' is a little misleading: the term refers to an absence of grazing – not just for decades but in some parts for centuries – and means that trees and their associated species have been able to survive into great age. With even longer to grow and provide local ecosystems, they have become incredibly rich for wildlife and your chances of spotting goldcrests or nuthatches, for example, are high.

"The knack to spotting red squirrels is to look high in the branches: pick the outer edge of a branch and follow it inward towards the trunk."

Cyclists are encouraged to approach from the east and the Red Squirrel Cycle Trail (⌀ redsquirreltrail.org.uk/other-routes/parkhurst-forest) makes a detour north from Newport specifically to take in the forest, and includes a 3¼-mile loop through the woods. All the cycle trails within the forest are along gravel trails. For walkers, the sole route with any waymarking leads from the car park for three-quarters of a mile to a log cabin-style hide (⌀ gifttonature.org.uk/discover/sites-in-and-around-newport/parkhurst-forest-red-squirrel-viewing-hide), where you can sit and stare up at the tree canopy, though try and manage expectations as there's no guarantee that the red squirrels will be co-operative. The knack to spotting them is to look high in the pine branches: pick the outer edge of a branch and follow it inward towards the trunk and be alert for any movement. They can be easier to spot in autumn, not only because broadleaved trees such as alder (which also bear low-calorie seeds) are dropping their leaves but also because the squirrels descend to ground level to bury and recover nuts.

The Island has long been a stronghold for the red squirrel; the greys have never been introduced here and the Solent acts as a natural barrier to their advance (there is also a £5,000 fine for introducing grey squirrels to the Island). In 1945, reds were widespread across the east and southwest of England; today the Isle of Wight is the only place in England you will find them south of Formby in Lancashire. The most recent census put the Island population at 3,500 (the UK number is around 140,000). Another reason red squirrels do well on the Isle of Wight is that the Island has no deer. Without grazing deer, the cycle of tree growth, coppicing and regrowth is uninterrupted and provides plenty of foraging cover for the squirrels as well as another, more furtive mammal, the reclusive dormouse.

There's plenty of other wildlife and flora to look out for in the forest, including green woodpecker, which you may see shuffling around on the forest floor, crossbills, goldcrests and great crested newts which live in the ponds in the centre of the forest. With a bit of knee-bending you can see the forest heath come alive as insects increase with warmer daytime temperatures, from harvestmen to assassin bugs, skimmers and emperor and common darter dragonflies. Should you visit between late April and July you may see the pearl bordered fritillary, a nationally scarce butterfly. Its emergence is synchronised with violets on which both the caterpillar and butterfly feed. Look out too for fly agaric, red cap and white-spotted mushrooms.

Buses #1 (between Newport and Cowes) and #7 (between Newport and Yarmouth) drop off outside the forest entrance and car park, a 400yd signposted walk north from the A3054, which is where you will find an information board and the start of paths into the forest.

5 DODNOR CREEK & DICKSON'S COPSE

The River Medina flows in a north–south direction and, just to the east of Parkhurst Forest and on its western banks, Dodnor Creek and the adjacent Dickson's Copse form an exquisite sliver of haven for wildlife.

Parkhurst Forest. ▶

A short, circular nature trail explores the site, which is managed by Gift to Nature (⊘ gifttonature.org.uk/discover/sites-in-and-around-newport/dodnor-creek-dicksons-copse). The Medina was one of the main trade routes on to the Island for many centuries and the small tributary at Dodnor was also utilised. The river has historically overflowed into the creek and brought with it saltwater fish such as plaice and flounder. Fishermen would set nets across the river, catch these and sell them across the Island. The creek was dammed in the 1790s to provide water for a flour mill and when that enterprise failed the cement industry moved in. For a brief period, the Isle of Wight became the epicentre of cement production in Victorian England, with the quick-setting cement used for all those sea fortifications (see box, page 16). Recent archaeological work has uncovered old cement kilns along the Medina's banks.

Dodnor Creek has been designated a RAMSAR site (an international status granted to wetlands of high quality) for its importance to winter wading birds such as teal and grebe. The waterway is fed by unnamed streams and much of the site is dominated by reed swamp and bulrushes. On the eastern side of the reserve is **Dickson's Copse**, which was once a continuation of Parkhurst Forest and where oak and ash still feature on the higher ground, with a rich shrub layer comprising holly, hawthorn, spindle, privet, butcher's-broom, hazel and field maple. The copse floor hosts ancient woodland indicator species such as lords-and-ladies, red campion, stinking iris, primrose and violets. In spring this is a good place to hear willow warbler, chiffchaff and blackcap, while year-round you may hear the drumming of great spotted woodpecker or catch sight of a barn owl.

The Red Squirrel Cycle Trail (page 26) runs alongside the copse, utilising the same former railway viaduct (called at this point the Dodnor Causeway) that takes you to Parkhurst Forest and Cowes. By bus, take the #1 and get off at the Stag Inn for a short walk to the creek and copse.

THE ARRETON VALLEY

Sweeping away to the east and southeast of Newport, the Arreton Valley represents the heart of the Island's farmland. The profundity of food production in the area is part of the reason why the parish of Arreton was the largest on the Island during medieval times, stretching from the north to the south coast. The parish's importance is reflected in the list of eight English monarchs who owned the village manor house (Arreton Manor still stands today and now offers B&B; page 305): the first records of the manor emerged in 872 in the will of Alfred the Great. In addition, monks from Quarr Abbey near Ryde held and farmed the land for the best part of 400 years until Henry VIII made one of his land grabs in 1595.

Ordinarily, a landscape dominated by agriculture does not equate to good news for wildlife: hedgerows and ditches are always in the crosshairs of farming that seeks to maximise yields and too often they get grubbed up or filled in. Things are a little different in the Arreton Valley and what is striking is how much nature survives and thrives here. Arreton offers vital habitats for farmland birds such as yellowhammer, skylark and the even rarer cirl bunting, and the insects they feed upon, and you will see more fields hemmed in by hedgerows than barbed-wire fences.

6 SHIDE CHALK PITS

Burnt House Ln, PO30 3BA ⟨gift icon⟩ gifttonature.org.uk/discover/sites-in-and-around-newport/shide-chalk-pit

Abandoned chalk pits are often good sites for orchids and Shide, on the southern outskirts of Newport as you head towards the Arreton Valley, is no exception, designated a SSSI and brimming with flowers and attendant wildlife. Shide also happens to be a typical Island nature reserve – understated, overlooked and in an unlikely location (off Burnt House Lane, just south of the ASDA superstore and off the busy A3020). The site was quarried for chalk during the first half of the 20th century and the prominent west-facing slope is a major landmark on Newport's skyline (you can't miss it as you head out of town towards the east coast). Since quarrying stopped, vegetation has colonised the floor and sides of the pit and habitats vary from bare rock to emergent woodland and a small stream.

Late spring and June to July sees populations of bee orchid, pyramidal orchid and southern marsh orchid emerge. Warm days draw out adders and common lizards to sunbathe amid the glare of reflecting chalk. Lepidopterists have a long list of flutterers to admire, including brimstone, orange tip, comma and chalk hill blue. You may notice small green mounds with soil on top – these are not the work of moles but the nests of the yellow meadow ant.

NICKEDWARDSPHOTO.UK/SHIPWRECK CENTRE & MARITIME MUSEUM

ROBIN HILL

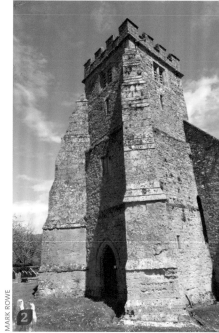
MARK ROWE

The modest woodland is dominated by sycamore, ash and hawthorn, and ivy covers much of the ground. The northern slope includes exotic shrubs such as holm oak and sweet bay while the southeast corner contains more native woodland species such as wild cherry, field maple and spindle. A sprinkling of magic is added by a shaded stream – in winter this is a good place to spot goldcrest and long-tailed tits.

You can access the site by bicycle – the Red Squirrel Trail (page 26) passes close to the site; just leave the trail at Shide Road by the Barley Mow pub, which is just across the road from the entrance. Buses #2 and #3 drop you at the pub, too.

7 ARRETON BARNS CRAFT VILLAGE

🏠 **Arreton Manor** (page 305)

Main Rd, Arreton PO30 3AA ⊘ arretonbarns.co.uk

Arreton Barns Craft Village is the Isle of Wight in a nutshell: a slightly discombobulating confection of vintage souvenir outlets, an excellent farm shop, arguably the most impressive church on the Island and a fascinating shipwreck museum. You'll find the craft village at the northern end of the straggling village of Arreton, which lines the A3056 south of Newport for the best part of a mile.

Rather in keeping with the Island's idiosyncratic approach to life, the village, which lies in the heart of the Island and at least four miles from the sea, is where you find the **Shipwreck Centre and Maritime Museum** (⊘ 01983 533079 ⊘ museum.maritimearchaeologytrust. org ⊙ Mar–Oct). The museum is tucked away at the back of the craft village and, before entering, you can admire the exterior of the stone barn in which it is housed. The gables and parapets contribute to the barn's Grade II-listed status, a designation reinforced inside by exposed rafters. The interior's nautical feel is deliberately enhanced by the more recent introduction of a mezzanine level to recreate the aspect of the bridge of a ship.

The displays, as they rampage through history and lay bare the tempestuous relationship the Island has both enjoyed and endured with the waters that surround it, have the power to move the visitor. It's widely estimated that at least 4,000 ships have come to grief around the Island's

◀ **1** Lights at Robin Hill, the POLAR event. **2** St George's Church, Arreton. **3** Shipwreck Centre and Maritime Museum.

coast since Roman times, with doubtless many more unrecorded. As you wander around you encounter an eclectic array of items recovered from the seabed, from periscopes retrieved from German U-boats, false teeth and bugles from British military ships sunk during World War I, and genuine pieces-of-eight silver.

While the most substantial eye-catching item is a 16th-century cannon recovered from the nearby waters, the most moving is a smashed porthole from the SS *Mendi*, a carrier that sank in 1917 after a collision with a cargo ship (see box, page 179). The smashed glass records the moment of the fatal impact that sank the ship.

It's no overstatement to say that the museum is largely homage to the extraordinary life of a single local diver. Over several decades, Martin Woodward (see box, below) was responsible for bringing most of what

THE DIVER & THE DEEP BLUE SEA

Most visitors to the Isle of Wight are content to simply stare at the sea, paddle at its edges or perhaps surf or kayak. Martin Woodward, the creator of the Shipwreck Centre and Maritime Museum at Arreton (page 241) is never happier than when he is rummaging around on its seabed. The saltwater of the Solent and the English Channel are in Martin's blood. The first time I spoke to him, he had just finished a morning swim off the beach at Bembridge. It was mid-December and the sea, Martin admitted, was 'a bit chilly' at what most of us would consider a toe- and tooth-curling 10°C. He repeats this dip day after day, whatever the weather.

Martin spent his childhood in Bembridge, in what he describes as 'the perfect environment for a kid to grow up in' and became involved at an early age with the work of the RNLI station at the end of the village pier. 'I bought a dinghy, some diving gear and cylinders, I just put things together

myself and went looking,' he recalls matter-of-factly (the irony is not lost on Martin that nowadays the RNLI would probably be called out if a child did what he had done in the 1960s).

A professional career as a diver followed, conducting remedial work on gas pipes under the Solent, which led to deep-diving work on rigs in the North Sea and the Philippines. Like an anchor being dragged along the seabed, however, the Isle of Wight drew him back. 'I'd always had a passion for shipwrecks and this is one of the best places – or worst if you're in one – for wrecks in the world. The Channel is the busiest shipping lane in the world.' Bad weather also plays its hand, he points out, for the southwesterlies will push stricken ships into the lee shores of the Island.

In the early days, finding anything involved an element of pot luck, as Martin would either use charts of wreck sites or educated hunches you see in the museum up from the seabed of the Solent and the English Channel. A highly engaging film of Martin's life and times underwater runs on a loop.

The process of recovering items of interest continues today, with the Maritime Archaeology Trust at the forefront of the activity. 'It's a privilege to dive in the waters around the Solent,' says Jacqui Arnold, the former education officer for the Maritime Archaeology Trust (⊘ maritimearchaeologytrust.org), which manages the museum. 'There are so many wrecks, there is something amazing about seeing them underwater in a submerged landscape. I don't think people always realise just how important our maritime history is but it has really shaped the Island. You can watch people playing on Sandown Beach and you wonder if they know there are three World War I wrecks just offshore.'

---

for spots to explore. 'You just jumped over the side and stayed underwater until you found something,' he says. As technology improved, radar enabled him to pinpoint sites of interest and he would trundle up and down the Solent and the Channel, waiting for something more substantial than a lobster pot to show up, a process he describes as 'mowing the lawn'. 'I'm looking to glean something from the grass of the ocean,' he says, smiling, 'it doesn't have to be valuable.'

Before long, Martin had accumulated so much from the seabed, from mastheads to periscopes, that he was struggling to squeeze through the front door of his house and he opened a museum in Bembridge. When that became full, 28 years later, the entire collection was moved to Arreton Barns (page 241). His most extraordinary find was the wreck of HMS *Swordfish*, a British submarine sunk by a U-boat in 1940. 'It was assumed to be 200 miles further southwest, off Brest in

France,' he says. Instead, it had been struck off the headland at St Catherine's Point. 'At times like this, the human element really sinks in, of the sailors' lives lost.'

Similarly harrowing was the wreck of the SS *Mendi* (see box, page 179), which Martin uncovered in 1974. The tale of the ship's catastrophic collision had long been covered up but Martin began digging into the story and it was his perseverance that established the truth, a process that ultimately led to the former UK prime minister Theresa May handing the bell from the *Mendi* to the South African president Cyril Ramaphosa in 2018. A few years ago, Martin himself travelled to Soweto to meet with descendants of Isaac Dyobha, the township vicar who had performed the death dance on deck. The experience reinforced an impression that Martin had long held, 'that no item I find has any kind of value unless you know the story of the people behind it.'

Elsewhere in the craft village the emphasis is on the olde-worlde, with shops and attractions including Sweet Memories, an old-fashioned sweetshop selling fudge made on site, as well as opportunities to witness glass blowing and brass rubbing. You will, however, not want to miss the farm shop to end all farm shops, Farmer Jack's (page 246).

St George's Church

Set among the bustle of Arreton Barns, St George's can be quite easy to overlook – it is tucked away just to the east of the main 'street' of shops, behind the Maritime Museum, as if hiding from the coach parties. Yet this Grade I-listed building, regarded as a masterpiece of Norman church architecture and overlooking an idyllic ornamental pond, is the one church on the Island you really should not miss. Built from Island stone rubble, which has a ploughed-earth light brown-grey appearance, it fits in harmoniously with the surrounding landscape of treelined fields and a skyline of rolling downs. Architecturally impressive both inside and out, it is set within a hugely atmospheric cemetery with a curious tomb. And with radiators heated by a Biomass boiler in the grounds of the Old Vicarage, it must be one of the greenest churches in the country.

The present church is thought to have been built on the grounds of an earlier Saxon site of worship but most of those pre-Norman origins disappeared when construction began anew in the 11th century (although the 10th-century west doorway survives, as does a blocked window above it). That discerning doyen of architecture Nikolaus Pevsner advised that 'One must go inside to appreciate fully the scale and quality of the building' but, with all due respect, this is not entirely true. The exterior is really exceptional, with a massive square tower (dating to 1299) and its immense buttresses, which the fanciful might compare to giant steps leading upwards to the heavens, filling the frame of view. You enter across an Elizabethan stone porch, overlooked by a sundial. Inside, there is beauty and fine craftsmanship wherever you look: three early English arches; exposed rafters; remains of a 13th-century font; a Norman window in the chancel; Tudor windows in the aisles; a Jacobean altar table; and a mighty oak chest. Careful excavation has exposed substantial remains of a carved stone of Christ in Majesty dating to the 13th century. The Ten Commandments are set in an arched recess amid polished marble columns and there's a stone-carved head of a dragon thrown in for good measure. A headless brass effigy represents Harry Hawles, a steward of the Island in the early 15th century under the reign of Henry V and a veteran of Agincourt. It's not known when the head disappeared.

The churchyard has a picturesque setting overlooked by Arreton Down and features a dozen listed monuments. The graveyard is dotted with mature trees and here and there shield-like tombstones stand hunched together in serried ranks, though there does not always seem to be a family link or explanation for these discrete groupings. The most striking grave is a large, box-shaped Georgian chest tomb, known as the Rayner Monument. A bronze plaque has been fixed to the tomb and is inscribed with a poem that pays homage to William Rayner, the deceased bellringer who lies within:

> Skill'd in the myster of the pleasing Peal, Which few can know, and fewer still reveal, Whether with little Bells or Bell sublime, To split a moment to the truth of time, Time so oft truly beat at length o'ercame, yet shall this tribute long preserve his Name.

The churchyard is also the final resting place of Elizabeth Wallbridge, who inspired a bestselling novel, *The Dairyman's Daughter* (see box, below).

THE SERMON THAT BECAME A BESTSELLING NOVEL

The Dairyman's Daughter was originally intended as a religious text advocating moral rigour and endurance, written by the Reverend Legh Richmond (page 266). While girls were the original target audience, the text became hugely popular in the 19th century and is still available now (classified as juvenile fiction), having sold more than four million copies with translations available in 19 languages.

The true-to-life tale recounts the eponymous daughter, Elizabeth Wallbridge, who lived, toiled, endured and died in Arreton (and who comes across as a real-life version of Charles Dickens's Little Nell). The narrator is the vicar and he writes approvingly of how Elizabeth had initially embraced a life of worldly values – nothing too bawdy of course, just a love of nice clothes when she could afford them and other similar traits that could not be deemed vain or irreligious. The novel approvingly records how she then abjured these worldly trappings when she found God. From that point on, her life was one of diligence, domestic servitude, altruism and Bible studies.

Elizabeth died in 1801 at the age of 31, after a long illness. Quite what either Richmond or Elizabeth would have made of the pub named after the novel and which stands a stone's throw from her grave in St George's Church, is anyone's guess.

Arreton Cross

Here, on the south side of the A3056 where this busy road meets Downend Road, is one of the Isle of Wight's more unheralded green corners. The scrub has been controlled to allow natural light to reach ground level and enable roadside plants to thrive in an unusual location. Flowers you may see include purple or yarrow broomrape, a stunning parasitic plant (it has no chlorophyll and so is a beautiful dark lilac colour). Look around and you will also see the scarce knotted and rough clovers, blue fleabane and, in some years, bee orchids. If your luck is in, you may see a lunar hornet clearwing moth emerging from the large willow on the bank at the back of the verge. The site is managed by Gift to Nature (*⊘* gifttonature.org.uk/discover/out-in-the-country/arreton-cross) and is a short stroll from the Arreton Barns complex. To get here, walk west from the barn for 200yds along the verge of the A3056; you'll find it where the A3056 turns left. The superb sculpture of a hare and a magpie, carved by artist Paul Sivell, will tell you that you are in the right place. Bus #8 also drops off here.

¶¶ FOOD & DRINK

Dairyman's Daughter Arreton Barns PO30 3AA *⊘* 01983 539361 *⊘* dairymansdaughter. co.uk. Surrounded by the Island's farming heartland, this pub is certainly in the right place when it comes to sourcing local food. There's an extensive menu catering for all tastes but vegetable dishes can have the edge, including stuffed peppers with goat's cheese and tomatoes, and sweet potato and butternut squash soup. Décor is overdone and the contrived feel can be a little irksome, but the food and general conviviality makes you inclined to give the team some slack. The pub also has a reputation for showcasing local musicians in the evenings.

Farmer Jack's Arreton Barns Craft Village, Main Rd, Arreton PO30 3AA *⊘* 01983 527530 *⊘* farmerjacks.co.uk. You can think of Farmer Jack's, housed in a barn-like building, as an uber-farm shop. The key mission of Farmer Jack's is to support the sizeable local community of farmers and food suppliers, and reduce the food miles. To describe the spectacle as a feast for the eyes doesn't quite do the place justice, and the mouth-watering choice ranges from locally grown tomatoes, Island cheeses, sausages, dates wrapped in bacon and goat's cheese, speciality breads (focaccia, malty bloomers) and homemade frozen pies. Some produce has travelled a little further, such as the 30-odd regional British cheeses and Italian specialities, including cured meats, antipasti and stilton biscotti. This is a good place to stock up if self-catering, assemble a picnic or buy to take home. Staff are happy to chat about the food they produce and sell. The shop is the product of the effort of two Island families, the Browns and the Pearces, who have farmed locally for several generations. Much of the produce on show is their own, including cherries grown in their orchards.

The White Lion Main Rd, Arreton PO30 3AA *℘* 01983 528479 *⊘* whitelionarreton.com. A deservedly popular pub, the whitewashed, low-slung White Lion sits harmoniously within the village. Despite it being near the honeypot of Arreton Barns, you get the vibe upon entry that it enjoys strong local community support. Best to work up an appetite here as dishes are hearty and a typical two-courses might feature beef Madras followed by Belgian waffles or apple and cinnamon crumble. The garden out the back is a pleasant suntrap in a good weather.

8 ARRETON DOWN

Much of the countryside immediately behind the Arreton Barns Craft Village is designated as the Arreton Down Nature Reserve, run by the Hampshire and Isle of Wight Wildlife Trust. With its holloways and grass-covered barrows, which hint at medieval thoroughfares, Arreton Down just *feels* ancient. The downland supports many species of wildflower, from orchids to horseshoe vetch and gentians. All this nectar-rich resource attracts an accordingly high number of butterflies, including chalkhill blues, which have been counted in their tens of thousands. Dingy skipper, brown argus and adonis blue can also easily be seen hovering above the grazed, south-facing slopes between April and July. Spring brings spotted flycatchers, wheatears and other migrant birds.

The easiest way to access Arreton Down is to follow footpath A12 behind the craft village, leading uphill from the White Lion pub (♀ SZ534866). This passes by the church and Arreton Manor, leading up to a kissing gate. Once the contours ease off, a couple of paths make a dart towards the east: follow either for as long as you wish to take in views across to the east coast and of further downlands that roll away towards the Solent. Avoid any route back that involves walking along Downend Road, to the west of the down: there's no footpath and the traffic can be fast.

A trio of paid-for attractions can be found on the northern flanks and the ridge of Arreton Down. Just north of Arreton Down Nature Reserve, **Robin Hill Country Park** (Downend Rd, PO30 2NU *⊘* robin-hill.com) is an 88-acre park which features ancient woodland. While you may object to part of the landscape being monetised, the park woodlands are a safe bet for spotting red squirrels. The counterargument of the owners – the Dabells, who also run Blackgang Chine (page 182) – is that they took on an overgrown site and have, since 2005, invested in making the landscape into one you can meander through. As you do, you'll come across more exotic specimens including a giant redwood and eucalyptus trees, ponds and dinky, Chinese-style miniature bridges that arch over streams. The owners also work hard at making the place entertaining, with the occasional seasonal theme set against a background of multi-coloured lighting.

On the eastern side of the grounds you will find some submerged earthen humps that represent **Combley Roman Villa**. The Roman villa essentially comprises a buried farmstead, bath house and aisled building, linked by a corridor with further associated features, including a courtyard to the south. The villa is thought to have been occupied for more than 400 years before, like Brading Roman Villa (page 269), falling through the gaps of collective memory, only reappearing by chance in 1910 during an excavation of the site. All of it has been reburied for protection, so there's little original to gaze at but the adjacent interpretation barn has a modest exhibition and a reconstruction of the mosaic found in the villa.

A couple of miles north of Robin Hill, off Long Lane, is **Monkey Haven** (Five Acres Farm, Staplers Rd, PO30 2NB ℰ 01983 530885 ⬧ monkeyhaven.org). Rather than a showcase for captive animals, the attraction offers a forever home for mistreated or rescued monkeys and other animals. The menagerie includes an assortment of rescued Barbary macaques, gibbons, white-throated capuchins and other simians. Some of the animals you see were discovered when traffickers attempted to smuggle them through UK customs in suitcases. Others have been legally imported from a pan-European rescue centre based in the Netherlands; you'll also see zebra finches that were used as therapy animals for inmates at Parkhurst prison and meerkats and lizards also recovered by authorities as a result of illegal behaviour or because of poor conditions.

The Isle of Wight is home to some important native butterfly species (pages 31 and 57) – for a wider view of what our planet has to offer to lepidopterists, you can drop into **Butterfly World** (Staplers Rd, PO33 4RW ℰ 01983 883430 ⬧ butterflyworldiow.com ◔ Easter–Oct). As well as a range of butterflies from around the world, the site has a Japanese-themed garden, fish pools and mature maple trees, making for a tranquil experience. Located close to Monkey Haven, you can easily combine the two for a half day (or longer) of wildlife encounters, which should particularly appeal to children.

9 THE GARLIC FARM

🏠 **The Garlic Farm** (page 305)

Mersley Farm, Mersley Ln, Newchurch PO36 0NR ✆ 01983 867333 ⊘ thegarlicfarm.co.uk

As you look around the Garlic Farm, you may feel like you are being watched. Everywhere, necklaces of garlic dangle down the walls. As Natasha Edwards, the third generation of the Boswell family to work on

TOMATO COUNTRY

If you thought a tomato was merely round and red (sometimes yellow) and only beef or cherry sized, think again. The Tomato Stall nursery (Hale Common PO30 3AR ⊘ thetomatostall.co.uk) near Arreton grows around 200 varieties of tomato of varying size, skin thickness, sugar and acids, many of which can be bought at nearby Farmer Jack's (page 246), as well as delis, farm and village shops across the Island and in the main supermarkets. The farm started small, selling at just two farmers' markets but, with 30% of the site certified as organic, it is now the largest organic grower of tomatoes in the UK. The crops are grown in coconut husks, a natural substrate that can be composted after its use has been exhausted.

The reasons for success are the same as those that favour the Island wine sector. 'It's down to sun and being an Island,' says Daniella Voisey, sales and marketing manager for The Tomato Stall. 'We simply get more daylight hours here and being close to the sea we get that light reflected back in.'

The Tomato Stall grows plants from seeds that have been developed elsewhere, often by innovative seed growers. The end products range from mixed heritage varieties to slow-roasted tomatoes with chilli and fennel. You can even get tomatoes that have the flavours of apricots or gooseberries. In addition to the tomatoes, the company produces tomato sea salt, tomato juice and tomato jams.

'We're always trying to find the best and tastiest tomato and that is what makes us different,' says Daniella. 'There are so many seeds out there and the retailers want to shout out that their product is exclusive, or high flavoured, to differentiate themselves in the market.'

The bad news is that this is one of those food producing sites on the Island that is not routinely open to the public (in this case for biosecurity reasons, as visitors can bring diseases in on footwear and clothing). The good news is that every other year, The Tomato Stall opens its doors for one day to the public, though no decision has been made when to resume this after Covid-19. To keep up to date, sign up to the company newsletter on their website, or keep an eye on their social media.

Mersley Farm puts it: 'A garlic bulb is quite striking, it's like an eyeball staring at you.' It becomes easy to understand why garlic features so strongly in folklore – just remember this is not Transylvania but a snug valley in the very south of England.

Justifiably one of the most popular attractions on the Island, the Garlic Farm is also the most archetypal of Island businesses: family run and expanding on the back of a good, if quirky, idea that has been well executed. The farm comprises a handful of converted barns where, along with those beady-eyed bulbs, you will find baskets full of varieties of garlic and shelves stacked with garlic-based preserves, chocolates, butter, oils and dressings.

If you get chatting to staff you may find there is one question you want to ask, and one they admit to pondering themselves: 'I do ask myself sometimes, "why garlic?",' admits Natasha, 'but I don't think any other product has the same allure or mystery. It's just a very satisfying thing to grow.'

A walk in the Arreton Valley

❊ OS Explorer map 29; start: The Garlic Farm, Mersley Farm, Mersley Ln, Newchurch PO36 0NR ♀ SZ557869; 2 miles; easy

This short walk takes you through an ancient landscape that has been long farmed by humans. The skyline is framed by chalk ridges and there's just the one brief climb. Up above you to the north is Mersley Down, which is a real hotspot for butterflies, such as chalkhill blue, adonis blue, brown argus and dingy skipper. This is a lovely walk for young families – it's not too arduous, and there's plenty of interest as well as the chance to picnic on Mersley Down.

1 Turn right (south) out of the entrance to the Garlic Farm. About 200yds south of the farm, bear left along a footpath that skirts the edge of woodlands and which keeps parallel to the road.

2 After another 300yds bear right (west) along the Bembridge Trail, which dog-legs across the road. This footpath is numbered NC6 and you follow it for the best part of a mile as it heads west. Like a gently curving wave, Arreton Down fills the view to the north while here and there you can pick out church spires across the centre of the Island.

3 When the track meets a T-junction, turn right and walk north towards Mersley Down, with disused quarries puckering its flanks.

The origins of the business date to the 1970s when Natasha's grandparents moved to the Isle of Wight and took over Mersley Farm (it is thought that garlic may have been grown on the Island as far back as Roman times). Initially, the family were tenant farmers, rearing cows and branching into sweetcorn. In the late 1990s a change of direction saw the focus turn to garlic, 'which had always grown really well in granny's garden', says Natasha. Garlic is pretty robust but particularly thrived in the chalky soils of the Arreton Valley. Soon Natasha and her four siblings were being dropped off at farmers' markets from Sussex to Surrey with boxes of garlic to sell.

Today the shop sells more than 60 garlic-themed products, from mayonnaise to beer. Should you wish to learn more you can sign up for 'tasting experiences', while children can participate in garlic workshops where they get to make garlic bread like they and you will have never tasted before. There's a saying that no two foods are incompatible but Natasha admits, after experimenting, that white garlic and ice cream

4 After 400yds, turn half-right along footpath A16, which cuts across a field, and follow this as it climbs uphill, with a quarry to your left. The path meets a minor road, Newport Shute; turn right along this and shortly afterwards up through a metal gate on the left, on to the flanks of Mersley Down. The rich birdlife here includes the likes of yellowhammers, goldfinches and linnets, joined in spring and summer by whinchats, redstarts and spotted flycatchers. Follow the path up the down as far as you wish.

5 Mersley Down is bounded to the north by a busy road so it's best to return to Mersley Shute via the metal gate through which you entered the down and then turn left (east) and follow the road. As it bears right at a shaded junction, follow it downhill to return to the Garlic Farm.

probably pushes at the boundaries of that adage. Instead, she suggests mixing ice cream with the sweeter-tasting black garlic.

Access to the Garlic Farm is easiest by car but is possible, if a little fiddly, by public transport or on foot. The #8 bus will drop you at Arreton, where you can follow the Bembridge Trail due east for 1¾ miles until you reach a minor lane; turn left (north) here and walk for a mile along Mersley Lane to the farm. The approaches along Mersley Lane and Knighton Shute (a lane to the north of the farm) are quiet and good for cycling.

♦♦ FOOD & DRINK

Farm Shop and Restaurant The Garlic Farm, Mersley Farm PO36 0NR ☎ 01983 867333 ⌂ thegarlicfarm.co.uk. Quality food, ranging from risotto and crab salads to paninis and ploughman's. Meat often comes from the farm's own beef herd. Needless to say, garlic features heavily. A good year-round choice, with a terrace for summer viewing of the picturesque valley and a log fire to warm things up in winter. In another example of localism, the restaurant is made out of Monterey cypress, planted around the farm at the end of the 20th century.

The award-winning Slow Travel series from Bradt Guides

Over 20 regional guides across Britain.
See the full list at bradtguides.com/slowtravel.

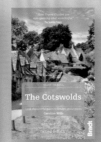

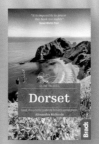

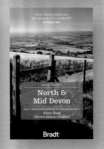

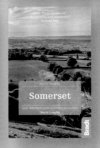

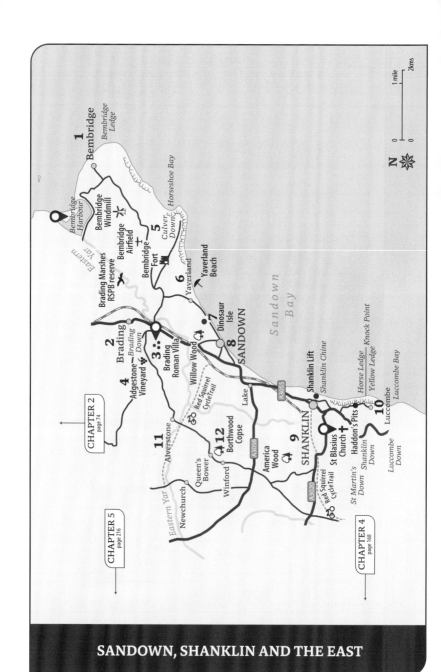

SANDOWN, SHANKLIN AND THE EAST

6

SANDOWN, SHANKLIN & THE EAST

Bookended between two mighty headlands, the beaches of Sandown Bay stretch unbroken for an impressive five miles and, for many visitors, represent the most striking sandscape on the Island. The enduring appeal of the beaches is demonstrated every summer when the bay's population of 23,000 residents swells to a seasonal 500,000.

The bay is backed by the conjoined towns of **Sandown**, **Lake** and **Shanklin**, where the Isle of Wight's traditional modus operandi as a bucket-and-spade destination remains robust. Kiss-me-quick hats, sticks of rock and saucy seaside postcards can all be found here. It makes for a singular experience that over the past couple of hundred years has exerted a magnetic allure, one way or another, on just about every strata of British society, from blue- and white-collar workers to the artistic types of Victorian England.

The coast here shapeshifts twice a day. At low tide the water retreats to expose the sand all the way from **Culver Down** at the north end to **Knock Point** at the southern tip; in contrast at high tide, especially when the wind is up, the prowling waters seem to claw and nip at the towns, inundation thwarted only by the sea wall and a hard-pressed system of groynes. While ancient cliffs top and tail the bay, in between them the Island's chalk spine, having run eastwards all the way from The Needles, finally collapses into the sea. Culver Down offers magnificent panoramas across much of the Island, while beyond Knock Point low tide plays a role again and permits you to explore fine ledges and an enchanting cove at **Luccombe Bay**.

On the periphery of these seaside conurbations is **Dinosaur Isle**, one of the best museums of its kind anywhere; a visit here will enlighten you with regard to the prehistoric giant lizards that once roamed the Island. Further north is **Brading Roman Villa**, a superbly interpreted site of equally high standard, as well as one of the UK's pioneering vineyards.

ℹ TOURIST INFORMATION

You'll find a good tourist information point at Brading train station (Station Rd, Brading PO36 0DY ℘ 01983 401222), with leaflets and guides.

Another handy tourist information point sits within Vernon Gift Shop Cottage in Old Shanklin (1 Eastcliff Rd, PO37 6AA). Brading Roman Villa and Dinosaur Isle also have a good selection of literature and information.

The town of Brading has an important history and is a gateway for good walks that work their way through wildlife reserves to the appealing village of **Bembridge**. Set back above these attractions are **Brading Down**, one of the most fetching, softly wooded of the Island's many downlands, and its near-neighbour Bembridge Down, a more stolid and wilder wedge of Island geology.

Closer to the sea, peer beyond the crowds and you will discover that wildlife is fighting its corner in this part of the Island. **Willow Wood** may be small but it is a wildlife-packed gem and reflects a very different side to Sandown.

GETTING THERE & AROUND
WALKING & CYCLING

Most of the sights mentioned in this chapter are accessible by **bike**. The Red Squirrel Trail, threading its way from Newport and Shide to Sandown and Shanklin, is the main thoroughfare for cyclists. You can spend an easy day on two wheels exploring much of the area, with cafés to stop off at along the eastern end of the trail. Behind Brading Roman Villa and Adgestone Vineyard you'll find a network of quiet lanes where traffic is light and regulations require motorists to go slow. These are perfect for navigating little-visited spots where you might happen upon a brook or the hedgerows give way to views of downlands. For those looking for a tougher challenge, some of these back lanes carry something of a kick as they work their way up towards Brading Down. The ascent of Culver Down will also demand plenty of huffing and puffing. Further south, the climb along the A3055 out of Shanklin towards St Martin's Down and Luccombe boasts a genuine unrelenting steepness (should you plan to try out an electric bike, this may be the place to use one). For cycle-hire options, see page 28.

Walkers too are blessed with similar opportunities afforded by those same hassle-free quiet lanes, while the beach walking is among the finest in the UK, with that five-mile stretch of beach at Sandown to barefoot along. Covering the ground between Sandown and Shanklin is easy, thanks to the sea wall that offers a wide, flat path which is ideal for both walkers and cyclists. The coast path seems to stubbornly seek out every rise and dip of the headlands at either end of the bay and this makes for stiff but scenically rewarding ascents, such as up to the Island's highest points around Shanklin Down. The concluding easterly stretches of the Worsley Trail (page 209) are another excellent means of surveying the spectacle of the bay from on high before dipping down to sea level. Also at sea level, a magical tidal walk around the cliffs to Luccombe Bay allows you to make your way across the shoreline's shimmering iron-coated pebbles.

PUBLIC TRANSPORT

Buses connect the area well. Route #2 runs from Brading down to Shanklin before heading for Newport, #3 also runs from Brading to Shanklin but continues to Ventnor, and #8 connects Yaverland to Sandown before winding its way back to Newport. The **Island Rail Line** stops at Brading, Sandown, Lake and Shanklin.

BEMBRIDGE, BRADING & AROUND

Jane Austen may have visited the Isle of Wight but none of her heroines ever exclaimed 'Oh! Bembridge!' in the way they were inclined to breathlessly talk of Bath or Lyme Regis. They really should have done. **Bembridge** has everything you'd want for an elegiac holiday: gorgeous beaches to wander along while pondering the meaning of life, an abundance of high-quality shops to potter around and a slightly faded – but not too faded – ambience.

Thanks to a charter granted by King Edward I in 1280, **Brading**, to the southwest and across the Eastern Yar from Bembridge, enjoys official town status, even though its population of 2,000 means it is less than half the size of Freshwater. Brading is also easy to reach by public transport, thanks to the Island train-line station, which sits just to the east of the centre and which is a good starting point for visiting RSPB Brading Marshes (page 260). The land to the west of town is also of significant interest and features a vineyard and one of the best Roman museums in the country (page 269).

1 BEMBRIDGE

🏠 **The Birdham Bembridge** (page 305), **The Crab & Lobster Inn** (page 305), **The Pilot Boat Inn** (page 305), **Harbourside View** (page 305) 🏠 **Heyvon Houseboat** (page 305)

As recently as the 16th century, Bembridge was almost an island, all but cut off from the rest of the Isle of Wight by the once-mighty River Eastern Yar. Some 1,500 years earlier the river and its estuary had been deep enough for a harbour at Brading Haven, where Roman trading vessels could moor and tides pushed sea water inland for almost four miles, as far as Brading and Sandown. Even before the Romans made landfall, however, the Eastern Yar had played an important part of the life of an area sometimes known as East Wight (an unofficial area covering everything east of a straight north–south line from East Cowes and St Catherine's Point), acting as an artery for grain and wool to be ferried up its waters to the old port of Brading.

Yet by the time the Tudors came to the throne, the river was beginning to silt up, a natural process later reinforced by those utilitarian Victorians who drained the land for grazing. The Isle of Bembridge was an island no more, but instead meshed to the rest of the Isle of Wight by a soggy hinterland of marshes and tidal mudflats. The surviving waterscape still had its playful moments: in the 1900s the winters were cold enough for the river's floodplain to freeze over, much to the delight of local skaters. And despite the Yar's dramatic narrowing over the centuries, it was still just wide enough for boating in its upper pre-harbour reaches well into the 1950s.

The lie of the land means that the village sits above and all but invisible from the harbour to which it lends its name. Today, a one-way road system around the village can leave the visitor feeling disarticulated and disoriented. This sensation is enhanced by the sprawling nature of the village, which hangs loosely around a long street that fades away at one end to a pier and to a windmill at the other, and is punctuated in the middle by a church with a lush, archetypical graveyard of tilted gravestones and mature yews. In between, quiet lanes and footpaths thread through extremely sleepy, broad residential streets stocked with large houses that hint at Bembridge's prosperous evolution as a retreat for the affluent Victorian classes.

The soul of the village is to be found in the High Street, which features several excellent independent stores, from a baker and a butcher to a fishmonger and a wholefood shop; it is with good reason that Bembridge won *Countryfile Magazine*'s 'Village of the Year' award in 2018.

Located on Church Road, at its junction with the High Street, the **church of the Holy Trinity** (PO35 5NA) is made of Purbeck stone and features an elaborate clock and lancet windows. It was built in the mid 19th century and replaced an earlier incarnation (a rare, failed effort by John Nash) that, made of the more friable Bembridge stone, began to collapse.

The village has three **beaches**, all of which are fetchingly attractive, but their geology is unsuited to lounging as they comprise stones, pebbles and shells. On the western shoreline, Bembridge Beach tumbles into the coast from the spit at the edge of Bembridge Harbour; softer sand reveals itself at low tide. To the east, Bembridge End Lane Beach, which bumps into the pier and lifeboat station, has a little more sand. Both of these beaches are perfect for beachcombing, with attractive backdrops of woodland framing the view inland. The pier, meanwhile, is 250yds in length and juts out into the water around the eastern periphery of the village and to some extent marks a logical geographical boundary to the community. The second of the Island RNLI lifeboat stations (the other is in Yarmouth) stands at the far end of the pier; the station can be visited in summer (bembridgelifeboat.org.uk ☺ check website). The coast remains accessible to the east of the pier, where it fragments into a series of wave-cut platforms around the appropriately named Ledge Beach: Bembridge Ledge, Long Ledge and Black Rock Ledge and the marshy shingle of the Foreland. Rock pooling comes into its own here at low tide. Another opportunity facilitated by low tide is a walk all around the Bembridge coast, from the lifeboat station to the harbour and the Pilot Boat Inn, a distance of around 1¼ miles that takes around 40 minutes. Beyond the ledges, and further to the southeast of Bembridge is Whitecliff Bay, a 200yd crescent of sand and shingle tucked below a high ridge and which offers a rear-view vista of Culver Down. The beach is accessed by steep paths via the holiday park behind it. From the shoreline you can also gain tidal access to Horseshoe Bay (page 273).

Half a mile south of the village centre, at the very end of High Street, is the lonely **Bembridge Windmill** (PO35 5SQ ✐ 01983 873945 ☺ usually Sun only, Mar–Sep but check website; National Trust). The last of its kind on the Island, this is the archetypical windmill, standing 38ft high with four sails pinned to a circular, tapering four-storey structure built from stone rubble, all topped with a wooden cap. Built in the 1700s, it operated as a flour mill and flourished until the advent of the Bembridge train line, which brought cheap flour from afar. The windmill bowed to economics and, after switching to the production of cattle feed, closed in 1913. Overlooking Brading Marshes, it's superbly situated and impossibly romantic; it's easy to see why J M W Turner chose to depict the windmill in his *oeuvre* (his unfinished painting of 1795 reveals the windmill teetering at the edge of the sea). In spring and summer you can climb the stone steps within the tower and take in the remarkably complete wooden machinery that survives from its days of practical use, including a turning wheel, windshaft and grain bins. There's also the chance to learn about the milling process in the small exhibition within the windmill. A small kiosk outside sells hot drinks, cakes and ice creams.

From the windmill, it's almost impossible to resist walking down the hill for half a mile to meander through the (often watery) hinterland of **RSPB Brading Marshes** (PO36 0BD ⊘ rspb.org.uk/reserves-and-events/reserves-a-z/brading-marshes), exploring the small wildlife-rich Centurion's Copse that is visible from on high. This silent, open expanse of reclaimed marshland and wetland habitat stretching between Bembridge and Brading has a touch of magic about it as the land tumbles away to become spirit-level flat. Flocks of sparrows and wagtails and even a wayward pheasant may shimmy among the trees. Look out for little egrets perched by a pond and lapwings, stylish birds with a raffish 'quiff' or quill. Meanwhile, alders dip their roots in the streams and the mires are dark and still. Though it feels like a vast woodland, you can explore the network of paths here inside an hour. Paths thread this way and that through the copse, past reed beds and clumps of woodland and hedgerows thick with old oak, ash and hazel, home to buzzards, yellowhammers, red squirrels and the embattled green woodpecker. You pass raised, dyke-like banks smothered with mosses of a fluorescent green that verges on the luminous, while a hilly curtain, in the form of the chalk edifice of Bembridge Down to the south and the woods above Brading to the west,

---

1 Brading Marsh. **2** Bembridge Windmill. **3** A houseboat at Bembridge Harbour. **4** Village sign at St Helens. **5** Lilliput Doll and Toy Museum, Brading. ▶

VISITISLEOFWIGHT.CO.UK

MARK ROWE

DYLAN GARCIA PHOTOGRAPHY/A

JONATHAN HOARE PHOTOGRAPHY

VISITISLEOFWIGHT.CO.UK

give a faint impression that this is a lost world. The reserve is just as easily accessed from the west, from Brading railway station.

Bembridge Harbour

The Eastern Yar finally meets the sea at **Bembridge Harbour**, a vast expanse of water spanning 250 acres from the beach at St Helens on the north bank to Bembridge Point on the southern side of its mouth. At low tide, the estuary shrivels to a trickle and any vessel within is marooned until ebb turns to flow. When empty, the harbour is a stirring spectacle of muds, mosses and wide-open skies. The harbour has been designated as a Site of Special Scientific Interest on account of these intertidal mudflats, sand dunes and, offshore, underwater sandstone ledges. Watery flora you might catch sight of along the shallow shores

A walk around Bembridge Harbour & St Helens Duver

✤ OS Explorer map 29; start: The Pilot Boat Inn, Station Rd, PO35 5NN; ♥ SZ643886; 2 miles; easy

Bembridge Harbour's contours and wooded backdrop are decidedly picturesque and a walk around its waterline allows you to explore an exquisite coastal corner bursting with wildlife. For refreshments, The Pilot Boat Inn can either send you on your way or welcome you back from the walk, while The Best Dressed Crab establishment offers sit-down and take-away food right on the harbourfront.

From The Pilot Boat Inn, head clockwise around the harbour along Embankment Road; you'll notice almost all the harbour houseboats lined up for inspection. At the western end of the road, cross the River Eastern Yar (today this takes just a few seconds – in medieval times you would have required a boat or a long plod inland) and turn right into Latimer Road. After 300yds, as the road bears left, keep ahead along the small lane to reach St Helens Quay. Go to the left of the building in front of you (the path is waymarked for the Coastal Path).

The new sea wall starts its journey across the harbour immediately behind this building. To the left are the remnants of the old sea wall. The new one provides a useful traverse of the harbour via a tidal causeway on to St Helens Duver. One way to know when the tide is rising is to watch the Brent geese: at low tide they graze on eelgrass along the shore but when the water is high they flap the short distance across Embankment Road to Brading Marshes to feed on hayfields. On its landward side, the new sea wall encloses a small salt marsh which is something include the submerged slender stems of the nationally rare foxtail stonewort, while on land you may see thrift, autumn squill and the delightfully named suffocated clover (the name comes from the tightly packed, overlapping nature of its white stalks and flowers). You can only imagine how vast this seascape must have seemed to arrivals and locals in Roman times when the estuary was five times larger than today.

The harbour is extremely easy on the eye. Woods overlook it from both headlands and a line of beach huts adds a parti-coloured dimension to the view. Behind the harbour is a magical sliver of salt marsh that makes a joyous playground for herons and egrets, while turnstones and waders such as sandpipers feast in the sandbanks on the seaward side.

The eye is drawn, however, to the 25 or so **houseboats** that radiate out like spokes from the crescent-shaped shoreline. Some look to have been

of a playground for herons and egrets who find easy pickings among the fish trapped by the outgoing tide; meanwhile, turnstones and waders such as sandpipers and redshank feast in the sandbanks on the seaward side.

Once on the duver you can make your way across the dunes and grasses on to either the beach or, just to the south, the adjacent modest promenade and a line of multi-coloured beach huts converted from 1860s' railway carriages. The small bank of woodlands that heaves up from almost sea level at the northern end of the duver is known as St Helens Common and comprises mainly oak and ash. Below the woods, the skeletal frame of St Helens Church (page 117) stands stout against the sea. All that could possibly enhance this gorgeous picture further would be the chance appearance of a high-masted yacht, its sails fluttering in a light breeze, weaving its way between rocks on its way into the harbour.

Return the same way to Embankment Road. For variation here, look for the path that runs along the line of an old railway track behind the unsightly green fencing on the west side of the road. This skirts the easternmost boundary of Brading Marsh and weaves past some brackish lagoons, where you can see tufted and other ducks, back to The Pilot Boat Inn. There is one creature you are unlikely to spot as it is small and underwater but which may be pleasing to know is there: the starlet sea anemone, which was discovered in these lagoons in 1035. In a nice touch, it was given the Latin name *Nematostella vectensis*, the second part of which alludes to the Roman name for the Island.

built from a *Grand Designs* manual, with gleaming sharp angles, potted plants and polished decking while others wallow in the mud in a rather more dilapidated fashion. These are a relatively recent phenomenon, growing in number around World War II when their small contingent included a racing yacht named *The Wander Bird*, which famously sailed 'the wrong way' (from east to west, against the prevailing westerlies) around Cape Horn. The houseboats were seen as a cheap alternative to a 'real' house, since there was no mains electricity and the only fresh water was from the standpipe at Dustbin Corner (so called because of the row of pig bins that used to stand at the entrance to Marsh Farm, which backs on to the harbour road). Today, with the merit of being floodproof, and now fitted with mains gas and electricity, the houseboats are increasingly sought after, with high-end versions put on the market with asking prices north of £400,000. Some offer tourist accommodation (page 305).

Behind the boats and across the narrowest point of the harbour are the remnants of the old sea wall, long collapsed, its sea-smashed foundations spanning, in intermittent fashion, the middle waters of the harbour and visible at low tide. The new sea wall is visible too and bisects the harbour, running in parallel to its predecessor; it is walkable at all but the highest of high tides and is a handy way to walk from Bembridge to St Helens Duver.

¶¶ FOOD & DRINK

The Best Dressed Crab Fisherman's Wharf, Embankment Rd, PO35 5NS ✆ 01983 874758 ⬦ thebestdressedcrabintown.co.uk. This hugely popular café/diner specialises almost exclusively in fresh seafood caught nearby. It's hard to think of a more idyllic location: the café is moored off a pontoon that pokes out into the water from the middle of the harbourside road, with outside decking for good weather. Even in high winds or rain, it's a snug place to enjoy locally caught shellfish – crab, lobster – presented in huge portions. If you can't hang around, the shop does a fine take-away service.

Captain Stan's Bembridge Fish Store 5 High St, PO35 5SD ✆ 01983 875572 ⬛. By the time you have eaten your holiday breakfast, Mike Curtis will almost certainly be back in port, with the daily catch for his fishmonger outlet in the process of being unloaded. Mike trundles up and down the east coast on the *Shooting Star*, a 26ft vessel that was once used to pot for lobster and crab in Hebridean waters. Typically his catch includes brill, bream, Dover sole, wild bass, grey mullet, turbot and lobster, much of which ends up attractively presented on his shop's ice counter; a good deal of the remainder is snapped up by Island restaurants. Mike catches the fish he encounters within a limited operating range, not venturing too far, nor harvesting everything he comes across; a low-impact, sustainable way of fishing. If you're unsure just how to prepare the fish you buy here, just ask – Mike and his partner Ruth have some great recipes to hand out, including one for Jamaican seafood curry.

Crab & Lobster Inn 32 Forelands Field Rd, PO35 5TR ✐ 01983 872244 ⌂ characterinns. co.uk/crabandlobsterinn. The easternmost pub on the Island is tucked away behind a maze of quiet, strangely suburban-looking roads. If walking here after dark, bring a torch. Good range of tasty pub favourites as well as their signature dish, a seafood platter for two including crab, mussels, salmon, prawns and the catch of the day. Also has rooms (page 305).

The Farm Shop & No 8 Café 8 High St, PO35 5SD ✐ 01983 874236 (shop), ✐ 07851 488560 (café) ⬛. A lentil crisis was the impetus needed for owner Jane Holman to set up this friendly shop and cosy café. On the ground floor you can buy a range of food that is good for you, from locally grown hispi cabbage to squash and garlic. The upstairs vegetarian café is squeezed into the upstairs space where its all-round cosiness is reinforced by olde-worlde photographs (most are actually of farming scenes from Somerset, where Jane grew up). All the mains are creative – the aubergine, olive, spinach and bean cassoulet is delicious, as are the gluten-free brownies.

The Pilot Boat Inn Station Rd, PO35 5NN ✐ 01983 872077. Unmissable as it is located on a bend in the Bembridge Harbour road, this unusual pub has been built to resemble an eponymous pilot tug. The inside has plenty of decorative rigging and model boats. Dinner ranges from the usual burgers to a house crab ramekin (crustaceans sourced from just across the road). Also has rooms (page 305).

W W Woodford & Sons 26 High St, PO35 5SE ✐ 01983 872717 ⌂ woodfordandsons. co.uk. Woodford the butcher is something of an institution across the Island, but it's the smell that may hook you: chances are you will be met with the waft of baking sausage rolls, which always seem to be just coming out of the oven. The owner, Graham Hawkins, places emphasis on what he describes as 'traditional' butchery skills, whereby the meat is hung on the bone for three weeks in order that it matures and yields its fullest flavour. 'The meat is cut up here, everything is made on the premises,' says Graham, who lays great emphasis on quality and locality – all meat is sourced on the Island.

Ye Olde Village Inn 61 High St, Bembridge PO35 5SF ✐ 01983 872616 ⌂ yeoldevillageinn.co.uk. The most centrally located of the village's pubs, this is a friendly pub serving local beers and high-quality wines. A cynic might raise an eyebrow at the name but it's the real deal as the hostelry does date to 1787. Much of the food used in the kitchen here has to be among the least travelled on the island as it includes meat and vegetables from shops just across the road. As well as steaks, there are stone-baked pizzas and curries to choose from.

2 BRADING

Brading is a seaport without a sea. Settlements here date back at least 2,000 years and the commanding location, on the edge of what was until the 17th century a substantial River Eastern Yar, would have allowed for the control and taxation of goods in and out of this part of the Island. During the Middle Ages, the ecclesiastical parish of Brading covered more than 10% of the Island but, as the Eastern Yar began to silt up and the land was subsequently drained, the town's influence began a slow process of waning. Today, half-timbered buildings line the High Street and, along with the Old Town Hall and the Rectory Mansion, hint at this earlier elevated stature.

The first baptism on the Isle of Wight is said to have taken place in or around AD687 at the Norman **parish church of St Mary's** (High St, PO36 0ED). The church boasts an unusual bell tower open on three sides and built on four piers; this requires the bell ringers to climb the near-vertical external ladder that stands by the front entrance). In the early 19th century, the church was served by a particularly enterprising vicar, the Reverend Legh Richmond (see box, page 245), who is credited with the bright idea of using boards with movable numbers to indicate hymn numbers during church services.

The churchyard is a magnificent haven for wildlife, with more than 175 species of wildflower recorded here. The clay-based soil lends itself to meadowland, rough pasture and woodland, and you can expect to see primroses, stinking iris, meadow vetchling and cow parsley, the last of which had a utilitarian value as fodder for cows and as a yellow dye, while its stalks were ideal for children's bobbins. Some of the flowers are thought to have been introduced centuries ago for medicinal or cultural significance: the sea couch grass growing along the top of the wall bordering Quay Lane is almost certainly a legacy of the tidal water that once flowed into the lane. You'll also come across the grave of Little Jane Squibb, just to the eastern rear of the church – Jane died in 1799 aged 15, from TB, but not before she had earned the approval of Rev Richmond for her pious facility for learning headstone epitaphs by heart.

Next to the church stands the **Old Town Hall** (High St, PO36 0DJ ✆ 01983 531785 ◷ hours vary, call ahead), a mix of red-brick foundations topped with exposed beams and whitewashed rubble. On view on the ground floor is a number of medieval punishment items, including a lock-up, stocks and a whipping post. All may have been needed at one time or another as records for the town show that in Elizabethan times, 'town folk were required to keep in their houses a club or blunt staff 7 or 8 ft long for… the better protection of the Queen's peace.' The burghers of the town laid down the law here during the 17th century, though by the 1800s it had been converted into a school. With its iron grill and three diamond-shaped bars, the lock-up still looks formidably secure while the stocks have five holes, which has prompted a good deal of reflection over the years: it may suggest the local miscreants were numerous in medieval days or perhaps the inclination of the townsfolk to give miscreants a through punishment. The whipping post, last used in 1833, extends all the way up to the ceiling and its grisly connotations are enhanced by the holes through which chains would have been threaded to secure the benighted prisoner. The building is now a small museum that also houses, above the stocks, on the first floor, a collection of original stones, brass scales and weights used in medieval town commerce.

At the southern end of the High Street, by the new town hall, you'll see a life-size wooden carving of a bull, which is testimony to a darker part of the town's history, when bulls would be tied up during the 16th century and baited by dogs to the amusement of onlookers. Adjacent is the original iron ring to which the unfortunate bovines were tethered so that the gruesome spectacle could take place. The meat of the deceased bull was often distributed among the town's poor.

The town train station offers something of a bygone times experience and is home to the **Brading Railway Visitor Centre and Tea Rooms** (Station Rd, PO39 0DY ☉ May–Oct Tue–Sun), which features fully restored railway buildings that house a tea room, stationmaster's office and a modest railway museum, all adorned with green shutters and hanging baskets. Although no longer operational, the red-brick signal box has been lovingly refurbished to its original appearance. While Brading High Street has a good deal of interest, the pavements are narrow and wider vehicles can rush by closer than a walker might wish, so consider using footpath B6 instead, which runs parallel to the east and links the train station and Quay Lane, from where you can make a more genteel access to the town sights.

The **Lilliput Doll and Toy Museum** (High St, PO36 0DJ ✆ 01983 407231 🖫 lilliputmuseum.net) is a must-see for children and enquiring adult minds too, not least for its 3,000-year-old Egyptian doll. Believed to be genuine, this was a doll intended to accompany the deceased into the afterlife. The museum's origins date to the 1960s so are more recent but no less curious. (The frontage is actually the original early 19th-century façade of a faggot bakery.) The owner's sister decided she wanted a Russian doll and wrote to Nikita Khrushchev, the President of the Soviet Union. They heard nothing for three months, then a parcel arrived with a consignment of matryoshka dolls, the little, ever-smaller figures that fit one inside the other. The hunt for ever more exotic dolls had begun.

There's an opportunity at **Rectory Mansion** (46–48 High St, PO36 0DQ ✐ 01983 300828 ⊘ rectorymansion.co.uk), an antique, vintage and retro emporium across the road from the Doll Museum, to have a good rummage of a wildly eclectic jumble of items ranging from copper pots to wrought-iron old road signs. The timbered building, with its thatched top, whitewashed walls and exposed black wooden beams, dates to 1200 and, supported by its creaking 1,000-year-old oak logs, offers a glimpse of how Brading must have looked in the Middle Ages. The shop has taken over the former home of what used to be one of the Island's most iconic attractions, the Brading Waxworks Museum, which closed in 2010 – a surreally eclectic waxworks museum that was more *Hammer House of Horror* than Madame Tussauds. There's a small micro-museum within the shop that pays homage to its former incarnation, as well as a pint-sized courtyard tea garden where you can enjoy tea and cake overlooked by those thatched roofs and exposed beams.

¶¶ FOOD & DRINK

The Bugle Inn 56–57 High St, PO36 0DQ ✐ 01983 407359 ⊘ buglebrading.co.uk. The standard pub food, combined with the sports screen, feels like an opportunity slightly missed to create the perfect pub, given the pub's history (ships would dock right by where today's beer garden lies; in medieval times, smugglers used the upper rooms as lookout points). That said, the pub works hard to create a traditional atmosphere, with good local ales, wooden bookshelves and a roaring fire in winter. It's always popular too, so the landlords clearly know their market.

Delysia Farm Carpenters Farm PO36 0QA ⊙ Mon–Sat. The smallest smokery on the Island can be found tucked away by the entrance to this delightful farm shop. The size of a large garden shed, owner John Day somehow finds space to smoke haddock, pheasants and homemade applewood cheese. He also finds time to gather crabs and lobsters from inshore pots off Bembridge Ledge, which are put on sale the day they're collected. The smallholding at Delysia Farm extends to chickens, geese and ducks (the eggs they lay are on sale) and vegetables which, along with Scotch eggs, local sea salt and honey, and John's cheese, are all squeezed into the shop. It is located on the busy B3330 east of Brading, so take care if cycling or walking. By bus, take the #2 (from Newport/Sandown) or #3 (from Ryde) and ask to be dropped off by the adjacent Oasis furniture shop.

3 BRADING ROMAN VILLA

Morton Old Rd, PO36 0PH ✆ 01983 406223 ⌂ bradingromanvilla.org.uk

Brading Roman Villa offers an absorbing insight into one of the Roman Empire's more unheralded conquests: the Isle of Wight. Set back to the southwest of Brading, the eponymous villa is beautifully laid out, remarkably intact and sheltered within a wonderful independent museum.

What you explore are the remains of the West Range, a high-status house that was complete by the early 4th century and occupied continuously for nearly 300 years. It's the last and grandest of the buildings on the site. Two other ranges have been identified: one to the south, which was built around the time of the Roman invasion in AD43, and a more substantial north range dating to AD200. The unexposed foundations of both are marked in chalk outside the main building. In the 6th century, for reasons unknown – perhaps political unrest – it fell into disrepair and slipped out of local memory, forgotten for the best part of 1,300 years until it was discovered by a local farmer in 1880.

The museum walls are built around the outline of a substantial part of what was a winged corridor villa, with a private family wing and a separate space for entertaining guests. The eyecatchers are the substantial mosaics, along with pieces recovered from excavations, including a bronze door key lock. There's a Medusa mosaic, here positioned to ward off evil-doers, as well as a depiction of a who's who of Roman and Greek mythology – Achilles, Ceres and the constellations of Perseus and Andromeda. The centrepiece is a huge fractured Bacchus, the god of wine, and some other unusual mosaics – considered to be of exceptional quality – that include a domed house and a cockerel-headed creature, known as a Gallus. There's also a display of an important Roman-era coin hoard found at Brighstone (see box, page 161).

Brading is a unique site: hundreds of Roman villas boasted a Medusa knocking around or a wine-quaffing Bacchus, but the cockerel-headed mosaic is the only one of its kind ever found and has long teased the finest antiquarians who have tried to unpick its true meaning. What the

A walk up Brading Down

✺ OS Explorer map 29; start: Brading Roman Villa 𝐐 SZ601862; 2 miles; easy

The Romans of Brading almost certainly grew wine on the slopes of Brading Down, and this short walk takes in both the villa and Adgestone Vineyard. The down is a good place to spot a yellowhammer, a bird that resembles an escaped exotic parrot; you may see one flapping out of the gorse.

1 Where the entrance path to the villa meets the car park, look for the waymarked footpath that leads north on to Lower Adgestone Road. Turn left along this quiet lane and, ignoring the first turning on the left, keep ahead on what now becomes Sheep Lane. After 300yds you'll reach a T-junction with the vineyard ahead of you: turn right here.

2 Take the footpath immediately to the right of the vineyard, uphill. This track – with chalk and flint protruding through the shallow topsoil – winds its way through brambles and thickets on to the brow of Brading Down, on the south side of Brading Down Road. At the top, there's an information board and several convenient benches by the car park for a breather. Looking north, freight ships and ferries glide across the English Channel, while to the south the towns of Sandown and Shanklin merge into one seaside conurbation. The view is enclosed by the

Gallus does surely disclose is that this was the owner's way of showing that he was a well-to-do, educated man. Other than that, however, we know nothing about the owner, though the discovery of evidence of ploughs, quern-stones and wagons indicates that barley and wheat were grown and processed here, pointing to him earning his wealth as a merchant or a farmer, rather than a soldier, as no evidence has been found of an army presence. It's possible the Romans by then had been long accepted by local people, which also implies that benign trade had gone on well before the invasion.

The villa was perched close to Brading Haven, at that time a deepwater port that dispatched goods to the Continent or southeast England. There was a rationale for this, for the Romans also had an interesting geographical perspective. To the Roman eye, the Isle of Wight made little sense if looked at in the conventional north–south way that we do today (with Cowes at the top, Ventnor at the bottom). For them, it was far more practical to view the Island as if looking along its plane, from west to east; in this view along the spine of the Island, the 'top' – Brading, swooping flanks of Bembridge Down to the north, and away to the south by Luccombe Down and St Boniface Down. Casting your eye further west, the ridgeline gently rises and dips across Stenbury Down and Gat Cliff. It's an ancient view: the folds of the downs were created 300 million years ago when the African and Eurasian tectonic plates bumped into one another (during the same collision, the European Alps were also created).

3 Drop down south from the top of the brow to the gate from the car park and bear left (east), following tracks that head downhill to reach Upper Road.

4 Turn right along the road and, after 300yds, take the first footpath on the left, heading southeast below an old quarry. After 800yds, take the turning on the right along Lower Adgestone Road to return to the villa.

Sandown – points directly along the Channel to France and seamlessly on to the northern European coastline and the mouth of the Seine, Boulogne and estuaries of Germanic lands. From there, a right-hand turn down any major river would sweep the traveller towards Rome. It's reckoned the return journey could have been done within two months.

Brading Roman Villa is extremely good for children, with opportunities to dress up and role play and for them to engage in their own self-assembly mosaics. The Forum Café is also excellent, offering big bowls of soup and excellent cake, with panoramic views across Sandown Bay. There's also a gift shop featuring both Roman-themed items and Island-wide crafts.

4 ADGESTONE VINEYARD

Upper Rd, Brading PO36 0ES 𝒥 01983 402882 𝄐 adgestonevineyard.co.uk ☉ 10.00–16.00 Tue–Sat, 11.00–16.00 Sun

Settled into the chalky south-facing slopes of Brading Down, Adgestone Vineyard is just a few hundred yards east of the Roman villa. It is highly likely that owner Russ Broughton is following in the footsteps of Romans, who were thought to produce wine on the Isle of Wight 2,000 years ago. The grapes grown on the Island produce a wide range of wines, including a full-bodied red with hints of caramel, a vanilla-tinted oaked white, a rosé mixing pinot noir and shönburger, and a fruit wine combining blueberries with lavender. Each year, the vineyard grows around 20 tons of grapes that produce 27,000 bottles of wine. 'Patience is king', says Russ. 'You must never pick the grapes when they look perfect, you need to wait until they look like the kind of grapes you wouldn't want in your fruit bowl.'

You can take a tour of the estate with an audioguide before finishing off with an inspection of the cellars and, the reason anyone really comes to a vineyard, the opportunity for tasting. The experience is much the same as you would find in Italy or France, as is the process of making the wine. As Russ points out, the Island is largely frost-free. 'Many English counties don't have the sunshine we do on the Island and that really helps bring down the acidity.'

A former engineering manager at Southampton Docks, Russ turned to winemaking in 2013 to counter a nagging concern that he was becoming too comfortable and no longer utilising his skills. 'Like a lot of trained people, I had got promoted to a point where I no longer used my training [as an engineer]. I came over to the Island to visit my sister and over a glass of wine I opened up the *County Press* [the local newspaper] and saw an advert for the vineyard up for sale.'

Knowing nothing about making wine, Russ embarked on a steep learning curve. 'I got the bug and gave it a go. Essentially you have to be prepared to make big decisions, occasionally make big mistakes – and then not repeat the big mistakes. All that's then left to do,' he adds airily, 'is work seven days a week for the rest of your life.'

The latest challenge was presented by Covid-19, which threatened to ruin the promising harvest of 2020. With staff furloughed the fruit was, literally, about to wither on the vine. Russ posted a plea for help on social media, offering a couple of bottles of wine in lieu of payment. Several thousand people replied and the rescued grapes worked their way through the system to appear in bottles in late 2021.

English wine still encounters snobbery, not least from the English, let alone the French, but Russ simply shrugs his shoulders and points to the long line of framed international awards on the wall of the shop. He has been at the forefront of the long-standing, long-ridiculed campaign to get English wine accepted and is keen to point out that Adgestone wine was served to the Queen to mark the 50th anniversary of the D-Day landings.

The company doesn't just produce wines – if you're brave enough you might want to take away a jar of their 'Arson-Fire' marmalade, jam or chocolate liqueur made with the Dorset Naga, one of the hottest chilli peppers in the world. The on-site shop morphs into the **Cabin Café**, which offers platters of everything from stuffed vine leaves to cream teas, which you can wash down with English wine. In summer live bands strum away in the background.

The vineyard is a 20-minute walk from Brading High Street – follow Lower Adgestone Road, which runs immediately to the north of the Roman villa; the vineyard is on the right as the road turns into Sheep Lane.

CULVER DOWN, YAVERLAND & AROUND

Stare for long enough at a map of the Isle of Wight – with a ridge through the middle and gently tapering east–west points – and it can come to resemble a large slice of vertebra from a fossilised backbone. A coincidence maybe, but the Island's primordial soup was perfect for fossilisation of animals such as dinosaurs, which inhabited the Island for around ten to 15 million years. Dinosaur fossils can be found around much of the coast, but one of the Island epicentres of discovery are the cliffs below Culver Down and Yaverland, where you will find what are termed Early Cretaceous and Wealden group rocks. You can learn – and see – a great deal more about the ancient reptile inhabitants of the Island at Dinosaur Isle, while the footpaths on Culver Down will pull you uphill from sea level to vistas that truly embrace the sheer scale of Sandown Bay.

5 CULVER DOWN

This chalk down towers above Yaverland Beach and bulges out like a furrowed brow into Horseshoe Bay (the latter lies just to the north of the headland and is not to be confused with a bay of the same name at Bonchurch). A three-quarter-mile walk from Yaverland takes you along coastal footpaths above Red Cliff to the 240ft brow of the down in around around 30 minutes. The ascent is steady rather than calf-tweaking, initially passing along 100ft-high sea cliffs where peregrines roost while around your feet are great bush crickets, harebells and cowslips. The route traverses 60 million years of geology, through a geological formation known as the Wealden group, where alternating sands and clays hark from the Early Cretaceous period (around 145 million–100 million years ago). The change, from Yaverland's grey-brown and orange sandstones to paler greensand and white chalk, is clear; here you are striding along a geological phenomenon known as the Cretaceous Succession, whereby grey-brown cliffs of around 125 million years in age give way to gault clay and, at the far end, the white of chalk dating back a mere 65 million years. The rock strata of Culver Cliff – brilliant white chalk, so shiny it seems to have just been painted – is a mirror image of its westernmost counterpart on the Island, the Needles.

Lumped on top of the down is the **Yarborough Monument**, a huge granite obelisk visible from afar. It's dedicated to the Earl of Yarborough, who inherited Appuldurcombe (page 207) through marriage in the 1830s and was the first commodore of the Royal Yacht Squadron at Cowes (notoriously, he was also elected an MP from the rotten borough of Newtown; page 65). Yarborough's son, incidentally, gave his name to a term familiar to Bridge players – the 'yarborough' is a weak hand at the card game, typically a hand with no card higher than a 'nine'. Frankly, the monument is rather dull and feels intrusive; it was originally erected a few hundred yards down the access road, where the ridge becomes Bembridge Down. When Bembridge Fort was earmarked for the same site in 1860, the monument was dismantled brick by brick and, rather than seizing the opportunity to tip it into the sea, dutifully relocated to its current location.

Despite its dreary appearance, the plinth base makes a good seat for a picnic, from where you can watch the steady conveyor belt of ferries and cargo ships plying back and forth at sea. The downland around and below the brow of Culver Down is good for birdlife, with rock pipits quivering on swaying sprigs of gorse and skylarks erupting vertically from the grass.

---

1 Culver Down, as seen from Luccombe. **2** Yaverland Beach. ▶

In 2019 Culver Down was the location for the release of six white-tailed eagles. The bird – Britain's largest bird of prey – was once spread along the south coast of England but, thanks to persecution, died out around 1780. The last known pair were actually recorded at Culver Cliff, making it the obvious and appropriate choice for the reintroduction. The new releases were juvenile birds, transferred from Scotland by conservationists, led by the Roy Dennis Wildlife Foundation (⊘ roydennis.org). A further six were released in 2020 and in total 30 will be introduced by 2025. It's hoped this leviathan of a bird will thrive along the coastline of the Island and the wider Solent, surveying their new kingdom from high cliffs and feasting on grey mullet, and overwintering wildfowl and waders among the Island marshes.

While Culver Down was identified as a suitable habitat, there was no expectation that all birds would settle in the area, not least because the territory of a single white-tailed eagle can extend to 27 square miles. And so it proved: they quickly spread their wings and were spotted, variously, over East Anglia (where farmers had vigorously opposed the bird's reintroduction), Hampshire and the New Forest, and even London (one bird settled in a field near the M40 in Oxfordshire, unnoticed for several weeks by hundreds of thousands of motorists). Oddly enough, the location for the birds' release, Culver, means 'pigeon' or 'dove', in Old English.

ISLAND FLIGHT

From Culver Down, you can pick out **Bembridge Airfield** far below and about a mile to the north. The airfield opened in 1920 and served locations as far away as Bristol, though after World War II it morphed into an enthusiasts' flying club. The airfield has its place in aviation lore thanks to the 1952 service ran by Silver City Airways, which operated a car-air service, carrying three cars and their passengers to Southampton.

A vacant hangar at the airfield was taken over in 1959 by a company that went on to design one of the world's most iconic small aircraft, the Britten Norman Islander. After experimenting with hovercraft designs, Britten Norman focused on the skies to design the Islander, hundreds of which continue to ply the world's skies, from Orkney (where it operates the world's shortest flight, a distance of just three miles between Westray and Papa Westray) to Canada and New Zealand. A concrete runway was only added to the airfield in 2010 and today the airfield serves as a base for enthusiasts and visiting private pilots of light aircraft.

At its eastern limits, Culver Down falls away into **Horseshoe Bay**. Note that it is dangerous to attempt to access Horseshoe Bay on foot from the Sandown side of Culver Down as the tide rarely retreats far enough, and even when it does you have precious little time to explore. Instead, you can reach it by following the tide out from the north side of the down, along Whitecliff Bay, but be sure to check tide times and don't be tempted to linger. You'll find two sea caves here to gaze into (again, don't hang around), chalk hollows strikingly incised by the sea and beautifully named The Nostrils.

Bembridge Fort
⊙ tours only, check website; National Trust

Around half a mile west of the Yarborough Monument, along an access road, lies another of the Palmerston Follies from the Victorian age (see box, page 16), built in this case because it offered unimpeded visibility of invasion from the south across Sandown Bay and the eastern approaches to the Solent. During World War I both cavalry and heavy artillery units occupied the site, and in World War II an anti-aircraft squadron and the local Home Guard were based here. After 73 years of never firing a shot in anger, Bembridge Fort finally saw action in 1940 when the fort's radar station was attacked by low-level ME109 fighters; gunners positioned on the turrets and magazine returned fire.

The fort, configured in hexagonal fashion and accessed across a dry moat and earthen ramparts, survives in substantial form but is unrestored, although National Trust volunteers are slowly clearing up the site and making the gun emplacements more accessible. Despite this, it can feel rather desultory, an impression not helped by the fact a part of the site has been leased by the Trust to a manufacturing company.

6 YAVERLAND

One of the best and most accessible places to explore the Island's dinosaur history is the base of the cliffs at Yaverland Beach, at the north end of Sandown Bay. This is a superb beach, with brown sands that slope gently to the sea. Centuries of fallen rock have accumulated at the bottom of the cliffs that back the beach and over time these have been smoothed, pulverised or upended by the sea, which encroaches ever higher up the beach as time passes. Above all, however, Yaverland is really all about dinosaurs and fossils. Walk 100yds north of Yaverland car park and you will soon leave the crowds behind and be able to explore the extraordinary geology of the cliffs by yourself. Between 110 million and 125 million years ago, when dinosaurs roamed the Island, things would have looked rather different: hot, sultry and tropical and rather like the Florida Everglades. Had humans been around at that time, conditions for a guaranteed holiday in the sun would rarely have been bettered. There would have been the occasional drawback: one of the Island's three native dinosaurs, the Yaverlandia, a small, waist-high yapping thing, would have kept stealing up behind you and grabbing your ice cream; the other two native species, the altogether more substantial and determinedly carnivorous Neovenator and the Eotryrannosaurus – a relative of Tyrannosaurus rex – would have grabbed you as well as your ice cream. In all, more than 35 different types of dinosaur have been identified on the Island.

Some fossil hunters are more passionate than others; when the winter gales kick in and wash away the clay face of the cliffs across the road from the museum, experts have been known to fly in on private light aircraft to inspect the newly exposed fossils. Yet the truly magical thing is that anyone can strike lucky and uncover a genuine find here. In 2012 a Danish girl on holiday came across only the second-known fossil scrap – part of the skull that sits behind the eyes – of a Yaverlandia, which lived some 125 million years ago. Among the fossils you may find are the bones and teeth of crocodiles, dinosaurs, turtles and fish, ammonites and bivalves. Once, while walking along the beach north of Dinosaur Isle, I picked up what a guide at the museum concluded to be a 100–125 million-year-old oyster shell. Just like the fool's gold (iron pyrite) that can be found here in abundance, it was a decidedly modest find.

Proof that the age of discovery is far from over came in 2019 when a new species of dinosaur was discovered a little further south, on the foreshore at Shanklin. Over the course of a few weeks, four vertebrae from the neck, back and tail were found by both individuals and a family and handed into Dinosaur Isle. Palaeontologists soon confirmed it was a new species of theropod, the same group that includes Tyrannosaurus rex and modern-day birds. The animal has been named *Vectaerovenator inopinatus,* which refers to the large air spaces found in the bones that made their skeleton lighter. As if that were not enough, in 2020 the remains of the first pterosaur (a flying reptile) to be discovered in the UK was found on the Island. Since named *Wightia declivirostris*, it turned out to be a later form of pterosaur, the more familiar pterodactyl. The bits and pieces were found by an amateur fossil hunter on the sands of Sandown Bay. 'It was just a crummy bit of bone – the tip of the beak,' says Megan Jacobs of Wight Coast Fossils. 'But they've only been found in Brazil and Morocco before – it makes you realise these birds were flying around the world.'

Just a couple of hundred yards south of Yaverland Beach, set back behind the sea wall, lies the **Wildheart Animal Sanctuary** (Yaverland Rd, PO36 8QB ✆ 01983 403883 ⊘ wildheartanimalsanctuary.org), which really should be on the visiting list of any wildlife lover. You may at first glance, from its forlorn and rather forbidding exterior of peeling paint, be inclined to give it a miss. It's no design of beauty, being incorporated into the ruins of another of those ubiquitous Victorian forts (in this case, Granite Fort) that once guarded the coast; but don't be misled. Until recently the building was home to the original Island zoo, but a rebranding exercise now more accurately reflects the ethos of what goes on behind the walls. The sanctuary is still home to big cats but the approach to their care and the rationale for keeping them captive is in tune with more enlightened times (see box, page 281).

Following many years under private ownership, the zoo became the Wildheart Trust in 2017, a charity founded to secure the long-term future of the zoo. The trust was set up by Charlotte Corney – her partner, the *Springwatch* presenter Chris Packham, is a trustee and her dad had founded the original zoo. The vision is to improve the well-being of animals in human care. 'Our animals can't go into the wild – they've never been there and their habitats are depleted. Many of them are physically or mentally debilitated in some way,' she says.

With this aim in mind, the zoo places an emphasis on excellent animal welfare in what keepers describe as 'a safe, forever home', as well as funding the protection of tiger habitats in India. The zoo is home to seven tigers, one from another zoo and six ex-circus performing animals. The individuals are not being used for captive breeding programmes because they come from problem backgrounds and impure bloodlines, which risks deformities in any cubs and offers no conservation value. The trust funds conservation projects of varying exoticism, from lemurs in Madagascar to the reddish buff moth, which is only found in the UK on the Isle of Wight.

Towards the southern end of Yaverland Beach, just behind Brown's Golf Course, a recently opened path meanders through **Willow Wood**, which links two reed beds. As well as grey willow, the woods comprise alder, some oak and some large white poplars. As you walk to the woods from the shore you are also walking across the 'lost duver' of Sandown. Over the centuries the duver, a spit of sand and shingle, has been churned and overwhelmed by everything from fierce storms to flooding by the Eastern Yar. One reason conservationists know for sure that there is a duver beneath the grass you walk across today is thanks to the artist Richard Livesay, the drawing master at Portsmouth Naval College in the early 19th century. Livesay had a reputation for realistic and factual painting and depicted the bay in 1800, complete with a duver.

Recent moves to restore the sandy landscape have been led by Arc Consulting (⌀ arc-consulting.co.uk) and involve planting flora that is well adapted to the harsh conditions on sand and by the sea: thrift, sea campion, viper's-bugloss, white stonecrop, bird's-foot trefoil, mouse-ear hawkweed, and lady's bedstraw.

7 DINOSAUR ISLE

Culver Parade, PO38 8QA ⌀ 01983 404344 ⌀ dinosaurisle.com ⊙ varies; check website

Dinosaur Isle must be one of the UK's most underrated visitor attractions. Viewed from a distance the building is a striking shape featuring two protruding poles and an arched canopy intended to resemble a pterodactyl (though you may be unable to resist a possibly ungracious comparison to a pair of narwhal tusks or knitting needles). It's something of a bizarre gem where you find both an important fossil collection and a main hall containing genuine skeletons and bones, alongside supersized dinosaur mannequins. Fossils from 35 types of dinosaur have been found on the Isle of Wight, and in total the museum's catalogue extends to more than 40,000 fossils gathered from right across the Island, with around 1,000 on display at any time.

The walk-through collection of Island finds is a highly informative eye-opener into the sheer range of animals that once roamed what is now called the Isle of Wight, including many of a more recent vintage, dating back a mere 10,000 to 15,000 years. Objects on display include the tusks of a mammoth and a hippopotamus; fossil teeth and femur of a straight-tusked elephant; the lower jaw of Bothriodon, a pig-like hippopotamus; and the jaw of another pig-like amphibious mammal, *Elomeryx porcinus*.

In the main hall, giant vertebra and casts of *Jurassic Park*-style footprints share cabinet space with tiny fossils of large-winged termites

WHEN TIGERS ROAMED THE BAY

Dinosaurs are not the only oversized and dangerous animals to have bestrode Sandown Bay. Some are of a more recent vintage. Had you strolled along the promenade in the late 1970s and early 1980s you might have seen a father and daughter exercising their four-legged pets. The felines were stripey but rather larger than your average short-haired moggy: for it was tiger cubs that were paddling in the sea at the end of a long rope leash. The human owners were Jack Corney, who took over Sandown Zoo in 1976, and his daughter Charlotte.

The beach exercises, with the tiger cubs thrashing around in the spray, were just what the public saw. At home, Charlotte grew up with several tiger and leopard cubs. She has fond memories of a tiger cub called Tamyra who lived at home. On occasion, Charlotte's mother would pick her up from school in a Citroen 2CV with a leopard called Flossy in the back seat. A black leopard cub called Bindu would be waiting at the top of the stairs to playfully nibble her ankles. 'I never had a bad bite, the worst I've ever had was from a German Shepherd,' she recalls. Two black bear cubs moved in at one point. 'They were highly intelligent. They'd open the dishwasher and "redecorate" the kitchen,' says Charlotte.

Charlotte looks back at that time with ambivalent feelings. 'At the start, it wasn't about rescuing animals, it was a question of getting sexy animals into the zoo; that way people would come in and generate income. But that was changing even then – there was awareness that tigers were becoming endangered and the message went out to zoos to do their bit and get them breeding like the clappers.' Tamyra certainly contributed, giving birth to 30 cubs. 'It was a privilege to handle and grow up with big cats but it was bittersweet because I know those animals should be autonomous and free. Ultimately, I had no right to look after them.'

This, she says is what motivated her to become founder of the Wildheart Trust and steer the former zoo in a new direction. 'We are a small charity and we understand that change does take time. We try and turn things on their head – at a traditional zoo people have a fun day out and want to see animals. Our point is that the animals shouldn't really be here. We show visitors what needs to be done so that in the future there is no need for big cats to be looked after like this. We try and educate them and motivate them, to feel a connection and go away and do something, whether that's supporting a project, signing a petition or putting up a bird box. We want this generation of children to be the last to see such animals in captivity.'

and water spiders that resemble the smeared imprint of flies on your car windscreen. Eye-catching exhibits include the skeletal display of a Neovenator dinosaur – its femurs each weigh three stone – along with the femur and humerus (each more than 3ft in length) and gastroliths (stomach stones) of a 45ft sauropod (these long-necked creatures were the largest dinosaurs ever to have lived).

Several knowledgeable palaeontologists – some amateur, some professional – are on hand to shed light on the displays and there is a working laboratory on view, which works on the same principles as an open kitchen in a restaurant. Staff like to point out that Yorkshire, the rival to the Jurassic Coast, has promoted its 'Dinosaur Coast' but you could count the number of bones the county has on the fingers of one hand. The captions display a refreshing candour that is absent from more pompous and self-important establishments; these regularly include statements about their more mysterious remains that have yet to be fully identified, in effect shrugging a shoulder and admitting 'we don't know' or 'we're not sure'. The museum runs year-round guided fossil walks on Yaverland Beach and further afield (book in advance; check website for details). As is the case at the museum, the guides are affable, neither precious nor guarded with their considerable knowledge, and keen to inspire future generations of palaeontologists.

SANDOWN, SHANKLIN & LUCCOMBE

Stretching for the best part of five miles along the edge of Sandown Bay, the twin towns of Sandown and Shanklin represent the epicentre of the Island's traditional seaside appeal – beach huts, risqué postcards and ice cream. You'll come here for the golden beaches and the Esplanade that runs from Culver Parade and Yaverland Beach in the north to Shanklin Chine in the south (though it occasionally has to dog-leg around some of the stubborn Island geology). Though the towns are always busy they are actually quite small, and their collective built-up area never extends more than a mile inland. It's easy – as the uniformed dignitaries who took the air here in the early 20th century most certainly did – to fall into the trap of sniffily averting one's gaze from the hustle and bustle of the towns, but the postcards, seaside tat and amusement arcades are here to stay, indisputably ingrained in the Island DNA. The southern tail of Sandown Bay curves away into a hodgepodge of underwater ledges, rock pools and towering cliffs below the tiny village of Luccombe, itself all but hidden with strips of coastal woodland.

Sandown Bay is also key to the dynamic, slowly changing shape of the island, for it receives sediment from longshore drift that arrives from both the south and the back of the Island (much of it from the spectacularly collapsed cliffs found along the Undercliff and Bonchurch Landslip). These soft cliff sediments work their way around the coast in an anti-clockwise direction and collect in the bay.

The bay is not always benign, and an autumn or winter storm here is right up there with anything on offer in the wilds of northern Scotland (having written Bradt guides to Orkney and the Outer Hebrides, your author speaks from battered experience). At such times the waves and swells can overtop the sea defences and bite sizeable chunks out of the cliffs at Yaverland. The bigger storms can also strip the cliff base down 4ft to bedrock (which is when the fossil hunters and dinosaur footprint enthusiasts head out to the beaches), only to bring it all back in again on the next tide. Rising sea levels and constant coastal erosion from Channel storms and winter rains cut away at the Island, to the extent of a loss of land of about 3ft a year. The inference is sobering: in several thousand years' time, depending on how the interacting dynamics of currents and longshore drift unfold, the Island will either be barely recognisable from its current shape, or there may no longer be an Isle of Wight at all. Get here while you can.

The groynes play their part in stabilising the bay and there is a strategy for maintenance at some of the more vulnerable spots, such as the north

SANDOWN BAY: THE WRITER'S RETREAT

Writers find seascapes and beach walks useful for stirring the creative juices and Sandown is no exception. In the 1870s, Lewis Carroll penned *The Hunting of the Snark*, his magnificent nonsense poem, while staying in the town. Meanwhile, users of shorthand (a dark art to just about everyone born in the 21st century) will be gratified to learn that Sir Isaac Pitman devised his impenetrable squiggles in the town in the 1860s. Around the same time, Charles Darwin began writing *On the Origin of Species* at Sandown's Ocean View Hotel in 1858 and it's sometimes speculated that the fossils and varying geology along nearby Yaverland Beach reinforced the conclusions he'd drawn from his sojourn around the Galápagos Islands.

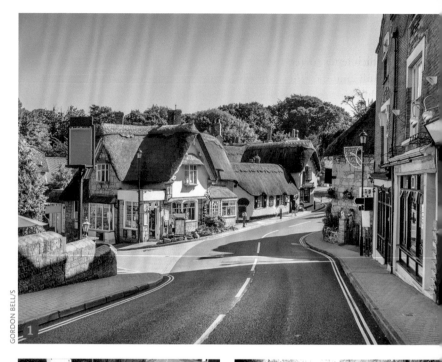

TO THE HORSES AND DOGS WHO ALSO
BORE THE BURDEN AND HEAT OF THE DAY
1914 — 1920.

GORDON BELL/S

MARK ROWE

MARK ROWE

CHRISTINE DODD/S

end which tends to get the major battering when the wind blows from the south and east. The good news is that this is a fairly stable system and, while change is incremental and negligible on the scale of a human lifetime, Sandown will be a reliable summer beach for many, many years to come. You can find out more about the guided environmental activities along the beach run by the Bay Coastal Community Team on their Facebook page (f shapingthebay).

Periodically, the weather has been too much for ships to handle as well. In 1878 HMS *Eurydice* sank here in a heavy snowstorm with the loss of 317 lives, one of the British Navy's worst peacetime disasters. Just two crew survived. The *Eurydice* is now one of the Isle of Wight's most infamous ghost ships, lore dictating that she haunts Dunnose Cape, a point south of Luccombe Bay. In 1998, Prince Edward, evidently one of the more credulous royals, claimed to have sighted the three masts of the ship while filming a TV series.

8 SANDOWN

Sandown is the classic seaside resort, with a promenade and reinforced sea wall to stroll along. Inland, there is little in all honesty to truly delay you in Sandown's retail heart, though you could have a look at the façade of Sandown's former **Town Hall**, a Neoclassical affair found on Grafton Street. This fine building was built in 1869 and subsequently hosted amateur and professional theatre and music shows; it sports a pediment inscribed with the design of the Prince of Wales feathers and six fluted columns that front two storeys and three bays. Sadly, at the time of writing, the hall was closed to the public, in poor condition and subject to plans for renovation and conversion that are bitterly opposed by local residents.

Long before they began to be invaded by Victorian tourists, the area's vast beaches gave cause for concern for invasions of a more military nature. The Palmerston Forts (see box, page 16) that are visible out at sea today and at the northern edge of the town date to the 1860s, built as an attempt to fortify the town against (usually) French incursions. The first known attempt at a fortification resulted in the now lost Sandown Castle, which quickly succumbed to the sea and was finally demolished barely 80 years after it had been built in 1543. The ill-

◄ **1** Shanklin. **2** War memorial, Lake. **3** Shanklin Chine. **4** Manmade vertipools, Sandown.

fated castle was superseded by Sandham Fort in 1631, which was built inland (rather than out to sea) and one of the first to be constructed with arrowhead bastions, though it too became obsolete and was demolished in the 1850s.

Royalty first came to dip their toes in the bay around the same time and in 1899 Sandown's credentials as a retreat for the well-to-do were established by the opening of the landmark Ocean View Hotel by the West End theatre impresario, Henry Lowenfield. The mass market wasn't far behind, however, and the bucket-and-spade industry took off in the wake of World War I amid the creation of boating lakes and miniature golf courses. Sandown reached the height of its popularity in the 1970s and, despite the advent of the cheap foreign holidays, still attracts plenty of holidaymakers.

In 2019 **Sandown Beach** was crowned 'Beach of the Year' by *Countryfile Magazine*. 'How many other five-mile beaches are there in Britain?' says Ian Boyd of Arc Consulting, a local organisation that leads environmental projects across the Island and seeks to encourage local people to become involved in them. 'We've got one of them here. Look along the beach and you are looking at 100 million years of geology.' Officially, just the one beach runs between the two headlands but the groynes that protrude into the water divide the sands into 52 distinct beaches, with two wilder stretches to be found at either end.

"Sandown reached the height of its popularity in the 1970s and still attracts plenty of holidaymakers."

You can't miss **Sandown Pier** as it is slap-bang in the middle of town, but it lacks the charm of its counterparts at Ryde or Yarmouth (although its prime years of entertainment saw luminaries such as Cilla Black, Frankie Howerd and Tommy Cooper take the stage). Underneath the pier's paraphernalia, however, it's a different story, for the pier extends almost 300yds into the sea and, as with its Island siblings, at low tide you'll find rock pools brimming with fauna to investigate.

Just west of central Sandown is **Sandown Community Orchard** (Golf Links Rd, PO36 9PR), a little gem that features fruit trees and a sizeable slice of wetland where you have a good chance of seeing kingfishers, dragonflies and damselflies. The site is a 15-minute walk from Sandown station – just follow the Red Squirrel Trail out of town; the orchard is right by it. Originally, the orchard formed part of a wider

VERTIPOOLS: SWIMMING AGAINST THE TIDE

As you walk along Sandown Beach you will see, here and there, what could pass for oversized washbasins attached to the concrete. These are in fact vertipools, an ingenious, manmade, wildlife-friendly response to climate change and the accompanying rising sea levels. The highest number are found on what, accordingly, is dubbed 'the Science Beach' (more or less opposite Browns Golf Course, by a part of the seafront known as Culver Parade).

Climate change is affecting the Isle of Wight and shoreline marine creatures are bearing the brunt of things. 'The sea level may only rise very slowly, by a millimetre or two,' says Ian Boyd of Arc Consulting, which developed the vertipools. 'But as it does, the tidal range gets smaller [and] low tide becomes higher up the beach.' This has profound implications for rock pools, whose communities of marine creatures require the twice-daily ebb and flow of the tides for their existence. 'If the rock pools are permanently flooded by higher tides,' says Ian, 'they have nowhere to go.'

Vertipools can offer these creatures a new home. Built to an industrial scale, they can hold over two gallons of water and are designed to resemble the distinctive long rock pools that nature has carved out of the soft chalk rocks on the shore. Vertipools have deeply textured surfaces and are full of sand; within them you are quite likely to see three species of crab, various prawns, shrimps and amphipods; barnacles, periwinkle, limpet and top shell, sponges, half a dozen species of sea squirt, sea spider and 15 or so species of seaweed, as well as a rock pool fish, the shanny.

parcel of cottage gardens for those employed at the nearby waterworks, which were built in 1861. Their construction (the waterworks, not the orchard) was driven by a keen desire to defeat the Victorian plague of cholera. Today, you are welcome to help yourself to the apples, cherries and plums that grow here, including the Alverstone variety of apple and Adgestone blue plum. There are paths through the site and the ponds are perfect for children to go dipping for sticklebacks and water scorpions.

¶¶ FOOD & DRINK

Boojum & Snark 105 High St, PO36 8AF ⊘ boojumandsnark.co.uk. Independent micro-brewery that doubles as an art gallery and offers plates of local cheeses and tapas for grazing. Brewer Julie Jones-Evans modestly describes her craft beer range as '80% cleaning, 20% chemistry', but there is much more than that in her India Pale Ale and stout flavoured with pulped cherries and apricots from Godshill Orchards. 'People can drink the beer just a few feet from where it is brewed,' she says.

SOMETHING BREWING IN YAVERLAND

A craft beer tap room is not something many outside observers would think to find in Sandown, a town as closely tied to the bucket-and-spade stereotype as any in the UK. But the rationale, says Julie Jones-Evans, who runs Boojum & Snark (page 287) with Tracy Mikich, is to boost regeneration in the town and bust a few stereotypes. 'We've both travelled in the United States and saw how craft beer outlets can really help regenerate an area and bring people in who might not otherwise come and spend money,' says Julie, who has retrained as a brewer and oversees the vats and pipes and the concoctions emerging from them, right behind the bar.

Having grown up on the Island and spent her teenage years clubbing in Sandown, Julie is frustrated by the preconceptions visitors often bring to the town. 'People say the town has been in decline but it's not what I see,' she says. 'Ventnor has a new vibe, it has reinvented itself, but Sandown has always been like this – with very diverse cultures all in the same place – and it's now undergoing a renaissance.'

Named after characters from the nonsense poem that Lewis Carroll wrote just across the street, the venue also operates as an art gallery and a natural history display. 'We've tried to take the idea full circle, and take Sandown back to its Victorian heyday,' says Julie.

Lake

Shoehorned between Shanklin and Sandown is Lake, once a small distinct village of its own, and today, although it has its own train station, a suburb of both its neighbours and indistinguishable from either. That said, Lake Beach – also known as Dunroamin Beach – is worth pausing at and enjoyable for both its sea-gazing opportunities and studying the steep cliffs rising to the rear. The beach can be accessed from either the Shanklin or Sandown ends of the Esplanade along the sea wall. Alternatively, there is a set of steps from the top of the cliff path, accessed along footpath SS60 from Currie Road; Lake station is a short distance away, along footpath SS62. Perhaps it's that modest flight of steps, but for whatever reason, Lake Beach is often very peaceful, with the few sunbathers often overlooked only by quivering, hovering kestrels above the clifftops. Lake also has a discrete but unusual war memorial in the form of a concrete horse trough, which is dedicated to the horses and dogs who served in the world wars. You'll find it on the pavement where Lake Hill meets the Fairway by the railway bridge, about ten minutes' walk from the cliff steps. The war memorial here is unusual too for it is dedicated to those who died between 1914 and 1920, an acknowledgement to the local men who were fighting in Russia until that time.

9 SHANKLIN

🏠 **Foxhills of Shanklin** (page 305), **Keats Cottage** (page 305), **Luccombe Hall Hotel** (page 305), **The Milaran** (page 305), **No 29** (page 305) ⛺ **Ninham Camping** (page 305), **Old Barn Touring Park** (page 305)

The Island's 'slow' ethos can be reasonably said to be paused in much of Shanklin, which in many respects feels joined both physically and spiritually with Sandown. That said, it wrestles back control in Old Shanklin, which contains some of the most distinctive dwellings on the Island. The old town is located to the south of the main town bustle, on a slightly lower level to modern Shanklin, where the hills, narrow streets and paths that tumble to the sea characterise much of this more rewarding part of town. Old Shanklin clings on to its past to the extent that a charabanc full of tourists would not look entirely out of place today. Thatched cottages abound; even the ice-cream stall on Chine Avenue sports a nifty straw bouffon. You also have to admire the determination of the Victorians, who, as at Sandown and Lake, sought to impose their solidity and certainty on some highly dynamic and unco-operative geology here: plonking grand Victorian villas and hotels on the tops of unstable cliffs requires an almost mulish obstinacy.

As with neighbouring Sandown, celebrity and academia have long been drawn to Shanklin. The Romantic poet John Keats spent two productive spells here. In 1817 he worked on his early poems, including *Lamia* and *Endymion*, although the opening line of *Endymion*, 'A thing of beauty is a joy for ever', was probably inspired more by the landscapes and seascapes visible across the bay than the embryonic tourism industry (the line is also found inscribed above the entrance to St Mary's Hospital in Newport). Keats's *Ode to Autumn*, while inspired by the scenery around Winchester, also followed a summer on the Island. On a less elevated literary note, it's sometimes claimed that, in the original version of the children's story, the porcine cast and the wolf of *The Three Little Pigs* all lived near Shanklin.

Sooner rather than later you will come across **Vernon Cottage**, which is not only a place of interest in its own right, but also a tea room (page 293) and a visitor information point. The building, the oldest cottage orné (page 172) on the Island, features several thatched humps and was named after the man who commissioned it, Edward Vernon Utterson, a writer, artist and collector of books. The cottage was built just before the Napoleonic Wars, at which time it looked out across a large meadow (now a car park) to the chine. A smuggling tunnel runs from beneath the cottage to Shanklin Chine. Underneath the present-day upstairs lounge is a small not-so-secret 'secret room' (accessed by a hatch from the ground floor), where vast amounts of contraband were once stashed. Whenever the men from Customs and Excise paid a visit, the mistress of the house would retire there, claiming to be suffering from the vapours; decorum of the day meant Her Majesty's inspectors could intrude no further. In addition to its tea room, the cottage hosts a local arts, crafts and produce fair on Tuesdays and Wednesdays from April until October.

Down by the sea, **Small Hope Beach** sits to the left (north) of the main seafront and backs up on to a spectacular cliff face which gives it a pleasingly enclosed feel as well as shelter when the westerlies blow across the Island. The gently sloping sands are also popular with families, partly perhaps because it tends to be quieter than the main beaches of the Sandown Bay area.

A Victorian report, *A History of Hampshire and the Isle of Wight*, once loftily dismissed Shanklin's main **church** (Church St, PO37 6QY), dedicated to St Blasius, noting how 'almost every trace of antiquity has vanished' and that 'it has been so altered and added to that it is now of little interest'. Perhaps the author, W M Page, was having a bad day when he wrote this, as this is a building of quiet charm that dates to the 12th century with a spooky lych gate, bell ropes dangling in the nave and a wooden bell tower that resembles a wizard's hat. And, surely, a church positioned by a small lake brimming with wildlife and which is named after the patron saint of sore throats and wool combers will always be worth a visit. While held captive at Carisbrooke Castle, Charles I was permitted to ride under escort to visit the chapel, where he received communion in the church porch.

The banks of high oaks (rare on the Isle of Wight), silver birch, elder, rowan, holly and sweet chestnut give **America Wood**, immediately west of Shanklin, a winning charm, and as such it is designated as a Site of Special Scientific Interest. Exploration of this undulating, often humid 50-acre woodland makes for a fascinating study of nature in recovery, for the great storms of 1987 and 1990 knocked down several mature oaks, creating open areas with sightlines; nature is slowly filling in the gaps with undergrowth and emergent trees. Wind-thrown trees are being left where they fell to create deadwood habitat for insects. To reach the wood on foot (or bicycle), follow the Shanklin–Wroxall cycle path (the southerly arm of the Red Squirrel Trail) for a mile from Shanklin railway station, and then take the footpath to the right just after you cross the A3020.

Shanklin Chine
3 Chine Av PO37 6BW ✐ 01983 866432 ⏁ shanklinchine.co.uk

Cutting through the Island geology from Old Shanklin to the sea, Shanklin Chine makes for a thrilling spectacle, dropping 105ft to sea level in barely a quarter of a mile (along a straight plane). In the 18th century the chine was a rough walk that was of appeal only to the intrepid. All that changed in 1817 when the superbly named William Colenutt excavated the present path and opened it to the public, though he demanded an entrance fee for his endeavours. Shanklin sojourner John Keats and author Jane Austen were among early admirers.

From the 1870s until 1958 the 'contribution', as Colenutt preferred to call it, was fixed at 6d (2.5p). Today you will pay a little more for access. You might retort – reasonably enough – that there are countless chines and beaches to explore for free across the Island, but if you are going to make an exception and pay for access to one, then give serious consideration to this one.

The chine is a work of nature dating back to the last ice age, around 10,000 years ago, when the stream would originally have flowed into the River Eastern Yar. This stream is continually cutting its way back to the foot of the downs and as you walk up and down the chine you will notice distinctive indentations of water-cut lines on the cliff faces. More than 150 varieties of wild plants and 50 species of fern, grass, moss and liverwort have so far been recorded, some of them extremely rare. Among them are wild garlic, horsetails, golden saxifrage, wild fuchsia and winter-flowering heliotrope, as well as the more exotic rhubarb-like *Gunnera manicata*, a native to the Serra do Mar mountains of southeastern Brazil, which flaunts its succulent 10ft-wide, 7ft-high leaves in the middle of the chine.

You can explore the chine along a nature trail that winds its way among elm, sycamore, alder, elder and beech as well as thick-set evergreen rhododendrons. From the trail or the hide you may spot wagtails and blackbirds, perhaps a peregrine falcon as well as now-captive rescue birds such as Senegal parrots and Asian blue quails. The darkest nooks and crannies are known to be home to *Meta menardi*, the rarely recorded cave spider, but you may have more luck spotting the three resident families of red squirrel.

Over the years, the temptation to tinker with nature here has proved irresistible and the chine is decorated with illuminations in a fashion similar to Robin Hill (page 247) and at night-time these are rather charming. Other manmade attractions to stumble upon include a Victorian brine tub in which heated saltwater baths were taken. The chine has also played an important role in modern history. During World War II, a pipeline under the sea to Normandy was constructed to provide fuel to Allied forces, a project codenamed PLUTO (the Pipe Line Under The Ocean). The pipeline extended all the way north towards Culver Down and during the war Browns Golf Course and an adjacent ice-cream factory were restructured to disguise pumping apparatus. A cross-section of the actual pipe can be seen in the on-site Heritage Centre.

The chine is best accessed from below, along Shanklin Esplanade. After you've worked your way up to overlook the waterfall, you can descend along the south side of the chine, tracking the PLUTO pipeline and passing an informative wildlife hut. The lower exit near here deposits you by the pub, the Fisherman's Cottage Inn (see opposite), which has fine views over the beach. You can explore further south here, towards Horse Ledge where the amber-coloured cliff face resembles large slabs of honeycomb and has the appearance of having been hacked away by a butcher who's been on the sauce. This is as good a place as any to gaze north for an unimpeded sea-level view and appreciate the sheer scale of Sandown Bay, which stretches away to the chalk cliffs beyond Yaverland. The other eyecatcher here is decidedly manmade: a lift which links sea level to Shanklin. Built in 1892 to provide easy access to the beaches, it is currently undergoing renovation (but still working). In stature it resembles a dockside crane, although another reason why you cannot miss it is because the word 'Lift' is etched, helpfully if perhaps superfluously, into the side of the main shaft in 8ft-high letters. As an alternative, you can take the Osborne Steps (footpath SS73), which you'll find just south of the lift, back up to the town.

¶¶ FOOD & DRINK

Fisherman's Cottage Inn Shanklin Chine PO37 6BN ☏ 01983 863882
⌕ fishermanscottageshanklin.co.uk ☉ Mar–Nov Tue–Sun. Wonderful 200-year-old sea-
level thatched pub with a fine outdoor seating area overlooking the bay and cliffs.
Morgan's of Shanklin 36–38 High St, PO37 6JY ☏ 01983 864900 ⌕ morgansofshanklin.
com ☉ usually closes in winter, check website. Modern restaurant with a strong emphasis
on wet fish and shellfish picked up from Ventnor each day. Try the cold seafood platter or
Ventnor Bay crab with tiger prawn linguine. Chef, local lad and owner Tim Morgan, worked
with Marco Pierre White and at The Ivy. For carnivores, there's a delicious shoulder of
Godshill lamb.
Old Thatched Teashop 4 Church Rd, PO37 6NU ☏ 01983 865587 ⌕ oldthatchteashop.
co.uk. Scones, teacakes and other hearty food in an emphatically quaint late 17th-century
building. Outside seating includes a Fairy Garden, among statues of elves and pixies.
Vernon Cottage Tea Room 1 Eastcliff Rd, PO37 6AA ☏ 01983 865411 ⌕ vernoncottage.
co.uk ☉ Apr–Sep. Another thatched cottage that offers the quintessential 'olde-worlde'
experience, though the spacious garden may well draw you outside. The eclectic menu caters
for every imaginable taste and somehow manages to be almost entirely home-baked. Cream
teas feature scones in the shape of the Isle of Wight (an innovation you'd expect to see more
widely across the Island).

▧ SHOPPING

Shanklin is the place to get that stick of rock, but most of the Island's food and craft
producers also sell their wares here; try **Cavanagh and Baker** (103 High St, PO37 6NS
☏ 01983 506590 ⌕ cavanagh-baker.co.uk) for food. Opposite the Old Thatched Teashop, a
narrow alleyway opens up into **The Mews Craft Centre**, where half a dozen artists' studios
are open to the public, including **Washed Up** (⌕ washedupdriftwoodart.co.uk) where you
can buy wine racks and surfboards made from driftwood by Emma Brown.

10 LUCCOMBE & AROUND

The village of Luccombe comprises just a handful of houses but the coast
and hinterland either side are simply magnificent, for this is another of
those parts of the Island where the land sweeps up from sea level to
a high point in dramatic, vertiginous fashion. If you are planning to
explore on two wheels, this is somewhere for which you might with a
clear conscience consider hiring an electric bike (it's so steep only the
hardest of hardcore mountain cyclists would dismiss you as 'lazy').

Beyond Luccombe itself, at the southern end of Sandown Bay, you will
see the distinctive feature of **Horse Ledge** pushing out into the water.

The rock pools here are full of anemones and tiny porcelain crabs that resemble flattened pancakes. If you follow the tide out at the far south of the bay, you will just have time to walk around Knock Point, the southern full stop of Sandown Bay (Horse Ledge is the sea-level protuberance of the point), into **Luccombe Bay** and back. Nowadays this is the only way to reach the bay: a path used to work its way down through Luccombe Chine but landslips among the sandy rock and gault clay cliffs have made this impossible. The path is closed off and it is both dangerous and a criminal offence to attempt to use it; matters are unlikely to change any time soon. (If you walk the coast path south of Luccombe village you'll see the closed-off path; a notice observes, rather primly if forlornly, that 'at present, a feasible restatement opportunity does not exist'.)

A walk from Shanklin to the highdowns

✤ OS Explorer map 29; start: St Blasius's Church, Church Rd, Old Shanklin PO37 6QY

📍 SZ579806; 6 miles; hard

The walk up to St Martin's Down and Shanklin Down from Old Shanklin must be among the most delightful on the Island. It's a steep climb but the contours are a little gentler than you might expect and the views will certainly distract you. Essentially, the hike follows the last couple of miles or so of the Worsley Trail (page 209), continues with a pleasing amble around the downs' summits and then returns the same way. Alternatively, you can extend this walk by a further 1½ miles to cross Luccombe Down and St Boniface Down and eventually drop down to Ventnor, and then take the #3 bus back to the church.

1 Pass through the lych gate of St Blasius's Church to take the graveyard path to the left of the church and then cross the couple of steps at the rear over the boundary wall. Continue over two fields and three stiles to reach some trees, where views open up towards Sandown Bay. The path enters woodland and immediately to the right (north) is Holme Copse, a mixture of oak, ash and hazel planted in 2004 and now maturing rapidly. At this point

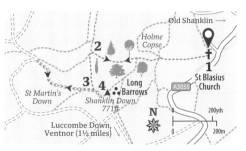

Within Luccombe Bay, look out for the **waterfall**, one of just three on the Island. The stretch of beach that runs from Horse Ledge to Yellow Ledge is covered in stones that are coated in iron; if your venture to the bay coincides with sunshine these mineralised iron pebbles are transformed, glistening and shimmering in the bright light. Do check tide times before exploring the area and, at the risk of labouring the point, you should follow the tide out to give yourself the most time.

Back on dry land, a sizeable tangle of bramble and elderberry known as **Haddon's Pits** sits immediately, if high, above Horse Ledge and its scrubby features are good for spotting birds such as whitethroat. You'll find the entrance to this pleasing slice of scrubland along the minor Luccombe Road (which at this point doubles as the coast path),

the path is, literally, a woodland corridor, providing important links to other hedgerows and habitats for dormice and red squirrels. As you emerge from this, keep ahead, ignoring any right or left turns, following footpath SS10 for Wroxall.

2 About 400yds further uphill from Holme Copse you reach a junction of gates and paths. Go through the gate directly ahead and turn sharp left uphill along footpath SS12 to St Martin's Down. The views are exquisite, with the large chalk finger of Culver Down now clear, protruding into the Solent, and much of the middle of the Island hinterland laid out below you.

3 The path meets a T-junction as it begins to level off: bear right along V5 (a public bridleway) and wander along St Martin's Down to the edge of the escarpment for what are simply wonderful wide-angle views down to the village of Wroxall with the Island free-falling away from the edge of the down to the valley below. Retrace your steps to the junction – there and back is a distance of a mile. This time, turn right and, after 100yds, take the gate on the left, following the path to the trig point on the top of Shanklin Down.

4 The views from here are incredible – you can see all the way to Tennyson Down, the fresh white brilliance of the cliffs clear even from here, some 25 miles distant. If your eyesight is keen you may be even able to pick out the distinct pinnacles of the Needles at the far end of Tennyson Down. A landslip along the edge of Tennyson Down may one day make them more apparent and enable visitors to gaze from one end of the Island to the other. Closer to hand, near the trig point, if you stare hard enough at the long grass to the north, the outline of two long barrows may emerge; they are more visible after cattle have grazed the area. Return the same way to St Blasius's.

immediately before it terminates in Luccombe village. Swallows and house martins congregate here in spring and summer before setting off south on their autumn migrations. Occasionally a peregrine falcon will ruffle avian feathers as it darts through the hollows here in search of prey.

The adjacent heathland of **Luccombe Down** is a good place to seek out smaller but no less charismatic birds, including Dartford warblers, which can be spotted hopping from one sprig of gorse to another. In spring, the down's wooded areas are smothered with bluebells. Yellowhammers, small copper butterflies and bilberries are other highlights that thrive on the land grazed by cattle.

Luccombe Down's northerly neighbours are **St Martin's Down** and **Shanklin Down**: the latter, at 770ft above sea level, is almost as high as you can go on the Isle of Wight (it is pipped to that accolade by St Boniface Down to the southeast). Accordingly, the views extend across almost the entire Island: Culver Down and the sheltered Arreton Valley in the north, Cowes (to the northwest), the South Downs on the mainland beyond and, away to the west, Tennyson Down.

THE EAST COAST HINTERLAND

🏠 **Rosemary Cottage** (page 305)

Sandown and Shanklin extend from the coast inland for less than a mile and their western delimitations are clearly defined: with just a few paces you step from urban development to sleepy backwaters. The area features four small villages: Alverstone and Newchurch in the north and Queen's Bower and Apse Heath to the south. Each of these amounts to little more than a smattering of houses (the sort of places for which you might subsequently look up property prices with a view to relocating), but the gaps between them are filled with woodland, farmland, streams and age-old sunken lanes and holloways. It is easy to over-romanticise, but this is somewhere where you really get a sense of how it must have felt to walk from point to point, from one village to another, in medieval times.

11 ALVERSTONE & AROUND

Little more than a mile from Sandown, the village of Alverstone is a world away from the seaside bustle of the coast. In truth, 'village' is a

RECYCLE & REPURPOSE

Should you be in want of a tote bag made from a bouncy castle or beach chair, consider the work of Newchurch-based **Wyatt and Jack** (Unit H, Langbridge Business Centre, Langbridge, Newchurch PO36 0NP ✆ 07500 207488 🖥 wyattandjack.com). Most orders are taken online and products are on sale at retail outlets across the Island, including the Garlic Farm, but you can also visit the workshop by appointment.

The company, run by Georgia Wyatt-Lovell, sells a wide range of wash bags, carry bags and retro zip pouches made from beach carousels, gazebo canvas, salvaged tents and deckchairs. Rope handles for some bags come from Goodleaf Tree Climbing after they have worn too thin to be of use for climbers there. The impetus for the business arose from one of the historically core businesses of the Island: beach sunbeds. The father of a friend of Georgia's worked as a beach concessionaire and was wondering how to dispose of the fabric from a sunbed that had reached the end of its working life. Georgia took the yellow PVC fabric and turned it into a bag. 'I've still got it,' she says, 'it's one thing I will never sell.' Following a hunch that the same wastage must be happening across the UK, Georgia drove around the country talking to beach concessionaires and collected their unwanted fabrics, saving them from landfill.

The key to running a genuinely environmentally friendly business, she says, is to be practical: make something people actually want to buy and avoid the pitfall of coming across as too worthy. 'I don't like it when people use trendy words such as "upcycle". I've never been looking to "do" the right thing – I don't see this as ethical or sustainable per se – it just seems obvious that you should re-use something.'

---

rather grand term, for Alverstone is really a modest collection of houses and leafy gardens scattered either side of a minor road. You can't help wondering if there are more red squirrels in the vicinity than people. On its southeastern edge is the rarely visited **Alverstone Mead Nature Reserve**, which sits in the heart of the Sandown Levels in the floodplain of the River Yar. This exquisite area of mixed woodland, featuring wild cherry, oak and hazel, has long been managed by traditional methods, and footpaths and boardwalks lead you around a network of old ditch drainage systems that create a wildlife wonderland of water meadows. Look out for herons, kingfishers, egrets and, at dusk, barn owls quartering above the field edges in search of a meal.

Just to the west of Alverstone, **Youngwoods Copse** is a good place to look for red squirrels among the young wild service trees (one of the first species of tree to colonise Britain after the last ice age). In spring, wood

anemones carpet the ground with their white- and purple-streaked petals and leave a strong musky aroma for you to inhale.

A circular loop runs around the village linking the nature reserve to its east and the woodlands to its south and west, and it's one of the most delightful and easy-going walks the Island has to offer. In the centre of the village, the Red Squirrel Trail intersects with the road – it's clearly waymarked and you can't miss it: head east on the trail for 600yds and then turn right through a gate into the nature reserve and south across a field to another gate. Bear right uphill and before long you turn right again (west) on to footpath NC17, which brings you to the Bern Thearle hide in the heart of Alverstone Mead Nature Reserve. The hide has wheelchair access and the well-stocked feeders here attract large flocks of tits, dunnocks and goldfinches, as well as a regular flypast by green woodpeckers. Continue west along the footpath to cross Alverstone Road and follow bridleway NC42 southwest. After 600yds, bear right along footpath NC12 and then turn right along NC50 through Youngwoods Copse to reach the Red Squirrel Trail again. Turn left and immediately right to cross a stream and follow footpath B54 back east, with the stream for company on your right, to Alverstone.

¶¶ FOOD & DRINK

Pedaller's Café Langbridge, Newchurch PO36 0NP ✆ 01983 864579 ⬦ pedallerscafe.co.uk ⊙ Wed–Sun. Located on the Red Squirrel Trail, a mile to the west of Alverstone, Pedaller's Café has long acquired legendary status among cyclists. Great food, drinks, teas, soups and cakes await to greet the weary pedaller. On chilly days there is a wood-burning stove to make you linger before easing back into the saddle. Outside is a decking area under the gaze of dangling tree branches; the air is often full of birdsong. The café even has a free cycle-maintenance service, ideal if you've picked up a flat tyre. Walkers are equally welcome, with no fuss about muddy boots.

12 BORTHWOOD COPSE

National Trust

Backing on to Queen's Bower and sitting just south of the Alverstone Road, Borthwood Copse is a magical place to wander and look out for wildlife. The copse features oaks, beech trees and coppiced sweet chestnut and is a remnant of the medieval forest that once covered much

◀ **1** Borthwood Copse. **2** Alverstone Mead Nature Reserve.

LIVING OFF THE LAND

Set back barely a mile to the south of Alverstone, the countryside around Apse Heath and Queen's Bower is fertile territory both for crop growing and creativity. There is a handful of truly excellent food producers and suppliers at work here, though only one sells on site. What is really striking, however, is that these food producers, while evidently of interest to visitors and lovers of all things Slow, evolved primarily to serve a local market – an audience who continues to be the bedrock of their business. Perhaps more than any other businesses listed in this book, these producers are proof that holidaying self-caterers don't need to stock up at a south coast supermarket before crossing the Solent.

THE QUEEN BOWER DAIRY & THE ISLE OF WIGHT CHEESE COMPANY

Alverstone Rd, PO36 0NZ ✆ 01983 402736 ⌂ isleofwightcheese.co.uk

Deep in a hidden valley on the edge of Borthwood Copse lies the beating heart of the Island's cheese-making community. Like so many other foodie entrepreneurs on the Island, Richard Hodgson grew up on the Island, then left, only to be drawn back. And, again like so many others, he is modest to a fault and seemingly unaware of how good his produce is. The cheese company began in 2006 with Richard and his mother, who had run a hotel on the Island with his father. 'It was the mid-2000s and the food revolution was just taking off,' he recalls. 'I thought that if we produced something palatable we could do well. People here have a strong allegiance to local produce and if it's good they will be proud of it and support it.'

Richard attended a couple of short cheese-making courses at agricultural college but believes that study and science only take you so far. 'Pretty much anyone could learn to make something that is palatable,' he says, 'but it takes years to get the feel for dealing with the variables. You are using all your senses, from handling the cows, to the smell and the look of the cheese. I could buy some expensive equipment but the cheese wouldn't have a soul. You buy supermarket cheese and it is homogenous. It tastes the same all year round because that's what they think their customers want. My cheeses taste different according to what the cows have eaten, whether it's fresh grass or silage. Cheeses are full of enzymes, they're alive.'

Richard has a herd of 52 cows and uses as much of their milk as possible to make the cheese. When he needs more, he tops up with milk from Briddlesford Farm (page 95). One of his latest products is Blue Slipper (named after the local moniker for the Island's gault clay), which is mild, milky and, rather like the cliffs that contain the clay, collapses easily and gracefully under pressure. It is sold at three to five weeks of age. Other cheeses include the pasteurised Isle of Wight Blue and the hard cheeses Gallybagger and Gallybagger Mature, made entirely from raw milk.

The cheeses are widely sold across the Island but Richard has a small shop window at the farm. Press the bell and wait (patiently). 'We never presumed we would be as popular as we are,' he says, 'so it's usually me who answers the bell in between making the cheese. I never want to give the impression I'm too busy to meet people.'

LIVING LARDER

⬦ livinglarder.co.uk

Based just south of Apse Heath, Living Larder supplies boxes of fresh fruit and vegetables to the doorstep and offers a service both to Islanders and, with a little notice, self-catering visitors. This is very much a family business, with Will Steward and his wife Aimee growing produce at their farm (the family first started growing on the site in 1922). In 2014 Will piloted a vegetable box scheme supplying around 20 family and friends – and he hasn't looked back. Today he typically distributes 160 boxes of fresh fruit and vegetables around the Island every week. About 90% of the vegetables are sourced from their own 12 acres of garden, the remainder topped up from farms across the Island. Depending on seasonal availability, you can expect to munch away on potatoes, tomatoes, onions, mixed baby leaf salad, Milan turnip, rainbow chard, green peppers, butternut squash, leeks, fennel, kale and carrots. The farm is currently in the process of being certificated as organic.

Although born on the Island, Will returned to run the farm after a career as an engineer on the mainland. 'A lot of people thought we were crazy to return but we were driven by what we wanted to do,' he says. 'It may have been a naive leap of faith but I saw it

as my way back to the Island.' While clearly a business rather than altruistic hobby, Will feels keenly that his job comes with a responsibility. 'When your family has lived on a farm on the Isle of Wight for four generations and looked after it, you have a strong sense of identity and duty. It was ingrained in me to look after the place. This Island is somewhere we are proud to live.'

WILD ISLAND FOODS

✆ 01983 868305 ⬦ wildislandstore.co.uk

Nuala Grandcourt moved to the Island 35 years ago, got the bug, stayed and now makes a living from living off the land. Her small company is based in Newchurch and produces dressings, dips, marinades and flavoured vinegars. Nuala settled on salad dressings as it made use of raw natural materials, such as rapeseed oil, that were easily accessible on the Island. Nuala is assisted by Ady Stothard who enjoys the superb title of chief balsamic alchemist and master oil infuser. The pair currently make spiced fig, blackberry and balsamic vinegars, as well as other dressings that draw on bay and juniper. Although she collects ingredients from all over the Island, she works at a small unit on the farm at Newchurch, where the rapeseed is grown and cold-pressed. Nuala does not have a shop front but you will find her foods across the Island – at delis in Yarmouth and at Farmer Jack's and other farm shops. Her website offers helpful recipes that can put her produce to good use, such as crispy tofu chilli wraps and smoky aubergine dips.

of the eastern end of the Island. You have a chance here of seeing – and hearing – great spotted woodpeckers. Look out too for one of the UK's smallest birds, the doughty goldcrest, which can often be seen in the copse, while the occasional mute swan can be seen settling in marshy fields. Bluebells run rampant here in spring.

ACCOMMODATION

The Isle of Wight is not short of charming, locally run places to stay, where the owners will give you space to recharge but still be on hand when required with that life-affirming cooked breakfast. Your options range from elegant town guesthouses and farmhouse B&Bs to camping and glamping in tucked-away woodland corners where you might unzip the tent in the morning to a view of the Island's downland spine. If it's self-catering you're after, then you'll find that stylish and tasteful conversions of milking sheds and 18th-century buildings abound, many located on working farms where you can, should you wish, either meet the animals or simply soak up the rural surroundings of an Island that holds the concept of 'slow' at its heart.

The list here is not exhaustive and features personal choices of places that stand out from the crowd, time and again. Many of these properties will also book ferry tickets for you at a discounted rate, so always be sure to ask if they can do this. No fee has been paid by any property to be included: all are featured on merit.

The hotels, inns and B&Bs featured in this section are indicated by 🏠 under the heading for the town or village nearest their location; self-catering is indicated by 🏡 and camping and glamping by ⛰️.

For detailed descriptions of the following places, go to ✎ bradtguides. com/iowsleeps.

1 YARMOUTH & THE NORTHWEST

B&Bs
Jireh House St James's Sq, Yarmouth PO41 0NP
✆ 01983 760513 ✎ jireh-house.com

Self-catering
Calbourne Water Mill Newport Rd, Calbourne PO30 4JN ✆ 01983 531227
✎ calbournewatermill.co.uk/holiday-accommodation

Tom's Eco Lodges Tapnell Farm Park, Newport Rd, PO41 0YJ ✆ 01983 758729
✎ tomsecolodge.com

Camping & glamping
Camp Wight Ningwood Hill, Yarmouth PO41 0XP ✎ campwight.co.uk/our-site
Glamping the Wight Way Copse Ln, Freshwater PO40 9DE ✆ 07585 956141
✎ glampingthewightway.co.uk

2 COWES, RYDE & THE NORTHEAST

Hotels

The Boathouse Springvale Rd, Seaview PO34 5AW ✆ 01983 873572 ⚲ theboathouseiow. co.uk

The Fishbourne 111 Fishbourne Ln, Fishbourne PO33 4EU ✆ 01983 873572 ⚲ thefishbourne. co.uk

Northbank Hotel Circular Rd, Seaview PO34 5ET ✆ 01983 612227 ⚲ northbankhotel.co.uk

Seaview Hotel The High St, Seaview PO34 5EX ✆ 01983 612711 ⚲ seaviewhotel.co.uk

B&Bs

The Caledon Guest House 59 Mill Hill Rd, Cowes PO31 7EG ✆ 01983 293599 ⚲ the-caledon.co.uk. See ad, page 118.

Grange Farm Staplers Rd, Wootton PO33 4RW ✆ 01983 882147 ⚲ grange-farm-holidays.co.uk

Onefifty Cowes 150 Park Rd, Cowes PO31 7NE ✆ 07795 296399 ⚲ onefiftycowes.co.uk

Self-catering

The Auction House 1 Ways Mews, Garfield Rd, Ryde PO33 2PT ✆ 07565 563879 ⚲ homeaway. co.uk/p8076088

Pavilion Cottage Osborne House, York Av, East Cowes PO32 6JX ✆ 0370 333 1187 ⚲ english-heritage.org.uk/visit/holiday-cottages/find-a-holiday-cottage/pavilion-cottage

Camping & glamping

Priory Bay Yurts Priory Croft, Priory Bay, Seaview PO34 5BU ✆ 07974 752510 ⚲ isleofwight-beachhomes.co.uk/ultimate-glamping-yurts

3 TENNYSON DOWN & THE SOUTHWEST

B&Bs

The Bay Boutique Bed and Breakfast Guyers Rd, Freshwater PO40 9PZ ✆ 01983 641143 ⚲ stayfreshwaterbay.co.uk

Gotten Manor Gotten Ln, Chale PO38 2HQ ✆ 01983 551368 ⚲ gottenmanor.co.uk

Homelea B&B Main Rd, Brighstone PO30 4DJ ✆ 01983 740718 ⚲ homeleaiow.co.uk

Westcourt Farm Shorwell PO30 3LA ✆ 01983 740233 ⚲ westcourt-farm.co.uk

Self-catering

Farringford Cottages Farringford House, Bedbury Ln, Freshwater PO40 9PE ✆ 01983 752500 ⚲ farringford.co.uk/self-catering-isle-of-wight/holiday-cottages. See ad, page 167.

The Mission Blythe Shute, Chale PO38 2HJ ✆ 07802 758113 ⚲ theshacks.co.uk/ hb_accommodation/the-mission

The Scout Hall Church Pl, Chale PO38 2HB ✆ 07802 758113 ⚲ theshacks.co.uk/ hb_accommodation/the-scout-hall

Weirside Cottage Main Rd, Brighstone PO30 4BJ ✆ 01983 740782 ⚲ westwightcottages. co.uk/our-cottages/weirside-cottage-brighstone-isle-of-wight

4 THE SOUTH

Hotel

The Chequers Inn Niton Rd, Rookley PO38 3NZ ✆ 01983 840314 ⚲ chequersinn-iow.co.uk

B&Bs

Kingsmede Kemming Rd, Whitwell PO38 2QX ✆ 01983 730285 ⚲ kingsmede.co.uk

St Maur Castle Rd, Ventnor PO38 1LG ✆ 01983 852570 ⚲ stmaur.co.uk

Self-catering

Castlehaven Retreat Castlehaven Ln, Niton Undercliff PO38 2ND ✆ 01983 730495 ⚲ castlehaven.me.uk

Godshill Park Farm & Cottages Godshill PO38 3JF ✆ 01983 840781 ⚲ godshillparkfarm.net

Koala Cottage Godshill PO38 3DR ✆ 01983 842031 ⚲ koalacottage.co.uk

Nettlecombe Farm Whitwell PO38 2AF ✆ 01983 730783 ⚲ nettlecombefarm.co.uk

St Catherine's Lighthouse Cottages nr Niton, PO38 2NF ✆ 01386 701177 ⌘ trinityhouse. co.uk/lighthouse-cottage-rental/st-catherines-holiday-cottages

Ventnor Botanic Garden Undercliff Dr, Ventnor PO38 1UL ✆ 01983 855397 ⌘ botanic.co.uk/stay

5 NEWPORT & AROUND

B&Bs
Arreton Manor Main Rd, Arreton PO30 3AA ✆ 07956 295633 ⌘ arretonmanor.net

Newport Quay 41 Quay St, Newport PO30 5BA ✆ 01983 528544 ⌘ newportquayhotel.co.uk

One Holyrood 1–2 Holyrood St, Newport PO30 5AU ✆ 01983 521717 ⌘ oneholyrood.co.uk

Self-catering
The Garlic Farm Mersley Farm, Mersely Ln, Newchurch PO36 0NR ✆ 01983 898477 ⌘ thegarlicfarm.co.uk

Tiny Homes Holidays Hillis Gate Stables, Hillis Gate Rd, Cowes PO30 5UB ✆ 07802 758113 ⌘ tinyhomesholidays.com

Camping & glamping
Kids Love Yurts Burnt House Farm, Burnt House Ln, Newport PO30 2PN ✆ 01983 300744 ⌘ kidsloveyurts.co.uk

6 SANDOWN, SHANKLIN & THE EAST

Hotels
The Birdham Bembridge 1 Steyne Rd, Bembridge PO35 5UH ✆ 01983 872840 ⌘ thebirdhambembridge.co.uk

The Crab & Lobster Inn 32 Forelands Field Rd, Bembridge PO35 5TR ✆ 01983 872244 ⌘ characterinns.co.uk/crabandlobsterinn

Luccombe Hall Hotel Luccombe Rd, Shanklin PO37 6RL ✆ 01983 869000 ⌘ luccombehall.co.uk

The Miclaran Littlestairs Rd, Shanklin PO37 6HS ✆ 01983 862726 ⌘ miclaran.co.uk

The Pilot Boat Inn Station Rd, Bembridge PO35 5NN ✆ 01983 872077 ⌘ thepilotboatinn.com

B&B
Foxhills of Shanklin 30 Victoria Av, Shanklin PO37 6LS ✆ 07845 101351 ⌘ foxhillsofshanklin.co.uk

Harbourside View Embankment Rd, Bembridge Harbour PO35 5NS ✆ 01983 339084 ⌘ harbourside-iow.co.uk

Keats Cottage 76 High St, Shanklin PO37 6NJ ✆ 01983 639661 ⌘ keatscottage.co.uk

No 29 29 St Paul's Cres, Shanklin PO37 7AN ✆ 01983 641773 ⌘ number29.uk

Rosemary Cottage Langbridge, Newchurch, Sandown PO36 0NP ✆ 01983 867735 ⌘ rosemarycottagebreaks.co.uk

Self-catering
Heyvon Houseboat Embankment Rd, Bembridge Harbour PO35 5NS ✆ 01983 339084 ⌘ harbourside-iow.co.uk

Camping & glamping
Ninham Camping Lake PO36 9PJ ✆ 01983 864243 ⌘ ninham-holidays.co.uk

Old Barn Touring Park Cheverton Farm, Newport Rd, Sandown PO36 9PJ ✆ 01983 866414 ⌘ oldbarntouring.co.uk

NOTES

INDEX

Entries in **bold** refer to major entries.

A

accessibility 38
accommodation 37, 303–5
Adgestone Vineyard 271–3
alpacas 71–2
Alum Bay 131–4
   geology 131–2
Alverstone 296–9
ancient monuments
   Five Barrows 144, **148–50**
   Long Stone **156–7**, 158
   long barrows 247, 295
   Neolithic period 149
   Tennyson Down mortuary
      chamber 125
Appley Park 109
Appuldurcombe House 207–10
Arreton Barns Craft Village 241–7
   St George's Church 244–5
Arreton Cross 246
Arreton Down 247–9

B

Back O' the Wight 152–4
Bembridge 258–62
   beaches 259
   food & drink 264–5
   windmill 259–60
Bembridge Fort 277
Bembridge Harbour 262–4
Binnel Bay 186–8
Binstead 101
Blackgang Beach 181
Blackgang Chine 182
Bonchurch 198–202
Bonchurch Landslip 202–5
   St Boniface Old Church 205
books 34–5
bookshops 85, 111, 117, 146

Bouldnor 59–62
   Ledge 62
Brading 266–9
Brading Roman Villa 269–71
Briddlesford Farm 95–6
Brighstone 157–62
   Brighstone coin hoard 161
   dragon tree 158
   medieval graffiti 160
Bromfield, William 32
Brook 151
buses 21–2 see also public
   transport

C

Calbourne 67–70
   All Saints' Church 68
   Calbourne Water Mill 67
   sheepwash 68
Cameron, Julia Margaret 124,
   136–9, 142
car-free travel **20–2** see also
   public transport
Carisbrooke 226
Carisbrooke Castle 226–30
Carroll, Lewis 142, 283
chain floating bridge ferry 78, 80
Chale 165
Chale Green 164–5
chimney sweep 222
chines 121, 148
   Brook Chine 147
   Shepherd's Chine 164
churches
   Arreton, St George's 244–5
   Bembridge, Holy Trinity 259
   Binstead, Holy Cross 89, 101
   Bonchurch, St Boniface Old
      Church 205

churches continued…
   Bonchurch, St Boniface Parish
      Church 203
   Brading, St Mary's 266
   Brook, St Mary the Virgin
      151
   Calbourne, All Saints' 68
   Chale, St Andrew's 165
   Freshwater, All Saints' 53
   Freshwater, St Agnes 136
   Gatcombe, St Olave's 232–3
   Godshill, All Saints' 211
   Mottistone, St Peter & Paul
      154
   Newport, Sts Thomas' 219–20
   Newtown, Holy Spirit 65
   Niton, St John the Baptist 175
   St Helens 117–18
   St Lawrence 186
   Shalfleet, St Michael the
      Archangel 63
   Shanklin, St Blasius 290, 294
   Shorwell, St Peter's 162
   Whippingham, St Mildred's 93
   Whitwell, St Mary & St
      Rhadegund 176, 182–3
cottage orné 176, 182, 289
Cowes 78–85
   Classic Boat Museum 82
   Cowes Beach 83
   food & drink 84
   hammerhead crane 82
   shopping 85
   Sir Max Aitken Museum 81
Cowes Week 19, **80**
cycle hire 28, 42
cycling 20, **25–8**, 37, 42, 49,
   123–4, 170–1, 174, 218, 235,
   256, 291, 299

cycle trails
Island Chalk Ridge Extreme Trail 26, 124, 171
Red Squirrel Cycle Trail 26, 171, 218, 235, 238, 241, 291, 299
Taste Round the Island Route 25, 100, 171

D

dark skies 123
Darwin, Charles 142, 283
Dickens, Charles 202–3
Dimbola Museum & Galleries 136–9
dinosaurs & fossils 29–30, **32–4**, 55, 56, 62, 147–8, 188, 273, 277–9, 280–2, 283
Dinosaur Isle 280–2
downland 24, 30–1, 144–5, 146, 152, 169 see also Tennyson Down
Afton Down 42, 54, 135, 138, 145
Appuldurcombe Down 210
Arreton Down 245, 247
Bembridge Down 256, 274
Bleak Down 215
Brading Down 256, 270–1
Brighstone Down 158–9
Brook Down 145, 148, 149
Chillerton Down 213–15
Compton Down 123, 144
Culver Down 255, 273–7
Luccombe Down 206, 294, 296
Mersley Down 250–1
Mottistone Down 158–9
St Boniface Down 200, 206, 294
St Catherine's Down 165, 166
St Martin's Down 294–5, 296
Shanklin Down 206, 294–5, 296
Stenbury Down 184–5, 210
Tennyson Down 122, 125–8, 135
Ventnor Downs 191, 200–1, 206
Wroxall Down 200–1

duver 113, 117, 262–3
lost duver, the 280

E

earthquakes 224
East Cowes 85–6

F

farm shops 95–6
Briddlesford Farm Shop 95
Delysia Farm 286
Farmer Jack's 246
Isle of Wight Farm Shop 213
farmers' markets 110, 111, 225
Farringford House 139–43
gardens 140–2
Fastcat ferry 20, 106
ferry services 20, 50–1, 80, 106
festivals & events 18–19, 138
Fishbourne 99
food producers 12–16, 249, 300–1
see also Slow food & drink
foraging 14
forests & woodlands
America Wood 290–1
Bouldnor Copse 59–61
Borthwood Copse 299
Brighstone Forest 158–9
Dodnor Creek & Dickson's Copse 236–8
Firestone Copse 96
Parkhurst Forest 234–6
Saltern Wood 53
Thorley Copse 47
Wydcombe Park 185
Youngwoods Copse 297–9
Fort Victoria Country Park 54–6
Freshwater Bay 135–9
food & drink 139
Freshwater village 143–6

G

Gandhi, Mahatma 191, 200
Garlic Farm, the 249–52
Gatcombe 232–4

Gatcombe continued...
St Olave's Church 232–3
withy beds 234
getting there 20
ghosts 70, 230, 233, 285
Godshill 210–13
All Saints' Church 211
food & drink 212–13
Golden Hill Fort & Country Park 57

H

Hamstead 62
Hendrix, Jimi 138
Horse Ledge 293
horseriding 29
hovercraft 20, 76, 106, 108
Hulverstone 151

I

Isle of Wight Festival 138
Isle of Wight Steam Railway 97

K

kayaking 29, 135

L

Lake 288–9
language
Isle of Wighty 17–18
Luccombe Bay 294–5
Lukely Brook 231

M

manor houses
Mottistone 154–6
Northcourt 162–3
Westcourt 162–3
Wolverton 162–3
maps 37
Marx, Karl 191
Military Road 146
Milne, John 224
museums see also visitor attractions
Brading Roman Villa 269–71

museums *continued*...
Brighstone Village Museum 157
Calbourne Water Mill & Rural Museum 67–8
Carisbrooke Castle 226–30
King Charles I 228–9
Carisbrooke Castle Museum 228–30
Carisbrooke Priory 231–2
Cowes, Classic Boat Museum 82–3
Cowes, Wight Military & Heritage Museum 84
Cowes, Sir Max Aitken Museum 81–2
Dimbola Museum & Galleries 136–9
Lilliput Toy & Doll Museum 267–8
Newport, Museum of Island History 221
Ryde, Isle of Wight Bus Museum 104
Shipwreck Centre & Maritime Museum 241–3
Ventnor & District Local History Museum 193

N
Nansen Hill 202–7
natural history 30–4
nature reserves
Alan Hersey Nature Reserve 112–13
Alverstone Mead Nature Reserve 297
Arreton Down Nature Reserve 247–8
Bohemia Bog 212
Munsley Bog 212
Newtown Harbour National Nature Reserve 60, 66
Ningwood Common 62–3
RSPB Brading Marshes 260–2
Shide Chalk Pits 239–41

UNESCO Biosphere Reserve 133
Needles, The 128–31
Needles Landmark Attraction, The 132
Old Battery & New Battery 129–31
Nettlecombe 182–5
Newbridge 70
Newport 218–25
food & drink 225
history 218–19
Quay Arts 223
Sts Thomas' Church 219–20
shopping 225
Newtown 64–7
bird hide 66
Church of the Holy Spirit 65
Old Town Hall 65
Niton 174–81

O
Osborne House 87–92

P
Palmerston follies **16**, 57, 129, 277
Parkhurst Forest 234–6
Pepperpot, the 166
public transport **20–2**, 43, 76, 106, 124, 171, 218, 257
Puckpool Park 109

Q
Quarr Abbey 99–100
Queen Victoria 75–6, **87–92**
place of worship 93
Queen's bathing machine 92

R
rivers
Eastern Yar 170, 175, 176–8, 258
Medina 76–7, 214–15, 222, 236–8
Western Yar 41, 42–3, 47, 52–4
rotten boroughs 46, 48, 65

Russian Royal Family 93, **94**, 165
Ryde 103–11
architecture 105–6
arts 107–8
bus museum 104
food & drink 110
history 103–5
pier 107
shopping 110–11
transport hub 106

S
sailing 29
St Catherine's Point 175–80
St Helens 116–18
church 117
food & drink 118
duver 117
St Lawrence 186
salt 198–9
Sandown 285–7
history 285
Sandown Bay 282–5
Seaview 112–16
food & drink 113–16
duver 113
Shalfleet 63–4
Church of St Michael the Archangel 63
Shanklin 289–93
food & drink 293
shopping 293
Shanklin Chine 291–2
Shorwell 162–4
Solent 11–12, 39, 40, **50–1**, 78, 103, 108, 112, 118, 128, 242–3
cricket 86
Slow food & drink 12–16
breweries 14
Edulis 189
gin 116
Isle of Wight Cheese Company 300–1
Isle of Wight Dairy Goats 63
Isle of Wight Meat Co 15

Slow food & drink *continued*...
  Living Larder 301
  Tomato Stall, The 249
  vineyards 97, 271–3
  Wild Island Foods 301
  Wight Salt 198–9
stargazing 123

T

Tapnell Farm Park 70–1
Tennyson, Alfred Lord 126–7,
  139–41
Tennyson Down 121, 125–8
  mortuary enclosure 125
  Tennyson Monument 126
tourist information 42, 77, 122,
  170, 218, 256
Totland 143
trains **22**, 76, 106, 257, 288
  Isle of Wight Steam Railway 97
tree climbing 109

U

Undercliff 169, **171–4**, 203

V

Ventnor 190–8
  food & drink 196–7
  history 190–1
  shopping 197–8
  Steephill Cove 195
  Wheelers Bay 195–6
  world leaders 191
Ventnor Botanic Garden
  188–90
Victorian A-listers 142
village signs 21
visitor attractions
  Blackgang Chine 182
  Brading Railway Visitor Centre
    267
  Butterfly World 248
  Dinosaur Isle 280–1
  East Cowes, Classic Boat Gallery
    83

visitor attractions *continued*...
  East Cowes Heritage Centre
    86
  Garlic Farm, the 249–52
  Havenstreet, Train Story 97
  Isle of Wight Donkey Sanctuary
    210
  Model Village, Godshill 212
  Monkey Haven 248
  The Needles Landmark
    Attraction 132
  Vernon Cottage 289

W

walking 20, **23–5**, 36, 38, 42, 152,
  169, 218, 256–7
  England Coast Path 66, 112,
    122, 147
  Isle of Wight Walking Festival 18
  with alpacas 71–2
walks
  Afton & Compton Downs 144–5
  Alverstone Mead Nature Reserve
    299
  Arreton Down 247
  Arreton Valley 250–1
  Bembridge beaches 259
  Bembridge harbour & St Helens
    Duver 262–3
  Bembridge Trail 218
  Bonchurch Landslip 202–5
  Bonchurch literary walk 202–3
  Brading Down 270–1
  Brading Marshes 260
  Brook to Hulverstone 151
  Chillerton Down 213–15
  Chillerton to Godshill 214–15
  crossing the island 24
  dinosaur & fossil walks 29–30,
    33, 277–8, 282
  East Cowes to Binstead & Ryde
    88–9
  Five Barrows 148–50
  Fort Victoria 56
  Freshwater Way 143

walks *continued*...
  Golden Hill 57
  Hamstead, Bouldnor Copse &
    Yarmouth 60–1
  Hanover Point to Chilton Chine
    147
  Headon Warren 134
  Long Stone to Brighstone Forest
    158–9
  low tide walk to St Helens Fort
    118
  Luccombe Bay low tide walk
    293–5
  Lukely Brook 231
  Mill Copse 47–9
  Nansen Hill 205–7
  Nettlestone to Seaview 114–15
  Newtown 64–7
  Needles, The 126–7, 128
  Niton to Blackgang Beach
    181–2
  Niton to Godshill 176–8
  Parkhurst Forest 235
  River Western Yar 52–4
  the road with (almost) no cars
    174
  St Catherine's Down 165, 166
  St Catherine's Lighthouse
    178–80
  St Helens Duver 117
  Shalfleet to Newtown 64–5
  Shanklin to the high downs
    294–5
  Shepherd's Trail 164
  Tapnell Trail 71
  Tennyson Down 126–7
  Tennyson Trail 123, 158–9
  under Ryde pier 97
  Ventnor & Wroxall Downs 200–1
  Warrior Trail 150
  Wheeler's Bay to Horseshoe Bay
    196
  Whippingham Heritage Trail 93
  Whitwell to Nettlecome &
    Stenbury Down 184–5

walks *continued* . . .
  Willow Wood 280
  Wootton Bridge to Briddlesford
    Farm 95–6
  Worsley Trail 209–10, 257, 294
  Wroxall Stream Trail 170
  Yar River Trail 170
  Yaverland to Culver Down 273–4
Whitwell 181–2
  Church of St Mary & St
    Rhadegund 182–3
Wydcombe Park 185
Whippingham 92–5
  St Mildred's Church 93
Wildheart Animal Sanctuary
  (formerly Sandown Zoo) 279

wildlife **31–2**
  Brent geese 66, 93, 107, 262
  butterflies 31, 57, 148, 152–4,
    205–6, 231, 236, 247, 250,
    296
  curlew 52, 107
  gull, Mediterranean 66
  red squirrels 41, 47, 55, 57, 63,
    68, 90, 100, 143, 154, 185,
    234–6, 247, 260, 292, 295,
    297
  tigers 281
  white-tailed eagle 66, 276
Wootton Bridge 96
Worsley family 209–10
Wroxall 207

Y

Yarborough monument 274
Yarmouth 41, **43–54**
  Castle 46
  food & drink 49–51
  history 44–6
  pier 47
  St James's Church 47
  shopping 51–4
Yaverland Beach 277–8

INDEX OF ADVERTISERS

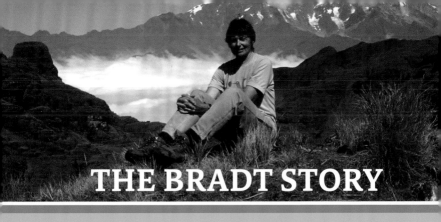

THE BRADT STORY

In the beginning

It all began in 1974 on an Amazon river barge. During an 18-month trip through South America, two adventurous young backpackers – Hilary Bradt and her then husband, George – decided to write about the hiking trails they had discovered through the Andes. *Backpacking Along Ancient Ways in Peru and Bolivia* included the very first descriptions of the Inca Trail. It was the start of a colourful journey to becoming one of the best-loved travel publishers in the world; you can read the full story on our website (www.bradtguides.com/ourstory).

Getting there first

Hilary quickly gained a reputation for being a true travel pioneer, and in the 1980s she started to focus on guides to places overlooked by other publishers. The Bradt Guides list became a roll call of guidebook 'firsts'. We published the first guide to Madagascar, followed by Mauritius, Czechoslovakia and Vietnam. The 1990s saw the beginning of our extensive coverage of Africa: Tanzania, Uganda, South Africa, and Eritrea. Later, post-conflict guides became a feature: Rwanda, Mozambique, Angola, Sierra Leone, Bosnia and Kosovo.

Comprehensive – and with a conscience

Today, we are the world's largest independently owned travel publisher, with more than 200 titles, from full-coun and wildlife guides to Slow Travel guides like this one. However, our ethos remains unchanged. Hilary is still keenly involved and we still get there first: two-thirds of Bradt guides have no direct competition.

But we don't just get there first. Our guides are also known for being more comprehensive than any other series. We avoid templates and tick-lists. Each guide is a one-of-a-kind expression of an expert author's interests, knowledge and enthusiasm for telling it how it really is.

And a commitment to wildlife, conservation and respect for local communities has always been at the heart of our books. Bradt Guides was championing sustainable travel before a other guidebook publisher.

Thank you!

We can only do what we do because of the support of readers like you – people who value less-obvious experiences, less-visited places and a more thoughtfu approach to travel. Those who, like us, ta travel seriously.

Bradt GUIDES
TRAVEL TAKEN SERIOUSLY